D1172049

THE FORM
OF HOUSING

THE FORM OF HOUSING

Edited By **Sam Davis**

With a Foreword by **Charles W. Moore**

Authors

**Sam Davis • Donn Logan • Gerald Allen
Roger Montgomery • Chester Hartman
Clare Cooper Marcus • Richard Bender
John Parman • Cathy Simon • Richard L. Meier**

VNR **VAN NOSTRAND REINHOLD COMPANY**
NEW YORK   CINCINNATI   ATLANTA   DALLAS   SAN FRANCISCO
LONDON   TORONTO   MELBOURNE

Van Nostrand Reinhold Company Regional Offices:
New York   Cincinnati   Atlanta   Dallas   San Francisco

Van Nostrand Reinhold Company International Offices:
London   Toronto   Melbourne

Library of Congress Catalog Card Number: 77-22037
ISBN: 0-442-22007-3

Manufactured in the United States of America

Published by Van Nostrand Reinhold Company
450 West 33rd Street, New York, N.Y.   10001

Published simultaneously in Canada by Van Nostrand Reinhold Ltd.

15 14 13 12 11 10 9 8 7 6 5 4 3 2

Library of Congress Cataloging in Publication Data

Main entry under title:

The Form of housing.

  Includes index.
  1. Housing—United States.   2. Housing policy—
United States.   I. Davis, Sam.
HD7293.F63   301.5′4′0973   77-22037
ISBN 0-442-22007-3

Foreword —Charles Moore

It is impossible, I am told, to deal with architects without the realization that we are hopeless pathological, incurable optimists, drenched in the belief that this inconvenient and somewhat tacky world will inch closer to perfection when our impossible dreams (our "white and gold visions" as Louis Kahn used to call them) are cajoled with reality. We are the wonder of our fellows for maintaining this belief within the face of overwhelming evidence to the contrary; and almost all the architecture literature—as well as the architecture—of our century is flawed by a king-size confidence in the supremacy of the new. The present volume contains in almost all its essays, perhaps the most thoughtful and most mature assertion I have seen yet of the dignity of the existing.

It is not an easy assertion to make. There is far easier mileage, given our optimism, in the breathless announcement that the present environment is hopeless but that its successor will be superior because of the application of some revolutionary new shape of organizing principle or grid or matrix. Some of the essays in *The Form of Housing* do miss favorite images: the reconditioned loft, for instance, keeps cropping up as a fine alternative housing form (I think I would rather plug for a garden in the sun

for almost everyone). But in all of the chapters, no panacea is being peddled; the future is seen as coming from the past, and the new as building on (or even in) the old, based on images that actually mean something to the inhabitants, that aid in the critical (and difficult) human act of dwelling.

One of the most vivid distinctions in the book is Karl Popper's, quoted in Bender and Parman's chapter, between clocks and clouds. The lockstep implications of the clocklike brought us along the route of industrialized housing to Operation Breakthrough, the institutionalized absurd. The other, more useful and more plausible movement (when one is dealing in something as complex and ambiguous as the act of dwelling, or the provision of housing) is akin to the movement of clouds, or schools of fish; the general direction (toward the industrialization of housing, for instance) can be guided or predicted, and the movements of the individual particles, or fish, is free, thank God, of regimentation. I remember the polemics of the 1930s and 1940s which described the wastefulness in the modern home of the separate dining room, used for only a small fraction of the day. There is a grisly refreshment, 40 years later, in looking at factory-produced mobile homes whose advertisements boast the elegance of a

separate dining room, furnished in homage to Old Spain. The variety and unpredictability of the housing alternatives within visible drifts toward greater density and (maybe) greater efficiency of production is a recurring theme, and even the futurist in the collection, Richard Meier, seems especially fascinated by people on houseboats, in oases, or in snowdrifts.

None of this is silly, or at least it is not so silly as the obsessive normalization of the recent past, where we have drawn our expressive elegance out of poverty, and as Bender and Parman say, our process out of crisis. I marvel at the process that tossed out architectural forms (columns and lintels and moldings and bases) as irrelevant and expensive, therefore antisocial and counterrevolutionary, and replaced them with spartan stripped-down glass walled boxes, which then found their (expensive) fruition in having the Spartan mullions made of bronze, then finally in bronzing the hitherto-transparent glass walls themselves. The housing development as we have known it represents a process born of crisis. And I like very much the tensions implicit in the realization that what we have inherited from the distant and even the recent past—the built world, the housing stock, in its complexity and variety—is a lot better than we ever said it was, and that what we have been doing and organizing and legislating and restricting is myopic and crazy.

There is another tension implicit in this collection too, that I find perplexing but somehow revealing, like those not-quite-randomly darting fish; if diversity in housing forms is essential to the kind of world we want (as it seems clearly to be), if diversity's enemy is stereotype, but if as is also implicit (and sometimes explicit) in these pages, stereotype's cousins prototype and archetype are essential components of tradition, which it seems to me comes into its own in these chapters as the essential base on which people become confident to make choices, and to dwell in their world, well then what are we to think? Probably we had better examine our prejudices about stereotype, as this book causes us to reexamine our prejudices against the already existing. Stereotype, possible, is almost all right.

Our acceptance of the validity of *almost,* our recognition that there is no single form of housing, no useful simple housing policy, no panaceas at all is critical to the reading of this book. In *The Place of Houses* Gerald Allen and Donlyn Lyndon and I proposed the thesis that a successful house is a receptacle of energy—the designer's and especially the inhabitants—and that a part of our task as authors was to identify, so as to exorcise the obstacles to the flow of energy: thoughtlessness, confusion, and inhibition. In a parallel way, as many have said, the success of housing depends on the success of the users' act of dwelling, and it is clear from *The Form of Housing* that the major inhibitions to that are the absence of choice, the rigidification of policy, implicit and explicit, and the proliferation of restrictions on human activity and the human imagination. I hope the ideas and images and possibilities visible darting through the clouds in this book will help the energies to flow.

Preface

The beginning of this book developed in June 1975, a few months after the Roosevelt Island Housing Competition sponsored by the Urban Development Corporation of New York. I was preparing a presentation on my own entry and the development of the ideas and research which preceded the design. As I went through the accumulation of months of notes, sketches, articles and books, it occurred to me that the presentation should not be given by myself alone, but by those who were affecting housing through their writings, buildings, or discussions, and to whom I was indebted. The competition was, of course, only a single event, but the notion of gathering statements from people involved in housing in various ways seemed to capture the spirit and intent of that event and of the sponsoring agency.

Architecture is public domain. Even the private house makes use of our diminishing natural resources and is affected by many individuals, laws, and institutions. As material resources dwindle further and more people become involved in various aspects of building, the problems grow in complexity and in their interdependence. Nowhere in the field of building and architecture is this more true than in housing. For those interested in architecture and its relationship to society, the place for fruitful investigation is housing.

Because of the complex nature of housing, it is not possible for a single person to treat adequately its many facets. This collection of essays represents some of the variety and diversity within the field. Although there are many books which emphasize some important aspect of housing—indeed many have been written by these authors—few books bring together into one volume the range of elements that must go into the planning and production of dwellings.

It is hoped that the readers of this book will not be limited to professionals alone, for professionals are not alone in determining the location and the form of housing. Ideally this book can aid in the efforts of the public to become serious participants in decisions which affect their communities and their personal environment.

For the student of planning and architecture, the book may serve as a general reference describing the areas of concern of prominent professionals and as a guide to extensive research in one or more of the topics.

For the professional this book begins to bridge the gap between policy statement and portfolio, making some connections between form and the forces which generate the design.

Sam Davis
Berkeley

Acknowledgments

It is not possible to do architecture alone, and it is not possible to do a book on architecture alone. Many people participated and to them I and the other authors are indebted.

For reviewing and commenting on the entire manuscript or individual chapters at various stages: James Anderson, Franklin D. Becker, Connie Byrom, Jack Cann, Barry Checkoway, Don Dommer, Barry Elbasani, Bernard Frieden, Guido Francescoto, Carol Shen Glass, William Glass, Dan Gregory, Sandy Hirshen, J. B. Jackson, Shelia Johnson, Michael Kirkland, Edward Ostrander, Anthony Pangaro, Michael Sears, Martha Senger, Wendy Tsuji, Sue Weidemann, Melvin Webber, William L. C. Wheaton, Sally Woodbridge.

For research assistance on various chapters: Vera Adams, Hugh Evans, Carol Reif, Arthur Waugh.

For editorial assistance: Emily Bachman, Jay Claiborne, Barbara Gross Davis, Kit Livingston, Michael Palmer, Joanna Taylor.

For administrative advice and assistance: Spiro Kostof, Sally Woodbridge.

A special thanks to William and Carol Glass for their drawings and graphic consultation.

A special thanks to Rob Super for photographic printing and advice.

During the course of preparing this book I was afforded a significant amount of uninterrupted time thanks to the financial assistance of the Committee for Humanities Research and the Office of the Vice Chancellor of the University of California at Berkeley.

A very special thanks to my spouse Barbara for ongoing support, concern, and advice.

SD

Introduction

"A decent home for every American" is the perennial call to arms among those concerned with the country's housing needs. Many attempts have been made in the decades since World War II to achieve this goal, but today, even though new dwellings are continuously being produced, the demand for decent housing still exceeds the supply.

In the past ten years the great boom of postwar babies has become a mature generation of Americans who, to some extent, can be characterized as having a common desire to reevaluate traditional social values. Increased levels of individual awareness and social consciousness regarding the physical environment are a consequence of certain social expectations promoted by the Civil Rights Movement, and later by the Free Speech Movement and the antiwar demonstrations of the mid-to-late 1960s. These new concerns have added further complexity to traditional housing issues. Art commissions, design review boards, rent control legislation, neighborhood preservation ordinances, and environmental impact regulations must now be included along with financial institutions, zoning ordinances, and government bureaucracies as forces directly affecting the design decisions of architects and planners. Since 1970, over 400 communities,

working through the courts, elected officials, and aroused public opinion, have instituted various types of environmental legislation. Two major urban projects have been closed down or drastically altered: Cedar Riverside in Minneapolis for having too much high-rise housing; and Yerba Buena in San Francisco for having no housing at all. Newly aroused sensitivity to the environment, limited growth, and energy conservation must also be considered.

In the past, Americans have tended to look upon the problems of providing decent housing as predominantly technical. With characteristic optimism, many looked to the example of the automobile industry and eagerly awaited the native genius of a Henry Ford of housing who, through some sophisticated variation on the assembly line, could provide the means of fulfilling the promise of adequate housing for all Americans. Ironically, it was the success of the space program in the mid 1960s which helped to undermine this confidence in the ability of technology to solve the major problems of housing. The dramatic contrast between the successful effort to put a man on the moon and the failure to provide decent houses for all citizens made it clear that the most serious problems of housing are social and economic,

not technical. Moreover, the old analogies between the building and the automobile industries were shown to be fallacious. With the possible exception of the mobile home industry, the home building industry has never been centralized and all attempts to centralize it have failed. A house produced for a broad range of locations often has difficulty satisfying the specific local codes, union regulations, climatic conditions, and cultural expectations of a particular place.

Home building is an industry which must respond to a fluctuating economic market. Small producers without the capital capabilities to stabilize or increase this market move in and out of production. Given a diversified demand, the capital expenditures needed to gear up for even territorial distribution have not been justified. According to government figures, of the more than 100,000 builders in the country, most produce less than 25 units per year.[1] Less than 10% consider their primary market to be the multifamily units needed to meet our housing demand. Single family homes are the major commodity of the building industry although their proportion to multifamily housing is declining. Attempts at industrialization have succeeded to the extent that all homes have certain standardized components, but these attempts have not significantly influenced the form or the cost of the total product.

Even more discouraging than the realization that the problems of housing go beyond the merely technical has been the confusion and ultimate failure in the last ten years of various governmental housing programs of great promise. At the federal level, the Department of Housing and Urban Development and the Housing and Urban Development Act of 1968 represented attempts to define housing as one of the primary concerns of government. These programs flourished until most of the legislation was abruptly suspended in the early 1970s. The creation of the Urban Development Corporation in New York State in 1968 signaled the beginning of one of the most hopeful new experiments in housing. Armed with the potential to cut through local and state bureaucracies, the corporation used existing programs and institutions to develop and package the financing of housing projects. More important, it departed from the policies of previous housing agencies by hiring the best architects possible to design the buildings and by developing a well-defined program of user needs which reflected the new social concerns of the time. Furthermore, the UDC

looked upon this mandate to its architects as having value only if it remained responsive to continuing analysis and evaluation.

Funding of UDC projects was drawn from existing federal government programs (now suspended) and from a state bond market which was backed only by a "moral obligation" to pay in case of default. The combination of factors including "expensive money," high construction costs, slow returns on investments, and the political climate in New York resulted in default and the suspension of any new construction in March of 1975.[2] But the efforts of the UDC were not completely in vain. Some 34,000 units were underway or built by 1975, and a whole new standard of the possible now exists. A *New York Times* editorial on the last major event of the UDC (the Roosevelt Island Competition) offers a good summary:

The UDC purpose which has been too quickly forgotten in the fiscal crisis . . . is to provide places for people to live. The irony of the winning designs [in the Roosevelt Island Competition] is that they clearly demonstrate that architects, encouraged by a concerned sponsor, are learning how to handle the exigencies of land, costs, and the scale of

mass housing to create twentieth-century dwellings of humanity and community.[3]

As this editorial suggests, the setbacks of the last ten years should not convince us that the goal of a decent house for everyone is less attainable now than it was in 1949. The events and accomplishments of the last ten years, as manifested in built projects, enacted legislation, and published research offer evidence of progress. Therefore, it is important as we enter the next decade to review the evidence for what it can tell us about our ability to understand and handle the issues of housing and what we can foresee as the form of housing.

The following ten essays represent statements by people whose interests and activities cover a broad range of housing issues. The intent of the collection is to provide a better understanding of why housing looks the way it does through multiple concerns and points of view. It is also to better define the forces which have determined housing's present form. Because it is not possible within such a format to consider all existing housing or to present a totally inclusive coverage of each of the contributor's fields, the bibliographies are meant to supplement each essay. Most studies

Fig. 0-1   Taos Pueblo.

of housing offer either descriptive solutions or extensive policy statements about a single issue such as social or economic factors, or technological advances. This collection of essays attempts to encompass both of these approaches.

The Need for More Involvement

Throughout these essays a major theme can be recognized: individuals need to be more involved in the formation of their own homes. The large-scale urban renewal housing projects of the previous decades—although well intentioned—lacked the involvement of those who had to live there. The emerging attitude toward housing characterized by these authors is more modest, responsive, and humanly scaled. In reaction to the large high-rise housing prototypes of the previous era, the development credo is now "small is beautiful."

Historically, the places where individuals or groups participated actively in the creation of their living environments have a special character. Their uniqueness emanates from the dignity of providing for one's self, of determining one's own living mode. Americans have always

valued the dignity of self-sufficiency, particularly when the individual effort conforms to an overall sense of order. Taos Pueblos continue to be an inspiration. Each dwelling is individual yet the resulting diverse form is still an integrated whole (Fig. 0-1). Decades of criticism notwithstanding, the American suburb has many of the qualities of individualism within overall conformity. Architects and planners, however, prefer to point to Mediterranean hilltowns as the form where independent efforts create a uniquely ordered entity.

Unfortunately the technological, social, and political complexities have reduced the possibilities for participation inherent in the form of the hilltown and pueblo. When providing shelter was a major human endeavor, one could not escape becoming involved. One had to participate and cooperate with others for mutual physical and political support. Life revolved around the home. Just as legislatures have replaced the town meeting, the provision of housing has evolved to a point where institutions and agencies act as the providers and representatives. These essays suggest that ways must be found to restore the potential for personal involvement in housing.

Hearing the People

When architects were commissioned to design houses for people a certain level of individual involvement was lost. Nevertheless, through the choice of architect and his/her ability to represent the client's values, a significant amount of personal expression for both client and architect could be achieved.

In multifamily housing the problem is exacerbated. The user has no contact with the architect. The desires, aspirations, and values of the potential users are only generally represented through the marketplace. The architect and builder assume a certain renter or buyer profile. This strategy does not take into account the real diversity among people, yet it is not completely unresponsive or the developer would not be successful. Changes in demographics of this country have definitely affected housing form because of market responsiveness.

Direct involvement of the user is still uncommon, but a more rigorous determination of user needs has been undertaken. This concern was first manifested through codes and health regulations and then later by various attempts to establish guidelines through surveys and

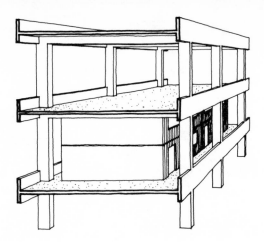

Fig. 0-2 Change and permanence.

evaluations studies. In this way the user was at least represented by surrogates of similar cultural and economic backgrounds and a level of participation (although indirect) was gained.

Throughout the past decade, the public has begun to affect the form of housing in other, more general ways. Through greater public awareness, and a willingness to participate in the environmental decision making in their cities and communities, people have banded together into interest groups. These groups have become a counter force to the bureaucracies and developers. Through litigation, lobbying, effective utilization of local media, and other techniques, these people are participating in the determination of the form of their neighborhoods if not their individual dwellings.

Physical Forms for Involvement

In calling for more participation and involvement in the process of creating housing, the authors have suggested a number of appropriate physical forms. Specific examples are surprisingly abundant and seem to fall into two major generic types. The first type is a multifamily housing form which allows economies of scale on the one hand, and the potential for individual choice and change on the other hand

(Fig. 0-2). These solutions indicate that certain aspects of the dwelling—the building structure, its interface with city services—can best be accomplished through larger scale development. They need not change drastically over long periods of time. Other aspects which relate to the individual dwellings must be able to accommodate change in shorter time spans, not only for the changing needs of individual families, but also for the potential change in occupancy. These elements include the nature of the interior space, amount of space, and the details of the dwelling which represent the cultural identity of the family. Examples of these types of structures cited in these essays include warehouse space, marinas and mobile home parks where the individual houses are elements of change within a stable context.

The second generic type of housing solution which encourages and even necessitates involvement is that which offers minimal spaces at the outset, but the potential for growth and alteration. In this way, people can invest in the rudiments of their environment and add equity and amenity as needed. These solutions are less abundant at present.

The cities into which these solutions must fit also need to accommodate involvement, en-

courage choices, and allow for change. Large-scale housing projects relying on the high rise have not succeeded in meeting these criteria. Rather, the original urban structure, which encouraged incremental growth and regeneration of cells within an overall city grid seems to work better. Consequently, the restoration and renovation of older segments of the city are finding renewed support. Human scale, an urban texture which continually offers choices and diversity, as well as the logic of conserving existing resources, are characteristic of this movement.

The common thread through this book is that there is no one way to make better housing. There is no single doctrine, no one approach to encourage participation, involvement and the control of the form of your own house. Diversity, choices, variety and the potential for change *in addition* to increased production are the new goals for housing. The form of housing will be determined by the myriad of preferences and desires of those who live there.

Organization of the Chapters

The book is divided into three sections: The

Form and Context of Housing, The Participants, and Choice and Change. The book concludes with a chapter entitled Planning for the Future of Housing. In Section One, three chapters discuss housing as it has evolved. These chapters include the developments which stem from the necessary movement away from the single family house, the changes in attitudes towards cities and urban housing, and the movement towards conservation of housing. In Section Two, the chapters discuss the important participants, both individual and institutional, who affect the form of housing. These participants include builders and developers whose changing attitudes influence the marketplace, the social scientist searching for more responsive housing, and the public struggling for a more influential role in their environment. Section Three includes three chapters discussing some of the housing forms and ideas which can accommodate the diversity and choices called for in the previous sections. The authors have tried to facilitate diversity in housing through their own writings, teachings, research and buildings. The aim of such efforts is better and more plentiful housing. The common goal for the public, architects, planners and social scientists working in the field is achieved when their efforts result in an improved dwelling and enhanced community environment. The title *The Form of Housing* represents the physical manifestations of a complex process.

Footnotes for the Introduction

1. National Housing Policy Review, *Housing of the Seventies.* Washington, D.C.: Department of Housing and Urban Development, 1975, p. 185.
2. Nichols, Mary Perrot, "The Houses Rocky Built," *New Republic* (July 17, 1976), pp. 23–27 and "The Martin Luther King Memorial Rip-Off," *New Republic* (July 24, 1976), pp. 15–21.
3. The New York Times, "The Ghost of U.D.C.," May 5, 1975, p. 30.

Contents

Section One
Housing Form and Context

1
The House Versus Housing

Sam Davis

"I can't find my house."

Although supplying shelter for everyone is critical, the quantity of dwellings does not in itself solve the housing problem. Dwellings must meet the expectations and living modes of the user. In North America, the favored form of dwelling is the single family house with its own piece of land. Although other types of housing were prevalent in parts of Great Britain and Europe when this country was first settled, early British settlers were ingrained with the image of a manor and cottage existence. Drawings of early habitats in this country reveal that the free standing house was the dominant form of home building, necessitated by the requirements of settling and pioneering. When other immigrants arrived, they too accepted the single family house tradition, even though they were often accustomed to other forms of housing and to more dense living conditions:

> . . . in the United States great importance has been attached to ownership of single-family homes in the belief, often consciously and explicitly put forward, that this type of living arrangement fosters the kind of citizenship which corresponds to traditional American values. Government agencies, such as the Federal Housing Administration and the Veterans Administration, have helped home ownership to become the dominant housing

style in American life. Particular types of financing institutions, such as savings and loan associations, have, with the encouragement and direction of state and federal government, concentrated their substantial resources in the same direction. It can be said that society looks with moral approbation upon the single family, owner occupied dwelling.[1]

The pervasiveness of the single family house idea, extending to government efforts to reinforce it, accounts for the fact that nearly 70% of all dwellings in the United States are single units.[2] It accounts for the success of such ventures as Levittown, a single family house development which reached a population of over 60,000 in 1965 (facing page). It also explains the continuing growth of the mobile home industry which, by 1973, represented 20% of all new homes being built.[3] The mobile home, free standing and served by a community support system in the form of the mobile home park, is the least expensive form of housing which still includes many of the characteristics of the Levitt-type suburb—identifiable units with multiple exposures, cross ventilation, and the potential for some private outdoor space. In both the mobile home and the suburban tract, the concept of ownership is inseparable

from form and can often provide acceptable housing even at the expense of certain physical amenities. Yet, certain physical design components are fundamental to the success of any housing (particularly family housing) and these elements are most easily accommodated by this traditional form or by comparable housing at very low densities.

After decades of testing and evaluation, a general set of requirements has emerged as predominantly important in family oriented housing. Since the single family house is the dominant housing form, the list of guidelines reflects this bias. It is, therefore, not surprising that the house best accommodates most of these criteria. The "program" has been codified in various ways, but the essentials can be seen in a list of statements developed by the Institute for Architecture and Urban Studies in New York. Their list includes:

Community: to organize dwellings and spaces to promote social interaction.
Child Supervision: to provide visual and aural contact as well as easy access between play areas and dwelling units.
Security: to avoid unseen, inactive areas.
Maintenance: to minimize undesignated interior public spaces.

1

Fig. 1-3 The housing design issues. Low-rise housing,
being a closer approximation of the single family house,
accommodates the issues better than high-rise.

Livability: to provide for individual privacy in
dwellings, for alternative views, and for
cross ventilation.
Responsiveness to Context: to acknowledge
and respect existing scale, light, views, etc.

Add to these the potential for displaying the
identity of the household and a convenient
access to the automobile (Fig. 1-3).

Elements of the House

In the single family detached house, the
domain of the dwelling is well defined (Fig. 1-4).
Intruders are easily recognized and must pass
through a series of spaces, progressing from the
most public (street) to the most private
(vestibule). This transition continues even within
the dwelling unit, beginning with the defined
entry (public) and ending with the sleeping
areas (private). The spaces which accommodate
this series of transitions also accommodate a set
of psychic needs. The *identity* of the household
is portrayed in these spaces by architectural
details ranging from the type of landscaping
(and the care lavished upon it) to the design and
embellishments of the semienclosed spaces.
These semiprivate spaces serve either as a
stage or, just the opposite, a box seat from

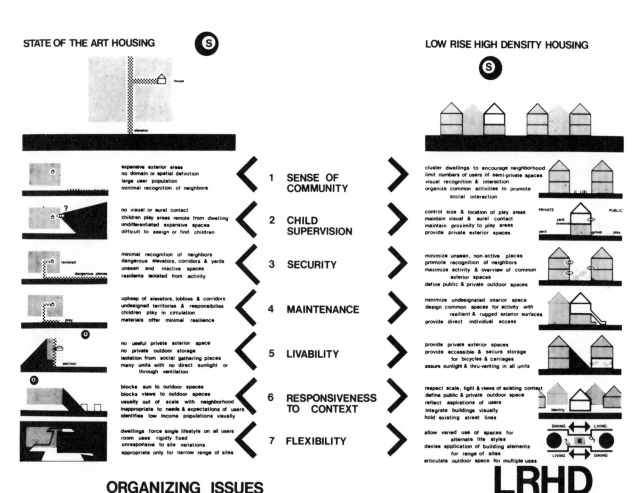

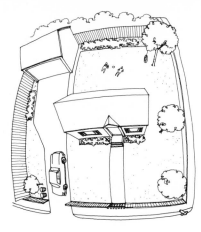

Fig. 1-4 The domain of the house.

which the user views, but does not participate in the activities of the public domain.

The absence of undifferentiated public spaces means that the single family house presents no ambiguities regarding *maintenance,* one of the major categories identified in the program. Indeed, the suburb, a form traditionally regarded as a symbol of *security* can be viewed as a strong expression of territorial definition combined with the advantage of easy surveillance. In housing of such low density, a sense of *community* is established by the limited number of immediate neighbors, easily known and recognized. Transportation modes (roads) as well as administrative boundaries (schools and community facilities) further reinforce this strong sense of domain.

In the single family house, *child supervision* is greatly simplified by immediate access to a protected outdoor play area which has direct visual and aural contact with the dwelling interior. *Livability* is insured by zoning areas within the dwelling for various activities, which can be altered without affecting other dwellings, and which allow many orientations of views, ventilation, and light. Finally, the dwelling allows easiest *access to the automobile,*

often accommodating the car within the structure itself.

The *context* of the single family house is easily responsive to the scale, light and views of other surrounding units and rarely will new units interfere with the relation of existing dwellings to these elements. Furthermore, free-standing structures on individual lots correspond to the overall existing grids of streets, sidewalks, and utility distribution.

THE CONFLICT

Although the single family house may best accommodate the criteria of the evolved and codified family housing program, it is a form which necessitates sparce development. As land, material, and energy costs rise, the average price of such a house approached $45,000 in 1976. This preferred housing form is now out of reach of most families, a frustration which further increases their dissatisfaction with their existing residential environment. A new goal for housing may be to maintain the features and amenities of the single family house while aggregating many more units on a single site for economy's sake. The conflict can best be called "the house versus housing." As eco-

nomic and ecological pressures for denser residential development increase, so does the seriousness of this dilemma. Sacrifice of personal amenities for economy and community enhancement may entail:

A reduction of private outdoor space to give more community space.
A loss of identity for individual units to allow repetition of structure and economy of production.
A reduction in ease of access to increase security.
A reduction in view and exposure of dwelling to increase privacy and numbers of units.

The conflict of "house versus housing" has become the focus for housing discussion and debate over the last decade. Variously described as "high-rise versus low-rise," "suburban versus urban," "variety versus uniformity," the basis of the arguments is housing density.

Density and Land Use Efficiency

Discussion of density and comparisons of housing using only statistics are difficult because there is no method or standard universally applied. Density may be expressed as people per acre, dwelling units per acre, FAR (floor area ratio of building to site), people per habitable room, and so on. Although indicators of density are intended to show the degree of crowdedness, some very dense environments may seem quite uncrowded and the housing within may meet many of the programmatic requirements usually associated with single family house developments. Though high density is most often associated with teaming slums, some of the densest neighborhoods in the United States are also the most elegant. Park Avenue in New York and Rittenhouse Square in Philadelphia house more than 500 families per acre. William Whyte and others have pointed to the Brooklyn Heights area of New York as a neighborhood with high livability and many features of low density settlement, yet, it has a relatively high density of 65 dwelling units per acre and over 200 people per acre. High density and overcrowdedness cannot be rigidly equated and numbers alone cannot indicate quality of life.

European cities are often praised for their comfortable blend of urbanity and density. Parks interspersed with low- or medium-rise building forms create a city texture which seems less intense than the American metropolis. Yet,

European countries support many more people per acre in both rural and urban areas than the United States. They are more dense. In some cities of the world, like Tokyo, where the perceived and actual density is higher than ours, people live in this close proximity quite successfully.

The negative image of high density in the United States is associated with long standing antiurban planning mentality. The garden city movement in England and the flight to the suburbs in the United States were a reaction to the city perceived as dirty, crowded, and crime-ridden. Recent literature suggests, however, that there is no evidence connecting crime or pathology to density. Fischer et al. concluded in a recent review of crowding studies that high density does not seem to have definite and consistent negative effects, although people may perceive it as unpleasant.

The problem may not be that density is too high, but that it is not high enough. Segregation of land uses through zoning has left many parts of the city underused, causing an average density which is quite low. Whereas our densest urban areas are comparable to those of Tokyo [Mahattan has 32 dwelling units per gross

acre and the Toshima area of Tokyo has 44 (1970)], the overall density in American cities is much lower. New York has only .7 dwelling units per gross acre.[4] Byron Hanke suggests there is ample area for growth *within* the city rather than spreading out from it.

Despite the extremes of our largest and densest cities, the density data on urbanized areas in the United States show clearly that there is enough land, a half-acre per U.S. household in urbanized areas with much unneeded reserve in large urban regions, 3 acres per household.[5]

High density has its advantages. As Whyte points out, "the center of things attracts because it is the center of things." He cites English architect Theo Crosby's analysis that public transport is economically unfeasible with less than 200–300 people per acre. At high densities, when good public transportation is affordable and convenient, cars become unnecessary. This alleviates the traditional planning dilemma of accommodating both pedestrians and private vehicles. Decentralizing urban centers into smaller cores not only duplicates facilities, but reduces the choices available to the city dweller. Furthermore, as development

Figs. 1-5 and 1-6 Density comparison. Which housing has the higher density? On a usable square foot comparison, the low-rise has a greater density.

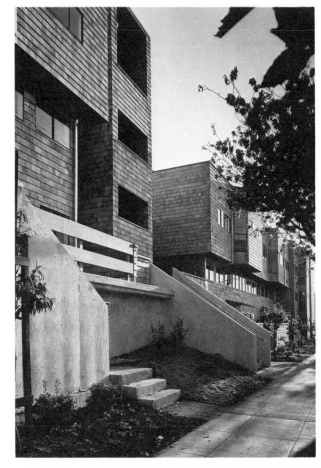

gets farther from the urban center, all services become more expensive as they are strung out farther to serve fewer people.

The discussions of high density or low density and the conflict of "the house versus housing" have also been stated as "suburban versus urban." Canadian architect Jack Diamond suggests that the choices become limited by a decentralist policy: if you want a house, you must move out of the city. The dichotomy is self-perpetuating: as the suburbs grow without an employment base, reliance on transportation into urban centers increases. As accessibility to the city increases, so does the value of urban land, thus forcing out housing and other less concentrated uses. Only high density housing can survive, and when associated with high-rise housing, this does not appeal to families as much as the suburbs. Cities may even favor high-rise and high density housing which caters to singles and childless couples who create less strain on schools and other comparable public services. Ignoring large segments of the population and eliminating a mixing of activities is shortsighted.

One of the major confusions in the continuing argument over density is the association of high density with high-rise. The reason for

	low-rise	high-rise
Ratio: Occupied square feet per square foot of site	1.51	.6
Ratio: Sq ft of recreation space per occupied sq ft	.035	.097
Cost of structure per occupied square foot	$33.01	$44.62
Cost of land per occupied sq ft		
... if land is $300,000/acre	$5.84	$5.97
... if land is $600,000/acre	$11.68	$11.94
Total cost per occupied sq ft		
... if land is $300,000/acre	**$38.85**	**$50.59**
... if land is $600,000/acre	**$44.69**	**$56.56**
Ratio: Adjusted net to gross	84.01%	84.5%

If underground parking is provided at one car per 1000 occupied sq ft, @ $5,000/car (or an added cost of $5/occupied sq ft), and assuming same ratio of recreation area to occupied sq ft ...

	low-rise	high-rise
Ratio: Occupied square feet per square foot of site	1.51	2.12
Total cost per occupied sq ft		
... if land is $300,000/acre	$43.76	$54.09
... if land is $600,000/acre	$49.60	$58.56

Fig. 1-7 California vernacular high density low-rise.

building high-rise is to achieve greater density and the logic which says rising costs are defrayed by placing more dwellings upon the land cannot be questioned. However, studies over recent years have shown that employment of the high-rise has not resulted in substantial increases in density and land use efficiency. When this building form is used, a great deal of land remains empty to allow the necessary space between the buildings. In a study conducted by Herbert McLaughlin, high-rise housing was compared to low-rise housing on the basis of the amount of usable floor area compared to the site area. (Since dwelling units vary in size and efficiency, using units per acre will not give accurate comparisons.) McLaughlin found that low-rise was more efficient than high-rise of more than 10–18 stories. While similar densities may be achieved by either high-rise or low-rise, the cost of high-rise was greater (Figs. 1-5 and 1-6). His thesis was that we do not build high-rise for economic reasons, but rather because high-rise corresponds to our image of appropriate urban form (regardless of the inappropriateness of such a form for certain user groups).
The argument over "high-rise versus low-rise" in building efficiency is not particular to the United States. In England, the government has encouraged the search for alternatives to the

high-rise through such administrative devices as the "housing cost yardstick." The housing cost yardstick has been a condition for government subsidies and emphasizes the need for higher density development through efficient housing forms. These, incidentally, turned out to be low-rise structures. More dramatically, a gas explosion and subsequent collapse of a portion of a 23-story apartment in 1968 stimulated a move in England away from towers. Their desirability was already being questioned with growing sociological evidence. In addition to recommending low-rise, work done at the Center for Land Use and Built Form in Cambridge, showed that the common street-oriented low-rise housing block was less efficient than courtyard-type housing. When courtyard housing is combined with other land uses, schools for example, the sharing of open space and access has allowed densities of up to 115 people per acre. Despite this intensified land use, the housing has a more satisfactory relationship to the ground and more private outdoor space.

The efficiency and acceptability of courtyard housing is recognized in the Southwest United States. A study by James Tice and Stefanos Polyzoides describes how this vernacular low-rise/high density dwelling provides many of

the amenities of the single family house but with increased land use efficiency. The courtyard is a collective substitute for the private yard. Accommodating controlled play areas and security, these enclaves have a high degree of community identity. Tice and Polyzoides' analysis takes into account variation in vehicle access and terrain, but maintains that the important elements of the single family house and intensified land use are consistent in the examples they studied (Fig. 1-7).

When high density housing is equated only with the high-rise form, it is also possible to see the dichotomy of "house versus housing" in terms of "variety versus uniformity." Endless suburbs of similar houses may not seem like variety. When compared to large masses of buildings each containing many dwellings within a single form, however, the house has infinite possibilities for expression. When building many dwellings at one time, variety is antithetical to maintaining efficiency of production.

The creation of monumental structures formally sited on great expanses of cleared urban land was the legacy of architecture's Modern Movement. Guided by the tenets of simplicity

6

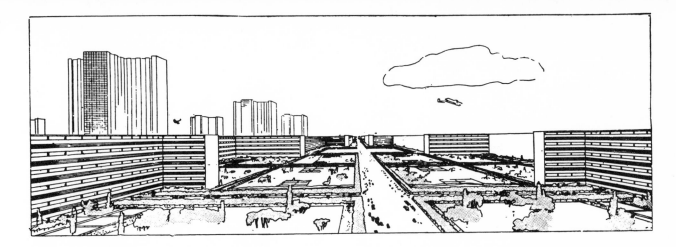

Fig. 1-8   Equality for all dwelling units, and a poor relationship to the ground.

and functionalism, architects created housing which was at the time hailed as the symbol of our ability to house the urban poor, but which is now seen as a disaster. Brent Brolin sums up what went wrong:

> The idea that the basic elemental needs of life can be satisfied by simple, elemental things is a dangerously simple misrepresentation. Some basic needs, such as an entrance to a shelter, may be simple to provide as well as universally required, but once the bare necessity is there, a complex web of social and psychological needs related to that physical entrance remains to be sorted out. The needs differ considerably from group to group but satisfying them is one of the important requirements for a happy life.[6]

The designers focused on the elements of composition and structural straightforwardness and failed to recognize the sometimes subtle social needs of those who had to live there.

Public housing was itself introduced as a socialistic concept. The Modern Movement housing form embodied unrelenting equality

and sameness. The image of "towers-in-the-park" represents a desire to give each housing unit the same amount of light, view and air by moving the buildings away from each other and by removing the dwellings from the ground. All dwellings have the same relationship to the ground (almost none) and all residents share common, often unarticulated open space (Fig. 1-8). As English architect Martin Pawley points out, these egalitarian forms were injected into a capitalistic consumer society where individualization and territoriality are cultural norms. Another analysis pictures it as a compromise of personal amenities for community enhancement.

> A rambling green carpet set at grade, flowing out between isolated buildings was thought to make amends for any loss of enclosure and, in the case of high-rise structures, to more than compensate for an inherently unsatisfactory relation to the ground.[7]

There has been a large increase in the numbers of multifamily housing being built. In 1960 only 22% of the new housing in the United States was in buildings of more than five units, but by 1972 the figure was up to 45%.[8] In suburban

rings (the area inside the standard metropolitan statistical area but outside the central city) only single family units were once preferred. Now the number of multifamily (nongovernment) housing starts between 1962–70 was as high as 75% in some of these areas.[9] In most cases, variety may be assumed to be sacrificed for increased production.

Variety can be seen in two ways. First, there is the potential for the dwellers to individualize and make distinct their own residences. As densities increase, this becomes more difficult. As units become a single building form, individuality becomes impossible. Variety may also be seen as a range of housing-type alternatives. Appropriate housing forms should not be limited by location. It should be possible, for example, to find a house suitable for family living within an urban center. It should also be possible for singles, childless couples, and the elderly to have appropriate housing environments outside the city if they choose to live there. In Manhattan, the demand for housing, mostly multifamily housing, comes from either the extremely wealthy or very poor. The poor have no option in that the city offers inexpensive (although often inadequate) housing and public transportation to jobs. The suburban areas, on the other hand, do not offer

7

low-cost housing and commuter costs are considerable. The wealthy, by contrast, have chosen the city for its amenities and services, and can afford to find luxury housing. This group consists mainly of professionals and childless couples who find recreation within the city and are willing to forego the advantages of the single family house.

As individual lifestyles create various markets, housing is produced to meet the demand. The elements of the traditional house and the general list of conventional housing requirements must continue to be accommodated as well as additional criteria specific to particular user groups. The growth of singles' complexes in Western Los Angeles and the development and renovation of town houses in urban areas is proof that variety and choice are being taken into consideration in some areas.

Even within the same development, choice and diversity should be encouraged. The range and type of outdoor spaces should allow for different age groups and activities as well as a range of dwelling unit sizes. It has also been suggested that no more than 10% of the units, or 100,000 square feet in large housing projects, be designed by the same architect to encourage variety.

As the desirability of variety becomes recognized and as the various user groups supplement the housing program, the development of large-scale housing will diminish. Small groupings of multifamily housing, often inserted into existing urban and suburban neighborhoods, will prevail over the large, uniform housing development.

Although it is not possible to make exact comparisons or analyses of the merit of housing on the basis of density alone, certain generalizations are useful in determining the range of densities which allow for various amenities. In the United States, the usual method of discussing density is dwelling units per gross acre (number of houses on total land including streets and easements). Single family units range from one house on an acre to as many as eight houses per acre, each on a 5000 square foot lot. High density, high-rise development may be as great as two to three hundred units per acre. Since the single family house is the most desirable and acceptable housing form (and the most prevalent) it becomes a standard against which any other form must be compared. Obviously, as density increases and as more units are aggregated on a site, the potential of retaining the amenities of the single family house diminishes. The major elements of this

form have been previously described as identifiability, transitional sets of open spaces and livability (defined as light, views and ventilation and zoning capabilities). Critical to all of these elements is the relationship between the unit and the ground. When the house is elevated from the ground, access, private yard, identifiability are all reduced. It is possible to sustain the loss of the individual free-standing house if the *combination* of dwelling units is made identifiable and if the spaces associated with these combinations are made to accommodate the functions of the suburban lot. Architect Alfred Koetter identifies the problem as the "big house" as opposed to many "little houses" and he offers a model:

The primary housing configurations at Bath or in Nash's London may be seen as attempts to deal with problems of extended repetition of great numbers through the use of large scale, highly identifiable sets of pieces . . . the terrace, the circus, the crescent, were pieces that made emphatic distinctions between the public and private realms.[10]

A number of recent similar studies on housing densities indicate the points at which amenities and certain building forms can coexist. A graduate course by Gerald McCue at the University of

Figs. 1-9, 1-10, and 1-11 Critical densities and amenities. Students studied densities in models on identical 10-acre sites. To facilitate comparisons, only one housing form and density were represented on each site.

20 units/acre—Above this density surface parking uses most of the open space. Parking structures begin to be necessary and this can be critical to the economics of the project.

30 units/acre—Above this density all units cannot be on the ground and therefore do not have private open space (at grade).

40–50 units/acre—Above this density more expensive construction is necessary. After 50 units/acre elevators may be required for a majority of units and units must share entries from public ways. Private open space on the ground is limited to a few units.

70 units/acre—Above this density elevators and parking are critical economic factors. At 75 units/acre parking and building mass take up the entire site. If parking garages are used, the resulting outdoor spaces are mostly "public."

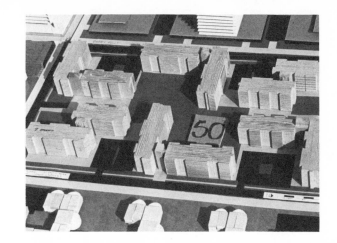

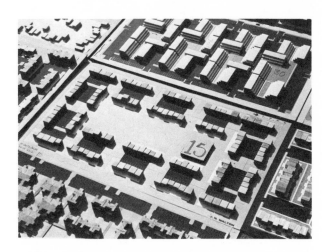

California, a report by Jack Diamond in Canada and studies by John Macsai and Oscar Newman in their books on housing all show the approximate densities at which ground related-ness, direct access to automobiles, and transitional spaces become lost. Although variation in unit sizes and mix, site configuration and parking ratio all influence density, the general conclusions of these studies were consistent (Figs. 1-9, 1-10, and 1-11). In terms of the magnitude of impact on the physical form, car storage was shown to be the single most important determinant. At densities of 8 to 20 dwelling units per gross acre, the car may be closely associated with the dwelling, but above that, aggregated parking becomes the only alternative. Above 30 units per gross acre, most of the open area of the site begins to be set aside for automobiles if they are not enclosed within the units or in some other structure. Often, the roof of a parking structure is landscaped and developed for recreational use to recover the lost open space.

Ground relatedness is the other major determinate of form by increased densities. It is preferable to have as many units on the ground as possible to allow for transitional spaces, controlled play, gardening—elements common to the house. As can be seen in the chart pre-

pared by Jack Diamond, between 20 and 35 units per acre the ratio of units on the ground to total units varies between 33 and 66% (Fig. 1-12). Beyond 35 units per acre, there are never more than a third of all units on the ground. It is possible at slightly higher densities to have stair access, but this too becomes problematic by 50 to 60 units per acre.

At 50 dwelling units per acre another major factor is evident. As the three-story height is surpassed, a different form of construction from Type 5 (wood frame) is used. At this point "medium-rise" buildings are determined by economical considerations and usually range from 7 to 12 stories in order to offset the costs of elevators and more expensive construction. Although an increase in open space of the site can be seen at these densities, this open space is not directly associated with the unit and most of the features of the single family lot have disappeared.

Beyond densities of 80 units per gross acre and up to 200 or more, the features are relatively unchanged. However, doubling the density from 100 to 200 necessitates an increase in building height to as much as 40 stories.

Small changes in density are more critical at the lower end of the scale than large changes

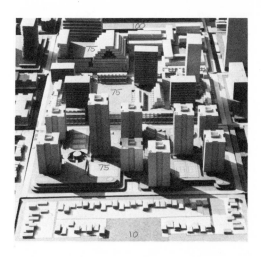

Fig. 1-12 Unit types, densities, and land use efficiency.

Dwelling Type	1 Single detached	2 Semi detached	3 Joined court	4 Duplex	5 Row house	6 Triplex	7 Quadruplex	8 Back to back Semi detached
Isometric								
Plot Plan								
Dwelling units/acre (dwelling units/hectare)	8 (20)	14 (35)	16 (40)	17 (42)	19 (47)	21 (52)	23 (57)	24 (59)
Floor area ratio / % open space	0.24 / 76%	0.38 / 81%	0.44 / 56%	0.48 / 88%	0.56 / 72%	0.60 / 80%	0.66 / 67%	0.66 / 67%
Unit relationship to grade	on grade	on grade	on grade	50% on grade 50% gr. related	on grade	33% on grade 66% gr. unrelated	50% on grade 50% gr. related	on grade
Access to unit	private on grade	private on grade	private on grade	50% priv. on gr. 50% priv. stair	private on grade	33% priv. on gr. 66% common stair	50% priv. on gr. 50% priv. stair	private on grade
Unit aspect	quadruple	triple	triple	quadruple	double (opposite)	quadruple	triple	double (adjacent)
Private outdoor space	on grade	on grade	on grade	50% on grade 50% gr. related	on grade	33% on grade 66% gr. unrelated	50% on grade 50% gr. related	on grade
Parking	private on grade	private on grade	private on grade	common on grade	private or com. on grade or u/g	common on grade	common on grade	private on grade

Dwelling Type	9 Stacked row house (1½ / bay)	10 Stacked row house (2/bay)	11 Garden apartment	12 3-storey walkup apartment	13 Medium rise stacked units	14 Combined apartments & row houses	15 Slab block apartment	16 High rise point block apartment
Isometric								
Plot Plan								
Dwelling units/acre (dwelling units/hectare)	31 (77)	35 (86)	52 (128)	65 (160)	71 (175)	84 (207)	90 (222)	120 (296)
Floor area ratio / % open space	0.86 / 72%	1.14 / 72%	1.06 / 62%	1.36 / 55%	1.95 / 68%	1.92 / 62%	1.78 / 82%	2.62 / 87%
Unit relationship to grade	33% on grade 66% gr. related	50% on grade 66% gr. unrelated	33% on grade 66% gr. unrelated	33% on grade 66% gr. unrelated	33% on grade 33% gr. related 33% gr. unrelated	25% on grade 75% gr. unrelated	small % on grade majority ground unrelated	small % on grade majority ground unrelated
Access to unit	33% priv. at gr. 66% priv. stair	50% priv. at gr. 50% com. stair	common stair	common stair	common elevator	25% priv. at gr. 75% com. elev.	common elevator	common elevator
Unit aspect	double (opposite)	double (opposite)	double (opposite)	single	double (opposite)	double (opposite)	single (and double adj.)	single (and double adj.)
Private Outdoor space	33% on grade 66% gr. related	50% on grade 50% gr. unrelated	33% on grade 66% gr. unrelated	33% on grade 66% gr. unrelated	33% on grade 33% gr. related 33% gr. unrelated	25% on grade 75% gr. unrelated	small % on grade majority ground unrelated	small % on grade majority ground unrelated
Parking	common underground	common underground	common underground	common underground	common underground	common underground	common on grade or u/g	common on grade or u/g

Assumptions For Calculations

Dwelling Type	Unit Area in S.F.	No. of Floors per Unit	Lot Size in Ft.
1	1200	1 or 2	50 × 100
2	1200	1 or 2	30 × 100
3	1200	1 or 2	25 × 100
4	1200	1	50 × 100
5	1200	2	21 × 100
6	1200	1	60 × 100
7	1200	1	60 × 100
8	1200	2	30 × 65
9	1200	1 and 2	consolidated
10	1200	2	consolidated
11	800	1	consolidated
12	800	1	consolidated
13	800	2	consolidated
14	800 & 1200	1 and 2	consolidated
15	800	1	consolidated
16	800	1	consolidated

Note: 10% circulation space added for dwelling types 11 through 16.

at the high end. Increasing the density from 15 to 50 units per gross acre changes not only the nature of open spaces, but the amenities of the individual dwelling units. Changing from 80 to 200 does not change the living environment drastically, but could produce changes in the quality of city life such as increased traffic and huge shadows, cast by 40-story buildings.

Unit Types

The discussion to this point has centered around external aspects of the dwelling and the site plan's potential to emulate the single family lot. The configuration of the dwelling itself must also accommodate elements similar to the single family house if the living environment is to be satisfactory. The nature of the interior is the subject of another chapter, but certain aspects of the dwelling configuration relate to the aggregation on the site, density, and the method of access.

These elements are extensively analyzed by Roger Sherwood. He limits the basic possible apartment configurations to three—the "single aspect," "double aspect 90 degree" and the

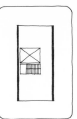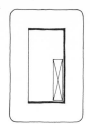

Fig. 1-13 Unit types: double aspect 90 degrees—must be on corners of the building and thus has limited application; double aspect open-ended—most like the conventional house; single aspect—most prevalent, particularly in high-rise.

"double aspect open-end" (Fig. 1-13). Of these, the double aspect 90 degrees has the least potential at higher densities since it must be at the corner of a building. The other two configurations are prevalent at nearly all densities. Within these two dwelling types are many variations depending on the structural system and, more important, the placement of "core" elements (bathrooms and kitchens).

The single aspect apartment is least like the traditional home. Not only does it have only one outlook, but bathrooms and kitchens are usually placed against the back wall and have no natural light and ventilation. This type of unit may have a direct access from the exterior through the open side, but it is also common in double loaded corridor buildings which have access along the wall opposite the windows. The depth of the apartment is limited because one wall is the sole source of natural light and ventilation. These dimensional constraints are critical in housing design since they determine the bulk of the buildings, and thereby influence the siting and amount of exterior space. The single aspect apartment along a corridor generates a building about 50–60 feet wide. The length of a structure depends on the number of units, but is also limited by fire regulations and the distance between fire access

stairs. Single aspect units are often used where orientation to one view is preferable such as in buildings near a freeway or noisy city streets. The apartment may then be oriented internally with the utility side against the noise source. A double loaded corridor building using only single aspect apartments usually should not be sited on a north/south orientation, as 50% of the dwellings would have only north light.

The "double aspect open-ended" apartment is a more prevalent type, and is also a closer approximation of the single family house. It can orient to the public front and private back and when used with the core element in the middle, creates a zoned dwelling allowing for simultaneous activities and privacy. Often this dwelling configuration is two stories high, further increasing both its zoning potential and its similarity to single family detached dwellings. When used as a two-story dwelling in a high-rise structure, a "skip stop" access system is used. In this system corridors occur at intervals greater than every floor. Units not on a corridor floor may span the entire width of the building and are reached through stairs from the hallway levels (Fig. 1-48).

"Double aspect open-ended" dwellings can be quite narrow, often only 12 feet wide. When

more than one room is necessary on each of the open ends, the width is increased. For example, a "double aspect open-ended" dwelling with four bedrooms upstairs would be 20 feet or more in width and 30–40 feet deep.

The combination of unit types, core locations and access systems may generate a range of dwelling alternatives. Nevertheless, few are close facsimiles of single family units in terms of the range of potential activities within, number of orientations, and potential for change without disturbing other dwellings. As in the other factors of "house versus housing" thus far discussed, increased production, standardization, and the need to aggregate more units together result in a corresponding reduction in amenities.

RESOLVING THE CONFLICT

The limited range of choices is defined and the conflict is manifested as the house versus housing, low-rise versus high-rise, urban versus suburban. Over the last 10 to 15 years, as an awareness of conflicts and the general issues increased, and as high-rise high density housing and the single family house became less feasible or acceptable, attempts to find

11

other forms of housing ensued. Clare Cooper-Marcus in the San Francisco Bay Area, Franklin Becker in New York, researchers at the Institute for Social Research in Ann Arbor and others extended user need studies to housing developments of varying forms and densities in the United States. The accumulation of these studies is beginning to give a clearer picture of which aspects of the designed housing environment meet with high satisfaction on the part of the user and which elements of the single family house must be retained regardless of density. Social scientists working in this field have been careful to avoid suggesting specific solutions. The feeling is that general guidelines of performance criteria allow for a variety of design responses to be considered, together with traditional factors of financing, availability of labor and materials, and site characteristics. A few architects are beginning to incorporate this body of knowledge into their architectural practice.

Although the general programmatic requirements as codified in the 1960s and early 1970s, and exemplified in the single family house, have remained consistent, specifics and emphases have changed according to location, site, density, costs and the special characteristics of the intended user groups. Consequently,

a number of different housing forms and ideas have been generated, many a result of retesting historical prototypes. With each application, priorities must be established and compromises reached. Access to the automobile, for example, is often sacrificed to controlled outdoor areas.

The following sections of this chapter describe some examples of housing at each of the critical density limits. Within these examples are various strategies to maintain the amenities of the single family house and meet the needs of particular user groups. The projects should be seen as physical manifestations of the priorities and compromises and as resolutions of the conflict of "the house versus housing."

Cluster Housing

The propensity for the single family house and a rural-oriented existence in the face of increasingly crowded conditions of the city and antiurban sentiment, resulted in the concepts of the "garden city." These garden cities, as envisioned in the late 1800s and popularized by Ebenezer Howard, were meant to contain the growth of the big metropolis by placing a green belt between the new community and the city.

It was also conceived that these new settlements would themselves be self-contained and self-supporting. With the growing personal use of the automobile, the garden city became a modern day suburb. Improved roads leading into the town eliminated the need for self-sufficiency, and only the concept of the single family house and land ownership remained. The typical subdivision created a strict segregation of land uses as well as large lot zoning. But as the pressures for space became greater, the large lots were reduced in size so that the houses became squeezed together and the spaces between them wasted and unusable.

These were the little boxes that so outraged people of sensibility and means. Photos of their rooftops and T.V. aerials, squeezed together—became stock horror shots. . . . But critics drew the wrong conclusion: what was wrong, they thought, was that the houses were too close together, when what was really wrong was that they were not close enough.[11]

The concept of the "green belt" persisted even within these suburban developments, its most prominent use being in "Radburn" planning, where pedestrian and vehicular circulation were segregated and housing placed on cul-de-

Figs. 1-14 and 1-15 Orindawoods. The courtyard house is the generator of the cluster.

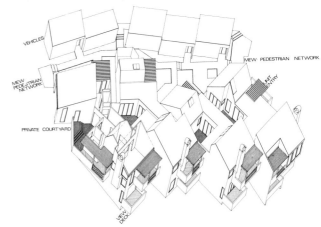

sacs separated by communal land. In Radburn, New Jersey, in the early 1930s and later in Baldwin Hills, Los Angeles, the concept of clustering housing together enabled the developers to create large expanses of open space rather than individual lots. For the most part, however, the tendency in suburban sub-developments of the United States was to further the acceptability and availability of the single family detached house, rather than to promote new housing forms. The pressure for desirable housing at increased densities came later when, due to the land squeeze the cost of developing individual lots became prohibitive. At this time, the nature of the market also changed. The use of a new zoning technique, the Planned Unit Development (PUD) emerged. The PUD allows for more comprehensive planning of large tracts of land, including the integration of commercial and recreational land use with housing. In addition, the PUD allows for various forms of housing, offering a choice to those with differing needs and lifestyles. PUD works on the principle of an overall planning process and negotiation rather than a preset type of zoning.

For housing, this zoning technique means that the dwellings can be clustered into relatively high density units (perhaps up to 20 to the acre).

Cost savings can be considerable since fewer roads and utilities must be employed, and since the houses are made more efficient by the sharing of walls. This feature reduces materials and energy consumption. Reduction in cleared land as well as planning for communal amenities not otherwise affordable by individual households has resulted in a high degree of user satisfaction with cluster housing. In terms of the dwelling units, the strength of the cluster concept is that the single family house and its domain may still be distinguishable at increased densities. Houses rest on the ground, and for the most part access to the automobile is still immediate. Often, because of reduced privacy due to the closeness of houses, the private outdoor space becomes an internalized court. The internalized court allows for light and air into dwellings which no longer have a four-sided exposure because of their clustering. In addition it supplies private outdoor space and an area for controlled play for children.

Two well-known California projects, Orindawoods by McKinley/Winnacher/McNeal (Figs. 1-14, 1-15, 1-16, 1-17) and The Californian by Backen, Arrigoni and Ross (Figs. 1-18, 1-19, 1-20, 1-21) exemplify the diverse approaches that have been used in clustering. Although Orindawoods

has a lower overall density (about 8 units per acre compared to 16 at The Californian), the units are significantly larger and the parking ratio higher so that the land use intensity is comparable to The Californian. Although using similar devices of the "double aspect open-ended" units and internalized courts, the architects took very different approaches in their treatment of the "big house" versus many "little houses" problem. This difference is exhibited in the aesthetics of the projects, as well as in the parking solutions and the nature of transitional open spaces. The reason for the differing concepts is due, in part, to the differences in user group and market. Orindawoods is a condominium development. The units are intended for sale to those who previously owned single family houses. Hence the images and functional relationships could not deviate drastically from those of conventional single family housing. Aggregated parking, for example, was considered unacceptable. Even the detaching of garages from some units, thereby creating semiprivate pedestrian walkways between parking and dwelling entry, has not met with positive user response. Most users claimed a reduction of convenience and security. The dwellings are large (most are approximately 3000 square feet) and the structures are designed to evoke conventional

13

Fig. 1-16 Orindawoods unit plan.
Fig. 1-17 Orindawoods site plan.

0   4   8 FEET

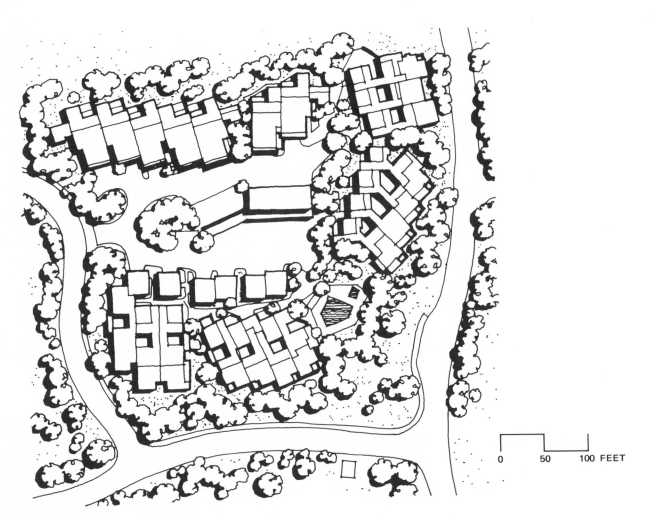

0   50   100 FEET

Bay Region domestic imagery, including shed roof and shingles. The domain of each dwelling is defined with individual trellis-covered entries, foyers, internalized courts and external decks with views. Although Orindawoods takes on a solid overall form, due to the consistency of recurring roof forms and materials, it emphasizes the individual unit as the generator of the cluster.

The Californian in the Southern California town of Tustin is aimed, on the other hand, at an adult rental market. Most of the units are on the ground and the internalized courtyard apartments (modeled after those in Chermayeff's and Alexander's *Community and Privacy*), are intended to offer a distinctly private realm. Nevertheless, the domain of each house is no longer recognizable. The entire complex is densely arranged into narrow walks and open public courts, with the parking pushed away from the units and onto the edge of the development. Although there is some variety in the sizes of open spaces, they do not seem to belong to particular dwelling units. Transitional sets of open spaces associated with individual units are not accommodated, and the distinction between public and private severe. The overall cubic white form further

Figs. 1-18 and 1-19 The Californian in Tustin. Two extremes—community and privacy—but no transition.

Fig. 1-20 Californian unit plan.
Fig. 1-21 California site plan.

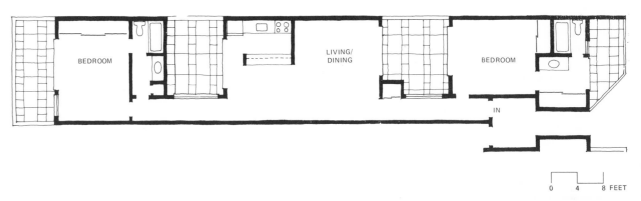

BEDROOM

LIVING/
DINING

BEDROOM

IN

0   4   8 FEET

0   50   100 FEET

diminishes the potential for recognizing the *houses* within the *housing*. Instead, the entire complex is viewed as a recognizable enclave, and the large common recreational facilities (made possible by removing parking and roads) are shared equally by all users.

Clustering allowed for increased densities in both of these projects. Each has resolved some aspects of the housing program, notably *livability*, through the use of "double aspect open-ended" dwelling types with internalized courts. Orindawoods, however, having emphasized the individual unit as the important generator of the cluster, has succeeded in retaining more of the imagery and amenities of the traditional house form, at two or three times the density. Because of the nature of their market, the developers of The Californian chose to use increased density to offer increased community and recreational facilities. While there is sufficient internalized privacy in the unit, there are few transitions between the community and private domains.

The clustering of dwellings, to achieve more density and still give private outdoor space, also resulted in a condensed form of the popular single family L-shaped unit—the joined court-

yard house. These are dwellings pushed together so that the side yard (as in the previous examples) has been completely eliminated, and the wall of the adjoining house helps define the private court. The advantages of the joined courtyard house are similar to those of the internalized court with the additional potential for a range of outdoor semipublic spaces which are closely related to the private yards and directly accessible to them. The entire site is a hierarchy of connected outdoor spaces. The domain of each house is further emphasized by the staggering of each dwelling. Parking is generally attached to the unit, but roads and driveways are separated from the pedestrian outdoor areas.

There are many examples of this housing form in Great Britain and Europe, one of the best examples being the housing design of Jorn Utzon in Elsinor and Friedresberg, Denmark (Figs. 1-22, 1-23, and 1-24). Utzon's design incorporates the joined court and "green belt" so there is a hierarchy of outdoor spaces all accessible to each other. The "Radburn" type site plan segregates parking by having alternating fingers of open space and driveways each separated by the staggered rows of houses. Sloping roof forms not only emphasize each house, but also give each court additional definition and privacy.

The use of joined courtyard clusters at increased densities covering the entire site with individual houses and private courts, is called "carpet housing" and can reach substantial densities (as high as 50 to the acre). As is always the case with increasing density, the range and variety of open space becomes more difficult to retain as does contiguous parking and the expression of individuality. The advantages of the variety of types of related outdoor spaces in Utzon's scheme and the substantial communal facilities in The Californian are reduced if all units remain close to the ground.

Essentially, cluster housing remains a relatively sparse land use. Internal courts, and houses with ground access begin to take up extensive amounts of site, and eventually force the dwellings into two- or three-story units. These then cast shadows on the private outdoor space. The appeal of cluster housing is in the individual access, potential for identity, ground relatedness and a generally pastoral setting at densities double or triple those of single family house developments.

Cluster housing is a generic term and implies no particular housing form. Although it has

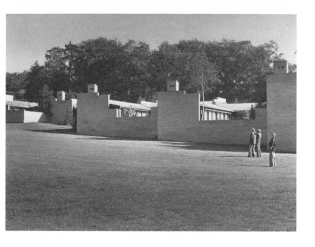

Figs. 1-22 and 1-23   Joined courtyard houses in Denmark. A range of outdoor spaces from private courts to public yards.

Fig. 1-24   Frederiksberg site plan by Utzon.

0   50   100 FEET

come to be equated with Planned Unit Development and courtyard-type aggregations, many planned unit clusters are actually made up of row house units. The row house, however, is traditionally an urban housing form.

Urban Row Housing

The town house usually takes the form of the row house, similar to the attached courtyard or internal courtyard models, but with rectangular housing envelopes that are pushed together. The major aspects of the detached house are still present: a front and back, a transitional set of spaces including a front porch or stoop and a well-zoned two- or three-story double aspect house. The front porch or stoop often takes on more significance than it would in the single family house, since it is often the only physical feature communicating the identity of the household. This form of housing is presently being revived and can be seen in almost any American city. This may be an attempt at rejuvenating the existing stock of older town houses, or an attempt at duplicating these characteristics in new intercity housing. In many cities, old row houses are being sold for one dollar and low interest loans are supplied for

17

Fig. 1-25 Placing the parking under the house, or in a garage under the yards, can increase the overall density of the project and the security of the open spaces.

Fig. 1-26 Penn's Landing Square in Philadelphia. Individual houses with private yards in an urban context.

Fig. 1-27 The row houses are oriented inward making a more secure open space but reducing street ambiance.

renovation. The intent is either to keep families in the city or to attract suburbanites back to the city, and into a housing form more appropriate to their needs than the urban high-rise building.

Although the conventional siting of row houses has been street-oriented, a number of newer developments of urban row housing show a change in priorities of the housing program. The traditional urban row house block created a strong consistent public side, with the potential for displaying the identity of the household. The requirements of security, child supervision, and access to automobile have, however, become more influential form determinants. Consequently, many town house developments are now internally oriented, toward the center of the block, to create more controlled access, sets of outdoor areas removed from the city street, and more secure open parking. As in the street-oriented model, individual parking is often incorporated into the lower levels of the units. When aggregated parking is necessary, it is often placed under a group of dwellings in the internally sited scheme with private yards on a deck above (Fig. 1-25). The potential for identifying the individual dwelling is reduced in the internal block model. It is replaced by the group identity of the separate enclave.

Louis Sauer has designed a number of row house schemes with varying siting and parking configurations. In one of his more recent projects, Penn's Square Landing in Philadelphia, the three-story town houses are internally oriented, have private yards, decks and aggregated underground parking (Figs. 1-26, 1-27, and 1-28). These condominiums have attracted buyers from the suburbs not only because they share many characteristics of the house, but also because of the security aspects of internally oriented housing. In his Harmony House in New Haven (Fig. 1-29), Sauer chose to place parking in an open courtyard in front of the internally oriented dwellings. He felt that a close physical relationship with the car was important not only for convenience, but because the user group was accustomed to it (Fig. 1-30). The sponsor opposed the design, but the architect prevailed, citing his own user evaluations surveys as evidence of this preference.

The characteristics which make the row house acceptable—increased density and retention of the characteristics of the single family house—convinced architects DeMars and Hardison and landscape architect Lawrence Halprin to try this form for the Easter Hill Village public housing project in Richmond,

18

Fig. 1-28 Penn's Landing Square site plan.
Fig. 1-29 Harmony House site plan.
Fig. 1-30 Harmony House in New Haven. Parking in the major open space in full view of the dwelling.

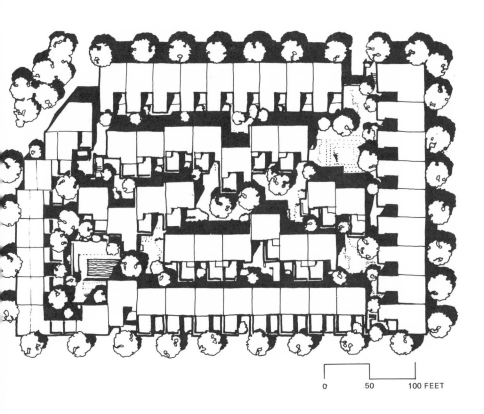

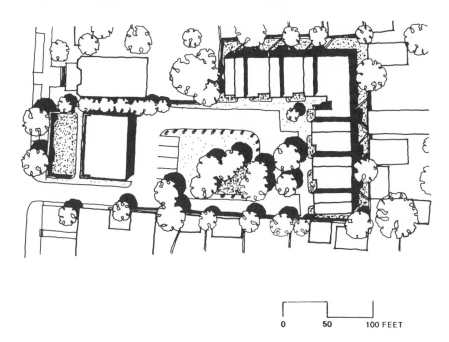

California in the early 1950s (Fig. 1-31). The project became the subject of an extensive evaluation by Clare Cooper-Marcus in her book, *Easter Hill Village*. The study covers many aspects of the development, including the resident's aspirations, needs, and attitudes, and there is also extensive information about the design assumption that the residents wanted single family houses. The architects tried, consequently, to make the dwellings as much like individual homes as possible, within the economic constraints of the program and the density required. Although the overall density is not high for row housing (12 units per gross acre), the buildings, parking and roads cover only 41% of the site. The architects wanted to supply a front yard, a private outdoor space in back and a semiprivate outdoor space. In addition, there were detailed aspects of the facade of the town houses, including variations in siding, color, roofing, and even porch and window details. The row houses were staggered in plan and elevation and units of differing size were clustered together to further increase the potential for variety and individualization. Compared to the norm in the 1950s for apartments of similar density—long rows of barrack-like housing — this project was very innovative. Of all the features which the architects con-

sidered in the design of the buildings, those most noticed by the residents were color and differences in height and unit size. Many of the other details went unmentioned by all but a few of the residents questioned. One assumption to be drawn is that the user does not perceive physical design in the same way that the professional does. DeMars feels that although the residents did not cite more subtle aspects of variation, their overall perception was one of diversity. Realizing the existence of variation, they simply mentioned color and height differences as the most obvious.

The importance of Easter Hill Village is that the designers were sensitive in their recognition that aspects of the single family house must be retained to achieve a high level of user satisfaction. Variety, even at the expense of a cohesive or unifying architectural statement, is in itself valuable. It is unfortunate that this project has since fallen into disrepair. The local authority budget was reduced and the maintenance of the project, a very important factor in insuring user satisfaction, has deteriorated. Many of the aspects of variety such as exterior colors, were lost in subsequent unimaginative repaintings.

The concepts sensitively applied by the architects, and recognized by the occupants of Easter Hill, can once again make urban row housing a popular form when coupled with some aspect of ownership or tenant control. This would apply even to those who have, up until now, preferred the suburbs and detached houses. The model offers many of the aspects of the single family house; it is an efficient use of land, and is certainly an alternative to the urban high-rise.

Walk-Ups

As moderate densities are achieved in row housing (40 to 60 units per gross acre), the open spaces on the ground are generally confined to private outdoor space as they are when joined courtyard houses are extended to create "carpet housing." User needs evaluations, including those by Becker at Cornell and Cooper-Marcus at Berkeley, have stressed the importance of variety in the site plan. This serves not only to provide transitional sets of spaces from public to private (issues of security, identity, community), but also to provide specific activity areas for different age groups. In order to create a more open site plan

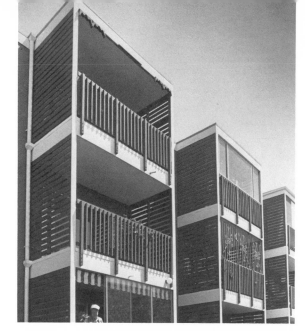

Some of the dwellings must be moved off the ground making walk-up apartments. These can take different forms such as stacked town houses or garden apartments, but they all share certain features which make them unlike any housing discussed thus far. Most do not have private outdoor space on the ground. They rely on commonly shared stairs and halls for access, and most parking is aggregated away from the units.

In walk-up apartments at moderate densities, the organization that has been used frequently to resolve the loss of traditional house amenities is that of interlocking open space to which buildings containing a few dwellings are oriented. In a site plan of interlocking spaces, a variety of activity areas are linked to each other by controlled paths. The paths are created by the constriction between the ends of buildings. Residents can walk from place to place within the community without crossing streets. They can experience different types of space and watch different kinds of activities.

St. Francis Square by Marquis and Stoller (completed in 1964 at 37 units per acre) has served as a model of this type of housing throughout the decade (Figs. 1-32, 1-33, 1-34). The development is family oriented (mostly two

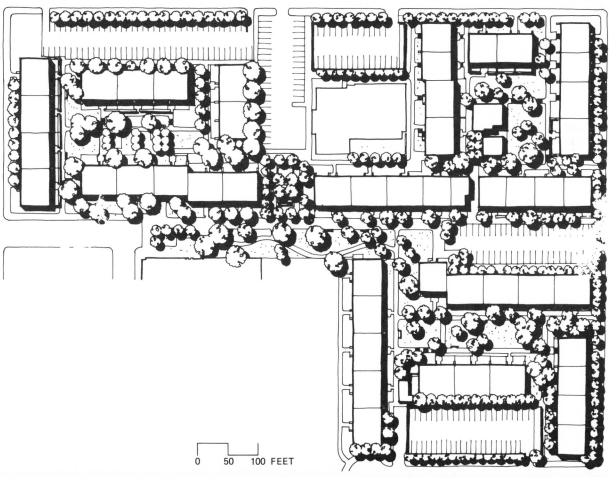

0   50   100 FEET

and three bedrooms) and is a cooperative. This fact undoubtedly accounts for much of the strong sense of identity and community which exists at St. Francis Square. Having six units off each access stair provies a controlled entrance, but more important, the scale of the open spaces makes the residents feel "at home." The "big house" has replaced the "little house:"

The fact that the architects also chose to further distinguish those six family units by stepping them back and forth and down the hillside also attributes to unit definitions . . . tenants tend to refer to the six family units as "my house."[12]

Although the single aspect units are not particularly large and do not respond to many of the issues of "livability" and "flexibility," there is a significant degree of variation in the use of private outdoor space, even when it is not at the ground level. Many families have taken balcony spaces and created individualized extensions of their homes in much the same way that the suburbanite embellishes through gardening or decorative additions. The designers chose to sacrifice convenient access to the car (they have been pushed to the edge of the site) in favor of protected interior yards, a decision which has proved to have been a wise one. The common courtyard space has become a collective extension of the suburban yard. Residents periodically volunteer to modify the landscape and facilities within these spaces after reaching a common agreement as to what should be done. The number, size and types of play equipment within each of these yards allows for activities to accommodate different age groups. This equipment, incidentally, has been radically changed by the tenants from the original design.

In her study of St. Francis Square, Clare Cooper-Marcus noted that most of the residents felt they "belonged" either to the whole development or at least to the square on which their "house" bordered. Asking the same question of residents of a 20-story high-rise, she found that most residents there responded that they "belonged" in their own apartment or "nowhere." She concluded that St. Francis Square, as the client–designer team had hoped, provides many of the amenities of suburban living in an urban context and, therefore, successfully resolves the conflict of "house versus housing."

A project with characteristics similar to those o St. Francis Square is Charles Moore's Church Street South in New Haven, Connecticut (Figs. 1-35 and 1-36). It also is innercity public housing with a density of approximately 37 units to the acre. The Church Street South project was somewhat controversial and under went continuous and extensive revisions before construction. The design which was finally built contains features intended to emphasize the individual nature of each unit and to maintain a close relationship both to th automobile and to the ground. The buildings ar admittedly plain, but are sited in combinations of units creating a diverse pattern of courts and streets. Along the streets, brightly painted graphics give special emphasis to the entry of each apartment. Even though man units are not resting on the ground, the combination of emphatic stoops and direct access to the ground through individual stairways does reinforce the sense of separate dwellings. To strengthen a village image and to increase the sense of community, each interior street or court formed by the buildings has a name and each dwelling has a corresponding address. In addition, the ends of the court and some of the streets contain commercial or community facilities. The varied ou door public space is organized around a

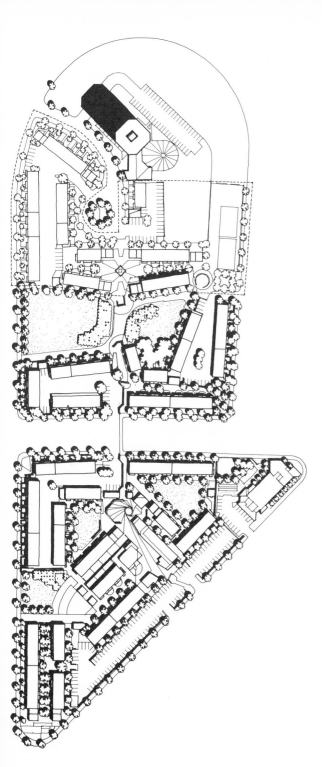

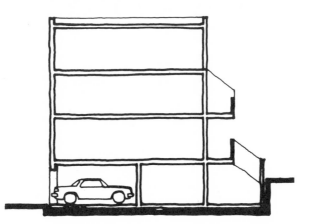

central spine. This places the housing in its urban context rather than creating an isolated enclave.

As is the case of St. Francis Square, the existence of the pedestrian street and courts did necessitate placing much of the parking at the perimeter of the site. However, 50% of the parking is in garages directly under the dwelling unit and is accessible through driveways separated from the pedestrian spaces by the buildings themselves (Fig. 1-37).

The low-rise high density (LRHD) prototypes outlined in *Another Chance for Housing*, incorporate most of the ideas of St. Francis Square and Church Street. Both the prototype and the specific designs for Fox Hills and Marcus Garvey Park Village (built in 1975, both with densities of approximately 55 units per acre) provide for private access to the outdoors from each unit (Figs. 1-38 and 1-39). This provision results in an unusual amount of interior stair space. It does, however, reinforce the individual nature of each dwelling unit even when that unit does not rest directly on the ground. Double aspect open-ended units are satisfactory in size and zoning capabilities,

23

and each allows for cross ventilation and light. It is the site plan and the emphasis on the individual domain of the unit within the plan, though, that represent the best resolution to date of the conflict between "house and housing." Mews and pedestrian streets serve to coalesce the mini-neighborhoods, and they are expanded when the density and size of the site allows parking in full view of the unit. Bordering the streets and mews are town houses containing more than one dwelling, but most have a front stoop, a private outdoor space, and a view both of the street and of the private rear yard. Commenting on these specific solutions, the designers explain:

We intended to bring to the city dweller many of the immediate amenities that the suburbs have to offer, most particularly the private house with its private yard, while at the same time, proffering to the suburban home owner a pattern of development which would create that specific sense of neighborhood that often seems best found within the city.[13]

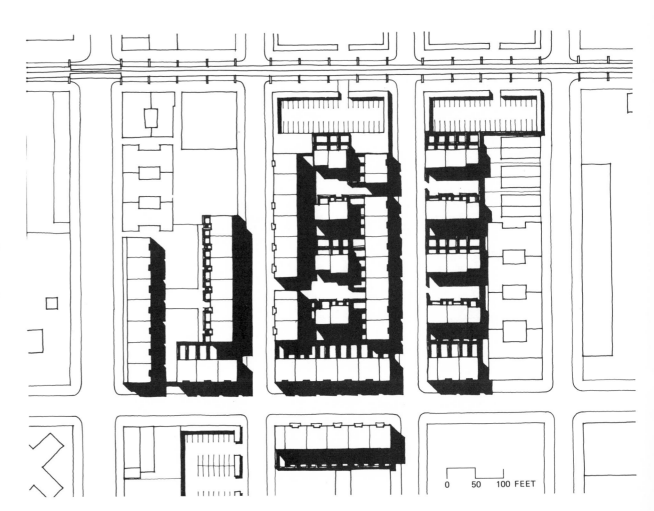

0   50   100 FEET

Fig. 1-40 Halen in Switzerland. Terraced housing gives each dweller a private outdoor space and a recognizable unit.

Terrace Housing

Once density becomes too great to provide for private outdoor spaces on or near the ground and once the dwelling unit becomes concealed within a greater building envelope, the major features of the single family house—identifiability and access to the yard—are lost. On sites where conventional building forms are impossible due to difficult terrain, terraced housing was devised.

Two strong visual characteristics typify this form. First, the overall form has an aggregated hill town image. This is strong enough to cause residents to identify the whole development as their own individual place. Second, as the mass is stepped back to conform to the hill, each dwelling becomes recognizable and claims an outdoor space immediately adjacent and private on the roof of the lower unit. Like "carpet housing," which completely covers the site with a fine texture of building and courts, terraced housing blankets the hillside and forms an inhabited surface.

The concept of this variation on "carpet housing" dates back to 1901 when Tony Garmer conceived of a stepped form for a hillside near Lyon. The most famous built appli-cation is Switzerland's Siedlung Halen built in 1961 by Atelier 5 (Fig. 1-40). It is a form which has now become popular in Switzerland because of the preponderance of difficult building sites. In Halen, the units are two- or three-story town houses each with an extensive garden on the roof of the house below and a courtyard entry. In the United States, a similar prototype was used for a public housing design in New York by Werner Seligman. He added a long slab at the top of the building to achieve the required density. In Seligman's scheme, the houses are small courtyard dwellings unlike those at Halen, and their open space does not overlap onto the roof of the lower unit.

Although terraced housing lacks multiple exposures when placed against a hill, and creates difficult access to parking, nevertheless, its advantages of private outdoor space and delineation of individual units has encouraged some architects to try the same form in an urban context (without the hill). Of course, without the accompanying site advantages, the underside or "belly" of the structure becomes a problem. In the urban setting, the underside can become commercial space while the artificial hill surface, open to the sunlight and air, remains housing. In the early 1960s, DeMars and Reay suggested this structure for Santa Monica, California, and they utilized the space under the terraced housing as parking (Figs. 1-41 and 1-42). Their scheme had a number of advantages, not the least of which was parking at the same level as the house entrance. This is common in single family housing but rare at high densities. In addition to the private yards, portions of the stepping structure were used for communal, semiprivate outdoor space in a manner similar to that of walk-up housing. Although the DeMars and Reay design was never built, it was widely publicized and had its affect on subsequent developments, including Habitat in Montreal.

Habitat by Moshe Safdie (1967) is the most famous of the stepped building prototypes used without the benefit of a sloping site (Fig. 1-43). Much of the publicity surrounding Safdie's structure stems from the technological approach of stacking room size concrete boxes. But the generation of the form was not due merely to the reliance on technology, it also repre-sents a program similar in intent to the requirements outlined in the most recent user need studies for family housing. Safdie calls it an "environmental bill of rights," including the

Figs. 1-41 and 1-42 Santa Monica Project. Terraced housing without the hill. Cars are parked underneath with direct access to dwelling. The forerunner to Habitat.

Fig. 1-43 Habitat in Montreal. An individual dwelling with a private outdoor space as large as a living room.

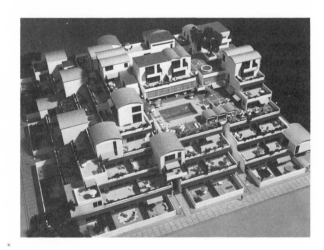

right to private outdoor space equal to or greater than the interior living space. He thus recognizes the need for protected children's play adjacent to the dwelling and the other amenities of yards, usually associated with single family houses. The "bill of rights" also states that in the single family house tradition of North America, "each dwelling unit must be recognizable and definable from the outside by the occupant."[14] The geometry of the stacked units at Habitat allows for dwellings which are a closer approximation of the detached house than is the case with other elevator supported housing schemes. The units are two-story and easily zoned; overlooks into other units are rare, yet each dwelling has many exposures rather than the one or two common to single or double aspect units.

Elevator Supported—Land-in-the-Air

As densities increase to above 80 units per gross acre, the design solutions successful in providing single family house amenities no longer work. Nearly all the dwelling units are off the ground. They are accessed by elevators and no unit is easily identifiable.

The high density tower block forms of the previous decades represent a disregard by designers for the functions of transitional sets of open spaces—territoriality and identity. These transitional spaces were traded for large expanses of what was supposed to be parklike ground. In the tower, the double loaded corridor becomes the public space. The functions of surveillance and social buffering are dependent upon doorways which, more often than not, open directly into the major living spaces of each dwelling. Methods for correcting this particular shortcoming of the double loaded, high-rise housing form have been prolific and sometimes successful. A major architectural response has been to transfer "the land" and its corresponding "street" to the air. The initial justification for pedestrian "street decks" in both Europe and the United States was that they would encourage social interaction and create the same sense of community as that found on a real street (Fig. 1-44). The English architects and disciples of Le Corbusier, Alison and Peter Smithson, saw their decks in the air quite literally as streets: "These pedestrian decks are no mere access balconies. Two women with prams can stop and talk without blocking the flow, and they are safe for small children, as the only wheeled vehicles allowed are the tradesmen's hand and electrically propelled trolleys."[15]

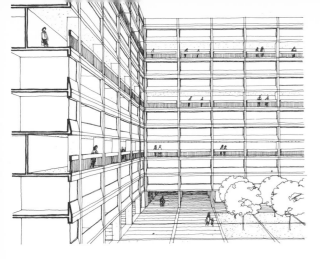

Fig. 1-44 Streets-in-the-air. Better access and the potential for individual houses, even if the sociability was not increased.

Fig. 1-45 Townland. Building a house on an artificial lot.

The concept of "streets-in-the-air" has been criticized as a mere romantic gesture meant to recreate city life on an artificial ground plane. On a real street there are many more activities than are possible on an elevated deck. Also, a real street has two sides. Yet, an access with light along one side, open to the air and adjoining a major open space, is certainly more pleasant than an enclosed corridor, even if the sociability intended is not increased.

The pedestrian deck may also be seen as a physical manifestation of the desire to retain the identifiable single family dwelling within the high-rise form. One of the most intriguing efforts of the United States government's Operation Breakthrough program (designed to encourage consortiums of finance, management and industrialized construction producers) was the artificial land scheme by Townland which created "lots in the sky" (Fig. 1-45). The potential to build a two- or three-story town house within certain restrictions (similar to traditional zoning laws) meant that a buyer could purchase a stacked lot on which a private single family house could be built. Some of the "lots" are left open so that each deck will have public outdoor space and community facilities. The scheme was developed on a

small scale in Seattle. A similar concept constructed on a minor scale held individual mobile homes on the land decks (Fig. 10-15).

The most prominent streets-in-the-air scheme in the United States is the Riverbend Project built in New York in 1968 (Fig. 1-46). The architects, Davis and Brody used "piggyback" brick town houses which rest on a concrete deck recurring every two stories. The full range of spaces from street to vestibule (public to private) exists in this solution through the use of slight level changes and half walls which surround the private open spaces. Reinforcing the territorial domain of the house, the blocks of stacked houses are sited around a public play area. The area is inaccessible from the public street at ground level and yet both accessible and visible to all the town houses. Each resident has his/her own two-story house on a pedestrian street near a public park that can be seen from each front porch.

The benefits of the land-in-the-air or artificial lot concept go beyond the mirroring of a suburban motif in an urban context. The work of Habraken in the Netherlands puts forth the notion that the two products, the land and the dwelling, are separate and have differing life

27

spans. Thus, the responsibility for the existence
and maintenance of each should also be
separate. In such a situation, ownership and
self-determination in the nature of each
dwelling are encouraged. Territorial domain
and identification of the dwelling are reinforced.

All of the "land-in-the-air" or "street deck"
schemes use a "skip stop" elevator (the elevators skip floors) since it is not necessary to
duplicate access on every level. In Riverbend,
for example, the access decks occur every two
levels with two-story town houses in between.
Many other configurations of skip stop are
possible, allowing for a great variety of
amenities to increase the livability of the
dwelling unit in high-rise structures (Fig. 1-47).
Many of these unit characteristics are similar to
those achieved in single family and low density
housing. They include the potential for double
aspect open-ended plans, thereby increasing
the amount of light and air into all spaces.
The community fabric of the site is also
enhanced because a larger range of spaces are
within visual, and often aural contact of the
dwelling. Life in such a building resembles the
experience of communicating to neighbors
across small streets and backyards.

Fig. 1-47 Skip stop elevator access. Variations on the system allow for single family house amenities and increased livability for high-rise.

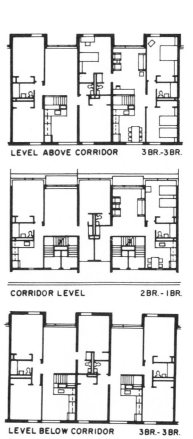

Figs. 1-48(a) and (b) Diagramatic plans of Eastwood Roosevelt Island and Peabody Terrace each using a skip stop system. In Roosevelt Island, the stairs are moved within each apartment.

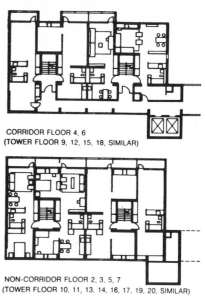

CORRIDOR FLOOR 4, 6
(TOWER FLOOR 9, 12, 15, 18, SIMILAR)

NON-CORRIDOR FLOOR 2, 3, 5, 7
(TOWER FLOOR 10, 11, 13, 14, 16, 17, 19, 20, SIMILAR)

The skip stop system also alleviates two of the problems generally associated with elevator-dependent housing, *maintenance* and *security*. It reduces by two-thirds or more the amount of corridors, and thus means a corresponding reduction in the upkeep and air conditioning of public interior space. It increases the use of the remaining corridors, thereby making them more observed and more secure.

Although the use of skip stop elevators is prominent in Europe (its most celebrated use is Corbusier's Unite d'Habitation), it has been used infrequently in the United States. One of the first examples of the skip stop, gallery access system in this country was provided by DeMars and Rapson in student housing at MIT, Cambridge, Massachusetts, constructed in 1950. Its most renowned application was Jose Luis Sert's Peabody Terrace, also in Cambridge, built in 1964 [Fig. 1-48(a)].

In Peabody Terrace the elevators stop every third floor. From there you enter a stair to walk up or down a level to apartments on noncorridor floors. For these units, there is double orientation and cross ventilation. Later, in his Roosevelt Island housing for the UDC, Sert moved the stairs within each dwelling so

LEVEL ABOVE CORRIDOR   3BR.-3BR.

CORRIDOR LEVEL   2BR.-1BR.

LEVEL BELOW CORRIDOR   3BR.-3BR.

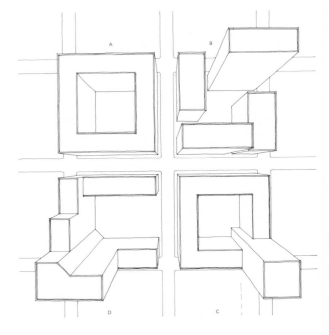

that all units had a private entry on the corridor floor leading up or down into the main portion of the apartment. Since these private stairs are not accessible to the public and are not continuous through the height of the building, separate fire stair towers had to be placed on the exterior [Fig. 1-48(b)].

Mixed Housing Form

Once the density becomes so great (75 to 150 units per acre) as to preclude the advantages of the single family house, certain elements take on added significance. The importance of the variety of outdoor spaces to accommodate different user groups has been emphasized in the evaluation studies of Becker at Cornell and Cooper-Marcus at Berkeley. Undifferentiated spaces do not achieve this goal. It is also extremely important that the new housing relate to its context, and at the same time represent an *aggregation* of dwellings with which each resident wants to identify.

Site massing is critical both for responding to the existing context and for establishing either a varied ground plane or protected semipublic spaces. Continuous building walls with cornice heights consistent with the existing neighbor-

hood (often zoning requires such consistency) have been used for decades to create a protected enclosed space for residents while holding the street line. This is called the "perimeter block" model and although used frequently throughout Europe at the beginning of the century, the form appears more recently in the "ding bat" housing of Southern California, where donut-shaped buildings often enclose pools (Fig. 1-49).

Breaking down the building mass into sets of smaller buildings which define and protect semipublic spaces is seen in all three of the examples in the "walk-up" section. When the density is increased so that a high-rise element must be incorporated, one of two approaches generally prevails. One method uses a combination of the perimeter block and a tower and the other uses a combination of free standing towers and walk-up buildings. In each case, the lower elements generally face the street in order to meet the existing scale, while the towers are located within the site to minimize their impact. The displacement of these structures often forms a varied ground plane allowing differing activities. A third type of massing has emerged which coalesces the two forms. It is the stepped building. The low-rise structures

Fig. 1-51 Roosevelt Island. Stepped forms provide increased sunlight and views for units, and protected outdoor space.
Fig. 1-50 Peabody Terrace. Stepping down to meet existing neighborhood.

and the tower element are connected into a single continuous building which steps from the lower scale into a tower. The advantages of the earlier massing schemes remain (variety of ground plane, protected spaces, responsiveness to existing street scale) with an additional advantage of increased internal security. This results because the whole building acts as a barrier, as it does in the perimeter block model. The objectionable use of fences (often seen by residents as "institutional") is avoided, while security and high density are maintained.

Sert's Peabody Terrace in Cambridge incorporates high elements to achieve density, but lower ones to meet the scale of the existing Cambridge neighborhood (Fig. 1-50). The two forms are connected and integral. The rationale of this same device is more evident on New York's Roosevelt Island where urban Main Street is built up into high elements with the buildings stepping down to the water promenade (Fig. 1-51). This concept affords views for the tower while allowing light and air to enter the open space that results. The space is defined for the use of the resident who is effectively separated from public traffic and from street noise.

In two Coney Island projects, Hoberman and Wasserman developed a high density scheme which maintained the existing street scale by pushing low buildings to the sidewalk and by having no setbacks. As a result, a maximum of interior space is gained for the resident (Figs. 1-52 and 1-53). The lower buildings then rise into towers, sited for maximum views and for minimum shadows on the open space. The combination of these two forms can provide a family-oriented housing near the ground in low buildings, usually available only in projects of much lower densities. In the high-rise portions, there is a solution more appropriate for the elderly, singles, and other types of resident groups not dependent on a close proximity to ground level, outdoor play space, and the necessary transitional order of this outdoor space.[16]

A scheme with similar massing graphically illustrates how changes in priorities within the housing program can influence the physical design. Plaza 1199, also in New York, evolved from the winning competition entry of Hodne and Stageberg. The original scheme included towers set within the site while low buildings were meant to relate to the existing neighborhood scale and street layout. However, the

Fig. 1-52 Coney Island. Stepped form meets existing neighborhood scale and provides protected interior spaces.

Fig. 1-53 Coney Island site plan.

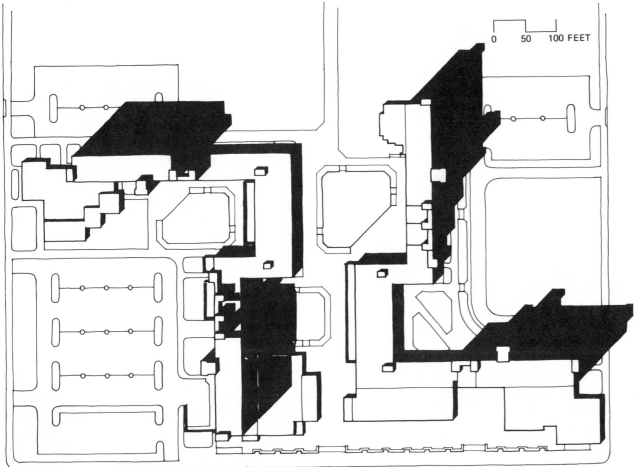

0   50   100 FEET

sponsor/resident group favored the final stepped form. This placed the high portions up against the existing low-rise neighborhoods and then stepped down toward the river, creating protected courtyards (Figs. 1-54 and 1-55). Although the building mass as realized is responsive to sunlight and view, the main reason for the shift was to *separate* the new housing from the old and further increase the imageability of the new development. Although the architects were sensitive to the existence of a generalized urban community and context in their original scheme, the programmatic aspects of *identity, security* and the specific *user group community* become a more influential form determinant.

Forum of High Density Forms

In the architectural community, competitions are used to stimulate ideas as well as to provide solutions for specific problems. Consequently, the results of competitions can be seen as bench marks of current thinking. In the years between 1963 and 1974, there were three major and very similar housing competitions which point out the advances made in understanding the housing design problem and the ways in which the evolving program for housing can be applied at high densities.

Fig. 1-54   Plaza 1199 site plan.

Fig. 1-55   Plaza 1199 in New York. Stepped form turns away from neighborhood and creates identifiably separate housing.

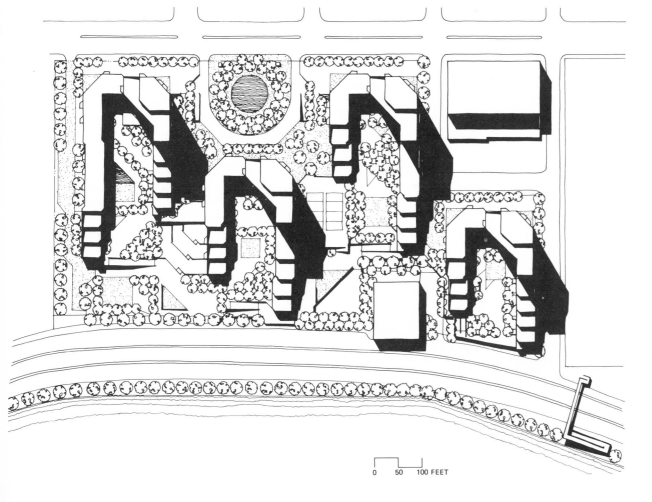

0   50   100 FEET

Fig. 1-56 Plaza 1199 original competition entry by Hodne and Stageberg. Low buildings to meet existing neighborhood, mixed uses.

These were the competition for 1199 Plaza on the East River in Manhattan (1963), the Brighton Beach Housing Competition for Brooklyn (1968), and the Roosevelt Island Housing Competition for the narrow island (formerly Welfare Island) on the East River (1974). The similarities among the three events include: an emphasis on the general housing issues described earlier, the existence of a strong urban context, a watery edge (not accessible in 1199 Plaza), the need for high density housing of 100 units per acre or more. The juries in all three competitions represented a broad range of concerns and included urban designers, sociologists and builders, as well as prominent architects. The winning submissions in these competitions represented a variety of stylstic trends in modern architecture, including the controversy over "vernacular" versus "monumental." More critically, all the cited schemes contained similar recurring elements which were designed to meet the needs and aspirations of the user, through the retention of the components of the single family house, or through an overall mass that was responsive to the urban context providing protected outdoor space.

The 1199 Plaza Competition, sponsored by the Ruberoid Company and supported by the New York Housing Development Administration, was won by Hodne Associates (now Hodne/Stageberg); their evolved and completed design was mentioned earlier as an example of the stepped building form. The original winning design used a variety of buildings in order to fit the context. These continued the established low-rise and mixed-use character of the upper East Side of Manhattan espousing the image of the urban life found in Jane Jacobs' *Death and Life of Great American Cities,* which had just been published (Fig. 1-56). The streets were continued into the low-rise portion of the site which included commercial and community facilities as an extension of the neighborhood. The general character of the scheme is in keeping with most of the programmatic issues codified and presented eleven years later for a similar competition. The responsiveness of the project to its urban context and its sense of community were certainly major form generators of the scheme. Equally important was an understanding that a variety of ground plane activities and lower housing forms were appropriate for family units. Although the principles remained consistent throughout the evolution of the final design, aspects of security became a more important form generator than earlier considerations. Responsiveness to the existing urban context, in particular, was felt to be in conflict with the security of the enclave.

The schemes for the Brighton Beach Housing Competition, which also involved the Housing Development Administration, displayed a wide variety of massing forms. The fourth prize, by Donald and Marja Watson, included towers and walk-ups somewhat similar to the earlier Hodne/Stageberg solution. However, the winners, Alfred Koetter and Jerry Wells, used a combination of a building wall and a "point tower" (a high-rise with a few units on each floor) (Figs. 1-57 and 1-58). The building wall formed semipublic courts in a massing reminiscent of Peabody Terrace. This lower building element is used to relate the mass to the surrounding neighborhood and to create controlled interior plazas. Other cited schemes for Brighton Beach included the use of the stepped tower. In this case, though, the top units opened to the roof of the stepped buildings to allow for large outdoor roof decks for at least some of the units, as in terraced housing. The Venturi and Rauch scheme, which created a controversy among the jury on the basis of its 19th century builder aesthetics, incorporated two towers which met the ground with garden apartments. In addition, their

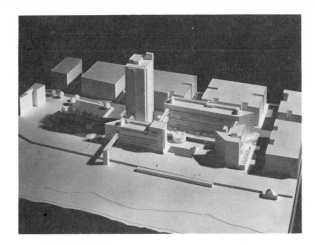

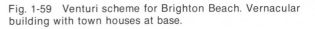

Fig. 1-57 Brighton Beach winner by Koetter and Wells. Building wall and point tower with protected outdoor spaces.

Fig. 1-58 Brighton Beach site plan.

Fig. 1-59 Venturi scheme for Brighton Beach. Vernacular building with town houses at base.

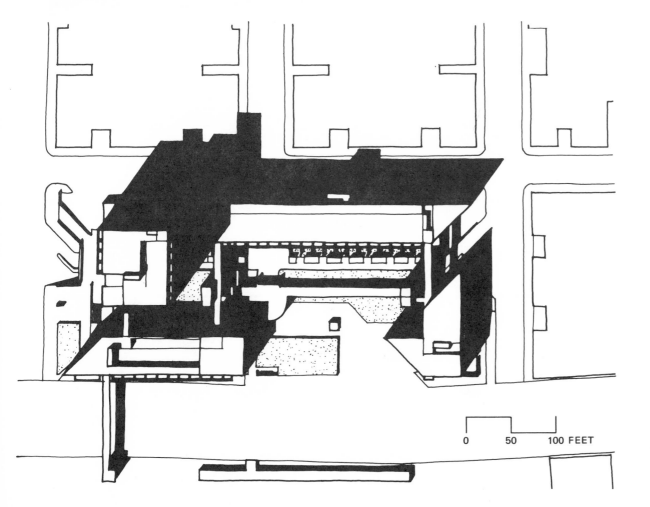

0   50   100 FEET

scheme included some low-rise walk-up units independent of the tower massing (Fig. 1-59).

The Roosevelt Island Competition may be seen for two reasons as a manifestation of a collective understanding of the housing design problem at high densities. First, it was sponsored by one of the country's most enlightened public agencies (the Urban Development Corporation) in direct response to their user needs research and the evolved codification of the housing "issues." Second, the cited schemes incorporated many of the aspects in the previous competitions and the various housing forms thus far discussed. The stepped building, the point tower and building wall, the use of a varying ground plane, family units toward the ground, skip stop elevators, were present in the four chosen schemes as responses to the program issues. Diversity in numbers and types of outdoor spaces was apparent in all the UDC winners (Kyu Sung Woo, Stern/Hagmann, Davis/ELS, Amico/Brandon, as was the concern for transition from the largest public spaces to the smallest private outdoor spaces. These were provided for the majority of family units. Clare Cooper-Marcus believes that the day-to-day activities facilitated by the single family house are impeded by the high-rise. Yet, the UDC Competition winners

Fig. 1-60 Kyu Sung Woo entry for Roosevelt Island. Level changes allow for town houses at upper floors and increased sense of street life.

Fig. 1-61 Stern and Hagmann entry for Roosevelt Island. Variety at the ground plane.

suggest that it is possible to incorporate many of the single family amenities (private entries, yards, transitional spaces) into a ground-oriented scheme, and then layer it with high-rise elements above which are accessible through separate enclosed lobbies.

In the Kyu Sung Woo scheme, for example, a system of moderate level changes using escalators moved pedestrian access to the third level. Town houses could thus be placed at higher levels than otherwise possible, while still giving easy access and a sense of a ''street'' type pedestrian entry (Fig. 1-60). The ground plane on the Stern/Hagmann scheme is filled with variety, created through free standing arches which define and continually change the open space as one moves through it (Fig. 1-61).

In the Davis/ELS scheme there are essentially two separate solutions: family-oriented housing in walk-up town houses and an elderly or nonfamily-oriented dwelling in skip stop towers which begin at the fifth floor. In addition to this horizontal layering, the site plan is also divided along the pivotal central pedestrial walk. On the river side of the walk the scheme is totally family-oriented (using the stacked row housing). The stacked row houses are accessible by stairs shared by only four houses each

Fig. 1-62 Davis/ELS entry for Roosevelt Island. Two solutions: a low-rise walk-up and a skip stop tower. As the buildings get higher, the spaces become larger and more public.

Fig. 1-63 Davis/ELS site plan. A diversity of exterior spaces from private yards to public plazas.

along a pedestrian street. Each of these units has a front yard or balcony, and a rear yard opening onto a semipublic space. In this way, each set of stacked town houses relates to another set, either across a pedestrian access street or across a rear yard. The remainder of the scheme represents a mixed family and nonfamily solution, located around larger neighborhood plazas. These plazas serve as a focus for larger groups of units and are bordered by schools, community facilities, or private yards of the adjacent town houses. The stepped building mass, used throughout the island and seen in earlier schemes, is repeated but with a finer texture, resulting in a wider range of exterior spaces. As the mass gets lower, the spaces become more private and the scheme becomes more family-oriented (Figs. 1-62 and 1-63).

The programmatic issues of ''community,'' ''child supervision,'' ''security,'' and ''responsiveness to context'' are handled through a variation in building form, variation in outdoor spaces, and the placement of larger units at ground level.

Existing housing types were used as models and images. These historical allusions help

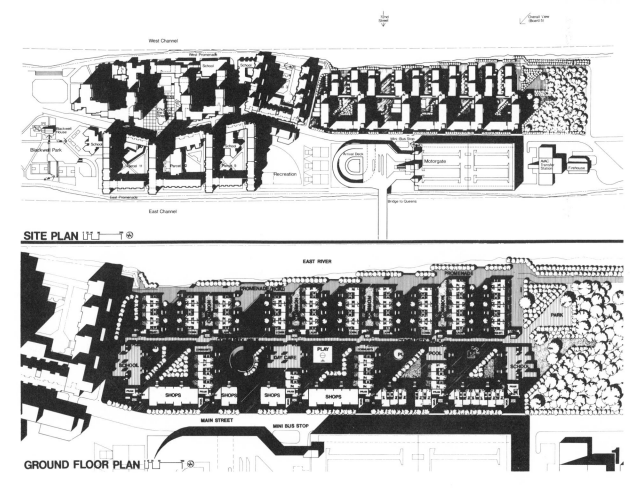

SITE PLAN

GROUND FLOOR PLAN

relate the new housing to some common cultural image as well as supply amenities inherent to that housing type. In the case of Stern/Hagmann, one recognizes the vernacular of speculatively built Brooklyn housing, similar to the earlier Venturi scheme; in the case of Kyu Sung Woo and Davis/ELS, the model is an urban town house on a pedestrian street. Writing about the results of the Roosevelt Island Competition, critic Suzanne Stephens characterized best what the winners represented:

> All the winning schemes are reasonably worked out, thoughtful, humane architectural solutions geared to be placed on a specific site. They are not innovative, for they are faithful accretions of ideas that have been tested elsewhere. And this is what they meant to be. As such, they are easily reproducible prototypes that could be built almost anywhere. But they are not visions of the future, sentinels of an emerging architectural destiny, revolutionary or poetic proclamations to inspire forthcoming generations of architects.[17]

The last 10 to 15 years have shown that the collective consciousness of this country and its new generation of architects are becoming more concerned with "thoughtful, humane buildings" than with the "visionary," the "revolutionary" or even the "poetic." One hopes that the design team's growing understanding of the very complex problems in housing and their proven ability to resolve them will provide inspiration for forthcoming generations of architects.

The elements of the house have not changed significantly over hundreds of years, and it remains the preferred housing form. Recent designs show that many aspects of the house can be retained even at higher densities and give the added advantages of city living. We can now predict with more accuracy not only the desires and aspirations of certain users, but also which physical designs are most appropriate and which aspects of the traditional house are most important. Strong cultural, social and psychological differences among occupant groups can and will affect the success of even our most sensitive application of prototypes. The continuous evaluation of our attempts and the development of more programs for different segments of the population are critical. Certainly, one of our goals should be to provide choice. Whereas the range of choice was once steadily diminishing to the extremes of high-rise or single family houses, it is now broadening. The elements of the still preferred single family house can now be seen in other more dense housing forms, creating a wider range of acceptable housing choices.

Footnotes for Chapter One

1. Smith, Wallace, *Housing: The Social and Economic Elements.* Berkeley, Calif.: University of California Press, 1970, p. 75.
2. National Housing Policy Review, *Housing of the Seventies.* Washington, D.C.: Department of Housing and Urban Development, 1975, p. 167.
3. National Housing Policy Review. See footnote 2, p. 17.
4. Hanke, Byron R., *Urban Densities in the U.S. and Japan.* Washington, D.C.: The Urban Land Institute, 1972, p. 47.
5. Hanke, Byron R. See footnote 4, p. 47.
6. Brolin, Brent C., *The Failure of Modern Architecture.* New York: Van Nostrand Reinhold, 1976, pp. 42 and 43.
7. Institute for Architecture and Urban Studies, *Another Change for Housing: Low Rise Alternatives.* New York: The Museum of Modern Art, 1973, p. 16.
8. National Housing Policy Review. See footnote 2, p. 166.
9. Schafer, Robert, *The Suburbanization of Multifamily Housing.* Lexington, Mass.: Lexington Books, 1974, p. 15.
10. Koetter, Alfred, "Broadway East—Historical precedents," *Progressive Architecture* (October, 1975), p. 68.
11. Whyte, William, *The Last Landscape.* Garden City, N.J.: Doubleday, 1968, p. 201.
12. Newman, Oscar, *Defensible Space.* New York: MacMillian, 1972, p. 138.
13. Institute for Architecture and Urban Studies. See footnote 7, p. 13.
14. Safdie, Moshe, *Beyond Habitat.* Cambridge, Mass.: MIT Press, 1970, p. 160.
15. Smithson, Alison and Smithson, Peter, *Ordinariness and Light.* Cambridge, Mass.: MIT Press, 1970, p. 57.
16. In the Coney Island Project, Hoberman and Wasserman chose to place the town house units in the tower using a skip stop system, and the traditional apartments in the lower portions.
17. Stephens, Suzanne, "This side of habitat," *Progressive Architecture* (July, 1975), p. 59.

Bibliography

Books

Becker, Franklin, *Design for Living: Resident's View of Multi-Family Housing.* Ithaca, N.Y.: Center for Urban Development Research, Cornell University, 1975.

Brolin, Brent C., *The Failure of Modern Architecture.* New York: Van Nostrand Reinhold, 1976.

Burchell, Robert W. (Ed.), *Frontiers of Planned Unit Development: A Synthesis of Expert Opinion.* New Brunswick, N.J.: Center for Urban Policy Research, Rutgers University, 1973.

Chermayeff, S. and Alexander, C., *Community and Privacy.* Garden City, N.J.: Anchor Book, 1965.

City of New York Housing and Development Administration, *Record of Submissions and Awards Competition for Middle Income Housing at Brighton Beach.* New York: HDA, 1968.

Cooper, Clare, *Easter Hill Village.* New York: Free Press, 1975.

Crawford, Davis (Ed.), *A Decade of British Housing 1963-1973.* London: Architectural Press Ltd., 1975.

DeChiara, Joseph and Koppelman, Lee, *Manual of Housing/Planning and Design Criteria.* Englewood Cliffs, N.J.: Prentice-Hall, 1975.

Habraken, N. J., *Supports—An Alternative to Mass Housing.* New York: Praeger, 1972.

Institute for Architecture and Urban Studies and Urban Development Corporation, *Another Chance for Housing: Low Rise Alternatives.* Museum of Modern Art, New York, 1973.

Lansing, John B., Marans, Robert W., and Zehner, Robert B. *Planned Residential Environments.* Ann Arbor, Mich.: Survey Research Center, University of Michigan, 1974.

Macsai, John, *Housing.* New York: John Wiley & Sons, 1976.

National Housing Policy Review, *Housing in the Seventies.* Washington, D.C.: United States Department of Housing and Urban Development, 1974.

Newman, Oscar, *Defensible Space.* New York: MacMillian, 1972.

Newman, Oscar, *Design Guidelines for Creating Defensible Space.* Washington: National Institute of Law Enforcement & Criminal Justice and the Law Enforcement Assistance Administration of the United States Dept. of Justice, 1976.

Pawley, Martin, *Architecture Versus Housing.* New York: Praeger, 1971.

Peters, Paulhans, *Hauser in Reihen.* Munich: Callwey, 1973.

Riccabona, Christof and Wachberger, Michael, *Terrassenhauser.* Munich: Callwey, 1974.

Safdie, Moshe, *Beyond Habitat.* Cambridge, Mass.: MIT Press, 1974.

Safdie, Moshe, *For Everyone a Garden.* Cambridge, Mass.: MIT Press, 1974.

Schafer, Robert, *The Suburbanization of Multi-Family Housing.* Lexington, Mass.: Lexington Books, 1974.

Smith, Wallace, *Housing: The Social and Economic Elements.* Berkeley, Calif.: University of California Press, 1970.

Smithson, Alison and Smithson, Peter, *Ordinariness and Light.* Cambridge, Mass.: MIT Press, 1970.

Stern, Robert, *New Directions in American Architecture.* New York: Braziller, 1969.

Thompson, Elisabeth Kendall (Ed.), *Apartments, Town-houses and Condominiums.* New York: Architectural Record Books, 1975.

Whyte, William, *The Last Landscape.* Garden City, N.J.: Doubleday, 1968.

Periodicals and Reports

Cooper, Clare, *The House as Symbol of Self.* Berkeley, Calif.: Institute of Urban and Regional Development, 1971.

Cooper, Clare, *Resident Dissatisfaction in Multi-Family Housing.* Berkeley, Calif.: Institute of Urban and Regional Development, 1972.

Cooper, Clare and Hackett, Phyllis, *Analysis of the Design Process at Two Moderate Income Housing Developments.* Berkeley, Calif.: Institute of Urban and Regional Development, 1968.

Cooper, Clare, "St. Francis Square attitudes of residents," *Amer. Inst. Architects J.* (December, 1971), pp. 22–25.

Diamond, Jack, "Housing form and density," *J. Architecture Educ.* (Spring, 1976), pp. 15–17.

Dunlop, Beth, "Competition on an island new town," *Amer. Inst. Architects J.* (July, 1975), pp. 27–35.

Fischer, Claude S., Baldeassare, Mark, and Ofshe, Richard J., "Crowding studies and urban life: A critical review," *Amer. Inst. Planners J.* (November, 1975), pp. 406–418.

Harvard University Graduate School of Design, *Comparative Housing Study.* Cambridge, Mass.; Harvard University, 1958.

Hanke, Byron R., "Urban densities in the U.S. and Japan," *Density's Perspectives,* The Urban Land Institute, 1972.

MacCormac, Richard, "Housing form and land use: New research," *RIBA J.* (November, 1973), pp. 549–551.

McCue, Gerald, "Architecture 282 1974," Dept. of Architecture, University of California, Berkeley, Calif, 1974.

McLaughlin, Herbert, "Density: The architect's urban choices and attitudes," *Architectural Rec.* (February, 1976), pp. 95–100.

Ministry of Housing and Local Government, *Homes for Today and Tomorrow,* Her Majesty's Stationery Office, London, 1961.

Pawley, Martin, "Need for a revolutionary myth," *Architectural Design* (February, 1972), pp. 73–80.

Progressive Architecture, "Housing—high rise versus low rise," (March, 1976), entire issue.

Sherwood, Roger, "Modern housing prototypes," *Architecture and Urbanism* (March, 1974), entire issue.

Tice, James and Polyzoides, Stefanos, "Los Angeles courts," *Casabella* (April, 1976), pp. 17–23.

2
Housing and Urbanism

Donn Logan

"Do you think I like being buried in the heart of town, two miles from the nearest shopping center, three miles from the drive-in movies, five miles from the airport . . ."

There is a renewed concern for urbanism in the design of housing in the United States. This empathy for cities and for the symbiotic relationship between housing and cities dates from the mid 1960s when several influences converged on the consciousness of designers. One significant influence was the failure of Urban Renewal programs to produce better housing or better cities. A second influence was the writing of Jane Jacobs on the qualities of mixed-use urban neighborhoods. Thirdly, as architects became more aware of the way cities really worked, they began shedding the formal stereotypes that had been imposed by the classical modern movement in architecture. Their sensitivities were heightened by revealing social studies of the reactions of residents to existing housing projects. The result of such influences has been a new respect for cities as we find them, a new interest in historical housing archetypes, and a search for contemporary prototypes that can embody urban lifestyle values while producing more organic urban patterns.

The current urbanistic direction in housing design is reinforced by post-modern movement theories like those of architects Robert Venturi and Charles Moore which advocate complexity over simplicity and inclusiveness over exclusiveness—inherent attributes of cities. This direction is evidenced in the enlightened design policies of some public agencies, such as New York's Urban Development Corporation. It is realized in part through new urban design tools and zoning devices such as those of the New York Urban Design Group.

The characteristics of recent urban housing designs are diverse but feature several common themes. Many examples show a preference for the vernacular over the unique. Many reaffirm the street and the piazza as open space over parklike environments. There is a growing practice to include diverse uses in housing projects such as retail stores, offices, and expanded communal facilities. There is a reaction against the elevator building in favor of walk-up units. There is also a reaction against large formally composed projects in favor of infill projects among existing buildings or modular clusters that can be aggregated incrementally. A new respect for the existing urban context has resulted in increased humility about altering it rashly and an intense interest in renovating old buildings. Similarly, there is free borrowing of historical prototypes that have produced lasting good environments.

URBAN HOUSING ROOTS

Throughout history the shape of cities has been strongly influenced by preferences and habits in housing. As a corollary, the relationships between houses, the way they fit together to make neighborhoods and the way they interrelate with other urban activities has determined the quality of city life. In 300 years of building on this continent, Americans have embraced or have had foisted upon them a number of housing types and patterns, each of which has had its impact on the form and style of our cities.

The first 150 years of urban housing in America consisted almost entirely of free standing single dwellings on individual lots. The houses usually were placed on a grid plan, that ubiquitous town planning device dating from ancient Greece. In Colonial New England, for instance, the pattern was composed of two-story wood-sided houses separated from each other by low fences or hedges and equally spaced along the city streets (Fig. 2-3). An important part of the pattern were the street trees which defined the space of the street and punctuated the order set up by the boxlike houses. Another major element was the sidewalk which, occupying the space between the fenced

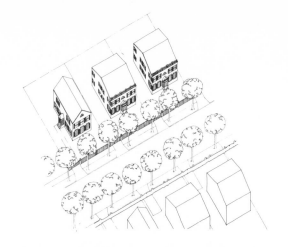

Fig. 2-3 New England street scene.
Fig. 2-4 Colonial New England housing pattern.
Fig. 2-5 Nineteenth century row house street.
Fig. 2-6 The row house system.

yard and the street trees, was part of the public realm but enjoyed some territorial identification with the house. The two together, house and grid, formed an open-ended system which put a premium on individual freedom but in the context of an ordering principle (Fig. 2-4).

The colonial housing pattern produced neighborhoods of great livability and low density towns of great charm. The concepts of separate houses and adaptable grid plans have proven extremely durable in the building of countless American cities. The grid was straightforward, pragmatic and infinitely expandable. The single house fitted the individualistic nature of the people. The combination of the two was particularly attractive in a plentiful land where expansion was inevitable and the Jeffersonian model of agrarian democracy prevailed. This image of residential environment pervades American culture and has persisted as an ideal into modern times. In government policy and literature, from movie sets for Mickey Rooney and Judy Garland to the paintings of Norman Rockwell, there has been continued praise for the virtues of the detached house neighborhood and the small town format to contain it.

American housing patterns became denser and more urban in the nineteenth century. In this

period the major cities experienced great population growth which, coupled with the flourishing of commerce and industry, produced the first truly urban streetscapes on this continent. The row house was the finest expression of this urbanization. Baltimore, Philadelphia, New York and Boston are among the cities whose urban character was shaped by tall row houses of masonry construction with elaborate cornices, sharply defined windows, and distinctive entrances (Fig. 2-5). As in the colonial period it was the grid plan that served to organize the development.

The row house block, even more than the colonial residential street, was a *city building system.* Like the colonial system, it had a fixed set of elements that fitted together according to particular rules to form whole blocks and neighborhoods. Unlike the former type, the dwellings gave vigorous definition to the streetscape by literally forming walls along the access corridor (Fig. 2-6). In spite of this apparent rigidity, the system was infinitely variable, capable of producing environments of specific character and flavor according to the architectural embellishments utilized. The row house system encouraged a quantum jump in urban street life. Its density brought people close together. Its common wall construction

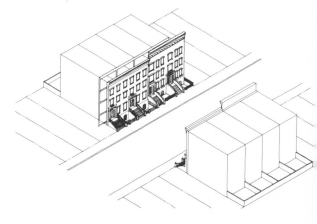

Fig. 2-7 The stoop as front yard.
Fig. 2-8 Row houses under construction.
Fig. 2-9 A row house district: Boston's Back Bay today.

and proximity to the street increased privacy in the rear garden while accentuating the public nature of the front façade. The projecting entry stair provided an intermediate zone between private and public where adults and children could visit or play (Fig. 2-7). It was a reduced version of the front yard. The sidewalk became an extension of the house and part of its territory.

[The sidewalk] was one of the nineteenth century's triumphs, and it always manipulated the scale of the town in favor of the individual. It personalizes the street, gives release from traffic flow and a place for loitering, provides a hierarchy of spaces and a multiplicity of uses in what would otherwise be a passage.[1]

The row house allowed the grid plan to be exploited fully. The houses could be erected by several builders in separate multiunit groups with confidence that they would all ultimately fit together (Fig. 2-8). They could be built in small groups or large ones; the pattern could be expanded in any direction, assuming land was available. In this way whole districts could be formed in a short time in the manner of Boston's Back Bay which was completed as a speculative enterprise (Fig. 2-9).

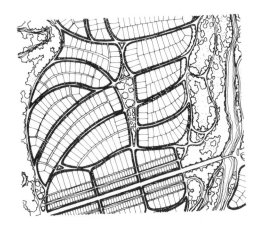

At any scale of development the qualities of the individual house were constant. The relationship to the street, the direct access, the nature of the rear garden, and all other aspects of community and privacy were unchanging whether 40 or 400 houses were constructed. This is in marked contrast to dwellings in modern housing archetypes which vary greatly in type of unit and quality of amenities as the scale increases. Similarly, while several modern developments built adjacent to one another would not necessarily make a coherent pattern, row house developments merged together forming a seamless urban fabric which relied on architectural details to make neighborhood variation. The system produced places of vitality, appropriate scale, sufficient density and considerable variety, all in all a compelling city structure with a finely scaled human quality.

Even with its many advantages, the row house did not become a universal model of the period. It was common only in the major commercial cities and housed mostly the successful gentry. In these same cities a burgeoning population of incoming immigrants gave rise to crowded tenements: six-story blocks which packed people in at high densities and high land coverages (up to 80%). The crowding, the dearth of light, air, and proper sanitation could not foster any kind of humane urban lifestyle. Ironically, the active and colorful street life of the period may partially have resulted from substandard housing (see p. 40).

THE FIRST SUPERBLOCKS

Reaction to the tenement conditions of the industrial centers and the ever-present American tendency to push outward manifested themselves in suburban expansion generally modeled on the grid plan with detached houses as in colonial times. A major new ingredient emerged however, through the picturesque philosophy of Andrew Jackson Downing as applied by Frederick Law Olmsted and others. Olmsted applied the same romantic gardening principles that he had used so successfully in Central Park, to residential neighborhoods like Riverside, Illinois (1869) and Vandergrift, Pennsylvania (1895). In these plans a romantic antiurbanism was demonstrated by sweeping curvilinear streets, manipulated vistas and an affected naturalism in a frank effort to create pastoral effects that left behind the growing problems of the industrial city (Fig. 2-10). Although the street patterns were a radical departure from the grid plan, the housing continued to follow the detached house form.

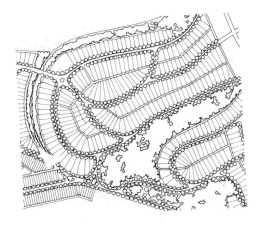

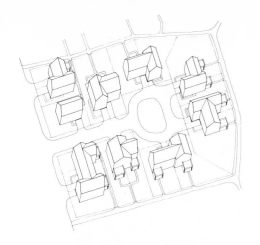

Fig. 2-11 The Radburn neighborhood unit.

The important feature of the romantic suburbs and new towns of the nineteenth century is that they became the first *projects*, superblock developments that could not merge with any adjacent patterns but were destined to exist as separate districts by virtue of their geometry and size. The plans were fixed compositions, not extrapolations of grid networks and not modular; they could not be expanded incrementally. This mode of planning had important consequences for the scale of development operations. A development had to be large enough to permit the plan to be resolved as a composition of streets and lots. The builder had to think in project scale; no longer could he undertake to build a few houses as an extension of the existing network.

The street layouts of the picturesque suburban developments seemed to anticipate the automobile. Later, in the early part of the twentieth century, the automobile became a dominant concern of housing design and planning. This was particularly true in what came to be known as *Radburn planning*, a concept derived from the ideas of Ebenezer Howard on the "Garden City" (1898) as applied in America by Clarence Stein and Henry Wright in the 1920s. The motivation of this planning was environmental: the provision of

light, air and recreation space rather than a romantic attachment to the picturesque as in the previous period. It was a movement intended to restore those healthful qualities that had been lost in the industrial city. The emphasis was on open space for recreation and the separation of pedestrians and cars. The car was seen as a dangerous but necessary nuisance that had to be rigorously controlled. The unit of development was a cul-de-sac street bordered by detached houses. The houses faced fingers of green space alternating with the dead end streets, forming intertwined but disconnected vehicular and pedestrian precincts (Fig. 2-11).

Radburn, New Jersey (1928) was the early ideal and the most famous example. Stein wrote that the Radburn idea was born of a need to find a way to live with the automobile. Cars, he said, made the grid obsolete and only the superblock concept with specialized roads could remedy the problem.[2] The clear advantages of this idea were the added safety of eliminating through traffic, the ability to make the street capacity only as great as needed, and the nearby green spaces that began practically at the door of the house. This logic and the laudable welfare motives behind it did not, however, give enough value to the social role that the street had played in urban neighborhoods. In Radburn-

type schemes the street and sidewalk lost their functions as places for interaction and neighboring. Often the sidewalks disappeared entirely and the streets became only vehicular service channels. While these omissions were compensated for by the common greens, community facilities, bike paths and other amenities, the motivating attitude was anticity. The Radburn-type plan, like the picturesque developments, had no modular characteristics. Each superblock project was a unique composition for a large precinct formed according to situational characteristics.

The postwar housing boom of the 1950s continued the suburban movement but ignored the principles of the Radburn planners. In the rush to deliver low cost houses quickly, the notions of green space and of pathways separated from roads were put aside. In their places came patterns of streets lined with small detached houses stamped out on a mass scale, a cheap version of the suburban dream. These developments were the lowest common denominator applications of the colonial, picturesque and Radburn patterns. As such, they continued the project or superblock scale of development, but offered few of the values of the original concepts and they prevented a rational growth of the core cities they surrounded.

Fig. 2-12 The Voisin plan for Paris, 1922–25.
Le Corbusier.
Fig. 2-13 Corbusian-type towers replacing older
apartments in East Harlem, New York.

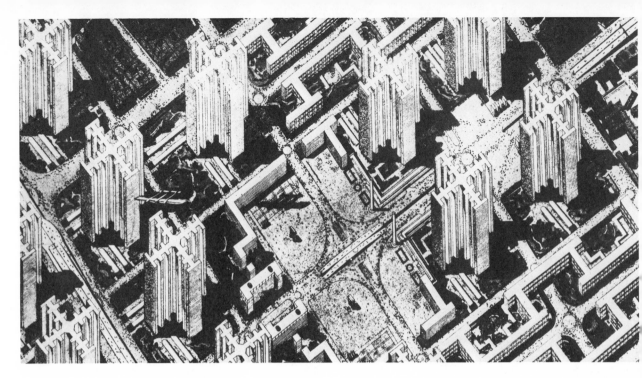

DOWNTOWN SUPERBLOCKS

A parallel attraction for superblock development
occurred within the cities themselves. Center
city areas had been decaying rapidly. The
Urban Renewal Program (dating from the 1949
Housing Act), prescribed to cure the problems of
slums in the cities, succeeded mostly in removing many blocks of urban buildings. The
wholesale erasure of neighborhoods, streets,
and houses destined the program to failure in its
social objectives. Part of this failure was due
to the superblock mentality. Project scale could
be useful in the suburbs where land was
vacant and at great distances from the core
cities. But it became more difficult to justify
in built up areas where great complexities of
physical and social interaction existed. Moreover, the program failed in urban design terms
by not bringing forward a new urban housing
form that could sustain and build upon
patterns and forms being replaced.

In the 1930s and 1940s even before Urban
Renewal, the forms of the modern movement in
architecture (also known as the international
style), and particularly the utopian schemes of
Le Corbusier, had an impact on urban housing
schemes. Developments like Alfred E. Smith
Houses and Stuyvesant Town in New York, Park

Fig. 2-14   Kips Bay Plaza, New York. Large apartment slabs in the context of smaller row buildings.

Fig. 2-15   Gratiot redevelopment plan, Detroit.

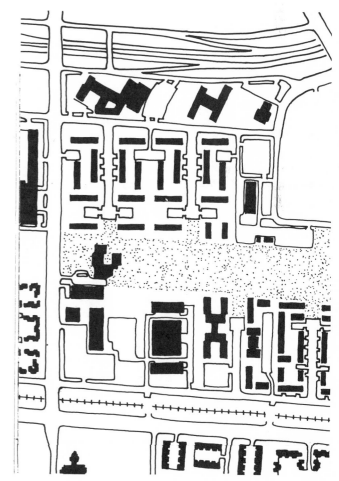

LeBrea and Park Merced in California, and many other public and middle income housing projects owed much to Corbusier's ideas, such as the Voisin plan for Paris (Fig. 2-12). Le Corbusier's concepts were essentially antiurban. He was not sympathetic to the messy urban streetscape and its chaotic mixed activities. He was advocating a new urban experience where motor cars would speed along broad avenues between apartment towers in parklike settings. His concept left no room for the pedestrian-scaled urban neighborhood of row houses and flats. Of course, Corbusier could not predict insensitive housing authorities, ruthless administrators or even the phenomenal growth of the automobile, influences that would transform his ideas into dull cookie cutter replications of cross-shaped towers isolated in asphalt settings (Fig. 2-13).

In the renewal schemes of the fifties and early sixties, the building forms of the modernists continued to grow in dominance. The older walk-up neighborhoods were replaced with various combinations of towers and slabs. In response to the middle income market for many urban renewal projects, the bland brick façades with their small window openings, common in many of the earlier high density projects, gave way to glassy façades on well proportioned buildings. These slabs were more often set in green settings rather than the asphalt of the former schemes. Kips Bay Plaza furnishes a classic example. Built in 1961, the I. M. Pei design features two parallel 21-story slabs straddling a common green space (Fig. 2-14). Two blocks were razed and a bisecting street was closed to form this small superblock whose architectural result bears no formal resemblance to the residual neighborhood surrounding it.

Some projects featured low-rise garden units as well, following Radburn planning principles. Detroit's Gratiot redevelopment project illustrates this genre. Begun in 1947 and completed in 1967, the plan features a combination of high-rise and low-rise buildings composed on a Clarence Stein-type superblock complete with central green space and penetrating cul-de-sac streets (Fig. 2-15). The architecture runs the gamut from high style modernist as in the 21-story Pavillion apartments by architect Mies Van der Rohe, to Regency Square, a cluster of two-story walk-ups and a six floor elevator slab. In between are other tall towers and two floor walk-up units spaced compositionally on the carpet of the common green.

In Kips Bay, Gratiot and other projects of the period, the combination of total clearance, the erasure of the original street patterns to form superblocks, and the architecture of the international style conspired to produce self-contained enclaves radically different from the neighborhoods they were replacing. Such projects inherently lacked connections to their urban contexts and could not have evolved incrementally from the original cities. A premium was placed on large open spaces, separation of circulation modes and superblock planning over other urban values that were less well understood. These planning practices were an outgrowth of earlier theories, such as the Radburn model, and demonstrated the inherent limitations of those theories for center city development.

REDUCING THE GRAIN OF HOUSING

The most successful urban renewal projects of the fifties and sixties were the cluster developments of two-story dwellings that were organized around small scale but well appointed open spaces. As a result of famous projects like St. Francis Square in San Francisco (1964), there has been increased interest in low-rise housing and particularly in the concept of low-rise/high density housing. This direction has received its best exposition in a publication entitled "Another Chance for Housing: Low-Rise Alternatives," a design study for sites in New York City which demonstrates that a density of 70 units per acre[3] can be achieved in four-story walk-up configurations (compared to an average of 100 dwellings per acre in typical high-rise projects).

The urban design ramifications of walk-up housing are considerable, as the earlier row house patterns confirm. Such dwelling configurations exhibit fine *grain*, a term that refers to the scale of elements in a site plan and the relative closeness of their patterns.[4] Differences in grain are readily seen when comparing these nineteenth century neighborhoods against the coarser high-rise superblock developments of this century. Moreover, fine grain is a natural consequence of building at the scale of row houses or small apartment blocks and accounts, to a degree, for the charm and specific identity associated with many historic urban districts in Europe and America. There seems to be a parallel between fine grain and the satisfaction of users with their environments. That is, fine grained places are most likely to be described as intimate, charming, rich or variable; while coarse grained places are more likely to be thought of as vast, anonymous, dull or monotonous, characteristics that correspond with the use of large repetitive forms, big open areas and the gross shaping of space.

The values associated with fine grain are an important factor in the current dissatisfaction with the superblock concept, large projects, and particularly high-rise projects. As the size of a development increases, the grain gets coarser almost in spite of any intentions of the designer. Most of the high-rise projects of the past few decades could have achieved their density in low-rise configurations and avoided the project stigma. Gratiot, for example, has a significant low-rise component, but it also has huge open spaces that could have absorbed more lower units in lieu of the towers (Fig. 2-15). The required open spaces and traffic separation could have been achieved in concert with the existing street grid rather than through the superblock created by erasing the street pattern. Similarly, the grain of Kips Bay Plaza is in severe contrast to the row house neighborhood surrounding it (Fig. 2-14). Most of the density could have been achieved with walk-up units that would have maintained the texture and scale of the area while providing more diverse amenities for the residents.

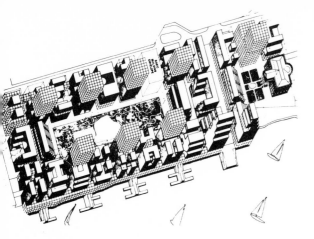

Fig. 2-16 Housing project on a miniature street grid.
Fig. 2-17 Penn Station South, New York. A proposal for reducing the grain of a housing project.

Recent efforts in housing design have attempted to reduce the grain of housing projects. In the Roosevelt Island housing competition one entry made such an effort to significantly reduce the grain of the development from its present coarse texture. O. M. Ungers headed a team which proposed the subdivision of the superblock site into a miniaturized version of Manhattan's street grid. A series of prototype designs for comparatively small 6- and 12-story buildings were developed to be located on different parts of the grid (Fig. 2-16). The design achieves great variety in spaces and dwelling forms and brings back the modular quality of nineteenth century cities. It may turn out to be one of the most important results of the competition in terms of its influence on subsequent housing schemes. It is even possible to reduce the grain of existing housing projects. Penn Station South in New York, is a typical 1930s style housing project with isolated towers set in large open spaces. Lawrence Halprin Associates, in a 1968 scheme, proposed a series of six-story blocks along the edges of the rectangular street grid (Fig. 2-17). These buildings would have realigned the project to its Manhattan context, reduced its scale and subdivided its amorphous open areas into defined courtyard spaces.

1. Portal
2. Supermarket
3. Tennis Court
4. Pedestrian
5. Plaza
6. Terrace
7. Play
8. Court
9. Garden
10. Church
11. Play Lawn/Parking Below
12. Indoor Swimming
13. Shops with Housing Above
14. Shops
15. Private Court
16. Public Plaza
17. Cafe
18. Apartment-Hotel

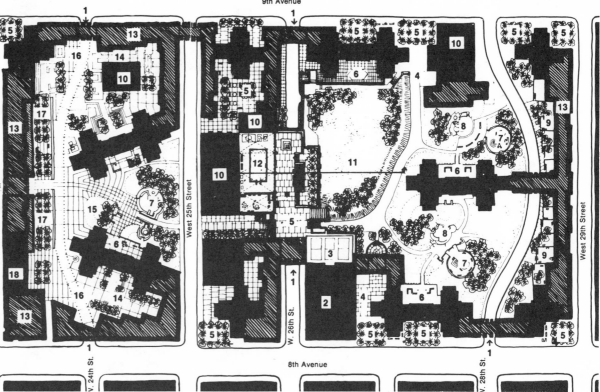

In the Western Addition renewal area of San Francisco, an attempt has been made to emulate the scale and texture of the older row houses and victorians in the area by limiting each piece of development to a single city block and by making three-story walk-ups throughout (Fig. 2-18). As a result, the project stigma is partially mitigated; the grain is similar to other parts of the city; there is architectural variety, and the concept is expandable without spoiling any grand plan. Nevertheless, even by using the block as the increment rather than individual units or smaller groups of dwellings, housing patterns are altered in this section of the city. Many of the houses face inward to a common area and turn their backs to the street in contrast to the traditional pattern where the interior of the block consisted of private gardens and houses faced each other across the street. The common green may be a holdover from the superblock mentality. But it also responds to the fact that many city streets have become too wide or too unfriendly. The internal common green gives more security to the residents. Some streets have been closed to traffic to provide parking or pedestrian paths, a way to get some of the planning advantages of the superblock while maintaining the grid.

Fig. 2-20   Main Street on Roosevelt Island.

Fig. 2-19   Shopping arcade at the Golden Gateway development.

THE RETURN TO MIXED-USE

Cities are mixed-use places by definition. In modern times, however, the mixing has been reduced through single-purpose zoning policies. Instead of a variety of activities within a block or a neighborhood, whole sections of cities have been restricted to one major activity. As a consequence most housing projects in this century have been almost entirely residential with very few community or commercial uses included. This practice is abating. An increasing number of newer projects are attempting to introduce diverse activities into housing developments. The Golden Gateway project, built in the middle 1960s, is a transitional example (Fig. 2-19). Although it belongs to the urban renewal period, its designers (a joint venture of DeMars & Reay and Wurster, Bernardi & Emmons) typify that Bay Region design philosophy that never fully endorsed the purity of the international style. As a result, the project displays an architecture of multiple colors and eclectic vocabulary and shows a penchant for rich materials, urban piazzas and street scenes. It can be considered an early example of the inclusive approach. Most of the public spaces are raised on a platform above parking and therefore do not relate well to the existing street life. Still they indicate a revived interest

51

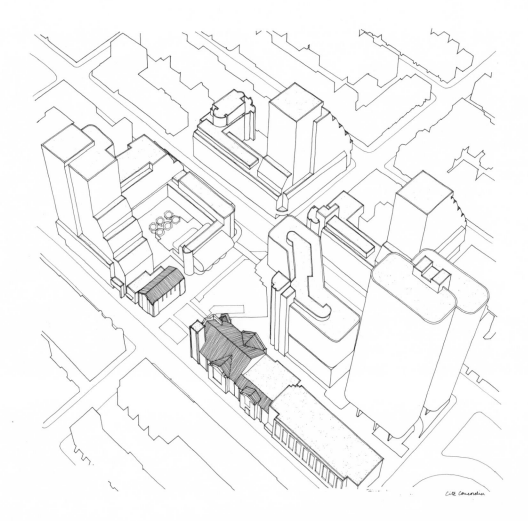

in urban places. Golden Gateway's main contribution as mixed-use is a covered shopping arcade that passes below the platform of houses, continuing the pattern of adjacent commercial streets and making a valuable contribution to the project and the neighborhood.

The Roosevelt Island development, on New York's East River, makes use of a similar shopping street to provide mixed activity. Here *Main Street* is the organizing principle underlying the development. The result is a contemporary version of a traditional New York street with continuous shops and services at ground level over which are stacked high-rise apartment blocks (Fig. 2-20). The wall of buildings that gives form to the street is broken periodically with plazas and recreational elements as well as a church which has been saved from earlier island development. Roosevelt Island and Golden Gateway both validate the traditional urban shopping street as an element that can be used in contemporary housing programs.

Cité Concordia in Montreal, is a more truly mixed development*(Fig. 2-21). It combines large amounts of retail, hotel and office uses with housing. In addition, it retains several existing row houses and churches within the project, integrating them with the larger new structures through a network of well-conceived open spaces. By relating the new structures to the street grid as well as to the existing buildings, the city form is recognized and reinforced. The streets bisecting the four blocks are retained as vehicular channels, but an underground shopping concourse connects all parts of the project and permits it to be rationalized like a superblock development. Cité Concordia is important for its merging of old and new, its variety of open spaces, its reinforcement of city form as well as its mixture of uses. When built it should have important influences on downtown redevelopment practices.

Another mixed-use urban project which merges old and new is the Brewery in Milwaukee. This four block project incorporates the old Blatz Brewery (1904) and the Pabst Bottling Plant (1932) and several smaller brick loft buildings. New construction is added within and between these structures to produce an inner city subdistrict of 470 apartments, 300 hotel rooms and a million square feet of shops, offices, and parking (Fig. 2-22). The design brings the different activities together to the greatest degree possible. Its success will depend on these connections between uses. The housing over-

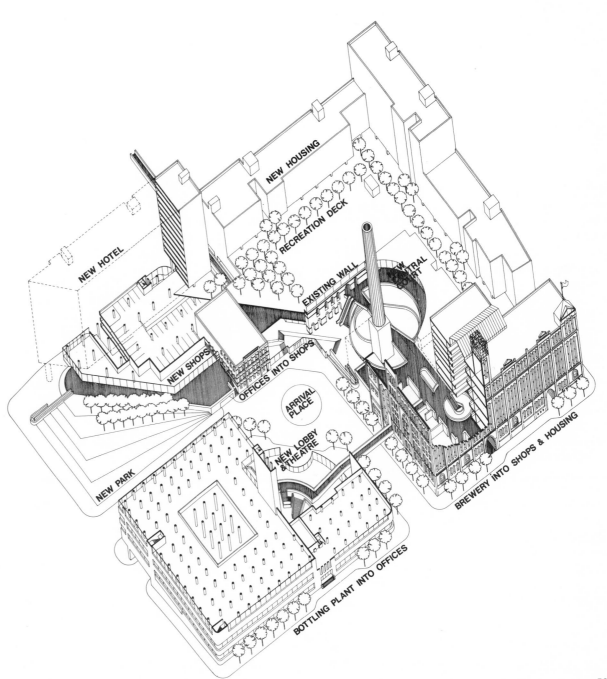

Fig. 2-23 A vernacular mixed-use building.

looks the shopping and entertainment court, sharing that vitality. Yet the apartments are separated to an extent by the recreation deck and the residential entries which are away from the shopping activity on the perimeter of the blocks.

Golden Gateway, Cité Concordia, Roosevelt Island and the Brewery are all large projects, yet they avoid many of the pitfalls of earlier and similarly sized projects. They are more sensitive to their surroundings; they display understanding of vernacular urban forms and try to adapt them to modern purposes. Three of the projects retain or renovate existing buildings within their boundaries, thus further increasing continuity with their city contexts. They all promise increased liveliness and social diversity as a result of mixing activities. Taken as a group, they demonstrate that there is still a place for well-conceived large projects, especially where sites are available due to antiquated uses as in the Brewery or at obsolete waterfronts or railroad yards, or where natural barriers have separated the site from the context as in Roosevelt Island.

Mixing housing with other uses is also becoming more common in individual buildings, particularly in New York where the city's pioneering

Urban Design Group has developed zoning devices that bring residential activity back into midtown Manhattan. These devices offer bonuses that increase allowable floor area where residential and retail uses are included in office buildings. Thus far two mixed-use towers have resulted. The Olympic Tower and the Galleria both feature shopping arcades at the street with offices and then apartments above, similar to Chicago's Hancock Tower (27 floors of office and 49 floors of apartments). Such efforts are increasing and are worthwhile, yet they are appropriate only in dense downtown areas. Luxury towers at this scale do not offer a way to make new urban housing precincts on a city wide basis.

NEIGHBORHOOD MIXED-USE

Vernacular urban buildings of the nineteenth and early twentieth centuries were often mixed-use. The central areas of many cities are still rich with small (two–six floors) buildings that feature shops or other commerce on the street level and offices or apartments on the floors above. A good example of the idiom is the building at the corner of Hyde and Green Streets in San Francisco. The shops open to Hyde Street, a well-developed neighborhood shopping street, while on residential Green Street

there are a series of common entries, each serving four to six apartments (Fig. 2-23). The two uses do not interfere with each other in any way; one clearly belongs to a commercial zone, the other faces a steep residential street. The combination produces a small-scaled repeatable building element that has had universal application in cities until recently. Although there are occasional contemporary buildings that place a shop or two under apartments (Fig. 2-24), this building type is almost totally unexplored by contemporary designers. The concept of small-scaled mixed-use buildings deserves to be taken out of the vernacular and utilized as a conscious housing and urban design strategy.

Such a strategy would combine the mixed-use idea, necessary for any vital urban lifestyle, with walk-up scaled houses and neighborhoods that have served so well as city building blocks in the past. The potential for a contemporary prototype is illustrated in a Booth and Nagle design for a site in a late nineteenth century neighborhood on Chicago's North Side (Fig. 2-25). The historical roots of this scheme are evident in the vertically proportioned row houses situated above street level shops. New ingredients have been added, however. There is

Fig. 2-24   418 Union Street, San Francisco.

Fig. 2-25   David's Plaza, an urban infill project of town houses over shops.

Fig. 2-26   120th Street and Seventh Avenue, New York. A postcard by Thaddeus Wilkerson.

a second row of units at the back of the lot and a common courtyard which serves as the entry for the houses. The shops are deep in accordance with contemporary standards and parking for ten cars is provided. The scheme has generic potential; its city building properties are similar to nineteenth century antecedents where the ground levels of row houses are used as shops (Fig. 2-26). This scheme brings the prototype up to date by adding the courtyard and the higher standard commercial space. It also replaces the sidewalk entries with courtyard entries in accordance with the security considerations that prevail in modern cities.

URBANIZING THE SUBURBS

The evolution that turned some eighteenth century colonial towns into nineteenth century row house cities and then into twentieth century high-rise metropolises is now making modern suburbs more densely urban. The barren housing tracts of the 1950s have become interspersed with commercial, cultural and industrial activities that provide a modicum of overlapping land use, albeit not as finely intertwined as the old cities. There are now many dwelling types available where the single family detached house was once the only choice. These housing forms are almost all borrowed from earlier urban models and all at densities significantly higher than the detached house. The only distinctions between these new suburban housing developments and current urban housing are the green settings of the suburban versions. The concept of Planned Unit Development has rationalized suburban planning. PUD's have enabled housing developments to aggregate open space, cluster units and otherwise reintroduce some of the characteristics of the 1920s garden suburbs.

This juxtaposition of an urban prototype and the green belt concept can be seen in Epernay, in Houston, designed by Fisher/Friedman. It is comprised of mini-neighborhoods each organized around a *town square* complete with brick paving and fountains (Fig. 2-27). A green open space replete with tennis courts and a swimming pool runs between the neighborhoods of two-story town houses. The common squares provide an active social setting missing from the original Radburn schemes without sacrificing the green belt idea.

Using devices like the town square in Epernay is one aspect of a prevailing interest in urban prototypes in suburban developments. Another aspect is historical allusion, where the whole concept responds to an earlier urban form,

55

Fig. 2-27 A *town square* at Epernay.

Fig. 2-28 Promontory Point. Fisher/Friedman, Architects.

Fig. 2-29 Mediterranean village imagery in San Mateo, California.

even in its architectural character. Promontory Point is a suburban apartment complex that appears as a Mediterranean hill town (Fig. 2-28). This 520 unit development in Newport Beach, California has seven stories of terraced apartments wrapped around a natural bluff and two-level parking structures. The configuration provides balconies for each unit shrouded by sloping tile roofs. Winding paths and steps pass between the groups of units from top to bottom to give access. There are paved squares, small piazzas with fountains and other environmental details to complete the allusion. A rational plan underlies the rich architectural expression. The five identical hilltop villages achieve a density of 17 units per acre and still give the open, spacious feeling sought after in all suburban cities. The piazzas and winding roads contribute to making a workable precinct for pedestrians, an all too rare occurrence in urban fringes.

The formation of such small-scale pedestrian precincts among the roads and freeways of the hinterland is one of the most important contributions of the denser suburban clusters. A Backen, Arrigoni & Ross designed rental complex in San Mateo, California displays these characteristics (Fig. 2-29). Like Promontory Point it alludes to a Mediterranean village imagery. There are narrow walkways and small

open spaces between the tightly packed white dwellings that recall Greek Island villages like Mykanos and contribute to the picture of a dense urban compound. Most of the apartments are one- and two-story attached patio houses. Along with a four-story terraced block, that overlooks the main piazza, they achieve a density of 26 units per acre. All cars are kept on the periphery or parked below grade to complete the pedestrian orientation of the interior.

Epernay, Promontory Point, and the San Mateo development are urban fragments in the suburbs. They illustrate the potential for dense pedestrian environments but are too small to deal with the larger issues of urban sprawl, strip development, land use policy, public transportation, and automobile pervasiveness. New towns like Reston and Columbia are more comprehensive attempts at rationalizing suburban planning. They have partially succeeded in dealing with land use and the integration of commercial and community uses into suburban housing situations. No constructed new towns have attempted to deal specifically with the adaption of urban forms and patterns to make highly compact suburban towns, although aspects of some indicate that direction. The original scheme for Valencia, California, by Victor Gruen Associates has a great many

neighborhoods that are compactly designed (Fig. 2-30). They provide a range of dwelling types from single detached houses to varieties of attached units. The higher density configurations produce short distances between places and therefore promote specialized circulation for pedestrians and cyclists. At a more utopian level, a new town designed by students at the Harvard Graduate School of Design in 1968, represents perhaps the ultimate compaction of suburban development (Fig. 2-31). A regional shopping center has been grafted to a series of high density clusters which are separated by fingers of green space. The groups of dwellings represent every imaginable variation of attached house, apartment, or tower. The complex is completed by the inclusion of rapid transit and moving sidewalks. This design embodies most of the major planning and architectural theories of the first half of the twentieth century. It has common green belt, cul-de-sac streets, separation of cars and pedestrians, superblocks, and the architectonic notions of the modern movement. In addition it incorporates more current thinking about high density/low-rise building, urban analogies from older cities, and high technology items like the rapid rail transit and the moving sidewalk. Although a potpourri of housing and urban design concepts it illustrates a direction for compact suburban towns of the future.

Fig. 2-30 Valencia, California, a compact *new town*.

Fig. 2-31 High density forms in suburban *new town* development.

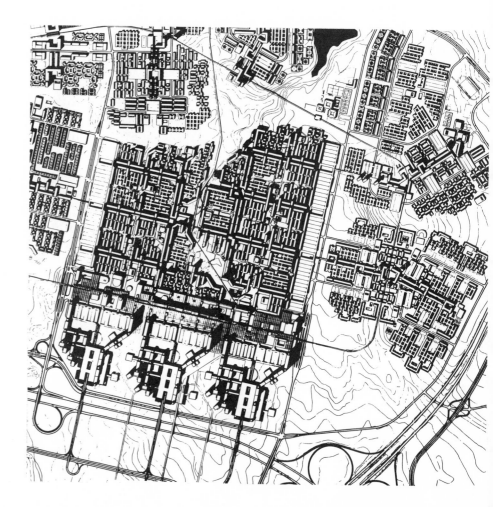

INNOVATION ON THE CAMPUS

Colleges and universities have, in recent times, provided a fertile ground for innovative housing design. In many respects a campus is analogous to the small historical town. It is a pedestrian community where people both live and work. It has a sense of community and common purpose. There is an active public life with people meeting on the streets to complete business and social transactions. In addition a campus is less restrained by the social and economic forces that operate in the housing market. For these reasons student housing is a natural setting for experimentation and testing of urban housing ideas that may ultimately be used elsewhere.

Like new housing in the cities and in the suburbs, there is a return to historical proto-types on the campuses. The concepts of *village* and *town square* are frequently utilized. There are also, however, contemporary extrapolations of the earlier models in the forms of *linear cities* and *miniature metropolises*. Mixed-use is also a major ingredient of student housing. The inclusion of food services, book-stores, auditoriums, classrooms and offices completes the urban analogy and further sets the stage for design innovation.

The renaissance in campus housing dates from the mid 1960s after a period of dull bureau-cratic slab and box making in the fifties and early sixties, parallel to the general decline in housing design. Two projects opened the way for the contributions that came later, the José Luis Sert scheme for Harvard's Peabody Terrace and Paul Rudolph's married student housing at Yale. Both use urban models as the basis of their organizations in contrast to previous dormitory archetypes. The Harvard project, completed in 1964, was reportedly influenced by the Italian town of San Gimignano. It features three 22-story towers and several lower buildings defining a brick paved central square and a series of other open spaces (Fig. 2-32). Common rooms, a food market, and child care facilities enliven the main square. The Yale project, designed about the same time, is a smaller development that also relies on town-scape principles, this time a hillside village (Fig. 2-33). The three-story buildings step down a hill via a series of narrow walks and steps.

Fig. 2-35 The village character of Kresge College.
Fig. 2-34 Kresge College site plan.

Fig. 2-36 Street level shops in Pembroke Dormitories.
Fig. 2-37 The courtyard in the Pembroke Dormitories.

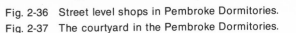

Fig. 2-36 Street level shops in Pembroke Dormitories.
Fig. 2-37 The courtyard in the Pembroke Dormitories.

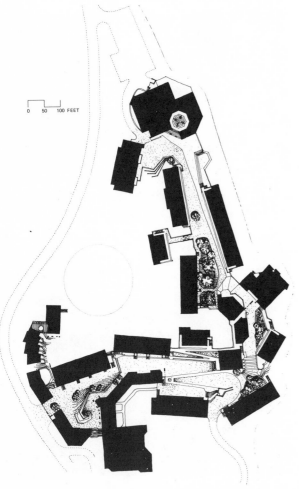

The Harvard and Yale housing confirmed the validity of urban paradigms for campus housing. Later projects like Kresge College and the Pembroke Dormitories continued the analogy in even more lively terms. These student complexes are based on two different models. Kresge College, on the University of California, Santa Cruz campus, relies on a winding Medieval street as the focus (Fig. 2-34). Architects Charles Moore and William Turnbull (MLTW) have clearly and purposefully made an urban village rather than a conventional dormitory complex. The street is mixed-use. There are classrooms, commons, library, and offices mixed with housing. At each change of direction of the meandering street there are squares featuring communal activities: laundry, post office, and café (Fig. 2-35).

At Brown University's Pembroke Dormitories (also by MLTW with Donlyn Lyndon in charge), the concept is an early twentieth century vernacular urban neighborhood. The buildings occupy a corner site. The brick façades of the project carefully reflect their context. One exterior façade continues a campus shopping street with its own shops filling the ground floor (Fig. 2-36). The other façade sets back behind a walled garden in deference to the residential nature of the street. Behind these

Fig. 2-38 The podium level at Joseph Ellicott.
Fig. 2-39 Joseph Ellicott: student housing as a city.

neighborly elevations, student suites are grouped around a central courtyard featuring a pop supergraphic treatment of cutout walls and complicated shapes (Fig. 2-37). As a potential housing prototype, the importance of Pembroke is the use of vernacular urban building language to create contemporary dwellings that offer a range of private, shared, and communal spaces. It is easy to compare Pembroke with the Booth and Nagle scheme for Chicago. Both are walk-up scale. Both have shops at street level. Both have a common courtyard. They differ in that one uses row houses and the other has flats. Both however, offer a small repeatable urban housing prototype. Similarly, Kresge would fare well as a modular neighborhood in a suburban context like that of Epernay. Taken together Kresge and Pembroke show new ways to reinterpret old forms to make the most modern and humane housing for cities.

There are new urban forms emerging on the campuses as well. In Buffalo, New York, and in Alberta, for example, dense sophisticated housing has been built which offers many lessons for cities. The Joseph Ellicott complex is one instance: (Figs. 2-38 and 2-39). If Pembroke is an urban neigborhood then Ellicott is a whole city. This group of six residential colleges at the State University of New York at Buffalo, has a

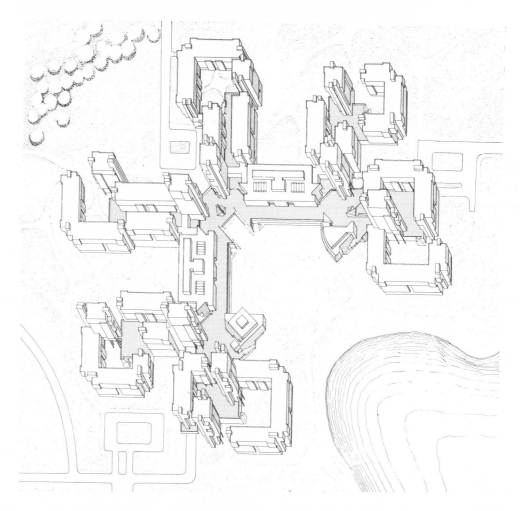

variegated skyline, mixed-use, and most of the
other attributes of a dense city, in miniaturized
form. With housing for 3300 students plus
classroom and support facilities for 2700 more
it is, in fact, bigger than many towns. Architects Davis and Brody have used an elevated
linear pedestrian street, lined with classrooms
and other uses (drama workshops, lecture halls,
etc.) to connect the six colleges. Below this
podium level, at grade, the street is duplicated
as an enclosed mall, with shops, cafeterias, and
a student center. The atmosphere of Joseph Ellicott is completely urban. None of the vestigial
village or town qualities common to the previous
schemes remains. It is big city urbanity, in the
vanguard of urban design practice in downtowns.
It is easy to view Ellicott in fact, in a downtown
redevelopment situation with its walks connecting to the city street system and its high
density neighborhoods projecting into older
neighborhoods.

The Student's Union Housing, at the University
of Alberta, by Diamond and Myers offers
similar potential for application in cities. It is a
single 950 foot long building consisting of a
glass covered pedestrian shopping street
flanked by walk-up apartments (Fig. 2-40). The

top three floors of units overlook the street
via shutters which can be thrown open into the
central space. The building acts as a weather
proof connector between old buildings on
distant parts of the campus and turns the
existing street into an exciting three-dimensional
space. It could play this same role in cities
and provide a unique alternative dwelling type
as well.

THE NEW URBANISM

During much of this century, housing design
has been destructive to existing urban patterns
and antithetical to city values. Somewhere in
the throes of rapid change we lost that spark
of vernacular genius that made the provision
of shelter an act of urban design. Yet the
strong-boned pattern of the nineteenth century
city still persists in many places and still tends
to define the American concept of urbanity. The
housing directions that have evolved in the last
decade promise to bring this older urban
concept together with the newer settlement
patterns rooted in the automobile and the
freeway. While no universal approach has
emerged and while it is doubtful that we will
ever go back to the unitary themes of a
brownstone New York or a victorian San
Francisco, there is evidence that many of the

values implicit in these images are finding their way into new concepts and configurations that bode well for a humane postindustrial urban lifestyle.

The new urbanism in housing design relies on diversity. The multiplicity of images and prototypes reflects the consciousness of post-Vietnam America and its pluralism of lifestyles. Less emphasis on the nuclear family, increases in both young people and old people, new variations in single and group living, desire for amenity and proximity, all argue for more multiple dwelling types catering to subgroups and regional differences. This polyglot urbanism does not abandon the contributions of the past. The planning theories that began in the twenties with an emphasis on green space, light, air, recreation and traffic segregation continue to be applied in selective form, but they are enriched with older urban values of the street, the piazza, and the public life.

The new urban housing forms should have an important effect on the form of cities. The emphasis on diversity of type, on smaller projects, on walk-up scale, on mixed-use will make cities more varied and rich. The same forces when coupled with recent concerns about energy and alternative transportation will make cities more compact. The renovation movement, the merging of old and new, and the unpopularity of wholesale demolition will encourage the continuous knitting together of the urban fabric. All of these forces tempered by the increased social awareness of the seventies and the growing contributions of social research in housing indicate the imminent arrival of the *Humanistic City*, the culminating form in the progression from the colonial rural town followed by the nineteenth century industrial city and the twentieth century technological city. The evidence of the humanistic city, a complex and multilayered package of Jeffersonian ideals, should be apparent before the end of the bicentennial decade.

Footnotes for Chapter Two

1. Scully, Vincent, *American Architecture and Urbanism.* New York: Praeger, 1969, p. 83.
2. Stein, Clarence S., *Toward New Towns for America.* New York: Reinhold, 1957, p. 37.
3. Institute for Architecture and Urban Studies; New York State Urban Development Corporation, *Another Chance for Housing: Low-Rise Alternatives.* New York: Museum of Modern Art, 1973, p. 17.
4. Lynch, Kevin, *Site Planning,* 2nd ed. Cambridge, Mass.: MIT Press, 1971, p. 37.

Bibliography

Books

Barnett, Jonathan, *Urban Design As Public Policy.* New York: Architectural Record Books, 1974.
Institute for Architecture and Urban Studies; New York State Urban Development Corporation, *Another Chance for Housing: Low-Rise Alternatives.* New York: Museum of Modern Art, 1973.
Jacobs, Jane, *The Death and Life of Great American Cities.* New York: Random House, 1961.
Le Corbusier, *The Radiant City.* New York: The Orion Press, 1964.
Lynch, Kevin, *Site Planning,* 2nd ed. Cambridge, Mass.: MIT Press, 1971.
Reps, John W., *The Making of Urban America.* Princeton, N.J.: Princeton University Press, 1965.
Scully, Vincent, *American Architecture and Urbanism.* New York: Praeger, 1969.
Stein, Clarence S., *Toward New Towns for America.* New York: Reinhold, 1957.

3
A Conservative Approach: Housing the Past as We House Ourselves

Gerald Allen

"We built it of reflecting glass—not knowing—"

During the past decade, there has been a veritable boom throughout the United States in the business of historic preservation, and in its sister arts of restoration, renovation, adaptive reuse, recycling, and (the most astonishing term of all) "retro-fitting." All of these terms are only more or less precise, but they all refer in some way to the phenomenon of adapting old buildings to some present useful purpose. The fact that there are so many words for this phenomenon correctly hints that it is wide-spread and dramatic. So much so that it is not unfair to say that what is going on these days in the reuse of old buildings is probably the most exciting thing in architecture, and ironically it is the most up-to-date as well.

The current surge of interest in old buildings manifests itself in many ways, and there are two compelling reasons why this interest makes good sense—a practical and a human one. The manifestations and the purposes are the focus of this chapter, but first it is worth asking why the phenomenon has occurred at all at this point, since the answers to this question have several interesting cultural implications.

The surge of interest in old buildings has to do with a general trend of attitude in the archi-tectural profession during recent years. This trend involves the development of a pragmatic, unheroic modesty on the part of architects, and with it the beginnings of a finer sensitivity to the social and visual contexts in which individual pieces of architecture get built. The arrival of both these attitudes is a key event in the evolution of housing design in the past decade. These attitudes, moreover, are not really even separate, but are instead closely related to each other, and they are related as well to a complicated nexus of experience (and reaction to experience) that form a part of what we can venture to call the collective consciousness of late-twentieth century America.

To be sensitive to the context in which our individual buildings exist implies that we think the one is as important as the other; so it implies a modesty about ourselves and about our creations. Similarly, to be able to be modest, unheroic, and pragmatic about what we build implies an awareness that other kinds of creations in other contexts are possible. Supple attitudes, therefore, are required. The way chosen in any one instance may not hold any ultimate promise, only a limited and appropriately local one.

Limited promise, in fact, may be a key to our current mood. For anyone who grew up in the United States in the 1950s or in the early and mid 1960s, beginning to learn about things and to do things was to crest a wave of virtually unlimited promise. Almost anything in any field seemed do-able: boundless economic prosperity seemed likely, political change possible, social justice thinkable, and worldwide peace at least conceivable. So did our cities, by the same optimism, seem perfectible and our whole man-made environment subject to the purgative blessings, the boldness, and the ex-citement of Modern architecture. The task was not so much to figure out what could be done as how.

This giant wave of promise, of course, finally broke, through a series of economic, social, political, and military misadventures, plus a few more that were gratuitously thrown in by fate. (This is perhaps another way of saying only that all of us who grew up in the 1950s or in the early to mid 1960s did, in fact, grow up.) And so, by the early 1970s, promises on many fronts seemed to many people to have been rudely broken, and options cruelly closed off like so many slamming doors along an endless corridor. The urgent questions seemed to shift radically from, "How can we do it?" to this: "*What* can we do?" or, even to this: "What is worth doing?"

Powerful and recent exercises in collective consciousness raising—like the so-called energy crisis of 1973, or the real constitutional crisis of 1974, or the ongoing crisis of world ecology (of which the energy crisis is only a part)—have only added to and confirmed the accumulating data that dramatize this one awareness: *all* of our resources are ultimately and inescapably limited. And among these resources, let us remember, are not just the physical ones with which we make things for ourselves, but the human ones as well.

These are our own resources of imagination, intellect, energy, enthusiasm, and even the resource of life itself—the things we use not only to make things for ourselves, but indeed the things we use to make things *of* ourselves. In short, one of the sweeping and profound perceptions of the decade just past—a perception so sweeping and so profound that it has yet to be fully appreciated—is that the real promises held out to us, however exciting and however hopeful, are in the end limited.

Significantly, the rise of this kind of awareness in the mid 1970s has occurred concurrently, in architecture, with the steady decline of the reputation of standard Modern architecture

(whose name can now be spelled with a capital "M" to signify that it has itself at last become one of the historical styles it began by scorning). The decline of Modern architecture, and with it the decline of its more rigid and authoritarian theories, is not particularly surprising, nor is it particularly to be regretted in the light of the more supple attitudes that now seem required. Suppleness is a quality that until recently was missing in high-style twentieth century architecture and high-style urban planning.

Until recently, for instance, most practicing architects received a good part of their education from the copybook of Modern architectural theory, which in its various chapters declared that ornament was a crime, that the historical styles were a lie, and that, as Walter Gropius had once said, a breach had been made with the past. The teachings of the Modern Movement represented a single-minded—and perhaps high-handed—attempt to sever the architecture of the present from what had gone before, and to create a new style independent of history, based on logic, reflective of the technological civilization of the Modern age, and capable of achieving honesty of thought and feeling.

The effort was not intended to accommodate the needs and visions of the present in some

comfortable continuum of history. Instead, it was to have it either/or: either Modern or old-fashioned, either okay or bunk. The effort was, in a word, revolutionary. It was fervent, it was doctrinaire, and it was (in its revolutionary way) orthodox. It called for a totally new, comprehensive, and exclusive system.

The trouble, naturally, with systems that attempt to be totally new, comprehensive, and exclusive is that they almost never turn out to be comprehensive enough. The order that they propose collides awkwardly with any number of other orders. Consider, for instance, the outright rejection of the past in Modern architectural theory and in effect, the rejection of architectural history.

Curiously enough, the collision here was least painful when it occurred with the most obvious competing orthodoxy: historic preservation. A restored town like Williamsburg, for instance, poses no general threat; returned to correctness right down to the upholsterers' tacks and neatly circumscribed as a place somewhere in Virginia, it is a self-contained package of the past that can be accommodated in the contemporary scene with ease. So it is with landmark buildings in most American towns and

ties: lovingly restored, they are like Old
Master paintings hung on the white walls of
starkly Modern houses.

But a great deal of the past—all of that part
which has not yet been granted Old Master
status—does not fit so easily into the system,
as residents of many American towns were not
pleased to discover when the bulldozers began
to arrive in the 1950s (and are still not pleased
to discover now). Architects, too, are among
the first to join the picket lines when a
historic building is threatened, just as they were
among the first to rediscover that Victorian
houses are fun to live in.

Their enthusiasm for old buildings seems to fly
in the face of what their teachers taught them,
for they are beginning more and more to
feel uneasy watching whole sections of the
built environment that obviously have merit bite
the dust. Their responses therefore have become supple rather than orthodox. They realize
now that the problem is not to rebuild the
world anew to one grand scheme. Instead it is to
conserve what we have for what we need,
to tune it more finely to our present purposes.

Simple-minded orthodoxies, we are now beginning to realize, are not needed. What now

seems required in place of them—and in the
face of our awareness that our resources are
limited—is wit rather than fatuous self-assured-
ness, agility of thought and imagination rather
than simple-minded firmness. These qualities
can create, and indeed are creating, a certain
calm modesty of aspiration in the architectural
profession. This calm modesty is combined
with a careful and traditional diligence in the
search for really available options, and with an
energetic awareness that no one set of rules,
no one way, will or indeed ought to apply in
all cases.

Among the available options, of course, are the
architectural traditions of the past, and the
buildings which remain as manifestations of
them.

What, in fact, do they have to give?

Consider, for instance, a perhaps bizarre example whose relevance can nonetheless be
demonstrated. The illustration on p. 64 shows an
old engraving of the colosseum built by the
Romans at Arles, converted into housing during
the Middle Ages. It sums up the two main goals
of the whole reuse and recycling game, and both
goals are extremely obvious. The first is purely
practical: if you have a useless colosseum on

your hands and you need some housing, it makes
perfect sense to try to make the latter out of the
former. The second goal is equally simple: it
would be a gas to live in a converted colosseum
—just as it would be fun to live in a cunningly
converted Vermont barn, or a factory loft in
SoHo, or in a found attic turret on Beacon Hill,
or on a barge in Sausalito.

THE PRACTICAL REASON

Reusing old buildings for housing can be highly
economical. In principle, this statement would
be hard to contradict, since it is almost always
cheaper to use something you already have
rather than throwing it away and starting over
again. It has been only recently, though, that
what seems true in principle has begun to be
realized in any large-scale way, and the reasons
for this delay can probably be described
accurately as blind prejudice. For nearly three
decades now there has been a passive prejudice
—confirmed by the policies of the federal
government, among other institutions, against
cities as places to live. And cities, of course, are
where older buildings are located.

The corresponding prejudice has been in
favor of suburbs, and it has been supported by government-financed mortgages

on new houses there, by government-built highways to get people from suburb to suburb and into the cities, and by cataclysmic urban renewal programs that were designed as much as anything to destroy the fabric of cities in order to make them attractive and accessible to commuting suburbanites (while incidentally rehousing the unfortunate poor who could not manage the exit). Private money for recycling old buildings into housing has traditionally been hard to come by, too, for the obvious reason that it is hard to convince someone to invest in something against which so many others are at least passively prejudiced.

In other words, the possibility of reusing older buildings for housing in a big way has simply not seemed to most people a real option, because of the recent prejudice in favor of housing in suburbs (along with the prejudice of Modern architecture for building bravely anew).

Lately, though, there have been signs that such strictures are being relaxed, and it seems now only a matter of time before the fundamental economic advantages of recycling and reuse can be more fully appreciated.[1] It has been estimated, for instance, that on a typical urban site, well covered with three- and four-story semidetached houses, the cost of demolishing the houses and replacing them with either low- or high-rise housing (with little or no gain in density) is approximately *three* times the cost of rehabilitation.[2] This cost is a function not only of the fact that rehabilitation is generally cheaper than any kind of new construction, but also of the fact that to the construction cost of the new housing must be added the cost of demolition of the old—plus the cost of interest and taxes while the land is being held through the planning and construction stages, which can drag on considerably.

Another powerful boost to the urge to reuse old buildings is beginning to be felt. Cities and towns all across the United States—as a product of no-growth policies and of broad ecological and environmental concerns—are imposing tougher and tougher restrictions on new housing developments of any sort. These restrictions, as any developer nowadays will report, are adding significantly to the cost of new housing. Conversely, planning permission for the reuse of older, existing buildings is becoming easier to obtain.[3]

THE HUMAN REASON

Living in a converted barn, or a loft, or a turret, or a barge (or a colosseum) could be fun, and this fact brings us to a very important point about reusing old structures for housing. "We can't know where we're going unless we know where we've been," go the historic preservation ads, in a kind of sermonizing tone that puts people off. The slogan really misses the point, too. It is not unreasonable to suppose that the citizens of Arles, when they put up their shacks in the colosseum, had no more than a passing interest in their Roman antecedents. Similarly, the person who lives in the converted barn in Vermont probably has little real interest in animal husbandry as practiced in northern New England, just as the one in the SoHo loft would probably just as soon forget the sweat shops that once flourished there.

Surely the real appeal of living in an older building lies not so much in the particular historical antecedents to which the building refers as in the fact that the references—whatever they are—are *specific*. Thus the building can stand in dramatic contrast to the undifferentiated blandness of much of the rest of the built environment; thus it can become a *place*, different from all the rest, and identifiable. And the person who lives there can be identified as well. This is the goal of any architecture, finally, but one that has been less and less frequently achieved by new buildings lately.

There are, then, two main reasons for reusing old buildings for housing. The first is that it makes sense on a number of practical grounds, and the second is that it feels right, for compelling psychological reasons.

Happily for purposes of the pluralism that our current cultural mood seems to require, there are many different ways of using old buildings for housing. The following examples will concentrate on four of the main ones: *conserving whole neighborhood contexts, conserving individual buildings, conserving parts of buildings, and conserving the images of old buildings*. Happily, again, for purposes of our desired pluralism, few of the examples which follow fit exclusively into just one category.

CONSERVING WHOLE NEIGHBORHOOD CONTEXTS

Assuming that one of the recent achievements of our collective thinking is in the development of a relaxed, modest and flexible attitude, and that the renewed interest in older buildings reflects this attitude, then we must be prepared to accept still further drifts from well traveled courses. Startling designs that seem to fly straight in the face of most of the conventional rules must be included.

Thus negative of the rules—and therefore appropriate as the first example of a building which attempts to conserve a whole neighborhood context—is George Schipporeit's design for a high-rise apartment building on Astor Street in Chicago (Fig. 3-3).

The problem here is familiar enough: a range of nineteenth century row houses threatened by pressures to develop. Legal restraints would force a setback from the sidewalk for any new construction (thus destroying the form of the neighborhood as well as the existing houses), and local soil conditions and local economies decree parking in above-grade garages (thus destroying most vestiges of human habitation at street level).

Schipporeit's design is one that will drive orthodox preservationists—and orthodox Modernists—to despair, and indeed it is not unfair to say that to some extent it does lack subtlety. It sheers off the backs of most of the row houses and converts the front parts, their façades intact, into two-bedroom town houses. The large house on the corner becomes the lobby for the apartment tower behind; its living room becomes a lounge, and its upper floors can be adapted to other amenities or put to commercial use. The above-grade

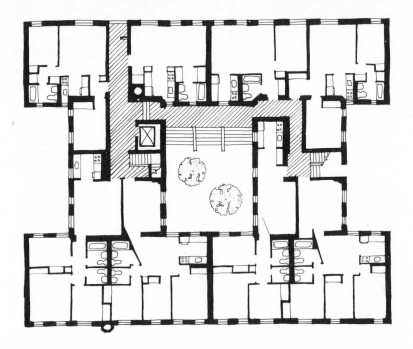

Fig. 3-4 A pair of H-shaped tenements in the Bronx, New York.

Fig. 3-5 "New Law" tenements in the Bronx, New York.

parking conveniently uses up the distance from the ground to the roof line of the houses, so that the first residential floors of the entirely new apartment tower have unrestricted views.

All of this may certainly seem at first glance to be destructive of cherished values on all sides, like a particularly cynical Congressional compromise. Certainly the scheme is not exactly pure. But for the person who is (literally) in the street, much that is worth saving will have been saved. Schipporeit's design is hybrid and relaxed, and it responds directly to a host of individual, social, and economic values.

During the past few years, the Bronx in New York City has become the scene for a more conventional, but ongoing and much more extensive, attempt to preserve a whole neighborhood context. The Bronx was on the whole developed in the 1920s in tenement buildings. A typical tenement was an H-shaped apartment building, usually six stories high, a recently renovated pair of which are shown in Fig. 3-4. In the South Bronx, which had begun to be developed earlier, these buildings were mixed in with an earlier type—known as the "New Law" tenement—which was T-shaped in plan, five stories high, and which covered about 80% of its lot (Fig. 3-5). These two

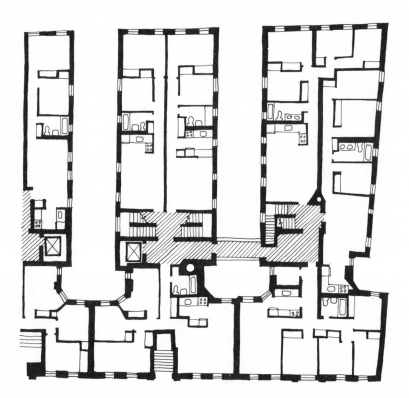

Figs. 3-6, 3-7, 3-8 and 3-9 show Jose de Diego-Beekman Houses in the Bronx, New York, renovated by Beyer, Blinder, and Belle.

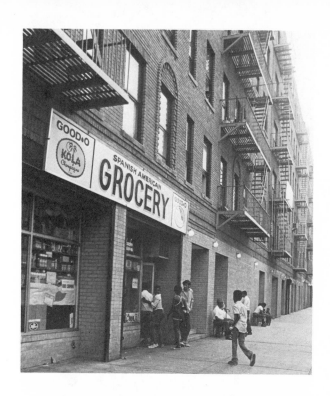

types of buildings were the basic housing stock available to middle class Bronx residents.

In less than 50 years, these buildings and their neighborhoods had been through a whole cycle of urban growth and decay. The families of the original occupants had grown up and left home, migrating to newer sections of the city and to the suburbs, leaving the old tenements in the care of the urban poor who could not afford to leave. Rising taxes, increasing maintenance costs, growing vandalism, and the rest of the usual plethora of self-compounding urban woes began to make these buildings unprofitable to their owners, until many abandoned them altogether. They were still at least structurally sound.

It occurred jointly to the Washington Heights Federal Savings and Loan (an institution in the Bronx with substantial mortgage investment there to protect) and to the Continental Wingate Company (a large developer and operator of rehabilitated housing) that these tenements, now at the end of one life cycle, could be recycled for another go around. The result is called the Jose de Diego–Beekman Houses (Figs. 3-6, 3-7, 3-8, and 3-9). The architects were the New York firm of Beyer, Blinder and Belle. In their final stage they contain 1350 units.

The rehabilitation of these buildings depended on the kinds of economic advantages of reusing old buildings that have already been described. It also depended on the experimental program begun in the early 1970s by the Department of Housing and Urban Development. Project Rehab was instituted to cut through the usual red tape and provide rent subsidies, lower mortgage rates, certain tax incentives, and other blandishments.

Yet the real key to the Jose de Diego–Beekman Houses is their insistence on contextual conservation. They are based on a simple conceptual economy, which was this: it makes sense to try to piece back together not only the houses, but at the same time the remaining threads of a social fabric which they represented, with its still-existing networks of community and commercial services. An additional advantage was that the rehabilitation could be accomplished building by building avoiding the necessity for large-scale relocation of tenants, and therefore helping to avoid the destruction of the social fabric.

Before rehabilitation began, all of the buildings were in more or less the same condition: though they were structurally sound, their interiors had been stripped and destroyed by vandalism,

fire, and theft. So the interiors had to be entirely rebuilt within the existing structural frames and exterior shells. Whenever possible, the "New Law" tenements, which had had no elevators, were connected by outdoor bridges, so that one new elevator could serve more than one building. Service and basement entrances, as well as fire escapes, were removed for security reasons, and interior courtyards, originally put there for light and ventilation only, were opened up to serve as controlled entrances and play yards for children. The exteriors of the buildings were cleaned and repaired, and a new thin aluminum window unit was designed by the architects to replace the rotted wood frames. Otherwise, the exteriors were not much changed.

The Jose de Diego–Beekman Houses will probably not win many rounds of applause in circles where artistic creativity is prized, but their creativity is of another sort—the sort that comes from rescuing and rejuvenating a whole neighborhood fabric. By carefully building on the resources that were already there—the human ones as well as the old tenements themselves—they have begun to recreate a social whole more surely than almost any set of new buildings could have done.

CONSERVING INDIVIDUAL BUILDINGS

The Jose de Diego–Beekman Houses are also, of course, examples of the conservation of individual buildings. This way of reusing old buildings, one by one, is nowadays so common that it is worth taking quick looks at a variety of such projects simply to demonstrate the breadth of building types that are being converted into housing.

Among these is the old Custom House in Boston (Fig. 3-10), which had been honored by being placed on the National Register of Historic Places, but dishonored by being left vacant and neglected. Boston architects Anderson Notter Associates were commissioned to convert the four-story granite building into 27 luxury apartment units (Figs. 3-11, 3-12, and 3-13). Transverse masonry walls divided the structure into nine separate buildings, each with a full attic. The architects pierced these walls with new arches to let corridors through. Modern fireproof stairs and a new elevator shaft were installed. New electrical services, central heating, sprinklers, and intercom systems were also added. The massive timbers framing the roof were exposed and the old masonry walls were cleaned with care and—presto chango—luxury apartments.

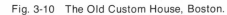

Fig. 3-10   The Old Custom House, Boston.

Fig. 3-11   An attic apartment in the Old Custom House, Boston, renovated by Anderson Notter Associates.

Fig. 3-12   A bedroom in the Old Custom House.

Fig. 3-13   Typical floor plans in the Old Custom House.

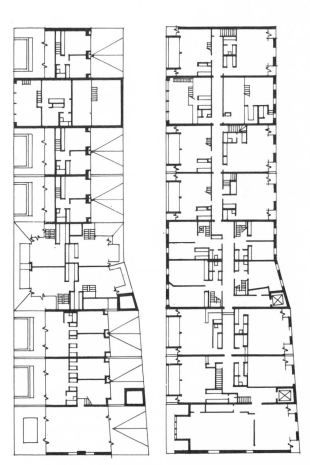

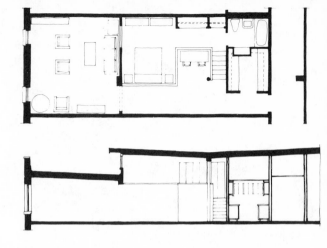

Fig. 3-16   A typical apartment unit in The Tannery, Peabody, Massachusetts, renovated by Anderson Notter Associates.

Fig. 3-14   The Rockingham Condominium Apartments, Portsmouth, New Hampshire, renovated by Stahl/Bennett.

Fig. 3-15   Rear of the Rockingham Condominium Apartments.

An equally dramatic change was wrought by the Boston architectural firm of Stahl/Bennett on the aging but still grand Rockingham Hotel in Portsmouth, New Hampshire, now recycled into the Rockingham Condominium Apartments (Fig. 3-14). Here there was the chance to apply the art of restoration to the finer front rooms of the hotel and in the rear portions of the building which surround a terrace (Fig. 3-15), to gut and thoroughly renovate the rooms that had been of little architectural distinction to begin with. What is perhaps most significant about the Rockingham conversion, though, is that it is one of the first successful examples of a type of reuse that may well become very common—since almost every town needs additional housing, and almost every town has a hotel that is disused.

The list of individual buildings that have been saved and converted into housing could go on to considerable length. Anderson Notter Associates alone have, in addition to the Boston Customs House, converted a leather tannery in Peabody, Massachusetts, a grammar school in Marlborough, Massachusetts, and a grammar school in Gloucester, Massachusetts. Currently they are at work on a proposal to turn the Vermont State Prison in Windsor into housing for the elderly.

The Tannery in Peabody contains 284 units of elderly housing in a strategic location near the central business district and community services of the town. The development consists of two large industrial buildings which contain the individual apartment units (Fig. 3-16) and which stand on either side of a smaller building known as the Crowninshield Mansion, a three-story brick Federal house built long before the site was transferred to industrial use. The Crowninshield Mansion is now enjoying a third life by providing community space, mail facilities, laundries, and administrative facilities for the development (Fig. 3-17). Crowninshield Pond (Fig. 3-18) was dredged and cleaned, and other more delapidated buildings on the site were demolished—though in some cases parts of their walls were retained to screen parking areas, or their brick and tile floors became terraces.

The former parochial school in Marlborough—now known as Academy Knoll Apartments (Figs. 3-19 and 3-20)—and the converted grammar school in Gloucester (Figs. 3-21 and 3-22) are both used as housing for the elderly. The former contains 109 units and the latter 84 units. Like the tannery complex in Peabody, they are located relatively near to the center of

Fig. 3-17 Site plan of The Tannery.

Fig. 3-18 The Tannery.

Fig. 3-19 Academy Knoll Apartments, Marlborough, Massachusetts, renovated by Anderson Notter Associates.

Fig. 3-20 Interior detail of the Academy Knoll Apartments.

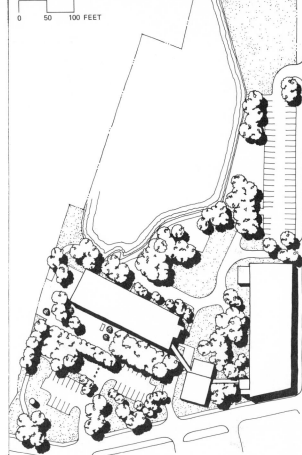

Fig. 3-21   Central Grammar School, Gloucester, Massachusetts, renovated by Anderson Notter Associates.

Fig. 3-22   Interior of the Central Grammar School.

Fig. 3-23   Penn Mutual Building, Philadelphia, by Mitchell/Giurgola Associates.

things, and by being reused they help revitalize the center.

What buildings like these document is simply this: the business of recycling and reusing individual old buildings for housing is no longer an eccentric pursuit practiced by effete historicists, but is instead in its many variations one of the broad avenues towards the achievement of an adequate supply of housing.

What may seem eccentric—or at least arcane— are the more subtle variations on this theme, where not whole buildings but just parts get reused, or where not even parts but just images get recreated. But these pursuits also have an important place in our current, multi-dimensional architectural scene.

CONSERVING PARTS OF BUILDINGS

At least two famous contemporary architects have discovered the drama—albeit a drama that is somewhat saucy in tone—that can be achieved by using only a part of an older building in the context of a new one. Their efforts are worth illustrating, even though they have nothing to do with housing, since they so clearly show the basic process (Figs. 3-23 and 3-24). Much more complex and interesting, though, is

Fig. 3-24   Derby Civic Center Competition entry, by James Stirling. Conserving at least a portion of the old within the new.

Fig. 3-25   Francisco Terrace, Chicago, by Frank Lloyd Wright.

Fig. 3-26   Francisco Terrace.

Fig. 3-27   Rebuilt version of Francisco Terrace, by Ben Weese.

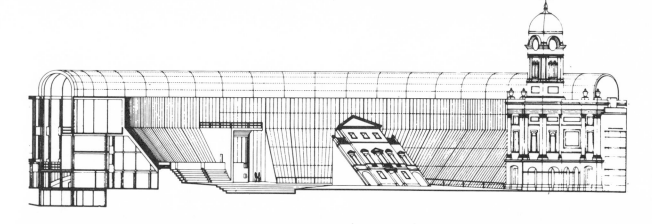

a design produced by Ben Weese, a Chicago architect and an ardently relaxed preservationist. It is a scheme for the "preservation" of Frank Lloyd Wright's Francisco Terrace housing in Chicago (Figs. 3-25 and 3-26). Wright's early attempt to deal with the problem of low-income housing consisted of spartan living quarters arranged around a central courtyard. The entire complex (like most of the neighborhood around it) was in an advanced state of decay. Attempts to renovate Francisco Terrace failed, and the building was demolished in 1974.

Weese's "preservation" scheme—which is still alive, even though the building itself is gone—takes the position that what was important about Francisco Terrace was its ornament (which could not be reproduced) and its massing (which could). Accordingly, the terra-cotta cornices, arch, and decorative columns and lintels were carefully removed before the demolition crews arrived, and Weese has designed a new building for a new site which conforms to the original massing, but consists of town houses with contemporary plans and contemporary amenities. These town houses, it now seems, can be feasibly financed and marketed (Fig. 3-27). Some will regard this as a Pyrrhic victory for the cause of historic preservation; but it is also a flexible, active

Fig. 3-28 Chester Terrace, London, by John Nash.

design response to a set of unalterable design problems.

Earlier, we noted that one of the reasons for recycling and reusing old buildings was that it seemed to feel right for psychological reasons, that it provided a direct route towards the necessary creation of a sense of place for human habitation. One of the powers of Ben Weese's scheme for the "preservation" of Francisco Terrace is that it tries to create this special sense of place by reusing only some of the parts of an older building, and in doing that it lunges beyond that point towards the daring notion of recycling just the *idea* of older buildings. That is, Weese's design comes close to simply being eclectic architecture.

CONSERVING THE IMAGES
OF OLD BUILDINGS

It now seems time to contradict flatly the notion of orthodox Modern architecture that eclecticism is the ultimate evil, and that the collecting of physical details or wistful images from past times or distant places in what we build is deplorable. This scorn is nonsense, and the banishment of eclecticism is contrary to human nature. Since it is demonstrable that we can know something only when it is related

to something else that we know already, it follows that every building, every unit of housing, has to be "like" something in order to mean something to the people who live there. This is a fact that came as no surprise, for instance, to John Nash when he designed Chester Terrace in London (Fig. 3-28), and indeed it seems to have been tacitly accepted by virtually every generation of architects but our own and the one just before us.

That architecture should be "like" something is a thing that the recent surge of interest in old buildings has helped teach us. But the lesson does not mean that all architecture must be like the same thing. This, again, means that architects must remain flexible and agile in their responses to different design problems.

Charles Moore, a notably historicizing architect (as well as an architectural historian), has commented on the difficulty many orthodox designers have in making their creations responsive to the real problems at hand:

I'm fascinated by how people clearly don't respond to what is clearly okay, but respond instead to their rigidified, Teutonized diagrams. Sociologists who sent out questionnaires to people who are going to move into subsidized housing do the same bad thing:

Fig. 3-29   Faculty Club, University of California at Santa Barbara, by MLTW/Moore-Turnbull.

Figs. 3-30, 3-31, and 3-32   Housing for Kingsmill-on-the-James, Virginia, by Charles Moore Associates.

they ask a set of questions that depend on a very limited set of things. 'Would you rather do A, like you did in your third-ago apartment, which you were driven out of by the rats? Or would you rather do B, like you did in your second-ago apartment, which fell down?' All they get back is either A or B again— and they don't get C, which could hardly fail to be better. The whole process of designing buildings depends on staying open, on being ready to seize on something when it seems to be a good thing, rather than pushing it away and making some 'original,' geometrically okay, but experientially hopeless concoction.[4]

Moore's own work, with his partners William Turnbull and Donlyn Lyndon, at the University of California at Santa Barbara (Fig. 3-29) seizes on the pseudo-Spanish Colonial architecture of many of the existing buildings of Santa Barbara, and emulates not only their theatrical spirit, but also their habit of using terraces, patios, arcades, and balconies to create varying degrees of indoors and out. A different project, for a housing development near Williamsburg, uses different models—American Colonial architecture in general, and the architecture of the Greek Revival in particular (Figs. 3-30, 3-31, and 3-32).

The parade of examples shows four of the possible ways in which we can conserve buildings from the past and use them to make housing now. We can use them to conserve whole neighborhoods, we can conserve individual buildings one by one, we can conserve only certain of their most desired parts, and we can conserve merely the images which they purvey. We are learning more and more, as well, to do all of these things, and frequently.

What then does this phenomenon have to say about the late-twentieth century form of housing? It says, in a sense, nothing, because this approach does not try to invent new forms and ideologies. That is, it says *no one thing*, because we have discovered that the influence of old buildings on housing is being felt in many different ways. We also discover that—from our late-twentieth century vantage—there are a great many different ways to make good housing.

If we feel some loss of security with this loss of orthodoxy, then we can also feel a corresponding excitement in the face of the many choices that are ours, and in the fact that the task is to continue to learn to cast our nets backwards in time—and outwards—to find what feels right for a given design problem, and what among the limited but still various options really seems efficient, appropriate, and therefore worthwhile.

Footnotes for Chapter 3

1. National Trust for Historic Preservation, *Economic Benefits of Conserving Old Buildings.* Washington, D.C.: The Preservation Press, 1976.
2. McLaughlin, Herbert, "Density: The architect's urban choices and attitudes," *Architectural Record,* vol. 159, no. 2 (February, 1976), p. 98.
3. Poorvu, William J., "Turning design ability into equity in your own development projects," *Architectural Record,* vol. 160, no. 8 (December, 1976), p. 51.
4. Allen, Gerald, "Found: The world as a candy box," *Architectural Record,* vol. 156, no. 8 (December, 1974), p. 130.

Bibliography

Cantacuzino, Sherban, *Architectural Conservation in Europe.* New York: Whitney Library of Design, 1975.
Chambers, Henry J., *Cyclical Maintenance for Historic Buildings.* Washington, D.C.: Office of Archeology and Historic Preservation, National Park Service, United States Department of the Interior, 1976.
Moore, Charles and Allen, Gerald, *Dimensions: Space, Shape & Scale in Architecture.* New York: Architectural Record Books, 1976.
National Trust for Historic Preservation, *Economic Benefits of Preserving Old Buildings.* Washington, D.C.: The Preservation Press, 1976.
National Trust for Historic Preservation, *Preservation & Building Codes.* Washington, D.C.: The Preservation Press, 1975.
Thompson, Elisabeth K., *Recycling Buildings: Renovations, Remodellings, Restorations, and Reuses.* New York: Architectural Record Books, 1976.

Section Two
The Participants

4
High Density, Low-Rise Housing and Changes in the American Housing Economy

Roger Montgomery

"You know how it is—money keeps getting tighter."

The decade that began in 1963 witnessed an important design change in the dominant house types built in the United States. Single family, detached, tract houses gave way to higher density, low-rise types typically clustered in planned unit developments. In large part this shift resulted from changes in the American housing economy and its institutions. Parallel changes occurred in both market and non-market or subsidized sectors of the economy, and they tended to produce similar design results though they had different starting points. For the architects and landscape architects who designed mass housing in the 1960s and early 1970s it was a busy and exciting time, particularly since the direction of these changes corresponded with their preferences, and the changes greatly enhanced their employment opportunities. A look back may help us understand that interesting period and what it may imply for the years to come.

In the United States between January 1963 and December 1972 nearly 20 million new dwelling units were built, more new houses than in any previous decade. Table 4-1 recapitulates some of the most important numbers about this production record. Points worth noting in addition to the relative decline of conventional single family housing include the rise of mobile homes and the small size of the nonmarket sector. Though subsidized production was small during this decade it exceeded the cumulative total in all the years since such housing began to be built in the 1930s. Higher density house types, town houses, row houses, patio houses, walk-ups, garden apartments, and various combinations of these types received new emphasis. Single family suburban sprawl slowed down. New kinds of site planning emerged. It was a decade of change and no aspect of the change was more apparent than the changes in design values.

These changes echoed ideas long advocated by designers. For years architects and landscape architects had decried single houses and suburban sprawl, and had advocated high density housing and cluster site planning. The other papers in this collection offer ample and ramified evidence about these values and enthusiasms. Though most of the examples illustrated come out of the 1963–73 decade they represent design ideas gestated earlier in the 1950s and before when designers raised lonely voices against the dominant trends in the American housing economy. The correspondences and parallels between what designers valued and advocated and what the housing economy produced during the 1960s and early 1970s give this period special interest for all those concerned with house form and the design of mass housing.

This chapter reviews some of the dimensions of the American housing economy that seem to have been particularly involved in these changes. The discussion divides into two main parts that treat separately the market and nonmarket sectors. The market sector refers to that part of the housing economy that serves "effective" demand, that is, the housing demand of those consumers able to pay the market price of housing. In this sector, decisions about the house itself including its design are made in the market place. Competition, profit, supply and demand affect design in the market sector. This contrasts with the nonmarket part of the housing economy, the sector that serves the "noneffective" demand of those potential consumers who are too poor to enter the market and buy housing. In this sector, decisions are made administratively usually by those providing and administering the subsidies that make up the difference between the market cost of the housing and the amount the "noneffective" consumers can pay. In a very crude sense the difference in decision making mirrors the difference that characterizes capitalist and socialist economic decision making.

THE MARKET SECTOR OF THE HOUSING ECONOMY: 1963–73

The American housing economy in the decade from the early 1960s to the early 1970s reflected, most importantly, changes on the demand side of the market. To understand these it is necessary to review the immediately previous period, the great suburban housing boom of the post-World War II era. During these years the housing economy produced an enormous number of single family detached dwellings sprawled across new suburban territory. This housing served the pent-up demand of war veterans and the wartime labor force. This group seemed to be composed of new households concentrated at the beginning of the child rearing years. These were nuclear families who fitted best into individual, single family, detached, suburban houses. This demand coincided nicely with a very generous supply of probably underpriced suburban land, and a building industry cost structure that made $7,000–$14,000, 700 to 1500 square foot houses possible (the equivalent in 1975 dollars is $16,000–$32,000 which contrasts with the actual mean price of new houses that year $39,300). The housing finance industry, laboriously reconstructed during the depression by the federal government, provided enormous quantities of money at prices people could afford. The result was suburban America and the ticky-tack boxes that built it.

The explosive building of the 1950s masked the fact that not all housing demand was being satisfied. Many kinds of people, the elderly, youth, childless couples, cosmopolites who loved central cities, poorer people who could not afford home ownership, to name a few, were ill served by the 1950s sprawl. These people, the nonnuclear families, composed a pent-up demand that burst forth in the 1960s. Perhaps the clearest indicator of this change can be seen in a favorite housing market statistic called "headship ratio." It refers to the ratio of households to total population. A society com-

TABLE 4-1. NEW HOUSE PRODUCTION IN THE UNITED STATES 1963–72
(Quantities in Thousands)

| Year | Market Sector | | | | | | % Market Sector |
	1–4 Family Units	Mobiles	Multiples	Total	Nonmarket [a] Sector	Total	
63	(n.a.)	151	(n.a.)	1,745	48	1,793	97
64	1,094	191	412	1,697	55	1,752	97
65	1,066	216	380	1,662	64	1,726	96
66	850	270	274	1,341	72	1,413	95
67	930	240	301	1,471	91	1,562	94
68	995	318	387	1,700	163	1,863	91
69	881	413	422	1,716	197	1,913	90
70	795	401	241	1,437	431	1,868	77
71	1,145	497	506	2,148	433	2,581	83
72	1,379	576	661	2,616	339	2,955	89
Totals	(n.a.)	3,220	(n.a.)	17,533	1,893	19,426	90

Derived from data in Anthony Downs: *Federal Housing Subsidies,* 1973, p. 11, Tables 2 and 3; HUD: *Housing in the Seventies,* p. 86, Table 2; and Department of Commerce: *Construction Review,* 1973 December, and 1968 December, Table B1.

[a] State-financed housing subsidies programs independent of federal subsidies not included.

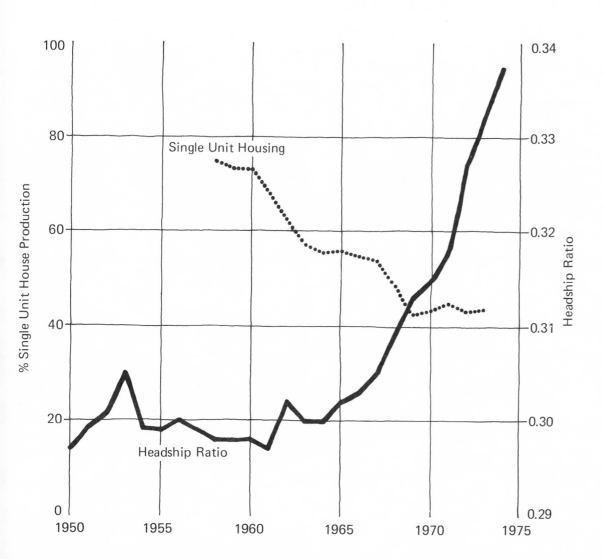

Fig. 4-3 Production of single-unit housing structures related to headship ration 1950–75.

Single Unit Housing

Headship Ratio

% Single Unit House Production

Headship Ratio

posed of a husband, wife, and two children nuclear family would have a headship ratio of 0.25 (1 household divided by 4 persons = 0.25). A society composed of 50 million such households would also have a 0.25 headship ratio. In contrast, a society of single individuals each living alone would have a ratio of 1.0. In the United States during the 1950s the headship ratio hovered at about 0.30. By 1973 it had climbed to 0.33. These small index numbers mask a shift from 10 to 20% in the number of households occupied by single individuals. Figure 4-3 charts this shift. It graphically indicates the big social changes that lay behind the changes in housing demand.

The change in the relative number of households had a magnified impact on new house design. Since the majority of recently built housing had been single family detached suburban units best suited to nuclear families, the standing stock of housing, which was largely composed of these units, could not easily accommodate the new nonnuclear households. Their demand required new production of new types of dwellings designed for nonnuclear family households. Thus it was that group housing, multiples, apartments, condominiums and such came to figure so importantly in the 1963–73 decade. They served both a pent-up

Fig. 4-4 The housing process major participants and influences.

demand that had not been met adequately in the 1950s housing boom and the new demand created by singles, old people, unrelated and unmarried couples including homosexuals, single parents, and other nonnuclear households. An indicator of this change, the percentage of single family units in each year's new house production is graphed in Fig. 4-3 along with the headship data. It dropped from about 80% to less than 50%.

Important changes also occurred autonomously on the supply side of the housing economy. Land, money, and building construction itself all became much more expensive. The first two factors particularly increased in cost faster than the overall price level. New dwellings rose substantially in relation to other goods and to incomes. This put a tremendous pinch on the market and tended to reduce consumption of new housing. As an indication of this, the price of new single family houses rose during the decade from $21,400 to $24,600 in 1967 dollars.

At least one perverse change accompanied the others. Throughout the 1960s the standard single family detached houses became progressively larger, more complex, and in some ways more costly in an absolute sense. Houses typically offered four or five bedrooms instead

of two or three, added several baths, a family room, all manner of built-in equipment like central air conditioning, wired intercom systems, and trash compactors. This curious phenomenon, given the decreasing household size and increasing relative costs, has yet to be sufficiently explained. Probably a combination of factors were involved. In any case, the effect was to further drive up prices and accelerate the drop in new, detached, suburban dwellings.

Taken together, the changes on the supply and demand sides of the housing market caused most of the big changes in the dominant house design motives of this decade. Demand led to smaller units and it showed preferences for clustering at locations that both required and permitted higher densities. On the supply side, the factors embodied in the secular cost trends led to similar outcomes, higher densities, smaller units, clustering, and the relative decline of single family suburban sprawl.

With that brief rundown of major changes in supply and demand, it makes sense to examine some institutional changes. In the United States, the market sector of the housing economy totally dominates in a quantitative sense. For the decade in question Table 4-1 shows this

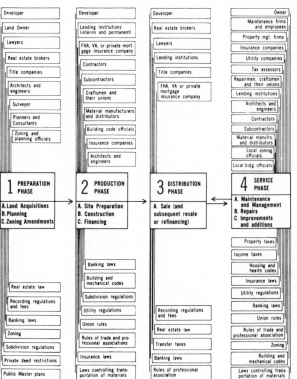

THE HOUSING PROCESS MAJOR PARTICIPANTS AND INFLUENCES

dominance. Throughout the 15 years prior to 1963 the market share never fell below 97%. The 1963–73 decade represented a high point in nonmarket production, still the market share overall was 90% and most years it exceeded that number. Given that substantial hegemony, it follows that most housing institutions relate to the market sector. This is compounded by the fact that the standing stock of housing represents in any year about 97% of all housing available for occupancy. An enormous number and variety of institutions own and manage this stock of existing housing.

Some idea of the complexity of this institutional landscape can be inferred from the chart reproduced in Fig. 4-4. Some of the salient characteristics of this curiously complex world were neatly summarized in 1968 in the following words by the President's Committee on Urban Housing from whence came this chart.

The fact that housing is tied to land and locally regulated has meant that most builders, real estate brokers, and mortgage lenders (at least savings and loan associations) restrict their activities to rather small geographical areas. Only a handful of homebuilders look for nationwide market possibilities.

The variety of the housing product has led to fragmentation of the industry into an elaborate complex of interlocking producing units. Different structures require different combinations of skills. Thus, the industry tends to work through *ad hoc* arrangements for each specific job. The practice of subcontracting, which is prevalent in the industry is not necessarily irrational, and in fact, is often an efficient response to the need to meet many specialized demands. It is not clear whether greater vertical integration in the industry— that is, permanent alignment of a broader range of skills under the umbrella of a larger organization—would greatly increase efficiency in production. . . .

With the major exception of some building materials manufacturers and a few distributors and lending institutions, most firms involved in the production and distribution of housing are relatively small. Smallness is characteristic not only of most builders, contractors, and subcontractors, but also of architectural and engineering firms, real estate brokers, and maintenance firms. The smallness of these firms results primarily from the industry's localized and fragmented nature. There are, however, additional reasons for the smallness and light capitalization of

construction firms. The rate of housing production is rather erratic, both on a national basis, and especially in each local market. . . . The erratic rate of output forces construction firms to try to keep their continuing overhead to a minimum, thus discouraging capital investment and assembly of large central staffs.

The firms which make up the heart of the industry—primarily homebuilders and contractors—are dependent on larger enterprises not primarily engaged in housing. They are usually too small to bargain on an equal basis with the larger firms on the periphery of the industry. Thus financial institutions probably constitute the single most important locus of power in the industry. . . .

Needless to say this extraordinary array of institutions and influences makes impossible a complete analysis of their multiple and interlocking influence on housing design. At best only a few highlights can be selected for consideration. Therefore, based on some of the conventional wisdom among housing economy participants, and on my own interests, insights, and experience, the next pages deal with a selection of institutional influences. They treat a major attitudinal shift among the builders themselves, two important legal–institutional

Fig. 4-5   The contrast visible in these pictures exemplifies
the design changes discussed in this chapter. (a) Typical
1950s single family detached suburban sprawl near
St. Louis, Missouri. (b) Typical 1960s planned
unit development.

changes, planned unit development and condominium ownership and, finally, several secondary effects of these and other changes that, taken together, enhanced the employment of design professionals in the housing field during the 1963–73 period [Figs. 4-5(a) and (b)].

Builders Become Cosmopolitan

Few sectors of the American economy have ever sustained such insistent hostile criticism as the house builders and land developers met during the 1950s. Pejorative phrases like ticky-tack suburban sprawl became household bywords. Lead by highbrow culture critics many in the society came to see the merchant builders and land developers as villains, insensitive to the higher things of life and interested only in short-term profit maximization. Despite the apparent double bind thus created, the suburban masses tended to share these views. Understandably the builders and developers reacted. After all, they had to face their fellow men and women at home and marketplace, club and church. And they had to sell houses. To an astonishing degree the builders and developers took the criticism seriously and tried to change their ways. They responded to the pervasive criticism by making

substantial changes in the practice of home building.

Understanding these changes necessitates a look at the world of the home builders who operated in the 1950s. Nearly a generation had elapsed since the last boom in house construction, a boom that began to decline in 1925 and collapsed in 1928. The ensuing depression, the Second World War and the postwar economic changeover kept the lid on building until the late 1940s. The old home builders mostly went out of business and died off. Then came the new boom. Very quickly house production reached unprecedented levels. By the middle 1950s, tract house sprawl had begun to change the face of every urbanized area in America. A new group of private sector housing entrepreneurs arose, self-made, not part of a continuing tradition. They had wrought enormous changes in the living environment of everyone in the country. The very changes and the criticism they engendered accentuated the psychological needs for group identity among these new born entrepreneurs. More significantly, common economic interests required that they band together. They did. The National Association of Home Builders of the United States became their main vehicle. By the beginning of the 1960s the NAHB had

become a powerful, relatively enlightened, industry association. It played a significant role in the rise of high density, low-rise housing. This happened, in part, as a response to the criticism of sprawl.

The NAHB behaved typically for an industry association. It undertook its struggles in order to increase its effectiveness as an interest group and to promote community and a positive self-image among its membership. For the sake of the present discussion the most important of these struggles was the effort to get its own members to adopt the design values of the cultural critics. To a remarkable degree it succeeded. Soon home builders were advocating alternatives to sprawl. They worked on consumers and other institutional participants to change their norms. The NAHB and the home builders played a leading role in changing the design values that dominated the United States housing market.

All the normal tools for changing attitudes came into play during this campaign: among these were publications, exhibits, conferences, workshops, prizes and awards, position taking by leaders, and financing of research and demonstrations. The following discussion of the results comes mainly from my experience as an off-and-on participant observer in the industry between 1948 and 1970. Among the various NAHB actions the research effort particularly merits attention. In this it joined forces with another industry association, the Urban Land Institute, an organization with a long history of useful applied research in urban design. Together the NAHB and ULI began the Land Use Research Program dedicated to overcoming the ticky-tack sprawl stereotype and replacing it with a better development prototype. By 1963 when our decade opened, this research had produced a substantial output. A notable series of technical publications appeared under the ULI imprint. Perhaps more important, a heavy flow of educational material directed at the NAHB members came from their central office in Washington appropriately called, given the nation's private business economy, "The National Housing Center." The July 1963 issue of the NAHB *Journal of Homebuilding*, for instance, carried a special section devoted to this research. It emphasized cluster plan land subdivision. Figures 4-6(a) and (b) taken from this publication illustrate the basic idea. High density, low-rise dwelling designs emerged as a by-product of these site planning studies.

The NAHB sponsored other influential efforts. Builders, made affluent by the profitable 1950s, flew around the United States and Europe looking at each other's work and at notable examples of housing design selected for their instruction. By the early 1960s a substantial proportion of the leading home builders had been on foreign architectural tours. The same examples architects visited on their European pilgrimages began to be well known among the builders too. English new towns and council housing, for instance, especially the work of the then London County Council, and Scandinavian examples, Finland's Tapiola particularly, became familiar to the NAHB opinion leaders.

Other agencies, groups, and individuals contributed to this struggle to change the image, the self-image, and the practice of home building. Henry Luce's *Time-Life* publications empire, for instance, became heavily involved. In 1952 they started a new magazine expressly for this purpose. *House and Home*, with generous initial backing, quickly became a force for change. It gave lavish attention to such themes as cluster site planning, planned unit developments, and the high density low-rise

Fig. 4-7 At the beginning of the shift to high density, low-rise house design, urban renewal played a critical role in making sites specifically available for such housing. The units built on these sites then became convincing feasibility demonstrations. Among the most influential of these early designs was the Bollinger and Martin Southwick project of 1960 in the slums of Louisville, Kentucky where land planners Wihry and Lantz produced a cluster layout for the historicist architecture of Augustus & Doumas. This NAHB prize winning design was built in a number of other localities, the picture shows it in St. Charles, Missouri in 1963.

alternatives to single family detached houses. Among their more splashy devices was an awards program. Figure 4-7 illustrates one of these.

This long campaign of public and self-education resulted in the house builders becoming quite cosmopolitan in tastes and outlook. By the mid 1960s they had, in large part, assimilated and internalized the idea of high density, low-rise housing. Their widespread use of "condominium vernacular" designs confirms this. Examples abound. Recently one of the larger San Francisco Bay Area builders confided to me that he really wished he could do some "mine-shaft" building. "Mine-shaft" is a high-culture code word for Sea Ranch Condominium designer Charles Moore's personal style of artfully artless design (see Fig. 4-12 and the discussion under condominiums). Builders and developers committed their hard market economics to exploiting the high density, low-rise idea.

In recounting the attitudinal change that brought the builders from a single-minded fixation to single family detached houses to a

positive view of high density, low-rise designs, it would be a mistake not to observe that economic self-interest supported the change. As the nuclear family demand shrank, as land and money costs skyrocketed, as preferences, whether manipulated by suppliers or not, shifted to larger more expensively equipped single detached houses, the home builders needed to make parallel changes in their product. And to do this they needed to change their attitudes so they and those who related to them like the mortgage bankers and zoning commissioners would see the changes in a positive light. Perhaps attitudes would not have changed so easily had they not been so functionally related to maximizing production and sales. In any case, it happened; and the home builders who started the decade as the villains behind sprawl ended the decade with a far more environmentally responsible self-image, thanks to their vigorous support of higher density house designs and site plans. (It is an irony that as this happened the environmental movement became widely dominant and its no-growth policies halted all development in many places just at the point when developers widely embraced the cosmopolitan cluster plan religion.)

PUDs: Zoning Laws to Control Sprawl

Local government in the United States exerts considerable regulatory control over urban development through zoning laws. These laws arise out of the responsibility and power of local government to protect the safety and general welfare of people and property. The concern for protecting property means protecting it "from impingement by competing private interests," in the words of John Delafons. In his book, *Land Use Control in the United States,* he observes, "the interest conserved may be that of private property owners against both speculative developers and unwanted new-comers. . . ." The concern became embodied in zoning legislation that was used first in the United States in San Francisco in 1885 to ban Chinese laundries from much of the city. By the 1950s most of the developed and undeveloped urban and potentially urban land lay under the control of zoning ordinances. These set quite rigid limits on what could be built. Almost always zoning was couched in terms of the lot–house stereotype, that is, a conventionalized image of a separate house standing alone on its own plot. Controls covered such things as side yard dimensions and number of dwellings per lot. They tended to force each new development into a pattern predictably looking almost exactly like everything else nearby. Zoning successfully cartelized the residential land and new house construction markets through orderly regulation that insured predictable results. But it insured also the monotony, the banality, the environmental insensitivity, that characterized sprawl.

Gradually planning professionals, architects and landscape architects, builders and developers, and environmentally aware members of the general public, began to sense the pernicious effects of lot-by-lot zoning. A search for alternatives began in the mid 1950s. From various sources, but mainly from federally sponsored garden apartment and group housing projects of the 1930s and 1940s, a new approach to zoning emerged. Probably Harland Bartholomew of St. Louis, the largest and most successful planning consultant of the era, wrote the first of the new regulations. It was geared specifically to higher densities and low-rise building. Later as the idea spread it became known as "planned unit development" zoning or PUD for short.

Instead of tying the control system to the process of piecemeal development on individual lots, PUD zoning is geared to the unified design and development of larger tracts. Such laws usually set minimum acreages to which they apply. These may be as small as ten acres or less. In practice, though, areas of hundreds, even thousands, of acres, are developed as PUDs. Instead of detailed controls on the arrangement and size of buildings such new controls allow such factors to vary. They often relax use restrictions permitting retail business, personal and communal services, and all sorts of recreational facilities to be incorporated in residential areas. Except for an overall gross density limit the controls are procedural. PUD zoning sets up a review process under which the developer presents a unified design for the total area, the zoning authority reviews this, and upon its approval the design itself becomes its own control.

At first PUD zoning ran into considerable opposition. In the late 1950s it was not uncommon for serious conflict to arise over just such matters as those that had initially led to zoning, particularly its capacity to make future

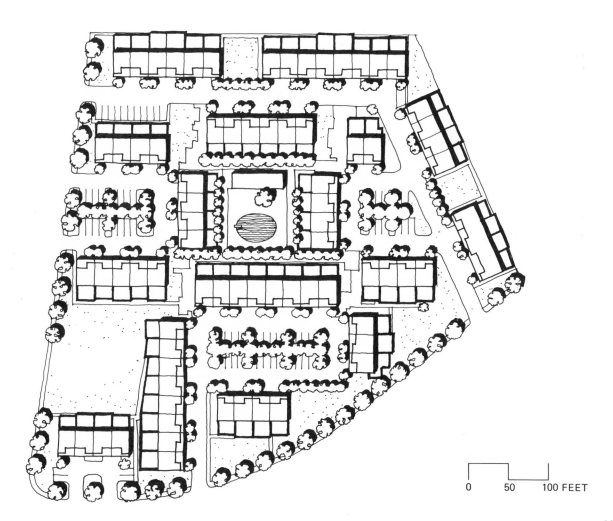

development predictable. At first people feared PUDs did not make the future sufficiently certain. However, by 1963 a considerable number of PUDs had been approved and built. Their outcome was no longer a market threatening mystery. During the rest of our decade PUDs became the normal way of developing housing in many parts of the country.

Under this kind of zoning, just as the title suggests, the whole site could be designed in a single planned unit. Perhaps the most common result was the "clustering" of dwellings. Instead of spreading houses more or less evenly over a tract of land, the same number of houses could be concentrated on a part of the land. Instead of an evenly distributed, monotonous sprawl, houses could be clustered into village-like groups. Figure 4-8 illustrates an influential early prototype PUD project. These new controls permitted designing of the site as a whole including the integrated design of house groups. It powerfully advanced the high density, low-rise idea by permitting clustered and attached dwellings where heretofore only detached and sprawled single family houses were allowed.

0   50   100 FEET

Figs. 4-9(a) and (b) These two diagrams appeared in the first edition of Kevin Lynch's superb and ubiquitous text, *Site Planning*. They neatly suggest the site survey design process, perhaps too neatly, for Lynch omitted such diagrams in the second edition and relied on a more ramified verbal description of the process.

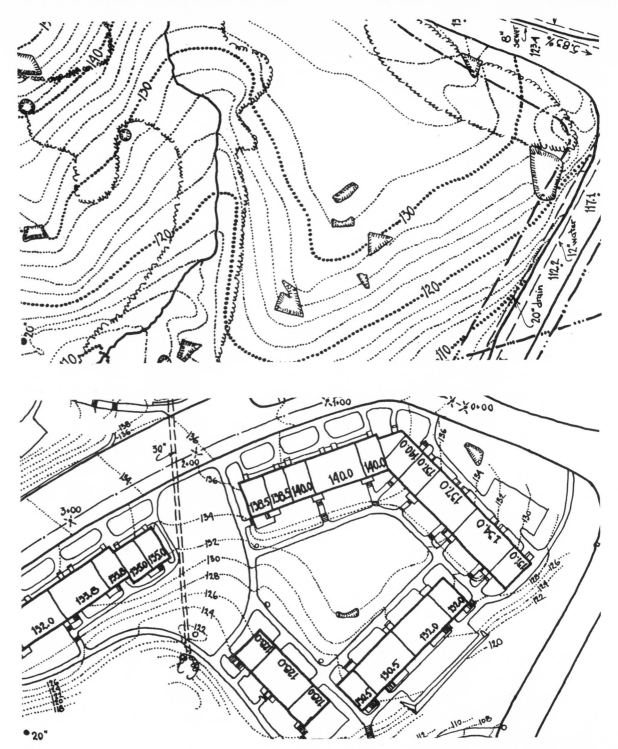

Several concurrent institutional, practical and ideological changes gave vigorous support to PUD zoning. Among the most important of these was the development and popularization of a new approach to site planning practice. By the 1950s landscape architects had codified an environmentally based technique. A survey of the many attributes of a specific site, such things as soils, slopes, vegetation, views, previous development and microclimate could be used to generate a site design. Instead of generating the design entirely on the demand side of the market, e.g., so many three bedroom dwellings; the design could be derived from the specifics on the supply side, e.g., the characteristics of an actual site. A spate of books, the home builder groups, and the media were quick to spread the word [Figs. 4-9(a) and (b)]. It was a methodology that dovetailed exquisitely with PUD zoning. It provided an ironclad environmental rationale for clustering, for preserving open space, and for turning to high density, low-rise house types.

Related to this were the beginnings of the environmental movement itself. From the beginning this movement looked on sprawl and the single family detached house as prime environmental villains. Clustered development under planned unit zoning became a strongly preferred alternative. Environmental institutions such as the American Conservation Association sponsored cultural leaders like William H. Whyte to advance the cause. [See Whyte's books, *Cluster Development* (1964) and *The Last Landscape* (1968).] Though by the end of our decade the environmental movement had moved beyond PUDs to a no-growth, totally antidevelopment position, in 1963 they were a powerful advocate of high density, low-rise housing.

Another supporting change emerged in the form of the homes associations, a new kind of institution to take jurisdiction over the common spaces and facilities in planned unit developments. Actually three alternatives exist for this: local government can take title and manage the facilities; or a special district government can do this; or, lastly, a homes association as it is called, a private institution composed of property owners and occupants within the planned unit development, can hold and manage common land and facilities. All have been used, but only the private association has proved widely acceptable in practice. (One of the landmarks in the movement toward PUDs was the research report *The Home Association Handbook* published by the Urban Land Institute. It developed from the NAHB–ULI research mentioned in the previous section of this chapter.) Homes associations added a new dimension to the planned unit movement. They offered a formalized social–political expression for the community that was spatially defined by the physical project. They laid the basis for a spatially defined social integration widely felt to be lacking in lot-by-lot sprawl. They gave the potential for a social community which designers felt should inhabit their high density, low-rise clusters.

Condominiums

Early in the 1963–73 decade a new wrinkle in American property law provided another stimulant in the rise of high density housing. Laws appeared that permitted condominium ownership. These allowed people to own a specific piece of a building, a particular apartment on a particular floor, plus an interest in the land and supporting facilities like elevators, lobbies, piping and foundations. Although condominiums have a long history in Europe and Latin America, until the 1960s home ownership in the United States had been tied to land ownership, and property law had no provisions for condominium ownership. After Puerto Rico started the parade in 1958, Hawaii became the first state to pass enabling legislation, felicitously named, the Hawaii Horizontal Property Act of 1961. The same year the Federal Housing Administration recognized condominium ownership. The following year it promulgated a model state law. By 1968 all 50 states had adopted it or similar legislation.

By providing some of the psychological and all of the tax advantages traditionally associated with fee simple real property ownership, the appearance of laws making condominium ownership possible had a significant impact on design. Heretofore, any other form of tenure open to individual householders except the fee ownership of a single house on its own plot of land entailed a number of disadvantages. The

TABLE 4-2. FEDERAL INTERVENTIONS IN THE UNITED STATES
HOUSING, 1972
(Numbers in Billions of Dollars)

Home owners deductions	$6.2
Other taxes forgone (e.g., capital gains on house sales)	3.0–4.0
Federal subsidies to the nonmarket sector	2.5
Federal welfare assistance payments for housing	2.6
Total for year 1972	$14.3–15.3

From HUD *Housing in the 70's*

TABLE 4-3. CONDOMINIUM CONSTRUCTION
(Numbers in Thousands)

	Prior to 1970	1970	1971	1972
Number	85	79	164	299
% of new construction	(n.a.)	5.4	7.9	12.5
% of existing stock	0.1	(n.a.)	(n.a.)	1.0 [a]

Derived from HUD Condominiums Cooperative Study (1975). pp. 111–112,
111–113.

[a] Approximate figure not derived from above source

least tangible of these is the most important. It has to do with the emotional, psychological, and status advantages of "owning your own home." In addition, financial advantages accrue to home owners primarily in terms of federal income tax deductions permitted for real estate taxes and mortgage interest payments on their homes, and the treatment of value increments as capital gains. In aggregate this represented an enormous amount. Table 4-2 illustrates its relative magnitude in relation to other federal interventions in the housing market. It is ironic that two-thirds of federal housing assistance dollars goes not to the poor but to the home-owning middle and upper classes. Since before the advent of condominiums these subsidies were tied to single family detached home ownership, they provided a massive federal subsidy for the 1950s suburban sprawl pattern.

The legislation that permitted condominium ownership provided the same basic tax advantages to owners of single apartments in high-rise and in high density, low-rise structures. It thus removed a powerful constraint that had tended to prevent these alternative house types. The timing of the condominium legislation could not have been more perfect. Ac-

tually it was not sheer happenstance. Just as the major market forces described in the first part of this chapter shifted to favor high density housing this new form of ownership emerged to facilitate the shift. This offers another example of the remarkable convergence of forces behind high density, low-rise housing in the 1963–73 decade.

By way of background, note that condominium ownership represents only one of several possible legal arrangements for community tenancy in single buildings. The most common of these are, of course, the conventional rental and lease tenancy. But a negative stigma attaches to being a renter in America. Most self-respecting citizens seek to raise themselves from the slough of rental tenancy. Government penalizes the renter by putting him at a tax disadvantage with respect to home owners. Only rarely, mainly in the nonmarket sector that services the inferior demand of the poor, has central government in the United States shown any interest in rental housing. Another tenure pattern, cooperative ownership, is often confused with the condominium. In a coop, tenants own shares in a corporation that owns the property. By virtue of that, and a "maintenance fee," they have rights to occupy a dwelling. It neither provides an actual individual

ownership in fee, nor does it offer all the tax advantages of the condominium. Cooperative ownership is particularly common in New York City. Outside of New York City it is limited to a very few projects, often those sponsored by a labor union, church, or ideological affinity group. In these cases the joint ownership has powerful communitarian payoffs as in the successful strike at Coop City (Fig. 4-10).

By the late 1960s and early 1970s condominiums represented a major fraction of total housing output. Table 4-3 illustrates this extraordinary increase. In some local markets the rise of the condominium was nothing short of spectacular. In California, for instance, they increased from 6% of for sale housing under construction in 1970 to 35% in 1974, and locally during that year in the active San Jose market they amounted to about 50% and at Lake Tahoe to about 60%. These two localities typify the two submarkets in which condominiums dominate. Tahoe exemplifies the second home resort settlement market, the ski-villages, beach-villages, mountain- and lake-villages which have become almost synonymous with the word "condominium" (Fig. 4-11). In the other market are dwellings designed to reap scale economies from clustering smaller units, reducing land costs per unit, and thereby permitting the

Fig. 4-10 The New York City housing economy contrasts sharply with that in the rest of the country. Massive high-rise projects and cooperative ownership as an alternative to rental tenancy occupy a dominant place there. Coop City, a high-rise new-town-in-town for over 50,000 inhabitants, offers the apotheosis of these unique regional characteristics. Designed by Herman J. Jessor, Zion and Breen did the landscaping, it was completed and occupied in the early 1970s. While it is safe to say the "tower-in-the-park" design concept gained no new adherents elsewhere as a result of this scheme, it does represent a national landmark in a very different way. Coop City's occupants, though nominally owners, carried out the biggest, longest, and most successful "rent strike" in American housing history. Their victory in 1976 may indicate new directions in housing economy toward a greater management voice for occupants, and a semipublic utility status for housing in some of the country's most urbanized submarket areas.

Fig. 4-11 By the late 1960s second home planned unit developments of condominiums typified both the new characteristics of the housing economy and the new directions in design. These trends show clearly in the Sasaki/Walker development plan and Killingsworth and Brady architecture for this Vail, Colorado, ski community of 1972.

marketing of less expensive houses better tuned to the emergent demand of small households. In both cases the enhanced design employment effect noted below tends to produce serious and consistent architecture.

Early in the spectacular rise of the condominium idea a California example provided it with a definitive architectural image. At Sea Ranch, a second home development on the coast north of San Francisco, Charles Moore and his partners built their "wooden rock," the Sea Ranch Condominium (Fig. 4-12). Instantly it became both archetype and epitome. Elsewhere I have referred to this phenomena as the "rise of a condominium vernacular," a vernacular style done by professional architect specialists. Today wherever condominiums are built in the United States, and to a large extent wherever any high density, low-rise housing is built, the shades of Sea Ranch show through. To most eyes this is a thoroughly satisfactory outcome. This self-conscious vernacular offers one of the happiest mass market design ideas abroad today. Figure 4-13 provides a sample of the worthy offspring of Sea Ranch. These designs indicate how the mass market housing economy can nurture the cause of good architecture and site design.

Fig. 4-12 Charles Moore and his partners of MLTW enormously influential "wooden rock" otherwise kn as the Sea Ranch Condominium. Instantly it became the ideal-typical housing image of the era. It sired the design response to the economy's new institutions, the "condominium vernacular" style.

Fig. 4-13 Ocean House by Sandy and Babcock.

Fig. 4-14 Airview of 1950s sprawl on the northwest side of St. Louis shows a transitional phase in the FHA campaign to substitute long block curved streets, popularly termed "spaghetti," for the most standard gridiron.

Enhanced Design Employment Effects—I

Many of the changes in housing market institutions during the 1960s had a profound effect on the specific terms under which architects and landscape architects were employed in designing housing. These changes positively affected the autonomy of designers and enhanced their power in relation to other factors in the market. In turn this meant that design values as distinct from commercial ones became relatively more dominant during the decade we are chronicling. The secular changes in the market and market institutions increased employment of all types of designers, encouraged the employment of independent architects, and reduced reliance on plan services, in-house staff designers, and the like. Designers became freer of the nondesign-based constraints of day-to-day business decisions. They worked more in the context of long-range design goals and independent professional values. Indirect though these effects were, they were profound and highly visible.

To understand this change it is necessary to start by looking at the design employment system characteristic of the 1950s single family house sprawl era. Generally land surveyors or engineers laid out the site plans for housing

using a rather few basic principles and guidelines. First and foremost among these principles was maximizing the number of lots per acre, constrained only by local zoning codes and subdivision regulations, and development costs such as earth moving, street, sewer, and drainage works. The local subdivision regulations pretty generally governed the engineering details of such works. Beyond this rather simple optimizing process of maximizing lots within the regulations, there were some design guidelines originally promulgated by the Federal Housing Administration in the 1930s. These guidelines set forth such objectives as long block, curved streets and T-shaped intersections, ideas that were intended to displace the endless gridiron of nearly all previous American urban development. Spaghetti—as the FHA design ideas were later tagged—replaced the checkerboard in 1950s land development practice (Fig. 4-14).

To return to the employment issue, the developers and builders of housing typically employed surveyors or site engineers to lay out their projects. Usually these professionals were small-scale, independent individuals or partnerships extremely localized in terms of their operations. They clustered in county seat towns because courthouses held the land

records. The most important product of the surveyors and engineers was land records, the subdivision plat, or official and legal record of marketable land units or lots. Recording, as this legal record keeping is called, classically typifies the function of government in a market economy: without this referee like record keeping the market could not function. Local surveyors and engineers, with their deeply embedded connections with a specific county recorder's office, were among the key independent, highly localized, housing market professionals along with the courthouse lawyers, the mortgage brokers, the title insurance and escrow people. Practice in such a localized social context made for insulated design norms, highly oriented to local traditions to the extent anything operated other than mechanical lot maximization. The ubiquitous, spaghetti-street suburban sprawl of the 1950s memorializes the physical effects of these particular housing market institutions, the county seat surveyor and engineer practicing under the aura of FHA.

The 1950s house design processes and institutions were somewhat different, though they often manifested some underlying organizational identities. Developers and builders ordinarily got house designs from one or more of three sources: plan services, highly specialized

Fig. 4-15 A small minority of 1950s style single family detached suburban houses attempted serious architecture, most did not. (a) Standard "lumberyard" architect's house versus (b) an Anshen and Allen house of 1952 illustrates, respectively, these majority and minority approaches.

and localized designers, and in-house staff. Plan services often operated on a national scale to produce endless minor variations on a relatively few stock house types. Economies of scale permitted extraordinary cost reductions. A price of $50 was not a high price to pay for a set of plans for a house that, if architect designed, would cost $1000 or more for the plans alone. Plan services would produce plans to order for slightly higher fees though still substantially below independent architects' charges. Developers could thus introduce some response to local preferences and still utilize these substantial economies. And of course hundreds of houses could be built from a single set of $50 plans.

Specialized local house designers existed, and exist still, in most market areas. These professionals typically operate outside the formal professional structure of architecture, outside the American Institute of Architects and such organizations; and they are, in fact, often not registered architects under the state licensing laws. For a per plan fee, in the typical case, these designers would provide a service slightly more tailored to local preferences than the plan services, though in many cases the distinction between the two kinds of designers grew

fuzzy indeed. Often these designers would do façade modifications on plan service prototypes. This produced the superficial variety so characteristic of the subdivisions of the 1950s. Sometimes these services were tied in with other components of the housing market. When I practiced in Ohio in the 1950s, building materials suppliers often had such designers tied to their operations. We called them "lumberyard architects." In return for patronizing a particular supplier, a builder could have plans drawn up at little or no cost.

The in-house design staff more commonly occurred in large firms. The prototypical developer of the era, William Levitt, exemplified the kind of scale economy and vertical organization common to such entrepreneurs. Characteristically they included home design as a staff function supporting management. Levitt had in-house site planning as well. Fewer firms did this. Staff house designers became quite common. Being in-house meant that they sat in on management decisions. Direct, internal communications linked them to both production and marketing, but they were almost totally cut off from the professional worlds of the independent designers. The reference group of the in-house designers was their firm's man-

agement not the American Institute of Architects [Fig. 4-15(a)].

In actual practice few developers and builders depended entirely on any one type of design arrangement. Combinations were common. In-house staff would handle details and daily work with the marketing and production people. Plan services and specialized independent designers would develop ideas for new models and feed these to the staff people. A few housing firms used bona fide independent AIA architects and ASLA landscape architects; the few that did became terribly well known in the 1950s. On the West Coast, Joseph Eichler carved out a special niche in the San Francisco Bay Area housing market with a line of builders' houses in undiluted, high-style architecture designed by such local AIA notables as Anshen & Allen and Jones & Emmons [Fig. 4-15(b)]. In the East, the Washington, D.C. market was unique in its wide use of independent designers. Architects like Charles Goodman, Chloethiel Smith, Keyes–Lethbridge–Condon, Cohen and Haft made reputations doing mass market work. Few tried in other local markets. Fewer still succeeded. A more common line found architects going it alone, trying to become developers and forming their own in-house, builder–developer operation. In Cambridge, Massachusetts, architects like Carl Koch and The Architects Collaborative (Walter Gropius' firm) personified this approach. Throughout the great 1950s house building boom it was rare indeed that independent architects and landscape designers had any direct involvement with the great mass of building that sprawled across the countryside around American cities.

In the 1960s the situation changed radically. The whole series of housing market occurrences chronicled in the preceding pages of this chapter led to the widespread employment of architects and landscape architects in mass market housing design. Given the architects' set of professional values which tended to be strongly antisprawl and antisingle family house (for others if not for him or herself); and given the architects' social position close to the makers of high culture, the people most hostile to sprawl; the architect's new prominence in housing corresponded to the strong market trends toward high density, low-rise housing. The importance of their influence during the 1963–73 decade makes it worth examining, in more detail, how it was that secular housing market trends enhanced the employment of independent professional housing designers, both architects and landscape architects.

Each of the main factors that pushed the market sector of the economy toward high density, low-rise housing had such an enhancing effect. The demographic changes and the secular increase in costs contributed most to the employment effect simply because the old economies no longer worked for the higher density designs these changes brought on. High density housing defied the simplicities of surveyor's plats and plan service stock dwelling designs. In single family detached house sprawl the space between dwellings and the perimeter of the lots gave a margin of error necessary to make the old design system work. When dwellings were tightly clustered there was no room to play. The necessary tolerance for fitting a stock house to a roughly platformed site had vanished. Catalog houses drawn up without specific knowledge of a particular site could only work with a generous margin for error. Dwellings joined tightly together in multiple-unit buildings or town houses, needed a lot of professional care to fit them to each other and to the land. There was no room to fudge discrepancies in site grades. Planting could not remedy privacy problems among dwellings placed cheek-by-jowl.

The growing cosmopolitanism of the builders intensified these employment effects that led to more and better designers working on housing. In addition to reinforcing the general drive toward high density, low-rise housing, the builders put increasingly high value on architecture for its own sake and for the sake of their new cosmopolitan image. By the middle 1960s developers in some markets were advertising the names of their architects. For instance, when Jack Foster started Foster City, California in 1961, though called a new town, actually a 1960s style Levittown-type development, he kicked it off with Edward Stone designed apartments [Fig. 4-16(a)]. In 1975, jazzy Fisher–Friedman designed clusters at Foster City [Fig. 4-16(b)] demonstrate the continuing strength of this need to demonstrate a cosmopolitan, high taste.

PUDs had big employment effects by shifting the entire game from the routinized, almost clerical lot-by-lot design process to a project master plan design concept. Just to apply for PUD development rights required a detailed comprehensive design, carefully related to a particular site. When the master plan design had been accepted as the PUD control in lieu of lot-by-lot zoning then the record plat was drawn from the design. The surveyor–engineer

Fig. 4-16 Serious architecture happened commonly in high density, low-rise planned unit development clusters as in Foster City, California, where (a) Edward Durrell Stone authored the earliest apartments, The Commodore, in 1962 and (b) Fisher-Friedman have authored the latest ones, The Islands, in 1976. These typify the enhanced design employment effects produced by the housing economy of the 1960s and early 1970s.

still had to draw the plat. But his role became subservient to the master plan or PUD designer. No single change in housing market institutions has had a more pervasive effect on designers and designs. The connection is so strong that sometimes the characteristic cluster house designs of the late 1960s are simply referred to as PUDs: the zoning term defines an archi-tectural style. This parallels, in a more official way, the similar effect of the style associated with the rise of condominiums discussed above in relation to Charles Moore's famous Sea Ranch design.

The nature of practice in mass market housing unit design changed in the 1960s and 1970s. The surveyor–engineer no longer held a pivotal role. A new breed, usually called land planner, had entered the field and gained the key role as initial designer and master planner. Some-times engineering firms diversified and added skills to do this work. More commonly it fell to teamwork groups of landscape architects, architects, urban planners, and engineers. On smaller projects conventional, independent, AIA, architectural firms would take on this site planning–master planning task. Around the country a whole group of firms grew up by perfecting their specialized skills and artistic talents in cluster design. In the San Francisco

Bay Area, for instance, probably partly because Sea Ranch happened there, a whole stable of such design firms came into being. Among those primarily based on architecture practice were Fisher–Friedman, Sandy and Babcock, Hall and Goodhue, Ian McKinley, Bull–Field–Volkmann–Stockwell, and Wurster, Bernardi & Emmons. Lawrence Halprin, Sasaki–Walker, Royston–Hanamoto–Beck & Abey, and EDAW developed national housing practices as landscape architects. Dan Coleman, a planner, specialized in this kind of work. Similar firms emerged in every major region. In but a decade a whole new field of practice was defined.

House or unit and building design got new emphasis, too. Often, particularly in the smaller projects, the same architects or designers would do the building and the land planning. This had enormous benefits in terms of functional and constructional coordination, and in terms of visual and esthetic criteria. Site and unit design became parts of a single process. Though economies from repetition and incremental rather than radical changes in unit design retained cost advantages, it became hard indeed not to design in a way that paid some considerable attention to the *genius loci* of a particular time and place. This attention to particularities is the essence of environmental design. Large-scale developments, particularly the very large ones of the late 1960s ambitiously called "new towns," understandably exhibited more division of labor. In these cases a multidisciplinary design and planning team would do the master plan while most of the houses, even the detail site plans, would be done in the same manner as smaller PUDs. Until the politically inspired housing market recession of 1973 it looked as though a specialization on new town design was emerging. Since then this design capacity has been underemployed and much of it has dispersed.

The promise of a decade of housing design when market demand and artistic values came so close to each other seems at first sight to have dribbled away. But vast structural changes were wrought. Employment in the field expanded enormously. These changes can be perhaps best seen in the sharply escalated design cost of mass market housing. Now instead of a $50 per lot surveyors plat and a set of reusable $50 house plans, developers spent thousands of dollars on PUD master plan designs, on the architectural work for prototype clusters, on the close—and expensive—coordination of building and site, and on the many public hearings and similar procedural embellishments that grew up around high density, low-rise housing. Though no hard data seem to exist, design costs per dwelling must have increased at least tenfold in constant dollars. This symptom of the enhanced design employment effects of change in the housing economy could be taken as the symbol for the whole decade. My own ballpark guess suggests that in 1963 mass market housing aggregated nationally to design fees perhaps $50 or $100 million dollars. By 1972 they almost certainly amounted to $500,000,000. Half a billion dollars buys a lot of design talent. What could more powerfully express this decade of change?

NONMARKET SECTOR

Housing produced outside the private profit system—actually no American housing is totally outside—plays only a tiny role in supplying shelter in this country. Despite this, however, for designers the nonmarket sector has had substantial importance for three reasons. First, practically by law all subsidized housing is done by independent designers generally bona fide members of the American Institute of Architects and the American Society of Landscape Architects. Second, from a value perspective, the modern movement in design has had a long association with social housing; and in the United States social housing translates into concern with the nonmarket sector. Third, small though it was between 1963 to 1973 the nonmarket sector produced a larger proportion of total production than in any previous period save the early years in World War II when war housing was under way.

In addition to this starting burst of productivity, the nonmarket sector experienced a number of other changes which had far-reaching design consequences. Among these were the demise of the central city, high-rise public housing strategies, the first crude steps toward housing allowances, and the massive development of the below market interest rate (BMIR) idea. The concluding sections of this chapter will deal with these various issues.

Demise of the Public Housing Act of 1949

After bitter political battles lasting through the 1940s, the depression-born public housing program was reborn in the United States Housing Act of 1949. It provided federal subsidies for local housing authorities to build low-rent public housing projects. The authorities would then own and run the projects, renting only to people below certain federally established income ceilings. In most areas the feds and the locals collaborated to limit such projects to

inner city, ghetto locations. Since a real housing shortage existed at the time, particularly in the dense slums where the projects were located, it was costly to acquire slum clearance land. This dictated high-rise building in order to spread the high land costs over more dwellings. Though later analysis suggests high density, low-rise designs could have been used many times to achieve the necessary densities, the feds plumped hard for high buildings. This dovetailed with local fears about ghetto expansion. High buildings would house more people on the same area thus in theory permitting the ghetto to house more people without enlarging its boundaries.

Designers had long favored high-rise buildings in central areas. Beginning in the 1920s the modern architecture movement had built up a formidable case for buildings made high enough to "free the ground." The unhealthy congestion of the nineteenth century high density, low-rise cities provided the main argument for this view. One suspects also that this doctrine gave designers the rationale they needed to justify high-rise construction now that it was technically feasible. This preference among designers conformed nicely to the federal government preferences. Designers and bureaucrats joined forces. The results of the

1949 Act were groups of high-rise public housing towers located in inner city slums of most large American cities. In Chicago, Newark, New York, Philadelphia, St. Louis and elsewhere these housing projects proliferated. They produced very powerful social housing landmarks that soon became the fixed image of public housing.

While these projects were being built, changes occurred in nonmarket housing demand. In the depression, when public housing began, vast unemployment afflicted the country. Millions of formerly employed, stable working class and middle class households were without income or lived on totally inadequate welfare stipends. It was this "submerged middle class"—the phrase is Lawrence Friedman's—that public housing originally served. It housed "deserving folk" while they "got back on their feet." By 1960 big demographic and economic changes heralded a radical shift in the demand for nonmarket housing. No longer was the submerged middle class submerged. They had well-paying jobs. Not only that, but if they were white and not too old, they had moved into market sector, single family, detached houses in the suburbs. Concurrently a new center city population appeared: unemployed black, Puerto Rican, and Chicano agricultural labor driven off the farms by technology. New to the central cities, often on welfare, this urban, lower class provided the demand for public housing after the mid 1950s. As they began to dominate project populations, the buildings themselves came increasingly to symbolize this group. The projects became stigmatized. Soon people began to talk and act as though they believed the projects caused the problems of these poor people. Racial prejudice played a central role. So did skinflint and oppressive project management styles. The result was that by the middle 1960s high-rise, inner city, slum clearance, urban renewal had fallen into very low repute. The projects themselves had become the slums.

At this point, policy changes redirected much of the public housing program. Vest-pocket projects, scattered sites, turnkey development (this was a jargon word for privately developed housing purchased or leased for public housing purposes), new lease forms, tenant participation in management, began to make a very different kind of design entity out of public housing. Gone was the high-rise in the park. Instead there were small, compact clusters of units, often looking very much like the output from the market sector. In fact, often they were market sector units purchased or

leased for public housing purposes. Important though these changes were they came too late and were too little to prevent the demise.

Of the many landmarks associated with the demise of the 1949 Act projects, Pruitt–Igoe in St. Louis has become the most tragic symbol of failed public housing (Fig. 4-17). Among designers a powerful mythology has grown up around this project. It began as a major component of St. Louis' ambitious use of the 1949 Act housing subsidies planned to house about 15,000 people in a group of 33 widely spaced, 11-story, high-rise buildings. Opened in the mid 1950s without any supporting facilities such as schools, shops, and recreational facilities, almost immediately it began to receive a voluminous negative press. Children fell out of unguarded windows and got scalded on uninsulated steam pipes. Thieves took refuge in its labyrinthlike, skip stop corridor system. Soon a vacancy problem emerged and then vandalism. In the early 1960s authorities belatedly began a costly effort to build support facilities and provide social services. Still the vacancy rate climbed. Though Pruitt–Igoe was in the target area for all sorts of the late 1960s Great Society programs, people continued to move out and new tenants did not appear. Desperate last minute rescue efforts such as Paul Fried-

berg's sculptured play yards and church-aided tenant management appeared in the early 1970s. But it was too late. No one was left. After the trial dynamiting of one building in 1972 (an experiment in urban renewal technology!), its final abandonment and demolition were assured. By the summer of 1976 the headache balls had ravaged the site, only a part of one structure remained to be done in by engineers in a full-scale simulation of earthquake forces.

Sometime in the middle 1960s (Architectural Forum's first critical article was published in December 1965) designers began to become aware of Pruitt–Igoe's problems. It served as an emblem of their consciousness change toward "user-oriented" design. They saw it as the archetypal case of a design that disregarded the real users of buildings. Pruitt–Igoe architect Minoru Yamasaki had received considerable attention in the architectural press for the preliminary design. His sketches showed happy, white, middle class mothers with their well-behaved children occupying the project. Everyone in on the new consciousness, myself among them, contrasted this architect's dream with the reality of harried, black, welfare mothers and hordes of undisciplined, black adolescents.

Fig. 4-17 In its better days, the infamous Pruitt-Igoe public housing project of 1957 designed by Leinweber, Yamasaki, and Hellmuth.

This failure of Yamasaki to consider who would really live in Pruitt–Igoe was further emphasized by detailed design failures—or what were interpreted as failures. These involved such things as the lack of insulation on the steam pipes referred to above, and the lack of ground floor public toilets implicated in the widespread practice of children urinating in the elevators. With a characteristic producer's bias the designers saw this as nothing more than a design failure. They did not see it as the structural result of a hostile, pinch-penny federal and local public housing program that wrote overdetailed, inhumane building specifications and selected politically okay architects, but cared nothing for black welfare mothers except to ghettoize them. By the late 1960s the designers' interpretation had developed mythic proportions. Pruitt–Igoe was understood to have brutalized the people who so sparsely inhabited it, and to have caused their antisocial behavior. It became the antiheroic symbol of a self-serving environmental determinism. This happened despite Lee Rainwater and others whose careful participant observer research showed most people in Pruitt–Igoe thought it was the best housing they had ever lived in. (A more important part of this research showed glimpses of the process by which racism and poverty forged welfare mothers and violent youths.)

Fig. 4-18 The public housing program in Oakland, California, illustrates the shift to high density, low-rise house types in the late 1960s and early 1970s.
(a) Oakland's first turnkey, four units by Bartlett and Ayer, 1968. (b) Another interesting turnkey, the Building Block Module, six unit, factory-built, concrete building by Fisher-Jackson Associates. Erected originally in 1968 on a test site in Richmond, California, the year following it was disassembled and reerected in Oakland.
(c) Most common among the scattered site projects of this period were the Dyna-Grow wooden modular units also designed by Fisher-Jackson Associates.

What actually went wrong at Pruitt–Igoe? Two things mainly: the official public housing policy of racism, ghettoization, and management brutality; and secondly, the transforming housing market events that emptied out the city of St. Louis. Between the time that Pruitt–Igoe was conceived and the time it was vacated about half of the city's white population left town. Hundreds of thousands of houses became vacant providing an enormous range of choices for even the poorest people. Declining prices of existing houses made noneffective demand effective. This enormous population shift has yet to be adequately studied and explained. But it is easy to understand why people chose not to live in Pruitt–Igoe. It had been built as a high density, segregated ghetto to keep poor blacks in the inner slums, and to facilitate moving them out of scattered suburban locations according to late 1950s relocation plans. It was run more like a penal institution than housing for free people. It was no wonder Pruitt–Igoe became vacant when the market became so soft even poor people could buy housing.

The final blow has come in the demolition, an action taken for fiscal reasons concerned with minimizing federal and local financial losses, not as the myth would have it because it did not work as design. In fact the myth played

into the hands of the racist management; it gave them a scapegoat behind which to hide. Even locally, design failures are publicly blamed as the chief cause of its demise. The new wave of user-oriented architects has provided the false doctrine that effectively masks institutional racism and poverty.

Rightly or wrongly, the Pruitt–Igoe myth traumatized the environmental design world. Never again could they build high-rise public housing with a clear conscience. No legacy of the 1963–73 decade seems more certain. Already by the mid 1960s public housing design had undergone a substantial reformation in attitudes and practices, some of them based on new legislation and administrative regulations. The vest-pocket, scattered site, and turnkey developments referred to earlier coincided with a shift toward high density, low-rise house forms and somewhat less stripped-to-the-bone specifications. Starting as far back as the middle 1950s the San Francisco Bay Area of California, for instance, saw such a series of more humane public housing projects. Some of these are shown in Figs. 4-18(a), (b), and (c). They indicate what public housing could have done in design terms had the political and administrative climate been more favorable.

BMIR Great Society Programs

The ghettoized, nonwhite, urban poor through civil disobedience and what some saw as violent rebellion, became the central domestic problem focus of this decade. The main events and actors are well known: Watts, Newark, Detroit, the National Welfare Rights Organization, Martin Luther King, Malcolm X, Jesse Jackson, and all. This turmoil had a powerful effect on housing policy in the nonmarket sector. Its main output was a subsidy program designed to produce vastly more housing than ever constructed under the public housing program. The new strategy depended upon paying the private market sector to produce nonmarket housing. The subsidy took the form of an interest rate payment from the federal treasury that lowered the cost of the dwelling to its occupants by paying a major share of the debt service. Debt service incidentally represents a substantial share of the market cost of housing, more than 50% according to the 1968 Presidential Committee on Urban Housing. Lowering debt service charges to the consumer opened and made effective a huge new housing demand.

Early in the 1960s experience began to accumulate with the BMIR idea (below market interest rate, the term came from the fact that the consumer was effectively charged a below market interest rate since the feds paid the difference). A small federal program, FHA's 221(d)3 developed to support urban renewal activities, acted as a pilot program. When the violence hit, President Johnson responded with a series of presidential commissions and committees. These in turn analyzed events and developed policy responses. In a series of reports that appeared in 1968 [the Kerner, Douglas, and Kaiser Commissions and Committees], a set of housing targets were set up calling for an annual production of 2.6 million units, 600,000 of which would be subsidized.

BMIR would provide the magic to reach these goals and it did. Amazingly, as a glance back at Table 4-1 demonstrates, the targets were reached soon after the legislation appeared. A nice irony lies in this story. The expanded housing and subsidy programs were products of the Democratic Johnson Great Society period. Their payoff in housing units occurred during Nixon's first term. Only after his 1972 landslide reelection did he halt these programs, an act that took place abruptly with the housing program moratorium of January 1973. Specifically, the BMIR programs embodied in the United States Housing Act of 1968 continued for a while the pioneering 221(d)3 and added to it the new programs, Section 235 in support of individual home ownership, and Section 236 which subsidized multiple-rental housing. A fourth program, Section 202, provided direct United States Treasury low interest loans to build nonprofit housing for the elderly. Most of the action in terms of new construction occurred in the multiple programs. Much of the 235 program went to support the purchase of old housing. Section 202 was relatively small; mostly it financed rather unprepossessing looking minihigh-rises on scattered sites. In practice, financial failure has dogged the BMIR projects. To the extent we understand this problem it seems associated with rapidly rising costs and widespread unemployment, not questions of design.

The BMIR programs utilized the institutional apparatus of the market sector with very little interference or change. Predictably, then, these programs tended to favor the same design ideas that had emerged in the private sector. High density, low-rise housing predominated. The St. Francis Square project mentioned and illustrated elsewhere in this volume (Figs. 1-32 and 1-33) provided the prototypical architectural image for this housing. Projects generally looked like somewhat stripped versions of the condominium vernacular. Again the Sea Ranch

Fig. 4-19 Charles Moore continued producing imaginative high density, low-rise designs in the public sector as well as market sector. Maplewood Terrace in Middletown, Connecticut.

image seemed pervasive, though simplified. In fact the master took a hand in the stripping process: Charles Moore designed some 236s that exemplify the best that could come from this program, Fig. 4-19, for instance.

Enhanced Design Employment Effect—II

Nowhere is the enhancement of designers' employment effect more powerful than in the nonmarket sector of the housing economy. By law government agencies must hire designers when they build housing. Not only that, the hiring is separated completely from building operations and management in public housing built under the 1949 Act. In contrast to most housing work for which the architects and site planners are integrated into the development team, hiring architects and landscape architects separately frees the designers from many of the constraints imposed by the development team. This has enormous influence on design. Summarized very briefly, it frees the designers almost completely to work in reference to their professional design peers. They are free to design architecture not housing. They must satisfy only a government bureau often disinterested in any real utilitarian or effectiveness criteria except perhaps some janitorial considerations. More damaging, these designers may totally or largely disregard the eventual actual occupants, "users" in modern lingo. As I have pointed out elsewhere in commenting on Rainwater's studies of Pruitt–Igoe, public housing architects worked not to satisfy the needs of the potential tenants, not even to satisfy the managers, but to satisfy the reference group made up of other architects with their architectural magazines and honor awards programs.

The uncoupling of the designers from ongoing involvement with their projects, and the lack of the kind of revealed preferences that disciplines production in the market sector, the built-in tendency of public building to seek values like monumentality, the ever-present opportunity payoff to political friends, and similar forces unrelated to housing as housing, conspire to make design in the nonmarket sector troubling and often counterproductive in terms of dwelling environment values.

CONCLUDING NOTE

Two of the designs mentioned in this chapter, both Northern California landmarks, St. Francis

Square in San Francisco and Sea Ranch Condominium on the wild Sonoma County coast, symbolize a fascinating decade in American housing practice. Are the themes of this period still working? Will they continue in the years to come? Many of the institutional factors that figured so importantly during 1963–73 show every sign of continuing on through the next decade into the 1980s. The long-term trend toward smaller households has accelerated rather than slowed. This means it will take more but smaller dwellings to house the population even if it stays stable. The long-term, relative cost increases in some factors of production will continue. Land particularly will increase as access diminishes and environmental protection interests make it harder and more expensive to develop. This probably means the market sector will be smaller in terms of new construction, and its output will be even more expensive. Certainly high density, low-rise designs will continue to dominate.

The nonmarket sector almost certainly will revive. After the Nixon moratorium enormous

noneffective demand has built up. Effective demand in the market sector is shrinking. Inflation and secular cost trends promise to again produce a submerged middle class in terms of housing. America may have to increase the level of subsidy to middle income consumers. Conventional public housing though limited to high density, low-rise designs, and some version of the BMIR idea, seem certain to reappear. In all likelihood, subsidies will be devised to increase production, maintain employment in the industry, and relieve the middle class now increasingly priced out of the housing market. It could take the form of forced savings at pegged interest rates, or shallow interest rate subsidies, or some similar policy. Since its effect should be widespread but gentle, it will probably not lead to a special design practice in the mold of the 1949 Act public housing. It may be coupled to some form of the housing allowance program which, since the 1973 moratorium, has received much attention and pilot utilization. This would continue one of the few legacies of mid 1970s public policy, the shift from subsidizing construction or the supply side of the market to subsidizing poor people thus making noneffective demand effective. The Section 8 program of the 1974 Act and a series of social experiments designed and managed by the Urban Institute and Rand Corporation are providing experience with the efficacy of housing demand subsidy. To the extent policy goes in this direction it will reduce the distinctions between the two sectors. Especially in terms of design practice they will tend to merge.

Finally, and probably most significantly, the next decade will put enormous impetus behind conserving the standing stock of housing. With each rise in cost, with each successful environmental protection effort, with each shift in preference, with each shift of subsidy to the demand side, it seems certain that the relative importance of housing conservation will increase. Relatively speaking new construction will decrease in importance. This has the most profound effects for design and design practice. Conservation, recycling in currently fashionable jargon, perforce goes slowly, piecemeal, in very small-scale units. To be in tune with the future, house architects and landscape architects will have to practice in equivalently small and piecemeal ways.

Bibliography

The following references have been selected mainly to offer housing design people access to the housing economy institutions and policy problems.

Hartman, Chester, *Housing and Social Policy.* Englewood Cliffs, N.J.: Prentice-Hall, 1975.

Meyerson, Martin, Terrett, Barbara, and Wheaton, William L. C., *Housing, People, and Cities.* New York: McGraw-Hill, 1962.

Montgomery, Roger, "Comment on 'fear and the house as haven in the lower class' by Lee Rainwater," *Journal of the American Inst. of Planners,* vol. 32, no. 1 (January, 1966), pp. 229–264.

Montgomery, Roger, "Mass producing Bay area architecture," in *Bay Area Houses,* Woodridge, Sally B., Ed. New York: Oxford, 1976, pp. 229–264.

Montgomery, Roger, "Review symposium: Behind ghetto walls: black families in a federal slum," Lee Rainwater. Chicago: Aldine, 1970, p. 11, *Urban Affairs Quart.,* vol. 7, no. 1 (September, 1973), pp. 109–119.

Report of the National Advisory Commission on Civil Disorders ("The Kerner Commission"). Washington, D.C.: The Commission, March 1, 1968. See particularly Chapter XVII "Recommendations for National Action, Part IV, Housing," pp. 257–263.

Building the American City: Report of the National Commission On Urban Problems ("The Douglas Commission"). Washington, D.C.: 91st Congress, 1st Session, House Document No. 91-34, December 12, 1968. See Part II "Housing Programs," pp. 56–197, and Parts V and VI, "Reducing Housing Costs" and "Improvement of the Environment," pp. 417–500, most especially the last eight pages of Part VI, titled "Chapter 2. Design and the Quality of Cities." U.S. Government Printing Office, 1968.

A Decent Home: Report of the President's Committee on Urban Housing ("The Kaiser Committee"). Washington, D.C.: The Committee, December 11, 1968. U.S. Government Printing Office, 1968.

United States Department of Housing and Urban Development, *Housing in the 1970s.* Washington, D.C.: HUD, 1974.

Urban Land Institute, *The Homes Association Handbook,* Technical Bulletin 50. Washington, D.C.: U.L.I., October 1964.

Whyte, William H., *Cluster Development.* New York: American Conservation Association, 1964.

Whyte, William H., *The Last Landscape.* New York: Doubleday, 1968.

5
Housing Struggles and Housing Form

Chester Hartman

"Save the Capitol—Save the Robie House!—What about me?"

"Housing struggles" have become increasingly common in United States cities over the past two and a half decades. They are basically political in nature—having to do with who shall live where, and how. As such, they have had and will continue to have important implications for the form of housing.

Usually such struggles arise over competing claims for turf. In its prototypical form, the fight involves a relatively low status, politically powerless group and its attempt to resist the move of a politically and economically more powerful group, often backed by the authority of the state, which is attempting to take over the land and structures the first group is occupying. The purpose of the takeover is to put the property to what the second group regards as a "higher and better use." The claims of the second group are often backed by a "public benefit" argument. They are frequently successful in convincing the public that such a land use change is in the public's interest (even if private interests are being served in the process). Needless to say, the first group usually does not share this notion of "higher and better use" and "the public interest." When the first group can organize itself sufficiently, and gain outside support, to oppose the displacement/replacement scheme, the result is a housing struggle. The forms such struggles take

have included demonstrations, rent strikes, appearances at public hearings and appeals, attempts to get public officials to intervene, attempts to have protective or remedial legislation passed, litigation, and influencing public opinion. It would appear that an increasing number of such struggles are achieving gains of some sort by delaying the displacement/replacement process, modifying it to mitigate its negative impact, bargaining for tradeoff concessions on the part of prospective developers or government agencies, or actually thwarting the scheme altogether.

Three such struggles are discussed in this chapter. They illustrate a range of strategies, tactics and outcomes. In one—San Francisco's Yerba Buena Center urban renewal project—the overall strategy was not to stop the project since the opposition began too late for this, and since the forces backing it were simply too powerful to oppose successfully. The purpose of the development plan was to break the central office district out of its narrow confines, via a major public–private development that would jump over Market Street, the city's 120-foot wide principal thoroughfare. The idea behind the opposition was to delay and harass the project via (highly legitimate) lawsuits and other means in order to wrench major concessions from the power structure. These con-

cessions involved requiring the city to provide replacement housing and giving the community the right to develop this housing itself. In a second illustration—the Goodman Building in San Francisco—the strategy has been to oppose the planned displacement/replacement process altogether and gain for the users the right to remain in the original structure. This has been accomplished via development of public support, imaginative use of public agencies and existing legislation, refusal to move, direct action (rent strikes and self-repair), and substitution of a workable counterplan. In the third illustration—the Cedar-Riverside New-Town-In-Town in Minneapolis—the strategy has been to stop the displacement/replacement process completely in midprocess, primarily via litigation, and substitute a locally based alternative development plan that meets the needs of current occupants and is to be carried out by them. In all three cases, the form of housing has been substantially influenced—possibly more so than by any direct design process—by political struggle.[1]

YERBA BUENA CENTER, SAN FRANCISCO

San Francisco's Yerba Buena Center (YBC) is one of the best known and most protracted urban renewal controversies in the nation. The

113

project was approved by the city's governing Board of Supervisors in 1966, following a lengthy planning period that began with receipt of a federal planning grant in October 1962. In its original form the project was to consist of two parts. The first part included the 25-acre Central Blocks, on which were to be constructed a convention center, sports arena, garage, apparel mart, pedestrian malls, and office buildings. The second part comprised the surrounding 62 acres, on which were proposed new office buildings and other buildings renovated according to the renewal plan. The site borders Market Street, the city's principal thoroughfare, directly opposite the major shopping, office and hotel area (Fig. 5-3).

A series of lawsuits have plagued the project since its inception, some of which continue to this day. The first major suit was brought by residents of the project area, in response to objectionable relocation practices by the San Francisco Redevelopment Agency (SFRA). The YBC site was characterized by mixed usage—warehousing, light manufacturing and other commercial uses, interspersed with some four dozen low-rent residential hotels (Figs. 5-4 and 5-5). These hotels were home to about 3000 people, mainly low-income, elderly, white,

Fig. 5-4 Yerba Buena Center 1968: South of Market Street before clearance.

Fig. 5-5 Yerba Buena Center 1975 after clearance.

male and single. Some 250 families also lived in the area. When the SFRA began its people removal and land clearance activities in 1967–68, the hotel residents, many of whom were ex-union members and organizers, formed themselves into a group called TOOR (Tenants and Owners in Opposition to Redevelopment), and with the help of local Neighborhood Legal Services attorneys began to make noise.

After getting no relief via administrative channels (through the Department of Housing and Urban Development), TOOR finally brought a lawsuit in November 1969, charging that the SFRA was violating federal statutory protections regarding relocation practices and rehousing resources. In April 1970, Federal Judge Stanley Weigel enjoined the $385 million project, pending submission of an acceptable relocation plan. In November 1970, the SFRA signed a consent decree, agreeing to provide within three years 1500–1800 permanent low-rent renovated units, throughout the city, and the injunction was lifted. By mid 1972 TOOR was back in court, claiming anticipatory breach of the agreement, since only 11 units had actually been completed and not many more were in the pipeline. In a settlement pact signed in May 1973, TOOR agreed to drop its relocation suit.

The Redevelopment Agency's half of the bargain was to grant TOOR four YBC sites, on the edge of the project area, permitting them to construct 400–500 units of low-rent replacement housing, subsidized by a ½% increase in the city's hotel tax. The units will be developed, owned and managed by TODCO (Tenants and Owners Development Corporation), TOOR's housing development arm.

This major concession on the Redevelopment Agency's part was what TOOR had been demanding for years. Until this compromise, the Agency had adamantly rejected this proposal of solving the relocation and replacement housing problem by providing a substantial number of units in the project area itself. Clementina Towers, a 276 unit public housing project on the project area's periphery, was the only housing included as part of the original YBC plan. The Agency's goal had always been to clear the area entirely of its primarily low-income elderly population and replace it with a "higher and better use"—the convention–sports–office complex. "This land is too valuable to permit poor people to park on it," in the words of the SFRA's powerful director from 1959–71, Justin Herman. TOOR, on the other hand, felt the former residents had claims on the area,

too. The neighborhood is suitable and attractive for the population who lived there prior to urban renewal: flat in a generally hilly city, sunny weather in a city with many foggy microclimates, and easily accessible to good public transportation, inexpensive restaurants and community facilities. The May 1973 TOOR–SFRA agreement opened the way for about 800 low-income elderly persons to return to their area in the 400–500 studio and one-bedroom apartments TOOR would be developing.

Acting immediately to implement the May 1973 agreement, TOOR moved into the development and design planning work. Under the terms of the agreement, the city and TOOR/TODCO were to interview architects and select five acceptable candidates. TODCO would then make its choice from that panel. Various delays arose because of the city's need to complete other steps called for in the agreement— amending the hotel tax ordinance and amending the renewal plan to include one of the four promised sites which lay just outside the original project boundaries. By early 1974, however, the architect selection process had been completed. As their first task, the appointed architects, Robert Herman Associates, developed a master plan for the four TODCO sites. The plan included relating the four sites to each

Fig. 5-6 One of TODCOs housing sites, in relation to Yerba Buena Center and other nearby housing developments for the elderly.

other, to the proposed YBC project, to other low-rent hotel accommodations and family apartments just to the west of the project area, to Clementina Towers and to two new nearby privately sponsored moderate- and low-income housing developments for the elderly (Fig. 5-6).

Bridging Herman's master plan and the actual design for the first of the four TODCO sites was a user needs survey. TODCO insisted that this study become a mandatory part of the architectural work. The purpose of the user needs survey was to close the gap between the designer and the ultimate users of the housing, to increase the likelihood that the TODCO housing would meet the needs and preferences of its low-income, elderly, primarily single occupants. In this, TODCO sought to go an important step beyond usual public agency and nonprofit developers. Since there were no HUD subsidies or programs involved in constructing the housing (beyond the urban renewal land write-down), federal building prescriptions and restrictions were not applicable, and a freer hand in design and development was possible. While the exact population which eventually would occupy the four developments was unknowable, surrogates for this group were easily available.

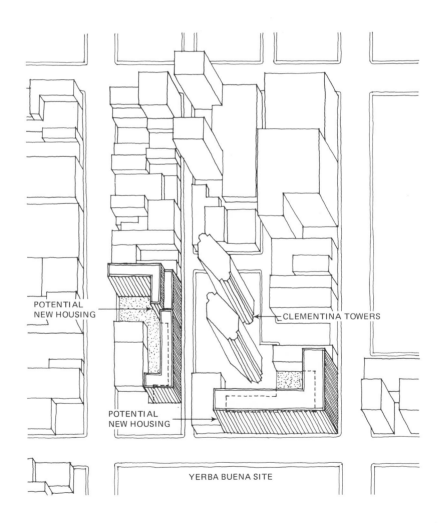

POTENTIAL NEW HOUSING

POTENTIAL NEW HOUSING

CLEMENTINA TOWERS

YERBA BUENA SITE

Figs. 5-7 (a), (b), (c), and (d)   Illustrations of design options for low-rise versus high-rise and traditional versus modern buildings shown as part of the small group sessions to elicit design preferences.

The device chosen for eliciting user needs and preferences was a slide show. Structured around 17 design issues, the slides presented a range of design alternatives covering various possibilities for the street area, outside space, the building's common spaces, and the individual units [Figs. 5-7(a), (b), (c), and (d);and Figs. 5-8(a), (b), (c), and (d)].

Public
   street development
   old versus new building style
   high-rise versus low-rise
   ground floor use
   relation of building entry to street
Semipublic
   lobby
   open space
   mailbox location
   laundry facilities
   game rooms
   corridors
Private
   balconies
   kitchen
   storage
   apartment furnishings
   apartment size
   apartment shape

Figs. 5-8 (a), (b), (c), and (d) Illustrations of design options for building entrance, shown as part of small group sessions to elicit design preferences.

The presentation and discussion was carried out in small (4–10 person) groups, assembled at and immediately following various senior lunch programs in the downtown area. A total of 17 sessions were held involving 123 persons, representing a cross section of the population to be rehoused by areas of residence and demographic characteristics.

Two social planners carried out the user needs survey (TODCO and its architectural firm also participated in several of the sessions). Following a brief introductory statement on TODCOs plans and the reasons for soliciting the participants' views, slides were shown, in blocks of two to five, illustrating the specific design item being investigated. Comments and votes were recorded on a form, and there was then further opportunity for discussion of housing issues not covered in the illustrations. The extent of interest and involvement by the elderly in assisting TODCOs design process was remarkably high.[2]

Among the more useful results of the user needs survey were the following:

—Strong sentiment in favor of developing Clementina Street into an active pedestrian way, with some commercial use, as the focus for a

119

mini-neighborhood for the elderly. This is a narrow one-way route around which the three existing developments and the new TODCO developments are centered.

—Modern-looking buildings were strongly preferred over traditional ones. The architect was testing the hypothesis that people might want to replicate the apparent comfortableness and homeyness of the older hotels and apartments from which they had moved. But there was little support for designing buildings to look that way; people felt the modern-looking buildings were cleaner, more prestigious and would have more amenities.

—Opinion was equally divided on the high-rise versus low-rise question. Those favoring views, efficient land use and the prestige often associated with high-rises were about equally balanced by those who feared the fire and earthquake dangers of such structures. Some felt high-rise buildings gave them less opportunity for social interaction.

—People wanted some commercial use in the ground-floor space. There was expressed concern that stores not cater primarily to outsiders or bring in undesirable and possibly dangerous people (i.e., no bars, liquor stores,

massage parlors). Food and other convenience stores were seen as most desirable. The idea of low-priced neighborhood cooperative food stores, staffed by resident volunteers (as exist in many San Francisco neighborhoods) was well received.

—Among the various types of building entries shown (recessed, arcade, courtyard, etc.) one flush with the street was universally preferred as offering the greatest safety. A landscaped courtyard, attractive from an aesthetic standpoint, was widely rejected with comments such as "lovely place for a mugger to hide." Quick, secure entry from the street was everyone's aim.

—Ground-floor lobbies were widely preferred (more so by men than by women). These spaces existed in many of the older hotels torn down for YBC and were important social spaces, where people sat around, watched TV, played cards, observed street life. Concern was also expressed, however, about the potentially threatening and disconfiting aspects of such lobbies. Outsiders might use them. They might become a gathering spot for unruly or inebriated tenants. It was considered an invasion of privacy to walk through a lobby past fellow residents, each time one entered or left the building. A lobby which avoided attracting

outsiders or running this gauntlet was a high priority.

—Mailboxes should be located in a protected inside area, not outside the front door, for security reasons.

—Individual apartment balconies, a fairly common feature in new San Francisco apartments (as in the Clementina Towers public housing project), were overwhelmingly favored. View, sunlight, an easily accessible place to sit or grow plants, a way to get outdoors when one is sick were all reasons for this preference. Larger, semicommunal balconies (such as those designed into another nearby, church-sponsored development) were not favored; they are a no-man's land, too small for genuine communal activities and not private enough to be regarded as personal space.

—Opinion was about equally divided on whether apartments ought to be furnished or unfurnished, with each group feeling strongly about its preference. Those who owned furniture wanted to retain it when they moved, for the obvious economic savings as well as the emotional meaning of those possessions. This group probably would not move to a place where they could not take their furnishings with them. Those whose previous lifestyles (long-term residence in furnished hotels and apartments) involved few personal possessions felt just as strongly about having furniture supplied, due to the combination of the capital required to furnish an apartment and an equally strong emotional commitment not to have possessions that hinder mobility. A far higher proportion of men than women wanted furnished apartments.

—Wall-to-wall carpeting seemed a high-priority item, for reasons of soundproofing as well as prestige.

—The need for good TV reception was stressed, as elderly people tend to spend a good deal of time watching TV. A master antenna or cable would be of obvious advantage.

—Entry doors should open easily (a surprisingly large number of entry doors from the street in hotels and apartments for the elderly are difficult to open).

—Roof areas should be designed to permit use by residents for sunning, sitting, possibly gardening.

—Phone booths should be provided, since many elderly residents cannot afford private phones.

The design guidelines and prescriptions developed through the user needs study will be incorporated as central elements in the TODCO housing design. Although work has been delayed because of other litigation,[3] detailed design work should resume by the end of 1976, and construction should begin on at least the first TODCO site sometime in 1977. The time gap between displacement/demolition and occupancy of the new replacement housing may turn out to be as much as eight years. When completed it may replace only 10% of the units demolished. The housing will surely be built, however, and it will be designed for the kinds of people who were displaced. While far from a total victory, the residents of Yerba Buena Center have squeezed far more out of public officials than almost any other antirenewal struggle in the program's 25-year history.

THE GOODMAN BUILDING, SAN FRANCISCO

The Goodman Building is another important, controversial, and well-publicized redevelopment struggle in San Francisco. In contradistinction to the struggle of TOOR around the massive Yerba Buena Center project, only a single structure is involved. It is, however, a structure with considerable social and architectural significance.

The Goodman Building is, and has been for many years, a working–living space for some two dozen San Francisco artists, known as the Goodman Group. They are painters, graphic artists, teachers, sculptors, instrument makers, muralists, musicians, poets, potters, filmmakers, photographers, actors, and dancers. The building is centrally located and it has excellent studio space (including ground-floor space originally containing stores but now used for exhibits and dramatic presentations). It is cheap—people pay an average of $55 a month rent for their individual rooms and use of the various common spaces. It is also a community—the people who live there run the building democratically, occasionally take their meals communally, and in the course of their five-year battle with the San Francisco Redevelopment Agency (SFRA) have developed a remarkable degree of dedication and cohesion. In truth, it is one of the more heroic struggles of people to hold on to their space and way of life against a huge, well-financed, politically powerful bureaucracy with no respect for them, their lives, and their plans.

The Goodman Building has the bad fortune to lie within the boundaries of one of the largest urban renewal projects in the country, the so-called Western Addition A-2 project. Together

Fig. 5-9 The Goodman Building and its neighbors.

with Western Addition A-1, these two projects have, since the early 1950s, been transforming the entire 385-acre segment of the city just west of the downtown and civic center area. The A-1 project cleared out some 4000 mainly Black and Japanese-American families and put in their place an eight-lane boulevard, new office buildings and churches, high-rise apartments and condominiums, and tourist-commercial complexes like the Japanese Cultural and Trade Center. The larger A-2 project, which surrounds the A-1 project on three sides, continues the work of removing thousands of low-income Third World people, but is attempting (with mixed success) to replace them with substantial numbers of moderate-income housing units, plus more office buildings and hotels. The Goodman Building lies on the eastern edge of the A-2 project area, a half block away from Van Ness Avenue, the city's principal north–south thoroughfare (Fig. 5-9). Its immediate neighbors are the huge Jack Tar Hotel, a new structure built by KRON-TV, and the new International Longshoremen's and Warehouse-men's Union building (one of the city's most politically influential unions). Most of the area between the Goodman Building and Van Ness Avenue is either vacant or scheduled for demo-lition, making the full 24,000 square foot site attractive for high-rise development.

The Redevelopment Agency's original plan for the site was a 20-story office–apartment complex, to be constructed by a politically well-wired developer closely connected with SFRA projects. In its haste to consummate this development and complement other nearby A-2 construction, the Agency even tried to convey the building in early 1971 to the developer before it had completed its condemnation action. This gave rise to the first in a long series of 90-day eviction notices to the tenants. The owner, septuagenarian Mervyn Goodman (who was born in the building), fought the Agency in court for over five years, in an attempt either to retain the building or be designated as the redeveloper for the site. He lost, and in mid 1973 the Agency took title to his building. Although the original developer dropped out of the picture as a result of the delays, changing economic conditions in the city, and his own difficulties in putting together his financing package, the Agency relentlessly pursued its plan to evict the tenants and demolish the building, despite the absence of an alternate plan or a redeveloper.

The next couple of years were a running battle between the landlord (the SFRA) and tenants (the Goodman Group), around eviction notices, building inspections, condemnation proceed-ings, offers of inadequate relocation housing,

Fig. 5-10   The Goodman Building and its five storefront workshops/galleries.

Fig. 5-11   The Goodman Building's top floor mansard roofed studio.

hearings, and appeals before numerous boards and commissions. The tenants simply stood fast against all attempts to bully them and evict them. In response to the Agency's failure to correct the building's many code violations, the residents, making use of state legislative authority, started to withhold their rents beginning April 1973. These rent moneys have been paid into a building maintenance/repair account, for use by the tenants themselves in removing violations. Most of the work is carried out by the tenants. In addition to removing hazards, the residents repainted the building's exterior to enhance its general appearance and highlight its attractive and architecturally important features. This was done in part as an appeal to the public to support the building's struggle.

In January 1975, the residents convinced the San Francisco Board of Supervisors to designate the Goodman Building a historical landmark, which provides protection against demolition for up to a year, in order to permit development of a plan to save the building. The 107-year-old building is an excellent example of the early Italianate style, with its huge windows, large rooms, mansard roof and immense skylighted fourth-floor studio (Figs.5-10 and 5-11).This action capped two years of effort before the City Landmarks Preservation Commission and pro-

vided an important political lever in carrying out their plan to purchase the structure. Building on the local effort, the Goodman Group next convinced the State Historic Preservation Commission to recommend inclusion of the Goodman Building in the National Register of Historic Places, which was done in June 1975. Inclusion in the National Register does not prevent demolition per se, but it raises the political stakes considerably.

In their appeal to the Board of Supervisors, a petition of artists and writers from all parts of the city stated:

San Francisco is pursuing a scorched earth policy. Bulldozers are ripping out the roots of our culture. Concrete is smothering the ground of our growth. High-rises hover ominously above us like great grey tombstones. We . . . call upon you, the supervisors of San Francisco, to truly oversee the cultivation of the city . . . Save its roots and its new tendrils—the enspiriting buildings, the neighborhoods . . .

In the words of a leaflet put out by the Goodman Group, the building is "an artistic, architectural, cultural and human bridge between past, present and future. It is the type of space a great

123

Fig. 5-12 One of the Goodman Building's resident artists.

city is supposed to embrace and protect." The appeal also referred to a recent Art Commission survey showing the scarcity of low-rent studio and artist space in the city (Fig. 5-12).

With official city, state and federal recognition of the building's architectural merit, the Goodman Group moved quickly to establish its status as a social and cultural landmark as well. They made successful application to the National Endowment for the Arts for a $10,000 planning grant to study the feasibility of turning the building's common spaces, ground floor and upstairs, into a neighborhood arts facility. The study is being carried out by a team of architects, social planners, architectural historians, engineers and economists, under the direction of Marquis Associates. Beyond providing the basis for carrying out renovation of the building, the study is intended as a model to demonstrate to other communities how endangered older buildings can be saved for use by the arts and in the revitalization of the neighborhoods in which they are located.

In many ways, this move represents a formalization and refinement of the building's de facto function over the past few years. While serving as individual living and working space, the building's downstairs and upstairs common paces have also been characterized by a steady flow of friends, visitors and "outsiders," giving the building a unique public–private quality. The five storefront spaces were (and are) being used for classrooms, rehearsals, performances and exhibits. One can study yoga and tai-chi; Japanese and medieval calligraphy; all kinds of dance from Afro-Spanish, to ballet, tap and boogie; theater, mime and pantomime; even community organizing theory and techniques. Theater and dance groups rehearse there. Excellent productions of Brecht's "Mother Courage," Tennessee Williams' "Gnädiges Fräulein," and "Marat/Sade" have been performed there. The tenants organize community events and parties celebrating everything from May Day, to Bastille Day, Valentine's Day and the winter solstice, plus film showings, dances, poetry readings, chamber music concerts and talent shows.

Moving beyond its necessarily defensive stance of the first years of the struggle, the Goodman group more recently has taken the initiative in putting together a development package of its own. They are backed by a citywide support group, the Citizens Committee to Preserve the Goodman Building—which includes such well-known figures as (the late) photographer Imogen Cunningham, poet Lawrence Ferlin-

ghetti, architectural critic Allen Temko and author Paul Jacobs. People all over San Francisco have donated considerable technical assistance. With this help, the Goodman Group has submitted to the Redevelopment Agency a solid development proposal and an offer to purchase the building. The total package comes to $475,000, approximately 40% of which is the purchase price, the remainder for building renovation. The major elements of the renovation include restoring the façade and other exterior architectural embellishments, rehabilitating the interior for use as congregate housing for 30 tenants, furnishing eight artists studios to be offered for rental, and leasing five storefronts as a neighborhood arts facility. Under the financing plan, average per unit (room) rent would be $90 a month.

The plan envisages obtaining the $475,000 from the following sources:

$225,000 from a long-term mortgage to be repaid with rental income from dwelling units and art studios.
$50,000 National Historic Grant-in-Aid, for which application had been made to the United States Department of Interior, with a

very good likelihood of the money coming through.
$50,000 Matching funds for the National Historic Grant-in-Aid, to be contributed in cash and services by or in behalf of the Goodman Group.

The remaining $150,000 will come from one or more of the following sources: a lump-sum advance against a long-term lease of the storefront space by the San Francisco Art Commission for use in its Neighborhood Arts Program; a grant from HUDs Innovative Projects Program whose purpose is to demonstrate innovative ways to preserve historic structures without destroying their low-rent and neighborhood use characteristics (the City of San Francisco has already made application on behalf of the Goodman Building); and Community Development funds from the city.

The denouement of the Goodman Building story still has not worked itself out. While the Redevelopment Agency is by no means delighted at the prospect of changing their bulldoze-and-rebuild plan for Western Addition A-2 and losing so protracted a battle to people they traditionally have fought off or bought off, it is a different ballgame now. No alternative developer is at hand; the new City Administration that took office in January 1976 fully supports the Goodman Group's new plan (in contradistinction to the former administration, which supported everything the Redevelopment Agency wanted to do); and the Goodman Group is stronger than ever, both internally and within the larger community.

The long struggle and its probable success is rooted in the uniqueness of the Goodman Building for the city. It is an internally cohesive community that contributes to the life of the city as a whole. As stated in the background document for their National Endowment for the Arts proposal: "... today [the Goodman Building] is the only space of its kind left in the city. The Building's physical and psychological attributes have lent themselves uniquely to the encouragement of dialogue among the resident artists and their constant flow of visitors of richly diverse involvements—without sacrifice to the privacy of the individual artists' creative space. The generous and varied scale of the interior spaces, fine natural lighting supplied by skylights and a northerly face—enhanced by the age/mystery of the Building—provide a unique environmental mix on the upper residential–studio floors."

Their struggle is summed up by Martha Senger, a painter who among all the dedicated residents has perhaps poured the most of herself into the long battle:

For three years we have been struggling to save the building. People have left—bought off, burned out. A core has stayed. More who welcome a chance to preserve/create a new culture in the center of the city have come. The Redevelopment Agency calls these people 'trespassers' . . . without them the Building would be down. If the Goodman Building is saved it will become a center for the coming together of art and life. Art can no longer remain alienated . . . it must become engaged in the stuff of being.

Where I come from most deeply is my horror at the relentless removal of people from their homes, their neighborhoods, their total ecology. Far more attention is given to swamp ecology than to the delicate balance of life-sustaining factors in a natural neighborhood. When will the connection begin to be made between disruption of a person's 'culture' and social disease, violence, apathy? Or is it recognized already—and ignored in the expectation that the unwanted will wither away?

I think the major threat we pose is that we are doing what is economically and humanely consonant. It is what the Planners et al. give lip service to but are not prepared to help happen.

CEDAR-RIVERSIDE, MINNEAPOLIS[4]

A recent Minneapolis court ruling that caps a five-year community struggle raises important new issues and possibilities regarding the design of housing. The setting is the 336-acre Cedar-Riverside Urban Renewal Area, adjacent to the main campus of the University of Minnesota and within a mile of the central business district (Figs. 5-13 and 5-14). The key element in this renewal plan, which was adopted in 1968, is the $800 million Cedar-Riverside New-Town-In-Town, being carried out under HUDs New Communities Program (Fig. 5-15). This 100-acre segment of the renewal site, upon completion in 1991, was to contain 12,500 dwelling units and 2.5 million square feet of commercial and cultural space, with a total population of 25–30,000. Stage I of the project, completed in 1973, contains 1300 dwelling units in low- and high-rise structures, housing 2500 people. The neighborhood has suffered a population drop from 20,000 to

Figs. 5-13 and 5-14   The Cedar-Riverside neighborhood.   Fig. 5-15   Cedar-Riverside Master Plan, Minneapolis.

Fig. 5-16   Phase I of the Cedar-Riverside new-town-in-town.

4000 over the years, due to a combination of freeway construction and university and hospital expansion and the deterioration in the residential environment which resulted. The remaining population—mainly single working people, elderly and students—is, however, well organized and committed to retaining and strengthening their community. The New-Town-In-Town, based on total clearance and new housing at 125 units per acre density, clearly was the antithesis of the existing community's desires.(Figs. 5-16 and 5-17)

Opposition to the new development took many forms, including rent strikes over substandard housing conditions in the area (with the exception of only 30–50 homes, all the residential property in the area had been purchased by the developers, Cedar-Riverside Associates), demonstrations, and negotiations with both the developers and the Minneapolis Housing and Redevelopment Agency. The principal weapon of opposition, however, was a lawsuit, brought in December 1973, challenging the adequacy of the project's Environmental Impact Statement (EIS). The suit was brought because serious breaches of federal and state requirements were alleged, but also to saddle the developer with additional constraints (beyond the usual financial and bureaucratic hurdles which accompany

Fig. 5-17 Site plan of Cedar-Riverside area west of Cedar Avenue.

FUTURE
COMMERCIAL

FUTURE
COMMERCIAL

FOURTH STREET

SIXTH STREET

CEDAR AVENUE

HOUSING FOR THE ELD

0 100 200 400

a project of this scale). Furthermore, the litigation was meant to educate the public about the defects in the plan, in order to undermine the political support for the development among the press, professionals and the city's liberal elements. The results of the suit have been far more sweeping and supportive than could have been imagined at the time it was initiated.

Because of the complexity of the issues, the federal judge to whom the case was assigned appointed a special hearing master, who carried the case through three weeks of testimony. Named defendants were HUD, the Minneapolis Housing and Redevelopment Agency, the City of Minneapolis, the developers, and the surrounding institutions that had helped develop the plan (Augsburg College, Fairview Hospital and the University of Minnesota). Plaintiffs included a group of residents, the local model cities and urban renewal project area committee groups, the Minnesota Public Interest Research Group—and their umbrella organization, the Cedar-Riverside Environmental Defense Fund. Aided by a grant from a national foundation interested in the issues being pursued in the litigation, the plaintiffs were also able to bring in a number of respected professionals in the planning and design fields to support their claims.

Fig. 5-18   Cedar Square West.

In August 1975, the special master issued his sweeping findings and order, signed by the judge in March 1976, upholding the plaintiffs' claims with respect to the EIS, and providing some of the broadest grounds for such a finding yet to come out of environmental litigation.

The special master's findings and conclusions covered a range of deficiencies in the EIS, many of which dealt directly and indirectly with important issues of housing design and planning.

The Court Findings

The court ruled that "the range of [development] alternatives discussed in the EIS omits reasonable options that would have significantly different environmental effects and could reduce negative aspects of the project as proposed."[5] Thus, the court found that proper public decision making for a project of such magnitude required looking at alternatives to the high density, high-rise plan of Cedar-Riverside Associates (Fig. 5-18). The plaintiffs and their expert witnesses in the hearings had discussed several prototypical development alternatives for the New-Town-in-Town including low-rise, high density cluster housing; a mixture of densities and designs; ownership alternatives (the planned development was to be all rental units); and a proposal combining several of these elements, put forth by the Cedar-Riverside Environmental Defense Fund (CREDF).

The CREDF alternative emphasized incremental planning, cooperative ownership, a mixture of rehabilitation and in-fill new housing in the area of the existing community. New high density, low-rise housing was proposed for areas now largely vacant. In order to preserve public access and the aesthetics of the river gorge, a more sensitive treatment of the river bluff was suggested. Neighborhood needs were the focus of the commercial development in the CREDF plan, accommodated largely through rehabilitated facilities.

In drawing the conclusion regarding omission of alternatives, the court relied on the studies and testimony about the advantages of low-rise, high density cluster housing for family life, the ways in which clustering, design of entrances, and the type of open space provided 'encourage[d] stability, commitment to place, proprietary feelings and feelings of community, all revolving around common concerns for

shared space over which people exert territorial claims."[6] The court also noted the advantages of low-rise, high density cluster housing over high-rise in terms of children's accessibility to outdoor recreational space and parents' ability to oversee their children from inside the home. The court concluded: "There is no description [in the EIS] of a low-rise, high density cluster alternative and no comparison of that alternative with the proposed project in terms of sociological and psychological effects. Such an alternative must be considered if the alternative section is to meet the requirements of NEPA [National Environmental Policy Act]."[7]

The court also found that the "characterization of alternatives solely in terms of gross densities is not descriptive enough to allow their comparison as to important environmental effects."[8] An EIS thus cannot simply compare the effects of "a 35 du/acre project" with those of "a 60–80 du/acre project." Design can vary widely within a given density: at 60 du/acre, high density, low-rise is possible or several high-rises; at 35 du/acre, a single tower or low-rises can be built. Details as to number of stories, number of units per floor, placement of entrances in relation to common space, number of units per entrance, availability and location of private or semiprivate open space all

must be presented and studied if there is to be any meaningful comparison of alternatives.

The EIS discussion of housing types and design was also deficient, according to the court, in that it did not take into account overall housing needs of the city, as expressed in the city's general urban renewal plan. That is, the Cedar-Riverside Associates New-Town-In-Town plan was designed for the needs and lifestyles of single people and childless couples. The EIS did not analyze the conflict between the thrust of this major development and the demographic objectives in the Minneapolis Urban Renewal Plan of insuring a "heterogeneous population in age, marital status, education, income and family size." Furthermore, it did not discuss the apparent conflict with the (HUD) New Community Project Agreement itself, which calls for a "sociologically and economically balanced community" serving "persons with a full range of family incomes, sizes and interests." Again, studies and expert testimony impressed the court with the somewhat anomic social quality of high-rise "adult" developments of this type and their lesser commitment to neighboring and local community. The court was convinced that "issues such as a housing development's tendency to satisfy its residents, encourage stability or transiency, elicit proprietary concerns, exacerbate (or ameliorate) friction and anxiety are important environmental concerns about which enough is known to make reasonable predictions."[9]

The failure of the EIS to discuss home ownership options was regarded by the court as a significant deficiency: "Considerable evidence was adduced as to the environmental implications of ownership of housing as it influences satisfaction of residents, community stability, concern for the environment, maintenance levels and the economic advantages of cooperative or condominiums for residents."[10] The EIS lacked any real discussion of ownership form in the alternatives section, thereby "prevent[ing] the decision maker from seriously evaluating ownership options in the decision-making process and thus prematurely foreclos[ing] such alternatives without investigation as to their environmental effect."[11] And again: "The EIS fails to disclose apparent negative effects of nonresidential ownership of the New Town on the human environment and fails properly to respond to comments in this area."[12]

The plaintiffs' victory has had a number of important results (and purposes). Most immediately, it stopped the project, probably perma-

nently. HUD has appealed the court's ruling, but most observers feel the trial court decision will be upheld. The developer has not formally pulled out, but appears to have given up on the project. The decision also forced the Minneapolis Housing and Redevelopment Agency to produce a new plan for the entire area, incorporating the court's findings. For the past six months, the Agency has been working with community groups in the Cedar-Riverside area to draft a new plan which gives community-based developers priority on new contracts. The residents have formed the West Bank Community Development Corporation, which has already received $30,000 in revenue sharing money for initial planning. The corporation intends to press for development of the neighborhood through community-controlled nonprofit and cooperative structures, with limited new construction (low-rise, medium density) and rehabilitation of the existing housing and commercial property. While the community and Redevelopment Agency have pretty much agreed on the content of the substitute plan, there is at present no way to finance it (or any other plan) with purely local funds, and HUD is unwilling to support this new plan while its appeal is pending (Fig. 5-19). The Agency and community are nonetheless trying to move ahead with their development

proposal, by drafting special Congressional legislation which would provide the Agency funds to buy out the New Community.

Another important role played by the suit was public education. The plaintiffs' objections to the EIS were originally framed very broadly, in order to open the door for important educational and political arguments during the public hearings. These proceedings were well covered by the local press. Beyond traditional EIS concerns about traffic congestion, energy consumption, noise, air pollution, and open space, the suit raised important issues of citywide and regional housing policy, cost-benefit analysis, and the financing plan for the proposed New-Town-In-Town. All of these issues were raised before the public and were dealt with in the court's final opinion. The court concluded that "the extent to which alternative development proposals meet the city and region's most pressing housing needs should be an important factor in comparing alternatives in the EIS."[13] The court found the EIS deficient because it "made no attempt to analyze the economic cost and benefits generally, and specifically made no attempt to analyze the government revenue increases versus the increased costs of providing services."[14] The judge's ruling also noted:

Fig. 5-19 Alternative proposal for redevelopment by Tim Mungaven, an architecture student working with the neighborhood design committees established by the Community Development Corporation. The design, which is being studied for cost, neighborhood impact and possible redevelopment densities, includes new housing in town houses as well as rehabilitated housing.

The Environmental Impact Statement (EIS) fails to indicate the cost and benefits of the proposed action and various alternatives to it, fails to indicate the weight given to economic and technical considerations, fails to indicate the effects the project finances will have on consideration of alternatives and their feasibility, and therefore, strikes an arbitrary balance of cost and benefits and clearly gives insufficient weight to environmental values compared to the economic and technical considerations, in violation of NEPA [National Environmental Policy Act]."[15]

The court thereby rejected HUD's defense argument that land economics factors dictated the high density development planned, and that no other alternatives were feasible. The decision notes that urban renewal land write-down subsidies would have to be used if further development of any type were to proceed and that "the high-densities and high-rise construction were dictated only by profit making and, probably, by tax-shelter considerations."[16] The "Special Master's Memorandum" laid this relationship out clearly:

It is easy enough to see why the investors in Cedar-Riverside would prefer to see the greater part of their investment go into high-rise buildings, even though that requires class A construction; the obvious advantage of such depreciable assets as high-rise buildings for the tax-shelter conscious need not be stressed. Land, on the other hand, cannot be depreciated and if its cost is held a low constant it must account for a higher proportion of the total investment in low-rise construction than in high-rise.[17]

The environmental costs of the Cedar-Riverside Associates plan were recognized by the court. These included the possible adverse effects on already marginal air quality in the area, possible fire dangers caused by increased traffic congestion coupled with dangerously limited access to buildings too high for available ladders and not fully equipped with sprinkler systems, sorely limited recreational open space of the neighborhood park category, the aesthetically adverse effect of "walling in" the river gorge area by high-rise buildings set close to the bluff, limitations of access and view to parts of the development and the possible adverse effects on children housed in high-rise buildings. The court concluded: "To accept such drastic costs because of unexamined and dubious economic assumptions is to reduce the entire [NEPA] process to a charade."[18] Thus, the court was saying that the

basic economic principles and assumptions underlying any major plan must be discussed in enough detail to allow an assessment of those interests that run counter to environmental concerns.

The long-range and nationwide effects of this Minneapolis case cannot yet be fully known. It should be borne in mind that the ruling defined what an adequate Environmental Impact Statement should cover. It did not mandate what an environmentally sound housing development plan and environmentally sound housing design should be. It mandates that an EIS adequately consider all alternatives before making a final project decision, and takes the EIS beyond its role as a mechanism for exposing environmentally unsound decisions. Perhaps most importantly, it broadly expands the concept of what are proper environmental concerns to be dealt with in an EIS. Environmental values and concerns regarding residential satisfaction, community, neighboring, child rearing have received judicial notice. The range of psychosocial aspects of residential design, and the extensive body of research in these areas has been recognized.

Following upon this opinion, there may be considerably more litigation (or threatened

litigation) involving the failure of proposed projects to meet the needs of prospective users and promote residential satisfaction. As the utility and necessity of alternative proposals becomes far greater, government sponsorship or funding of user feedback studies that refine our understanding of what makes for a satisfactory living environment may result.

THE CONSEQUENCES

Probably the main impact of successful housing struggles of the type discussed here is on the basic decision of whether to demolish or not demolish, whether to build or not build. If the Goodman Group is successful, housing will continue to exist on the site. Rather than a high-rise commercial structure, it will be a particular kind of housing for a special group of users. An Italianate style building, important in the city's history, will continue to affect its neighborhood and the city as a whole. The same is true with respect to its inhabitants and their multitudinous activities. As a result of TODCOs struggle, several hundred units of housing will be built that otherwise would not have existed. The residents of the Cedar-Riverside area have taken actions that have stopped an entire New-Town-In-Town and will likely lead to retention and rehabilitation of much of the existing housing.

Struggles of this type can substantially affect a housing design or program as well. TODCOs opposition led to its control of the development process, and the design of its housing will likely be significantly affected by the group's direction of, and participation in, this process. The people of Cedar-Riverside, in their stress on low-rise, medium density development, cooperative ownership forms, community control of the development process, and renovation of both commercial and residential space, have totally altered the housing program for that huge area. Struggles of this type often present a clash of user-oriented values versus the "renewal mentality," which is a clearance and rebuilding process that does not involve participation by the community or the ultimate users.

In each case, the community and the lives of those residing and working there were disregarded and disrespected by both private developers and the public agencies that facilitate their work. This disregard probably is inherent in the large-scale approach to urban design and rebuilding, and it is not surprising that all three struggles chronicled here took place within the context of massive redevelopment projects, insensitive to change processes and local desires.

Each of the cases also shows specific use of design criteria and considerations as part of the struggle. In its negotiations with the San Francisco Redevelopment Agency, TOOR insisted on control of the development and design and on prefacing its work with a user needs survey. The Goodman Group insisted that the building had unique architectural value to the neighborhood and city, and it used mechanisms and bodies designed to protect a heritage of this sort. The Cedar-Riverside Environmental Defense Fund forcefully introduced the psychological and social dimensions of housing design into the litigation and community education process.

Some of the techniques used in the three case studies are worth highlighting. Sophisticated, politically conscious use was made ot historic preservation laws and bodies. Grants were secured not only to assist community preservation work but to legitimize a specific struggle by giving it the imprimatur of a prestigious body at a higher government level or a nationally known foundation. Public relations techniques and the active search for widespread community support turned small struggles into communitywide issues. Educating the general public as to the issues involved helped not only to generate public support but also to provide longer range benefits by influencing future public and private activities. The standards and protections of environmental impact legislation were brought to a new level of sophistication, and the courts have now given a legitimacy to user needs considerations and studies previously not achieved.

While struggles of this type have been proliferating over the past years, it is only recently that they have been winning substantial victories. This is attributable in large part to development of more sophisticated and effective techniques of opposition, to a greater willingness of the courts to offer protections of this type, and to the widespread support and assistance such struggles now are attracting in the community at large. As in many cases, success here will doubtless breed both more activity and more success. Planners, architects and community activists would do well to continue chronicling and studying such struggles, to assess their impact on housing form. If the three case studies discussed here are in any way typical, the impact of housing struggles on housing form can only be beneficial.

Footnotes for Chapter 5

1. It may be appropriate to note my personal involvement in all three cases and the "bias" that may thereby be introduced. With respect to Yerba Buena Center, I was from 1970–74 Senior Planning Associate at the National Housing and Economic Development Law Project, at the University of California (Berkeley), which was co-counsel in the relocation litigation described. As a direct result of that association, I and several coauthors wrote a case study of the project through early 1974, entitled *Yerba Buena: Land Grab and Community Resistance in San Francisco* (San Francisco: Glide Publications, 1974). I also served as the representative of the community group on the Yerba Buena Relocation Appeals Board established by the federal district court. As a result of continued involvement with and support of the community organization I was asked by them and the architect they selected to carry out the user needs survey described in the text. With respect to the Goodman Building, I have assisted their struggle on many occasions over the past three years, including help in critiquing the environmental impact statement of the San Francisco Redevelopment Agency, putting together their proposal to purchase the building, and covering their struggle in a newspaper for which I write. I also will be carrying out the social planning element of the feasibility study they have commissioned under the National Endowment for the Arts grant described in the text. With respect to the Cedar-Riverside case, I appeared as expert witness on behalf of the plaintiffs in the special master's hearings that led to the court order described in the text. These various involvements have given me intimate knowledge of the events and also indicate my clear support for the struggles I describe here.

2. For a fuller discussion see: Hartman, Chester, Horovitz, Jerry, and Herman, Robert, "Designing with the elderly: A user needs survey for housing low-income senior citizens," *The Gerontologist,* vol. 16, no. 4 (August, 1976), pp. 303–311.

3. Other litigation around Yerba Buena centered around its environmental impact and financing plan. The latter issue, which brought forth three lawsuits, all of which are still pending in one form or other, is whether the "lease revenue bonds" device for financing the YBC public facilities in effect are a general obligation bond issue, since the city would commit itself to backing the bond repayments if project revenues fell short of the amount needed. General obligation bond issues require two-thirds voter approval, while lease revenue bonds need not come before the voters at all. The last suit filed on this issue is still before the California Supreme Court on appeal. Because of a "fail-safe" clause inserted by the city in its May 1973 agreement with TOOR, these suits have caused delays for the tenant group. The agreement reads that the TODCO housing cannot go ahead until the bonds for the YBC public facilities are sold. The city's aim, in large part, was to discourage further attempts to block the project and to turn TOOR into an advocate of YBC. The various lawsuits on the YBC financing plan effectively stopped the sale of the YBC bonds. Although the Redevelopment Agency and city were persuaded to provide the funds to allow the TODCO master planning and user needs survey to proceed, when this work was completed (in June 1975) the Agency would not agree to allow further progress. The YBC project itself is now being completely reevaluated by a select committee appointed by the new mayor, who took office in January 1976. That committee is holding extensive public hearings and will produce a revised YBC plan by late summer of 1976, with the convention center element to appear on the November 1976 ballot. There is solid agreement among committee members that the TODCO housing will be included in any new YBC plan.

4. See Cann, Jack, "West bank update: Judge rules out high-rises," *Common Ground,* no. 7 (Winter–Spring, 1976), pp. 12–13.
   Conn, Jack, "Throwing out the developers," *The Public Works,* no. 3, Spring 1976.

5. United States District Court, "Findings of fact, conclusions of law and order for judgment," District of Minnesota, Fourth Division. *Cedar-Riverside Environ-*

mental Defense Fund et al., vs. Carla Anderson Hills et al. (Civil No. 4-73-592), p. 9.

6. United States District Court, District of Minnesota. See footnote 5, p. 9.

7. United States District Court, District of Minnesota. See footnote 5, p. 11.

8. United States District Court, District of Minnesota. See footnote 5, p. 20.

9. United States District Court, District of Minnesota. See footnote 5, pp. 44–45.

10. United States District Court, District of Minnesota. See footnote 5, p. 13.

11. United States District Court, District of Minnesota. See footnote 5, pp. 13–14.

12. United States District Court, District of Minnesota. See footnote 5, p. 46.

13. United States District Court, District of Minnesota. See footnote 5, p. 25.

14. United States District Court, District of Minnesota. See footnote 5, p. 8.

15. United States District Court, District of Minnesota. See footnote 5, p. 64.

16. United States District Court, "Special Master's Memorandum," District of Minnesota, Fourth Division. Cedar-Riverside Environmental Defense Fund et al. vs. Carla Anderson Hills et al. (Civil No. 4-73-592), p. 19.

17. United States District Court, District of Minnesota. See footnote 16, p. 4.

18. United States District Court, District of Minnesota. See footnote 16, p. 5.

Bibliography

Fellman, Gordon (in association with Barbara Brandt), *The Deceived Majority: Politics and Protest in Middle America.* New Brunswick, N.J.: Transaction Books, 1973.

Goodman, Robert, *After the Planners.* New York: Simon and Schuster, 1971.

Hartman, Chester et al., *Yerba Buena: Land Grab and Community Resistance in San Francisco.* San Francisco: Glide Publications, 1974.

Hartman, Chester; Horovitz, Jerry; and Herman, Robert, "Designing with the elderly: A user needs survey for housing low-income senior citizens," *The Gerontologist,* vol. 16, no. 4 (August, 1976), pp. 303–311.

Harvey, David, *Social Justice in the City.* Baltimore, Md.: Johns Hopkins Press, 1973.

Jacobs, Jane, *The Death and Life of Great American Cities.* New York: Random House, 1961.

Lipsky, Michael, *Protest and City Politics.* Chicago, Ill.: Rand McNally & Co., 1970.

Mollenkopf, John, "The postwar politics of urban development," *Politics and Society,* no. 5 (Winter, 1976), pp. 247–295.

6
User Needs Research in Housing

Clare Cooper-Marcus

"The purpose of planning and design is not to create a physical artifact but a setting for human behavior."

(C. M. Deasy, *Design for Human Affairs*)

"Do I have to live in a 'statement'? Can't I just have a home?"

INTRODUCTION

In the days when most architects were designing for wealthy, private clients, the designer and his patron frequently came from the same social class, shared similar values, and had little trouble communicating. Furthermore, the client and the eventual user of a designed environment were one and the same person. The communication of the needs and preferences from client/user to designer was a relatively simple person to person exchange.

With the onset of the industrial revolution and the emergence of more complex institutional and corporate environments, such as schools, hospitals, prisons, factories, and transportation terminals, the designer–client/user link became more convoluted. The client became a board of directors or committee and not a single person. More significantly, the client and the user were no longer the same person. The client sought to represent the interests of the eventual users, who were often of a different age, lifestyle and socioeconomic background (Fig. 6-3). To complicate matters still further, the users or consumers of new environments themselves often belonged to different interest groups. The variety of needs and priorities in a hospital of surgeons, doctors, nurses, patients,

janitorial staff and visitors exemplifies the complexity of the problem of anticipating "user needs."

As cities in the developed world became more crowded, scientists, doctors and biologists began to investigate links between health and variables in the physical environment such as overcrowding, lack of sunlight, shared sanitary facilities, and water supply. Hypotheses regarding the environment and health began to find tenuous support and agitation began for the enactment of protective building codes and public health laws. Robert Owen, George Cadbury, and other philanthropist–industrialists created whole new towns for their workers, espousing many of the emerging demands for space, sunlight and greenery. Although the exact causal connections have in some cases still not been clearly identified, it became increasingly apparent that there were significant links between physical health and characteristics of the environment controlled by architects and builders.

As a great variety of materials and components became available, building codes began to specify such things as wall thickness, structural systems, and building materials to protect building users from the worst hazards of fires

and natural disasters. The state, via official codes and laws, was taking on the responsibility for ensuring that reasonable standards of physical health and safety be attained in the nation's dwellings.

USER NEEDS AND PREFERENCE STUDIES, 1950–76

Soon after World War II, with moderate and high density housing projects being constructed in many major western cities, questions were asked for the first time regarding the *social* and *psychological* effects of the residential environment. It was assumed by this time that housing quality had tangible effects on *physical* health, but only in the late 1940s were questions posed on the effects of housing on *psychological* health. Urban anthropologist, Anthony Wallace, for example, was hired by the Philadelphia Housing Authority to study some of its problem housing projects (Wallace, 1952); for the first time some of the effects of housing design on individual and family behavior were pointed out. Other housing authorities were concerned. The Federal Public Housing Authority (1946) initiated a study of its past efforts at housing provision; housing authorities in Chicago (1952) and San Francisco (1948) conducted resident surveys on such issues as "livability."

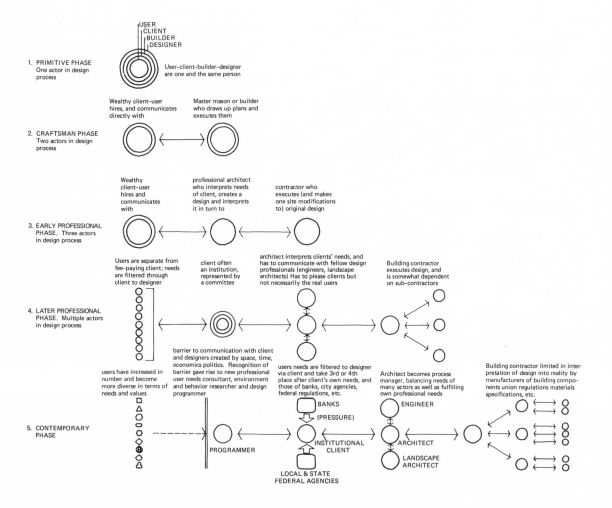

1. **PRIMITIVE PHASE**
One actor in design process

USER
CLIENT
BUILDER
DESIGNER

User-client-builder-designer are one and the same person

2. **CRAFTSMAN PHASE**
Two actors in design process

Wealthy client-user hires, and communicates directly with

Master mason or builder who draws up plans and executes them

3. **EARLY PROFESSIONAL PHASE.** Three actors in design process

Wealthy client-user hires and communicates with

professional architect who interprets needs of client, creates a design and interprets it in turn to

contractor who executes (and makes one site modifications to) original design

4. **LATER PROFESSIONAL PHASE.** Multiple actors in design process

Users are separate from fee-paying client; needs are filtered through client to designer

client often an institution, represented by a committee

architect interprets clients' needs, and has to communicate with fellow design professionals (engineers, landscape architects) Has to please clients but not necessarily the real users

Building contractor executes design, and is somewhat dependent on sub-contractors

users have increased in number and become more diverse in terms of needs and values

barrier to communication with client and designers created by space, time, economics politics. Recognition of barrier gave rise to new professional user needs consultant, environment and behavior researcher and design programmer

users needs are filtered to designer via client and take 3rd or 4th place after client's own needs, and those of banks, city agencies, federal regulations, etc.

Architect becomes process manager, balancing needs of many actors as well as fulfilling own professional needs

Building contractor limited in interpretation of design into reality by manufacturers of building components union regulations materials specifications, etc.

5. **CONTEMPORARY PHASE**

PROGRAMMER

BANKS
(PRESSURE)

INSTITUTIONAL CLIENT

LOCAL & STATE FEDERAL AGENCIES

ENGINEER

ARCHITECT

LANDSCAPE ARCHITECT

Although none of these reports could exactly be labeled "research," they were important consciousness raising critiques of public housing. Other, more academic accounts soon emerged. A conference on "The Role of Social Research in Housing Design" was held at Ann Arbor in 1951. Also in that year, an entire issue of the *Journal of Social Issues* was devoted to "Social Policy and Social Research in Housing," beginning with a provocative article by Catharine Bauer on "Social Questions in Housing and Community Planning." Although she cautioned against too great a reliance on research ("few, if any, of our problems will ever be solved *wholly* by objective analysis"), she called for the use of sociological survey methods, not only in the production of gross figures on housing demand, but also in the sensitive areas of what people actually need and want in their housing environments.

Researchers became fascinated with particular aspects of resident behavior in residential settings. The arrangement of dwelling units on a site and its effect on neighboring patterns became an important aspect of research in the early 1950s. Festinger, Schachter and Back (1950) studied married students' housing in Cambridge, Massachusetts, and their book became a minor classic in the field. They were

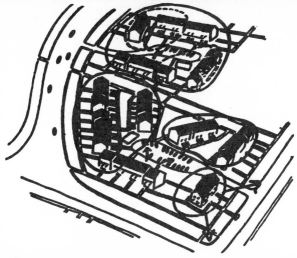

What makes a court clique: In the rental courts formed around parking bays social life is oriented inward. In the large court at the bottom, for example, wings whose back doors face each other form natural social units. Buildings sited somewhat ambiguously tend to split the allegiance of their inhabitants, or else, like the lonely apartment unit at lower right, isolate them. Smaller courts like the one at the top are usually more cohesive; and though there may be subgroupings, court people often get together as a unit.

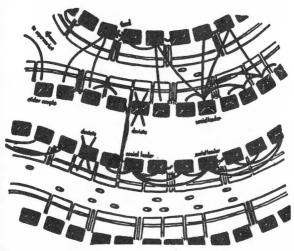

How homeowners get together: (1) Individuals tend to become most friendly with neighbors whose driveways adjoin theirs. (2) Deviates or feuding neighbors tend to become boundaries of the gang. (3) People in the most central positions make the greatest number of social contacts. (4) Street width and traffic determine whether or not people make friends across the street. (5) People make friends with those in back of them only where some physical feature creates traffic—such as the short-cut pavement one woman on the lower street uses on her way to the supermarket.

soon followed by Leo Kuper (1953) with a comparable study of working class housing in Coventry, England and by William Whyte (1956) who studied neighboring in a middle-income Chicago suburb (Fig. 6-4).

Social Critiques

The social effects of newly built housing projects began to receive attention from a few socially conscious professionals (mostly non-architects). Catherine Bauer Wurster was undoubtedly one of the most vocal critics of the monolithic public housing design which began to dominate redevelopment areas. Her criticism was remarkable since her influence had helped create the 1930s legislation which resulted in such housing. She spoke frequently at professional meetings, conferences and on federal committees. She was a persuasive critic of large-scale, high density projects, and a proponent of smaller scale, lower density developments which she hoped would not become labeled as "projects."

Bauer's writing and personal appearances were the start of a whole series of muckraking critiques. Until that time, the large project had been considered the most efficient way of solving the postwar housing shortage for lower income families. Later, such widely read books as Jane Jacobs' *The Death and Life of Great American Cities* (1961), and Robert Goodman's *After the Planners* (1971), influenced the thinking not only of academics but also of city officials and the general public, for whom the monolithic projects were being built.

Meanwhile, attention had focused on two United States cities where social scientists and planners began to strongly criticize the process of slum clearance and high density redevelopment; these were Boston, Massachusetts and San Juan, Puerto Rico. In Boston's West End in the late 1950s, a group of community-oriented psychiatrists at Massachusetts General Hospital, together with planner sociologist Herbert Gans, joined others in opposing the redevelopment of this viable working class Italian community. Gans (1962) in a classic participant observer study documented some of the crucial environment behavior linkages. A resident of the area himself, he was nevertheless unable to help prevent clearance of nineteenth century neighborhoods labeled "slums" by city officials. Dr. Marc Fried (1961) and his colleagues focused on the emotional reactions to forceable relocation, and found some residents, even two years after the move, still suffering from depression.

Observers and researchers in San Juan were questioning why many families, supposedly rehoused in "better" housing, were returning to the shacks and shanty towns deemed substandard by the planners. Kurt Back (1962), A. B. Hoslingshead and L. H. Rogler (1963), and Chester Hartman (1960), made it clear that the findings in Boston were not an isolated case. Indeed, there were compelling social and psychological reasons why poor and working class families found life in so-called substandard housing and neighborhoods preferable to that in the projects provided for them by professional architects and planners. Long-term neighboring and family visiting patterns were often disrupted by the move. Public housing regulations were often petty and severe: painting or altering the dwelling was restricted, as was the right to have guests or relatives for extended visits. The raising of animals for food was possible in Puerto Rico's shanty towns, but not in the new housing projects. Quite apart from these regulatory constraints, the location of new housing projects often placed residents at a disadvantage in finding jobs. The arrangement of dwelling units vis-à-vis other units and the common facilities often infringed unnecessarily on traditional patterns of neighboring and child rearing. With the growing criticism of redevelopment,

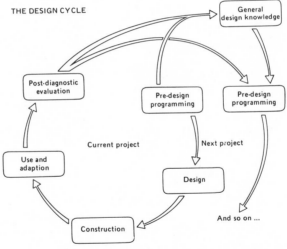

THE DESIGN CYCLE

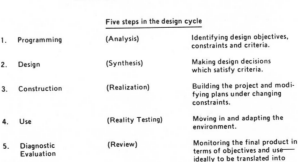

1.	Programming	(Analysis)	Identifying design objectives, constraints and criteria.
2.	Design	(Synthesis)	Making design decisions which satisfy criteria.
3.	Construction	(Realization)	Building the project and modifying plans under changing constraints.
4.	Use	(Reality Testing)	Moving in and adapting the environment.
5.	Diagnostic Evaluation	(Review)	Monitoring the final product in terms of objectives and use—ideally to be translated into future design criteria.

Five steps in the design cycle

triggered by the Boston and San Juan studies, and popularized by the mass media, urban decision makers were forced into reevaluating their roles and products. One form of this reevaluation was collaboration between designers and social researchers. Certain innovative or prototypical housing developments were examined to see how they were used and viewed by their residents (Fig. 6-5).

Consumer Preference Studies

This new area of consumer preferences or user needs studies began as a series of small-scale case studies. Hypotheses that might later be tested over a broader scale would emerge only through detailed investigation of people-environment relations in particular settings. The decade from 1965 to 1975 yielded many of these case studies. The first influential work came exclusively from Britain, and most notably from the Architectural Research Unit at the University of Edinburgh and the Sociological Research Section of the Ministry of Housing in London.

The Architecture Research Unit employed both social scientists and architects and was initially financed by the Nuffield Foundation—an independent research trust. The aim was to set

Figs. 6-6 (a) and (b)   Feedback from systematic observations of site use. A comparison of adult and child use of public open spaces in a prototype low-rise, high density development (Fenwick Place in Lambeth, London). This study was conducted by the Architecture Research Unit, University of Edinburgh.

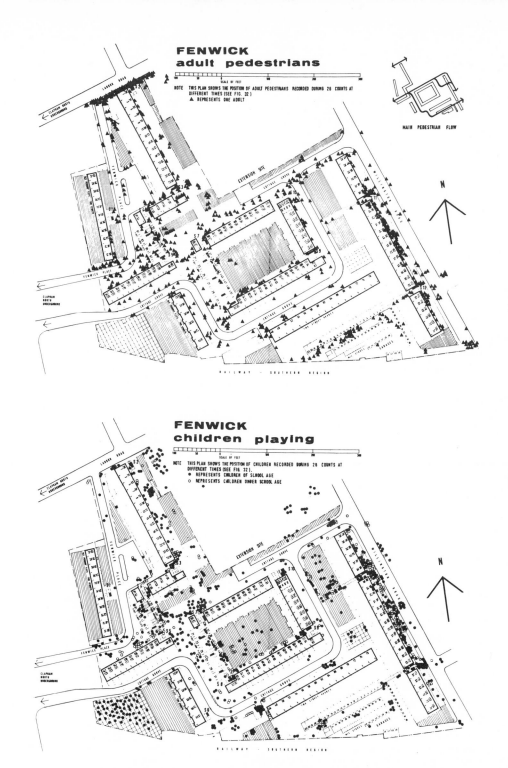

up a practice, research, and teaching unit which would initiate a fresh approach to the field of housing by taking into account user needs and by combining the findings of research studies with actual design work. Their first project was a courtyard housing scheme for a local housing authority at Prestonpans, Scotland. This scheme included several experimental features, all of which were carefully evaluated over a relatively long period. The results were published in a report (Architecture Research Unit, 1966), which significantly was well-illustrated and contained useful recommendations for the design of comparable housing in the future. (The significance of visual material and recommendations still eludes many working in the field.) Over the years the Unit's work has expanded and their interests widened. Their work includes: rehabilitation studies; the assessment and value to residents of different forms of housing layout and tenure; resident reactions to low-rise, high density housing [Figs. 6-6(a) and (b)], and more recently, a series of projects concerned with the maintenance, management and use of shared open space in different types of housing.[1]

Equally significant are the case studies undertaken by the Ministry of Housing in London.

143

"... Substituting adjustable for fixed shelving ..."

"... easy access to the back of base cupboards ..."

Fig. 6-7 Designers need to be informed about frequent user complaints in housing.

Fig. 6-8 An early user reaction study. Resident feedback from two-, four-, and five-person households at Woodway Lane Estates in Coventry, England. This 132-unit row house project was designed by the Midlands Housing Consortium. The designer–developers requested that the sociological research section of the Ministry of Housing and Local Government carry out an appraisal of this pilot scheme from the tenant's point of view so that improvements could be made to later versions of the housing.

Figs. 6-9 and 6-10 Resident reactions to the design of a 39-unit prototype development after one year of occupancy. This housing was intended to demonstrate a new set of standards [Parker Morris Standards, 1961]. This project was designed by the Development Group of the Ministry of Housing and Local Government.

Since the ministry was (and is) a major producer of subsidized housing, they felt it necessary to find out how their more innovative developments were being received. The motivation was not pure "market research," in which a new product is evaluated in terms of sales effectiveness, rather it was the conviction that any government agency involved in innovative programming must, as part of their social responsibility, seek consumer feedback (Fig. 6-7). (Unfortunately, the United States equivalent of the Ministry of Housing has not yet seen fit to follow suit.)

In an early set of guidelines on the social programming of subsidized housing, the Ministry of Housing (1961) offered recommendations to local housing authorities on the provision of playgrounds, storage space, parking, laundries, and so forth. In fact, all the amenities *outside* the dwelling were considered even when the significance of these to user satisfaction was only vaguely understood. In the detailed case studies they undertook in the late 1960s and early 1970s, many significant people-environment variables in the residential setting began to be understood in greater depth. Studies in Coventry (1967) and Sheffield (1969) emphasized the interior of the dwelling,

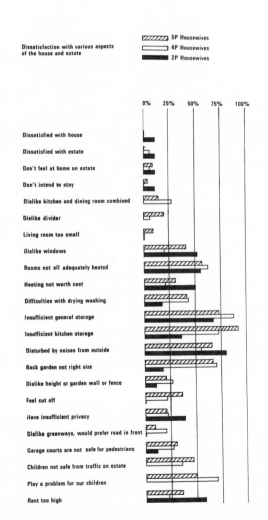

Fig. 6-11

including feedback on room sizes, room arrangement, storage, heating, and family activities (Fig. 6-8). There followed two longitudinal studies in which families were interviewed before and after a move from substandard to new housing in West Ham (1969) and Oldham (Dept. of Environment, 1971). These began to uncover the issues of how prior living experiences and expectations affect housing satisfaction; how the same house design is viewed differently by different family types; and how the design of space outside and between buildings can strongly affect the success of the development (Figs. 6-9 and 6-10).

By the early 1970s the British studies were focused on high-rise, high density housing, for this had been a frequent solution to pressing housing needs, but was being increasingly criticized by social scientists, the media, and the lay public throughout the world. After 1968, further high-rise building for families was strongly discouraged by the Ministry of Housing in Britain. In 1972, a similar law was enforced by the public housing authority of Melbourne, Australia, where high-rise towers were common. By 1976, a strong antihigh-rise directive from France's president was triggered by the proliferation of problem-ridden high-rise "new towns" in the Paris suburbs. What was the

extent of the influence of user needs and preference studies on these rather stringent changes in policy regarding housing form? Did the Ministry of Housing's *Families Living at High Density* (1970), or Pearl Jephcott's *Family Life in High Flats* (1971) influence the Ministry's ban? Did Stevenson's book *High Living: A Study of Family Life in Flats* (1967) influence the antihigh-rise sentiment in Australia? It is impossible to say with certainty. It seems highly likely, however, that such studies acted to publicize and identify the problems of such building forms, particularly for families with small children. In both Britain and Australia, however, it was a particular *event*, or series of events, which was the turning point. In London, the partial collapse of a building at Ronan Point focused media attention on the possible dangers of high-rise living. In Melbourne, a highly publicized series of suicides from high-rise towers, together with the vocal opposition of middle class, professional home owners on the periphery of the high-rise projects, eventually forced the housing authority to retract from its high-rise policy. As in any change in housing design policy, there was a long gap between the first indication of trouble ahead (Maizel, 1961), and the final change in policy.

From the late 1960s on, the trend in Britain with regard to subsidized housing was low-rise, high density. Walk-up apartments, generally approached through common stairs and open balconies, were arranged around communal courtyards or open space. The postwar Corbusier-inspired towers-in-the-park of the 1950s gave way to an era of "mixed development," where one or two towers were mixed with low-rise housing and, finally, to a return of low-rise (Fig. 6-11).

Research in the United States: A Varied Interdisciplinary Approach

It was clear that the architects who graduated from the mid 1960s to early 1970s were imbued with greater social consciousness than was true for those who trained before (or possibly after) that period. It seems likely that this consciousness raising was more the result of general humanitarian trends in society (civil rights, antiwar movement, ecology movement) than the result of academic research into user needs in housing. Nevertheless, it is important to trace briefly the recent trends in this research in the United States.

In the mid 1960s, Sim Van der Ryn, Murray Silverstein and a team of other socially oriented

KITCHEN   FAMILY ROOM   SALA   ENTRY

Figs. 6-12 (a) and (b) The intimacy gradient: observation of lower income family homes in Peru indicated a gradient from the most formal at the front to the most private at the back, and suggested the need for a strict sequence in new housing from entry-sala-family room-kitchen-bedrooms. This was one of 67 general design principles, or patterns, recommended in a United Nations sponsored competition for low-cost housing in Lima, Peru and submitted by Christopher Alexander and colleagues at the Center for Environmental Structure.

architects used both survey and observation techniques to evaluate user reactions to a particular form of housing—high-rise dormitory buildings for students at Berkeley (Van der Ryn and Silverstein, 1967). Just as important as their findings was the way in which they chose to publish the results. They provided the results in a relatively short, attractive, illustrated booklet with clearly articulated recommendations for the future. (This crucial question of the communication of research will be discussed later.)

Also at Berkeley, Christopher Alexander (1969) and his co-workers at the Center for Environmental Structure (primarily architects), produced a significant work in the area of user reactions. Using a research method known as participant observation, they approached a design competition for low-cost housing in Peru by the unconventional means of moving in with families in Lima, and observing how their lifestyles and environments interrelated. Using these observations and other research they then formulated design proposals, called "patterns," covering all aspects of the design of the housing. Their final design was developed from these patterns. Their final report was well-illustrated and attractively presented (since they were architects). Although they did not win the competition, their work became a

rallying point for those newly working in the field of user needs in housing [Figs. 6-12(a) and (b)].

Around this time, the whole interdisciplinary field, known variously as man-environment research, environment and behavior studies, social factors in design, and environmental psychology, began to emerge as a viable entity. Two books in particular, E. T. Hall's *The Hidden Dimension* (1966) and Robert Sommer's *Personal Space: The Behavioral Basis of Design* (1969), focused attention on new concepts in the environment-behavior interface. Their work began to be used as texts in innovative courses in some architecture schools. The first interdisciplinary conference of EDRA (Environmental Design Research Association), a loose-knit organization of people working in this area, was held in Raleigh, North Carolina in 1969.

Four centers of research specializing in housing began to make their presence felt in the United States. The oldest was at Cornell where work by Glenn Beyer and others in the Department of Home Economics (later, Environmental Analysis) had focused on house interiors in the 1950s. More recently, collaborative work on predesign programming and postconstruction

Interviewees usually respond well to photographic questions. Residents in several New York Urban Development Corporation projects were asked to comment on these pictures. Their preferences do not necessarily coincide with those of architects!

Fig. 6-13 Positive characteristics of exterior appearance. These photographs received highly positive comments in all categories. Among visual attributes mentioned: "staggered buildings," "variation," "separation," "less regularity." Function attributes included: balconies, separate entries, private patios.

Fig. 6-14 Negative characteristics of exterior appearance. These photographs were the least preferred and received almost totally negative responses in all categories. The comments were the mirror image of the positive comments. Some of the responses to these photographs were: "flat," "repetitious," "does not look like a place to live," "stacked apartments," "blank," "no separation," "shared entries."

evaluation has been done by Edward Ostrander (psychologist) working with the Architects' Collaborative in Cambridge and Franklin Becker (psychologist) working with the staff of the Urban Development Corporation, New York City [Figs. 6-13(a), (b), (c), and (d) and 6-14(a), (b), and (c)]; various staff members working with architect Louis Sauer in Philadelphia. Edward Ostrander and Bettye Rose Connell are currently documenting how programming decisions were made in the site planning of a Section 236 housing development in Baltimore with architect Louis Sauer. They later expect to do a postoccupancy evaluation of the same project to test how decisions work out in reality. There is undoubtedly a pressing need for more studies like this; unfortunately, the paucity of research funds and of designers willing to be "observed" while making their decisions, render such studies a rarity. There can be little doubt that these interdisciplinary efforts will result in housing more in keeping with user needs and preferences. The following examples serve as encouragement.

In preprogramming research for the Oxford Veterans Home, increased choice and control by residents was to be highly valued. Individually controlled thermostats and room arrangements were planned. Each room served as "home," each wing as "neighborhood," the entire building and grounds as "community," for the inhabitants. The staff expressed a willingness to modify arrangements for feeding and other activities, thus giving residents more options, even when this made more work for them.

The basic objectives that were important for elderly housing were arrayed on one axis of a matrix while design features were enumerated on the other axis. When compared, some objectives were met by many design features, some design features supported a great many objectives.

This exercise helped to sensitize all of us to the important link between design and the purposes for which the building was being created. Though the building never was built, the researchers would like to believe that some of the ideas and perspectives that grew out of the collaboration were not lost with the termination of the project but are living on as the architects at TAC go about their work. This may be a fond hope that any collaborative researcher harbors, but the fact of the matter is, that it may be so.[2]

Another current project at Cornell is described by Franklin Becker:

Working in a general hospital, we have attempted to follow a Lewinian model of research; i.e., where theory is developed and tested through practical application. As part of a NSF grant to investigate environmental messages and personalization, we have actually done a small scale renovation of a nursing unit (using a small donation of material costs from the grant, and a large donation of labor by the maintenance department at the hospital). In this case, the research team included a design team so that those involved in the collection of data (surveys, participatory workshops, and informal interviews) were also involved in design. The distance between information and design was totally collapsed. This research is exciting because we are trying to develop some general principles of how the environment affects people, and yet, the outcome of the research is a tangible change in the physical environment. Our project is done on a very small scale, but I anticipate that because its results are based on tangible environmental changes, when they are made available to hospital designers and/or plan-

Fig. 6-15 Children's play activity in public spaces in Rockford, Illinois, public housing project. This feedback study was performed by architects and social scientists on the staff of the Committee on Housing Research and Development at the University of Illinois for the City of Rockford. Its dual objectives were to establish a continuous mechanism which would enable public housing to be more responsive to the needs of residents and to indicate ways in which public agencies and research organizations can mutually assist each other in arriving at these mechanisms.

ners, that they would carry more weight than a study that only involves a post-construction evaluation, where the effects of proposed changes remain hypothetical. . . . The essential point is the reduction of distance between design and research, and the development of working teams.[3]

In the Harvard Graduate School of Design, a group of researchers in the Architecture Research Office, working with John Zeisel (sociologist), have produced valuable case studies where architects' intentions have been matched (or mismatched) with residents' needs (Griffin, 1973 and Zeisel and Griffin, 1974). There has been considerable collaborative work with local architects and developers interested in behavioral critiques of their proposed designs. There is evidence that social science research is beginning to have tangible effects on the built form of housing, especially in the crucial details of elements relating to privacy, territoriality, and community.

A group of social scientists and designers at the Housing Research and Development Program of the University of Illinois at Urbana-Champaign have been involved in housing evaluation research since the mid 1960s. Their evaluative

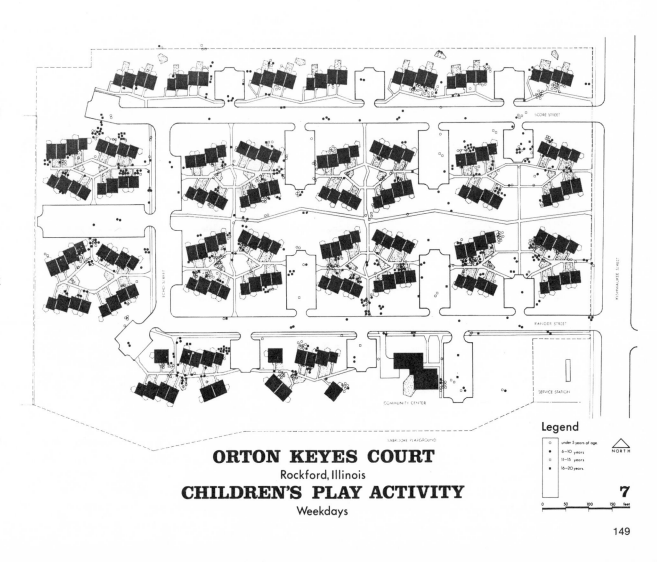

ORTON KEYES COURT
Rockford, Illinois
CHILDREN'S PLAY ACTIVITY
Weekdays

Legend

○ under 5 years of age.
● 6–10 years
□ 11–15 years
■ 16–20 years.

NORTH

0   50   100   150 feet

7

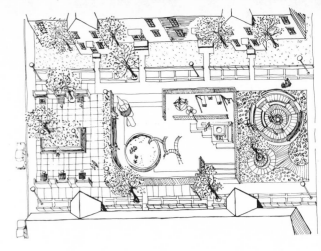

Fig. 6-16 Evaluation of resident responses to design before and after changes: modification of the central square of Clason Point Gardens in the Bronx provides intensive use for three age groups. (From left) the elderly, 3–10 year olds, and teenagers. Hopefully this will transform the most crime-ridden area of the project into an active and safe focal point.

case study of two public housing projects in Rockford, Illinois. (1972) based on methods developed by the Ministry of Housing in London, was one of the first such detailed case studies completed in this country (Fig. 6-15). A housing evaluation project inaugurated in 1972 and directed by Sue Weidemann and Guido Francescato, has studied 37 publicly assisted housing developments in ten states by means of self-reports (questionnaires and interviews), behavioral and physical observations, and archival records. This project fills a definite research need: the application of the same data collection and analytical methods to a large sample of housing developments, varying in density and location, but comparable in terms of residential makeup. Only when we can compare the results of such broad-scale studies with those of in-depth case analyses will we be able to determine which design elements are more or less "universal," and which are place or building form specific.

Another ongoing study at the Housing Research and Development Program, this one directed by James R. Anderson and Richard Chenoweth, involves physical changes at two multifamily housing sites administered by an urban housing authority. The changes are intended to reduce crime and vandalism. Having created an ex-

perimental setting, the researchers will evaluate the impact of the physical changes on four sets of key variables: 1) quantification of the emotional impact of the changes; 2) the degree to which individual residents are willing to assume personal responsibility for control in their own territory; 3) the number, strength, and distribution of social interactions; and 4) the incidence of crime. The physical changes were based on some of the recommendations by Oscar Newman (1972) and, like some of Newman's experimental studies, data were collected before and after physical modifications (Fig. 6-16).

Since about 1965, a group of designer researchers at Berkeley have been involved in housing evaluation and consultation with United States and foreign architectural and planning firms. Under the aegis of the Center for Environmental Structure, Christopher Alexander (1976) and co-workers Sara Ishikawa, Murray Silverstein, Shlomo Angel, Ingrid King, Max Jacobson, Christie Coffin, and others, developed "A Pattern Language." Intended as a user–designer reference manual, the many guidelines or "patterns" are proposed not as hard and fast rules, but as statements regarding people-environment relations in different contexts. These will be modified and amended over time.

It is the intent of the Center that the pattern language be comprehensible and usable by the lay public in the development and design of their own homes, neighborhoods, public buildings, and work places.

Finally, the development of user needs and preference studies and their effects on the built environment have also been the focus of my own work at Berkeley. *Easter Hill Village: Some Social Implications of Design*, first appeared as a monograph from the University of California in 1965, and then as a book (somewhat modified and expanded from the original publication) in 1975 [Figs. 6-17 (a), (b), (c), (d), and (e)]. It was the first study of a housing environment which compared the designers' social objectives translated into built form, with the self-reported needs and preferences of the residents. It was posited that either the designers might have: 1) wrongly interpreted resident needs; or 2) correctly interpreted needs, but translated them into physical solutions which were not meaningful to the residents; or 3) both correctly interpreted and translated resident needs. Examples of all three situations were found to exist. This study influenced other researchers (in terms of method) and certain architects and landscape architects who have reportedly used specific

Fig. 6-17 When shown these photographs of different forms, Easter Hill residents voted overwhelmingly for suburbia (a), but saw their own row housing dwellings (b) as preferable to walk-up apartments (c). They voted over-whelmingly against both a high-rise project (d) and an inner city neighborhood (e).

findings (for example, the need for well-defined private open space) as persuasive material in discussions with clients.

A later study, focusing on two moderate-income San Francisco housing developments, began with a similar approach. Seeing the designers as the only actors in the design process was a naïve (nondesigner's) assumption, however. For each of two sites—Geneva Towers and St. Francis Square—a total of eight "actors" were interviewed in depth, and an analysis of their differing views of the design process was reported. This is one of the most detailed studies of the machinations of pre-construction decision making (Cooper and Hackett, 1968). Later work reported the resident's reactions to the objectives of the design process (Cooper, 1971).

Subsequent to this study, the San Francisco Redevelopment Agency commissioned Clare Cooper and Stephen Marcus to do behavioral observation studies of three recently completed housing developments—Martin Luther King Square, Banneker Homes, and Friendship Village—and to compile guidelines for site planning and landscaping of future projects (Cooper and Marcus, 1971). These guidelines

151

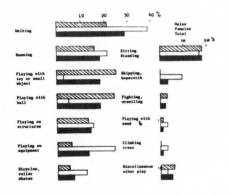

Childrens' outdoor activities by sex: St. Francis Square

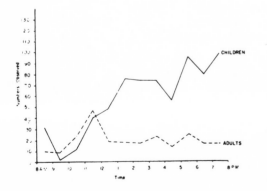

Number of persons in public places on a summer weekday, 8 AM to 8 PM: St. Francis Square

were distributed to designers of subsequent housing sponsored by the Agency, and presumably resulted in some past mistakes being avoided. Sadly, few housing agencies can be persuaded that the relatively low costs of such studies can repay them many times over in lower maintenance and replacement costs in future housing.

More recent studies have resulted from consultation with the San Francisco Public Housing Authority and Urban Rural Systems Associates on upgrading the livability of two problem housing projects (Cooper, 1972); and children's activities in a successful San Francisco low-rise high density development (Cooper, 1974) (Fig. 6-18).

THREE MODELS FOR THE CREATION OF MORE USER-RESPONSIVE HOUSING

Undoubtedly, the "user needs" approach *does* have validity. It is seen by at least some environmental decision makers as a valid alternative to present practice. Yet, we need models of how housing *can* be made more user responsive within the existing housing production contexts. Three possible models will be described here: 1) guidelines and "patterns," 2) evaluation feedback; and 3) "adaptable housing."

Guidelines and Patterns

One model for the production of more user-responsive housing is simply to translate the research that does exist and is applicable into design-sensitive recommendations. By now, a considerable number of comparable case studies exist and similar findings have recurred. For example, many observation studies of moderate to high density family housing indicate that children are by far the chief users of common outdoor spaces while adults are the chief users of private outdoor spaces. The implications for design are obvious. Many studies show that lack of a clear definition between private and communal space creates problems for users in both areas. Site plans that are too accessible to the adjacent neighborhood invite use by children and teenagers who do not live there. Regardless of what we as designers and researchers may feel about such reactions, there is almost universal resentment and anger at such "invasion of territory." To this add Newman's findings regarding the need to define territory for ease of surveillance and crime prevention, and there emerges a case for a particular kind of spatial quality in a site plan (Newman, 1976). A recommendation or guideline regarding such a quality is not worded as a *solution* or as one physical result,

Fig. 6-19   One method of approaching user needs in housing. Analysis of how activities coincide in the home at successive periods of the day for a typical family at a particular stage in its development.

but as a quality which a designer could achieve many different ways.

Designers may resist the idea of guidelines, or the "cookbook" approach, assuming that the researcher may usurp their creative role and *tell* them what to do. Such should not be the case, except where a purely functional necessity demands an exact solution. Even if the research results are stated, the designer may still come to a different conclusion from the researcher (Fig. 6-19).

The movement to give architecture a more rational basis stems in large part from the writings of Christopher Alexander, and especially from his development of a "pattern language." Each pattern comprises three distinct components: a context that defines the situation in which the pattern applies; the pattern (or recommendation) itself; and a problem statement which gives the background for the pattern and the specific data on which it is based.

The pattern language was developed so that existing social science research that was relevant to design could be translated into a format usable by designers and lay persons. It is stated in such a way that the patterns would, hopefully, be constantly reviewed and modified

Time and place of activities

The older family
(Parents (mother working part-time) and boy aged 23, girl 20, boy 14)

7.00 a.m.   With 4 workers and a secondary school child wanting to wash before they leave home, a second W.C. and wash basin is needed. Hot water and warmth are again essential.

7.30 a.m.   There is a crush in and around the kitchen. Sandwiches are being cut, lunches packed up, breakfasts eaten, before all collect their things and leave home.

8.30 a.m.   While the house is empty during the day, the
4.30 p.m.   bread, milk, parcels and perhaps laundry will have to be delivered and put in safe places, and the meter reader may call.

4.30 p.m.   When the wife gets back from work she wants to be able to warm the house, clear up and get a snack with as much speed and as little trouble as possible.

6.30 p.m.   The evening meal may be the only time during the week when the family sit down together. They may like to eat away from the kitchen area.

8.00 p.m.   In a practically adult family several individual activities may take place in an evening at home and room is needed for them.

9.00 p.m.   The family will sometimes split up into groups during an evening and the children may entertain their own friends separately. Room and privacy are needed for more than one group.

10.30 p.m.   Before going to bed, people at work often have to get things ready for the morning and meantime perhaps have a snack. Room is needed for several people to do their chores at once.

11.30 p.m.   Separate bedrooms are needed by each child when reaching adolescence, but they do not need to be near the parents.

as further research appeared. It seemed pointless to Alexander and his co-workers that every designer should have to "reinvent the wheel." In the classroom, the patterns have allowed students to experience confidence in dealing with complex user requirements, and avoided the necessity of always going back to original research sources (Montgomery, 1970).

Based on similar goals of translating existing user needs research into formats which designers can use, other workers in this area have started to produce sets of guidelines—most of them specific to a particular *type* of environment. These include guidelines on low-rise, multifamily housing (Cooper, 1975); guidelines on play areas for housing projects (Housing Research & Development program, 1974; guidelines for the planning and design of elderly housing (Lawton, 1975); guidelines for the design of urban open spaces (Cooper Marcus, 1976); guidelines for improving residential security (Newman, 1976); guidelines on controlling access to high-rise buildings (Brill, 1976); and guidelines on site design for the handicapped (American Society of Landscape Architects' Foundation, 1975).

In my own work in this area the following have emerged as the most persistent and puzzling

153

Fig. 6-20 The problem of translating research data into design recommendations: some researchers are now including verbal and graphic guidelines in their reports. (a) Positive characteristics of tot lot location. Access to tot lot without crossing parking lot, large number of units have direct visual access, adult seating area permits physical separation from children but allows for visual access to them, away from the main traffic roads. (b) Negative characteristics of tot lot location. Children have to cross parking lot, limited visual access to tot lot for most units makes casual supervision of children difficult, tot lot very near to main road on site.

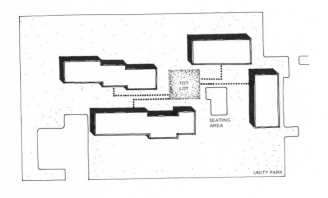

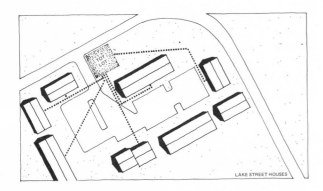

questions regarding this crucial "bridging" process:

How does one state a guideline so that it is just a suggestion and does not presume to tell the designer what to do? Granted that illustrations are crucial if we wish to communicate with visually oriented designers, do we depict "good" and "bad" examples, or diagrams of suggested arrangements? Should we use sketches of possible solutions? And how do we avoid the possibility that someone will perceive it as being the "one and only solution?" [Figs. 6-20(a) and (b)]. How should we arrange guidelines? Should we use subtopics familiar to the designer (circulation, room sizes, orientation) or behavioral headings which focus on what a resident actually does (entering, eating, sleeping, sunbathing, etc.)? How do we deal with aesthetics? Do we leave this entirely to the designers, or communicate what appears to be predominant user preferences regarding color, variety, size, massing, and so forth?

After working on these questions with a group of students at Berkeley, we determined that guidelines must encompass all of the following forms of "data" gleaned from user studies:

(1) Observed behavior—(tots like to dig).
(2) User preferences—(most people like greenery).
(3) Aesthetic principles which have been backed up by user studies—(variety is preferable to homogeneity).
(4) Functional requirements—(garbage cans have to be emptied).
(5) Informed hunches.

There are human requirements which we could not specifically attribute to a particular study, but which seemed abundantly clear. We did not feel that the researcher—any more than the architect—should be reticent about "informed hunches," as long as they are documented as such.

In conclusion, it is clear that researchers must start to collaborate, not only with the designers who will be the "consumers" of their work, but also with graphic artists, photographers, and media experts, who are essential in the successful translation of research findings to design practice (Fig. 6-21). One of the most interesting recent attempts to present guidelines in a format usable during the design process is a package of guideline sheets produced for the designers of a proposed Canadian demonstration housing project.

Fig. 6-21 Housing consumers need to be made more aware of what they are buying. Cartoons from a booklet prepared for prospective house buyers or renters by the British Ministry of Housing.

. . . Each of the guidelines is presented with selected evidence for the field data so that the designer may make his own evaluation of the strength and priority of each recommendation. Beside each topic, an empty space is provided for the designer's own use. These may contain doodlings, comments or sketches which constitute the designer's physical responses to the social guidelines. . . . The aim . . . is not just to provide a summary of user needs . . . it is also to function as an instrument or manual for the architects of these dwellings so that they might refer simply and efficiently to a set of socio-spatial criteria in the process of making their design decisions.[5]

User Needs Generation Through Evaluation Feedback

The comon-sense, long-range model for an agency producing large numbers of housing units is to systematically evaluate its own products in order to better fulfill resident needs. Few housing agencies have done this. Historically, most housing evaluation studies have been conducted in academic settings. If these studies reached housing decision makers, it was often a matter of chance.

There are a few housing agencies which are exceptions to this rule. In the late 1950s, the London County Council (now, Greater London Council) employed sociologist Margaret Willis to evaluate certain features of its very large housing production. Her innovative studies of balconies, laundries, garden spaces, and so forth, appeared as mimeographed in-house documents. Sadly, this work was before its time: the results were largely ignored by the designers to whom they were addressed. Later, in a more consumer-oriented era, the Council contracted with academic researchers (Architecture Research Unit, University of Edinburgh) to evaluate certain of its prototype low-rise, high density schemes. These studies, meticulously conducted and using a variety of methods, *did* influence later action. By this time the general societal pressure for more user-responsive environments was considerable. Specific effects of the studies included more thoughtful design of communal areas, especially as they visually and functionally relate to interior private space; the provision of more useful and safe areas for small children's play, particularly in the form of semiprivate open spaces common to a well-defined group of dwellings; improved design of all shared facilities (particularly vulnerable in high density schemes).

The Ministry of Housing and Local Government (later the Department of the Environment) in Britain, through its Sociological Research Section, has conducted a series of innovative housing evaluation studies which have appeared as "Design Bulletins" published by Her Majesty's Stationery Office (Fig. 6-22). Some of these have been longitudinal studies, monitoring housing needs and preferences before and after moving to new prototype dwellings (Ministry, 1969; Department of the Environment, 1971), while others have been comparisons between several housing developments of the same type of density concerning a particular aspect of the environment (Department of the Environment, 1972), or a particular form of activity (Department of the Environment, 1973). These studies have influenced thought about housing form and were particularly influential in the virtual ban on further high-rise housing for families subsequent to 1968. Nevertheless, the studies are not beyond the following criticisms: 1) they did not receive sufficient coverage in the architectural and design journals and; therefore, often did not reach the audience at which they were directed; 2) the authors were reluctant to suggest guidelines or design recommendations; 3) they took a long time reaching the United States. Although criticized by some for their relatively unsophisti-

Fig. 6-22 Resident feedback on noise problems at St. Mary's Estate in Oldham, England. A redevelopment scheme of 520 low-rise units designed by Max Lock and Partners together with the Research and Development group of the former Ministry of Housing and Local Government. Three-fourths of the residents were interviewed 18 months after completion of the project in 1968. Feedback on such items as room use, gardens, noise, privacy, children's play and traffic was published in *New Housing in a Cleared Area: A Study of St. Mary's Oldham.*

Fig. 6-23 Place of occurrence of crimes in buildings of different heights. Based on New York City Housing Authority Police 1969 data (felonies).

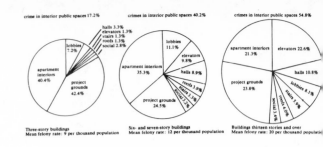

Place of Occurrence of Crimes in Buildings of Different Heights. Based on New York City Housing Authority Police 1969 data (felonies).

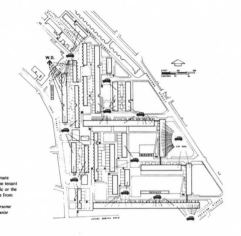

Diagram showing approximate position of dwelling in which the tenant interviewed complained of traffic or the T.A. centre as a source of noise from outside.
Thick broken lines denote bothersome noise, thin broken lines denote noise heard but not bothersome.

Childrens' play area

Children

Noise from children's play showing approximate position of dwelling in which the tenant interviewed complained of children's play areas and children playing as a source of noise from outside. *Thick broken lines denote bothersome noise, thin broken lines denote noise heard but not bothersome.*

cated methodology and straightforward reporting, such studies are probably more directly useful to designers than other more obtuse and "sophisticated" studies where data manipulation sometimes becomes an end in itself.

The philosophy, methodology, and substantive results of these British studies eventually began to have an effect in this country, notably in the work of the Urban Development Corporation of New York State.[6]

The Urban Development Corporation of New York State has been not only one of the most prolific housing producers in this country, but the only one (public or private) which has had a strong behavioral program and an ongoing policy of in-house evaluations of built projects. Founded in 1968, the corporation had, by 1974, produced 35,000 new units in 55 communities, accommodating 100,000 people.

In 1971, they began to accumulate data on housing evaluation to educate staff involved in programming and design review. The most fruitful source turned out to be the work of the Ministry of Housing and Local Government in London. Building on this work, on United States studies by Cooper, Keller, Michelson, Perin, and

on evaluations of existing UDC Housing and New York City Public Housing, UDC evolved their own "Criteria for Housing."

The criteria outlined requirements for the size (usually larger than FHA minimum), organization, arrangement, and use of rooms; and, even more importantly, the type, amount, and appropriate locations of public facilities and amenities. This last concern was critical since Newman (1972) had substantiated that it was undefined public and semipublic territories which were the primary crime areas in subsidized housing (Fig. 6-23).

UDC staff felt their criteria were meaningful only if they were written in a language which dealt with the way people actually *used* space (how people enter a dwelling) and a language which transmitted to architects qualities to be sought (rather than a codified series of minimally acceptable standards). The broadest subdivision of users for which they could accurately define needs were small families (child-oriented), elderly, and "others" (students, dependent elderly, and so forth). Since their scope was statewide, they had to develop criteria for inner urban, fringe urban, suburban and rural contexts.

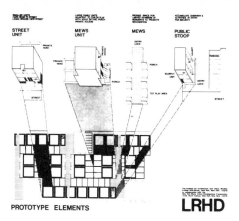

Fig. 6-24 The low-rise high density prototype.

Taking a more informed look at their own products, UDC staff found their housing was responsive neither to its residents nor to adjacent neighborhoods. Major problems included child rearing, ambiguity of public spaces resulting in security and maintenance problems, and lack of attention to scale between project and adjacent neighborhood. UDC staff decided to develop a low-rise, high density prototype which addressed the salient behavioral and contextual issues, and focused on the large family, urban situation (Fig. 6-24). They claimed that ". . . the architects we hired seemed unable to develop designs for us that dealt with these serious livability issues."[7]

A further impetus to the development of this prototype was the opening of a UDC high-rise where the developer proposed dealing with the crime problem by fencing the entire project and instituting patrols of armed security guards with attack dogs. The crisis became an opportunity. A detailed program for a low-rise, high density prototype was developed jointly by The Institute of Architecture and Urban Studies and The UDC (Fig. 1-3). The prototype, designed for either urban or suburban situations, was applied in an urban context in Brooklyn—Marcus Garvey Park Village, designed by The

Institute of Architecture and Urban Studies (Figs. 1-38 and 1-39). It was not the first low-rise, high density project to be built in this country, but it was one of the first to be generated and supported by behavioral research. It produced a convincing alternative to the common New York City housing solution of high-rise, double-loaded corridor buildings. UDC determined to minimize the construction of elevator-dependent buildings for families with children, then commissioned architects to design a second generation of low-rise, high density housing on a number of sites in New York City. These ranged from 120 to 350 units in size, and were based on experience gained at Marcus Garvey Park Village.

The UDC staff recognized that only a systematic series of evaluations of their housing could keep them informed about the livability and general acceptability of what they were producing. They started their own project evaluations which involved a unique program of "live-ins." UDC staff at all levels lived in each new housing development for a week or two, and were asked to make "implementable suggestions" for improved livability. Suggestions ranged from one more towel rack in the bath-

room, to additional neighborhood shopping facilities. At the end of each live-in session, a day was spent with all participants sharing their experiences with the project architects.

In 1974, the live-in program was expanded to include ". . . all architects who do business with us, believing that no matter how well we inform our architects about our intentions, there is no substitute for direct experience in producing responsible design. One benefit we hope will develop will be architects who will challenge our programs."[8]

Of course, no amount of staff live-in experience can substitute for direct resident feedback. Recognizing this, UDC contracted with psychologist Franklin Becker of Cornell University's Department of Design and Environmental Analysis to monitor and evaluate seven of the oldest UDC projects to determine tenant satisfaction with both the physical and social environments. Becker's study (1974) ranged from inner-city high-rise housing to small town, garden apartments. Methods of data collection comprised resident interviews, questionnaire checklists filled out by residents, systematic observation of outdoor behavior, and man-

Fig. 6-25 Evaluative study of New York Urban Development Corporation housing reveals resident preferences on cooking and eating arrangements. (a) Most residents sampled preferred a separated dining area. This arrangement was convenient for preparing and serving food, and separated eating activities from the more formal living area. (b) Existing kitchen/living/dining arrangement was the least preferred. The disadvantages included: inconvenience of carrying food from one room to another, food odors in living room, reduces potential hobby space. Advantages included: visual separation of cooking activities from eating and living area, opportunity to watch television while eating.

Figs. 6-26 (a), (b), and (c) Since low-rise, high density housing is becoming more frequent, we need to know much more about resident reactions to the dimensions, shape, landscaping and management of common open spaces and courtyards. Evaluative feedback was requested from interviews in several New York Urban Development Corporation projects.

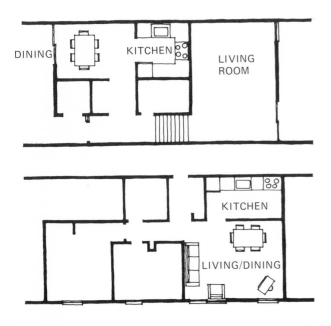

agement interviews [Figs. 6-25(a) and (b) and 6-26(a), (b), and (c)].

All of these research and evaluation methods have given us a better sense about predicting housing environments that will be successful. We now have some understanding of the anxiety of parents who cannot easily supervise their children in play. We have been repeatedly told how an endless repetition of look-alike apartments begins to submerge individuality and have observed how this need can sometimes only find experience in destructive acts. Territoriality, a much-discussed environmental attribute, has made us aware of the importance of being able to distinguish neighbor and stranger. . . . There was a clear desire for more unit flexibility . . . our large family units now have two living spaces. . . . We also try to ensure flexibility in furniture location by requiring our architects to lay out several arrangements that work during schematics. . . . We realize the economic and social consequences of maintaining public space for which no one feels responsible . . .[9]

UDC's heavy emphasis on design programs based on behavioral and livability issues was unique in United States housing experience. Since its enforced cutdown on production due

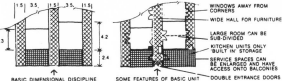

CONVENTIONAL LAYOUT. HALL USED AS LINK ONLY AND SPACES SIZED TO FUNCTIONS

ADAPTABLE UNIT HAS AMBIGUOUS SPACES GROUPED AROUND CENTRAL HALL

BASIC DIMENSIONAL DISCIPLINE AT PARKER MORRIS + 10%

SOME FEATURES OF BASIC UNIT

WINDOWS AWAY FROM CORNERS
WIDE HALL FOR FURNITURE
LARGE ROOM CAN BE SUB-DIVIDED
KITCHEN UNITS ONLY 'BUILT IN' STORAGE
SERVICE SPACES CAN BE ENLARGED AND HAVE ACCESS ONTO BALCONIES
DOUBLE ENTRANCE DOORS

EVOLUTION OF ADAPTABLE UNIT TYPES

Fig. 6-27   Illustration of tenant choice provided in "adaptable housing."

BASIC 4 ROOM UNIT IS PARKER MORRIS + 10% SPACE IS THE LONG-TERM INVESTMENT

EXAMPLE: DAY/NIGHT ZONING CHOICE

EXAMPLE: PARENT/CHILDREN ZONING CHOICE

POSSIBLE: ALTERNATE UNIT WITH SERVICE ROOMS DIAGONALLY OPPOSITE

POSSIBLE: ALTERNATIVE UNIT WITH SQUARE HALL

ILLUSTRATION OF TENANT CHOICE PROVIDED

to New York's fiscal problems, former staff members have carried UDC's innovative programs to other housing authorities (. . . an unexpected "payoff" of UDC's demise! . . .)

"Adaptability" as an Answer to More User-Responsive Housing

Architecture is going through a kind of minor revolution. Increasingly, designers are grappling with the problem of the "unknown user," not necessarily by incorporating behavioral research, but more often by wrestling with notions of "flexibility," "adaptability," and "responsive environments."

After studying many European housing developments using flexible components, Rabeneck, Sheppard and Town (1973) proposed an approach termed "adaptability" in designing family housing (1974). This method is intended to cope with the problem that occupants' needs and aspirations often change through time. Simple planning, spaciousness, and ambiguity of use, once common in the traditional domestic architecture of most cultures, are the basic components of their approach. Their work is a rejection of the institutionalized process and product of mass housing, as well as what they perceive as the emerging stereotypes provided

by behavioral research of the "average resident."

Our eclectic concept of an adaptable home is one in which there is a conscious avoidance of a stereotype of the occupants, whether it be that of a speculative builder or a social psychologist.[10]

The authors looked at both traditional and contemporary forms of house design that are—by accident or design—adaptable and flexible, and came up with 14 basic design requirements for the flexible dwelling. Among these requirements are: rooms should avoid extremes of size and be neutral in terms of form (i.e., simple volumes); expression of a particular room's function through external walls, fenestration, and built-in furniture, should be avoided; plan form, circulation space, and positioning of doors, should allow a variety of room uses and interconnections. They stress that these requirements could be achieved in a number of ways, and do not necessarily require the "traditional" hardware solution stressed in flexible housing, i.e., demountable partitions (Fig. 6-27).

The inventive 'popular mechanics' approach is all too often an alibi for actually thinking

about how people live or might want to live. The fact that these systems can achieve anything within the shell is convenient, because it eases the conscience of the designer, besides it satisfies the canon of 'flexibility,' an important attribute of Modern Architecture . . . Fifty years of fascination with machines-for-living dies hard. The results are usually some form of the fallacy—"freedom through control."[11]

Although their proposal for "occupant choice through ambiguity" has many merits, it too can be criticized. It pretends to avoid the pitfalls of unresponsive housing, but it does so without communicating directly with the users. This is just the criticism the authors direct at architects who have previously relied on user needs research. The approach, however, does recognize that a family's needs change through time, that the dwelling may well be used by a variety of family types throughout its life, and that one means of coping with this is to plan for considerable personal choice within the dwelling. For example, in describing a flexible housing scheme near Paris by the Arsene-Henri brothers, they report that ten hypothetical floor plans accommodating different concepts of eating, cooking, and entertainment, were shown to prospective tenants. No family chose

Fig. 6-28 (a) Activity on drying area. (b) Play on side patio. (c) Cycling activity in court. (d) Play activity on parking court.

any of these plans, and each devised their own.

Flexibility and choice within the dwelling is necessary, and copes with the problem faced by many user needs researchers: How can we be sure that needs expressed to us by group A will be valid for group B, or, indeed, will still be valid for group A at some future point in time?

THE SITE PLAN

Missing from the approach of "occupant choice through ambiguity" is any understanding that the "act of dwelling" encompasses more than just the four walls of a living unit, and what goes on inside. Coming from a tradition of designing homes for wealthy individual clients on generous sites, relatively few contemporary architects have come to terms with the fact that the design of the *site plan*, encompassing interior and exterior *communal space*, is just as important as is the design of the dwelling interior. This is one area in which the "user needs researcher" has made a considerable contribution. They have shown that in moderate and high density multifamily housing, public and semipublic spaces around and between dwellings—their design, delimitation, landscaping, use, maintenance, and supervision— are often the crucial elements in the livability of

such neighborhoods [Figs. 6-28(a), (b), (c), and (d)].

A user survey commissioned by the design firm of Shankland Cox & Associates to aid in the design of a new housing estate for the Liverpool Corporation, found that the design of the approach areas—"the threshold"—exerted an unexpectedly great effect on overall satisfaction (Shankland Cox, 1967). An extensive study of six British high density estates found that the two variables which correlated most highly with overall satisfaction were "overall appearance of the estate" and "exterior maintenance" (Department of the Environment, 1972). Similarly, the majority of residents in the highly successful San Francisco family co-op, St. Francis Square, had moved there not only because of the reasonable rent and inner-city location, but also because of the exterior appearance, landscaping, and site planning. Ironically, their most frequent complaints related to the *interiors* (kitchen too small, no separate dining area), but most residents felt these were relatively minor inconveniences compared to the great merits of living in a green, quiet, and safe oasis in the city (Cooper, 1971). Among the basic findings of Oscar Newman's study *Defensible Space*, are that residents in potential crime areas feel more secure and

experience lower rates of crime when site planning encourages feelings of territoriality and responsibility for semipublic exterior spaces and entrances.

The site planning of St. Francis Square is successful due to its *lack* of ambiguity. Although Rabeneck (1973, 1974) is correct to argue for ambiguous *interiors*, it would be most unfortunate if designers accepted the same goal for exterior space. The site must be designed so that there is a clear delineation between private outdoor spaces and communal outdoor spaces as well as a clear delineation between space "belonging" to the housing development itself, and that "belonging" to the adjacent neighborhood. Clarity about which portions of the site are available for play and which are not and an understanding between residents and management about territorial control are likewise very important. Residents in many evaluation studies of housing developments report that problems occur where there is a misunderstanding between management and residents regarding delimitation of territory or maintenance responsibilities; between adults and children when there is a misunderstanding about where the latter are expected to play; and between residents and nonresidents regarding use of facilities and space which the former

group believe is their particular right. Residents have frequently had no previous experience of living in an arrangement whereby they *share* interior access space and exterior recreation space with their neighbors. Most of us "act" in a certain space with reference to previous comparable spaces we have been in or lived in. But, if you have only lived in a single family house or a sterile apartment building, there is no prior experience to understanding how one should view or use common landscaped areas and communal facilities. Lack of ambiguity in the site plan, management sensitivity, and the provision of resident manuals can alleviate these problems.

Children

Many studies of medium to high density multifamily housing conclude that it is "problems with children" that are among the most pressing for residents (Fig. 6-29). Since children are by far the chief users of communal space *around* the home, these areas tend to be critical. User needs research makes it clear that: 1) the more a multifamily housing design accommodates the needs of children, the more satisfied will adult residents be with that environment; 2) the key to providing for children's needs is in the sensitive design of the

Fig. 6-29 Observation studies of mid and high density family housing indicate that children are likely to play anywhere and everywhere and that large amounts invested in playgrounds will not guarantee that children will use them.

Fig. 6-30 Conflicts in family high-rise developments frequently occur in the common spaces such as corridors, elevators, lobbies and entrances. (a) Lobby as play facility. (b) Raised grassy area separates running and wheeled activity and provides ledge for sitting and socializing. (c) Concrete ledge fine for sitting but should coexist with a variety of other facilities.

Percentage of mothers finding play a problem, by density

Density in bed-spaces per acre	Number of estates	%	No.
0– 40	2	32	39
41– 80	12	63	236
81–120	8	58	373
121–160	8	·76	441
161–200	6	71	211
200+	4	92	56

Cost and use of play areas, by estate

Estate	Cost per sq ft* £	Percentage of use %	No.
Winstanley	1.74	11	3,562
Curnock	1.58	15	2,846
Acorn	1.32	13	3,732
Canada	0.95	13	3,780
The Bonamy	0.95	8	3,163
Warwick	0.92	3	4,773
Edith	0.87	3	4,861
Sceaux	0.75	4	1,732
Park Hill	0.74	18	4,424
Woodway	0.50	5	3,215
St Mary's	0.47	18	5,169

* The costs per sq ft quoted in the table are not actual scheme costs, but are a comparable valuation based on prices ruling for average local authority schemes in early 1972. They therefore eliminate the many variables between individual schemes. They include the cost of: construction; play equipment; seats, litter bins and lighting; enclosing walls, fencing and ballustrading; planting; paving, grassing and turfing; drainage and general excavation.

Where the 0–4 age groups played on those estates which had play areas

	%
Access areas*	33
Paved areas	32
Roads & pavements	14
Play areas	9
Grassed areas	7
Other	7
Gardens*	6

Number = 8,419

* These percentages were adjusted to exclude the numbers of children observed on the estates which did not have locations in these categories. Therefore the total exceeds 100%.

Percentage of mothers finding play a problem, by building types

Building types	Number of estates	%	No.
Low-density houses	11	56	161
High-density houses	11	61	576
Deck access	2	61	125
Balcony access with lifts	4	72	161
Walk-up blocks	6	72	81
Corridor blocks	3	73	92
Point blocks	7	81	137

overall site plan; and 3) the key to the successful use (and minimal "misuse") of the overall site is in *lack* of ambiguity.

There is ample evidence now to indicate that 80–90% of the users of public and communal outdoor space in a family housing development will be *children*. Yet, designers continue to plan such areas as if satisfying the aesthetic and functional needs of adults (and their own peers) were the principal—and sometimes the *only*—goal of site planning. The fantasies of neighbors chatting around a splashing fountain, barbecuing in a public space, playing shuffleboard, or working together in a communal garden are largely architects' pipe dreams; they do not coincide with the reality as recorded in research surveys and behavioral observations [Figs. 6-30(a), (b), and (c)].

Government regulations are not much help. In "Minimum Property Standards for Multi-Family Housing," there are 495 pages of detailed design directives—and just one short sentence that refers to the needs of children. It says, "Well-equipped playgrounds of adequate size and number shall be provided, where it is antici-

Fig. 6-31

"A ha, privacy! So you want to spend government money on frills."

ated that children will occupy the premises."[12] There is no definition of what is considered "well-equipped" or what constitutes an "adequate size and number," and no indication here or elsewhere that the *whole* environment must be designed with children in mind. They will use it to a far greater extent than will anyone else.

In addition to overlooking the predominance of children's use, designers and regulatory agencies have also overlooked the data on *where and how* children play in residential environments. For example, it is generally disregarded that studies in the United States and Western Europe show that children from ages one through six nearly always play around the most frequently used entrance to the dwelling; that hard surfaces are far more popular for play than grass; that communal open space is used much more frequently for play than private open space; that play equipment that moves is more attractive than that which is stationary; that children shun wide open spaces (except team-playing boys) and often seek out small-scale secluded locations. All of these findings have obvious implications for landscaping and site design, and should form the basis of good planning in residential areas.

IMPEDIMENTS TO COLLABORATION BETWEEN RESEARCHERS AND DESIGNERS

The interdisciplinary field of man-environment relations is now firmly established, at least at the academic level. The formal organization where researchers and designers meet (Environmental Design Research Association) has held seven annual conferences; the journal *Environment Behavior* has been published for almost a decade; many hundreds of articles have appeared in various journals authored by psychologists, anthropologists, sociologists, geographers, planners, architects, and others. Yet, all is not "well" in the field. Researchers do not feel their work is being adequately used, while designers still do not feel they are being supplied with the right kind of information, at the right time, or in the right format.

What are some of the impediments to researcher–designer collaboration? Appleyard (1973) suggests the following communications problems emanating from the researcher.

(1) United States man-environment research (unlike that in Europe) has been largely university-sponsored, and professional or pragmatic relevance has not been a high priority.
(2) Research findings are often either too general ("stating the obvious") or too specialized to be usable by the decision maker.
(3) Environmental variables in research are often poorly described, and environmental implications of findings rarely explicitly stated.
(4) Most research has been postconstruction rather than preconstruction, and, although decisions can be based on their analogy with previous schemes, the use of analogy may discourage innovative solutions.
(5) Research is often obscurely written and appears in a wide range of publications not generally read by design professionals.
(6) Too much emphasis has been placed on how to improve researcher–designer communication when what is really needed is further clarification on *when* user input has most relevance in the design process and to *whom* the information should be directed (Howell, 1974). For example, if federal regulatory agency staff, institutional clients, building component manufacturers, building contractors, parallel design professionals (landscape architects, city planners, engineers), are not seen as recipients of user needs information equal in importance to the archi-

tect, then architects' decisions will be hampered throughout the design process by uninformed co-decision makers (Fig. 6-31).

On the "consumer" side, there have been equally strong resistances to the use of valid behavioral and attitudinal research in housing (Ostrander, 1974).

(1) The language of social science is often seen as incomprehensible or misleading. Statistics and research designs are not common language for designers, clients, or users.
(2) Useful research findings rarely appear in the journals read by designers or the manufacturers of building components. This is partly because researchers have not bothered to write for these consumers, preferring the prestige of academic social science journals. Also the professional magazines have not been overly enthusiastic about the publication of research material.
(3) Social science research is generally held in low esteem by design professionals, who prefer to think that their own experience and perception of the world is sufficient for making common sense and intuitive decisions. Many architects see themselves as either artists (Louis Kahn) or social reformers

(Buckminster Fuller) or both (Soleri), and pay little regard to existing environment behavior research.
(4) Even if a social researcher is brought in on a job in the programming phase, most researchers need a much longer time than is available in the typical design process to obtain viable research results.
(5) Most researchers communicate in a verbal/statistical mode, while most design professionals are more graphicaly than verbally oriented.

A recent conference report on the possibilities of architect and social science collaboration noted that the architectural profession is in a period of transition, reexamining old values and seeking a new philosophical direction. The participants concluded that neither building technology nor design capability were the chief constraints in determining architecture's future direction.

. . . We understand how a façade can move and cannot move. We do not understand the performance of buildings in non-architectonic terms, that is, from the user's point of view. Now we are asking questions never asked before. We have solved most of the other design and aesthetic problems.[13]

There was a high degree of agreement that one of the emerging directions in architecture is the attempt to create environments that are most responsive to the needs of their users. But just how to do that is the dilemma, when "user needs" is just one of a number of innovative approaches to the design process.

IMPROVING THE VIABILITY OF USER NEEDS RESEARCH IN HOUSING: SOME RECOMMENDATIONS FOR THE FUTURE

There are important and valid roles for environment-behavior research in the field of housing. In order for the output of this research to have a real and beneficial effect on the improvement of housing environments, some changes are necessary in the identification of research consumers, the communication of research findings, the philosophy of architectural criticism, the criteria for design awards, and the education of designers.

Research—Who Does It—And For Whom?

One of the most basic tasks is to determine who is producing environment-behavior research for housing, who is using it, and what difference

Fig. 6-32

it is making to the built environment. As Beck (1976) writes: "Researchers produce information in one context and it is consumed in another. There is no knowledge by whom it is consumed, how much of it is consumed, and what translation the information goes through in the process."[14]

Sandra Howell (1974) has argued that although behavioral information may be relevant and properly communicated, it still may not be used by architects. At many points in the design process, the architect is constrained by the demands of the paying client, the availability of building components, and the pragmatic on-site concerns of the building contractor. Howell argues the clarification of *when* user needs have most relevance in the process and to *whom* the information should be directed is of the utmost importance.

An important step towards clarifying this situation has been expressed by Beck (1976). He suggests that we consolidate ideas and procedures and direct our attention to areas where we know we can have influence. An insightful table by Beck has been reworded in the medium of the housing field in Fig. 6-32.

Role of Researcher	Typical Clients	Context	Methods	Output Format
1. User-Program Consultant	Architect, developer, federal agency	Design of new housing; renovation or additions to existing stock; planning of new housing programs	Postconstruction evaluation of analogous existing environments; literature review of existing comparable studies	User-program for specific environment; user-programming guidelines applicable in variety of settings
2. Environmental Management Consultant	Housing authority; home owners association, state or federal agency sponsoring housing	Improvement of management, maintenance, security and general user-satisfaction in existing housing context	Interviews, observation, mapping, organizational analysis	Program of design and management changes, which might include space allocations, regulations, hardware, maintenance schedules, recreation programs, etc.
3. Citizens Group Consultant	Citizen action groups; neighborhood organizations; non-profit sponsors of new housing	Citizen-sponsored design and development of new housing; opposition to proposed housing; citizen input to local/national housing policy	Archival and original data collection relevant to case; case studies of typical housing residents	Design and development guidelines; social impact statements; legal testimony; citizen planning kits
4. Building Codes and Standards Researcher	Federal and state government; HUD, HEW, Bureau of Standards, American National Standards Institute Building Officials Code Administrators; American Society for Testing & Materials	Evaluation and modification of existing codes and standards; models for systematic feedback from researcher to appropriate regulatory agencies	Postconstruction evaluation of comparable housing types in different regions; design-process analysis to analyze effect of existing standards	Proposals for reformulation of codes and standards; manuals of voluntary standards
5. Building Materials Evaluator	Contractors, developers; technical information journals and information services; manufacturers of building materials and components; structural engineers; housing authorities; building inspectors	Technical testing of materials, building components and structural systems; tests for safety, fire and earthquake resistance; consumer ratings, materials and items in Sweets Catalog	Scientific tests; laboratory studies; analysis of sales figures; cost-effectiveness; market research	Technical bulletins; technical backup for reformulation of mandatory building codes and regulations; manuals of voluntary standards; hardware guidelines based on user preferences for architects, contractors and housing management; consumer reports in materials and components catalogs
6. Academic Researcher/Teacher	Students of planning, design, and engineering	Education of future decision makers regarding user needs and preferences in housing	Presentation of case study material; training in design evaluation and user programming; role playing of different user-researcher groups	Course materials, readers, textbooks
7. Information Researcher and "Broker"	Professional, state or local agencies; professional associations and journals; decision makers of all stages of the design process	Collection, processing and diffusion of research produced by any of above six researcher types; Broker link between researchers and practitioners	Research review and assessment; identification of significant research consumers; translation and dissemination in usable format; quality control through research review boards	Continuously modified data banks; literature abstracts; guidelines and patterns; annotated bibliography; consultant services; training workshops

The Communication of Behavioral Research Findings to The Design Community

Architects and other designers have, quite rightly, criticized researchers for not communicating their findings in a format which designers can comprehend and use. The United States Department of Housing and Urban Development has cosponsored two recent publications which present research findings in a format specifically directed at designers. These documents, one by Oscar Newman (1976) and one by American Society of Landscape Architects' Foundation (1975) cover crime prevention through design and the needs of the handicapped. Several recent books present research findings in the form of guidelines or recommendations, worded specifically in design or planning vocabulary (Newman, 1972; Cooper, 1975; and Alexander, 1976). Several papers and at least one book discuss the problems and promises of designer–researcher collaboration. In one of these, architect D. M. Deasy (1974), recounts his long-standing collaboration with a social psychologist consultant and offers some fascinating examples of their joint ventures in campus and office design. He writes:

There are many economic, technical and aesthetic considerations that shape the build-

ings we know; they in turn shape the behavior patterns of the people who use them. To reverse this relationship, to start with an understanding of human motivation and let this concern shape the form, will require a profound alteration in the basic approach to design.[15]

It is a "profound alteration" of this type which motivated the work on guidelines and patterns described earlier.

One of the fundamental changes which must come about is collapsing the distance—geographical, temporal, conceptual—between those that "produce" and those that "consume" user needs research. As Franklin Becker wrote concerning his position as an "in-house" researcher for the design section of UDC:

. . . the most unique and exciting aspect of the UDC research was that I was connected in a real way to an organization that actually created physical forms. There was relatively little "distance" between my research and the ongoing operations of UDC. At several points during the research, I was asked to write memorandums indicating my reactions, based on the data we had collected at that point,

to proposed modifications of existing UDC developments . . . Although sometimes difficult, I involved the persons who subsequently would use the research within the organization in the research process, and they were very interested in having a say when they realized how much top level support the project had.[16]

Architectural Criticism

Architectural criticism in this country is in a sorry state. Aided by some unspoken "old boy" code of not being overly critical of each other's work, supported by the editorial policies of most architectural and design journals which tend to print only favorable critiques, architectural criticism has emerged as a literature— "hermetically sealed against reality—autointoxicated, self-congratulatory, elitist and suffocatingly smug."[17] Architectural writers, for the most part, are still looking at buildings as sculpture, and judging them on the basis of current stylistic fads. Professional colleagues coyly critique each other's work, pictured with only traces of humanity.

Architectural critics appear to be totally ignorant, for example, of the burgeoning literature on user-response to medium and high density housing. Lengthy, well-illustrated articles on low-income housing turn out to be what most architectural magazine writing essentially comprises—a detailed *description* of recent developments, part aesthetic, part technical, with minimal cliché social commentary. It is not clear how this "head-in-the-sand" attitude has arisen in the United States. Many West European design magazines publish much more critical and socially responsible reviews. They also routinely publish the results of behavioral and attitudinal "feedback" studies on existing buildings. However, the message may at last be getting through in the United States. *Landscape Architecture* has for some years encouraged the publication of design critiques from the users' viewpoint. More recently, *Design and Environment* has emerged as a magazine committed to the promotion of writing and research on the social and psychological implications of design. A recent issue of the *American Institute of Architects' Journal* (August 1976), featured four evaluative studies of built environments from the users' viewpoint and maintained in an editorial that this heralded an even stronger emphasis on this field in the future.

Design Awards: Will User-Response Become a Criterion?

Traditionally, design awards have been made on the basis of form rather than function. Judgment by peers excludes any "user input" while the perusal of photos and plans is a poor substitute for experiencing the real environment (if, indeed, the environment has yet been constructed). Rarely does the jury visit the site or speak to users, and the submitting designer is generally not expected to give any evidence that he or she has researched user needs during the programming phase.

As pressures for more responsive environments are felt, the awards criteria may also change. Submissions for awards given by *Design and Environment* now require the designer to answer the question: How does this design fulfill the needs of potential users? The United States Housing and Community Development Act of 1974 calls for ". . . standards of design which meet the needs of the intended occupants." Hopefully, HUD will begin to require similar evidence for the Design Awards. It is up to the professional bodies of the AIA and ASLA to make their presence felt in this matter, and insure that user acceptance is in some measure a necessary prerequisite for an award.

Design Education

If we are to produce future designers who have sensitivity to user needs in housing, we must ensure that their formal education embraces a real understanding of the social and psychological implications of design. It is not enough that most major schools of architecture and landscape architecture now include courses in "social and psychological factors in design"—though this is certainly a vast improvement over a decade ago. It is also essential that this significant area of design education be made a mandatory section of AIA and ASLA registration. The professions can no longer perceive the field as a social aberration of the late 1960s, which (hopefully?) will gradually die away.

A designer with a capacity to observe and question may well be a better user needs researcher than a traditionally trained sociologist or psychologist. It is generally easier for a designer to learn research skills than it is for a social scientist to learn to visualize the world in design terms. Ideally, evaluation research teams should be composed of both social scientists *and* designers. If a designer learns how to observe environments in use with a questioning eye; how to ask the right kinds of questions; how to find and use existing research; how to communicate with social scientists—it will be a vast step forward. Potentially, the designer will become less of a leader on the design team, and more of a "process manager." If this role change occurs, the needs and inputs of a variety of actors—from users of surrogate environments, to potential users of the planned environment, to environmental managers, government bureaucrats, and fellow designers—can become welded into a finished product acceptable to all. The education received now must train the designer for this task.

Footnotes for Chapter 6

1. Letter from Connie Byrom, August 1976.
2. Letter from Edward Ostrander, August 1976.
3. Letter from Franklin Becker, August 1976.
4. Letter from James Anderson, August 1976.
5. "Revelstoke demonstration housing project: Phase 2—social guidelines." Report to Central Mortgage & Housing Corporation, Ottawa, 1976.
6. This section on the Urban Development Corporation derives in part from an article by Theodore Leibman in *Progressive Architecture* (November, 1971), and in part from correspondence with three former UDC staff members: Michael Kirkland (University of Toronto); Anthony Pangaro (Southwest Corridor Development Coordinator, Boston); and Michael Sears (Denver Housing Authority).
7. Leibman, Theodore. See footnote 6, p. 72.
8. Leibman, Theodore. See footnote 6, p. 76.
9. Leibman, Theodore. See footnote 6, p. 76.
10. Rabeneck, Andrew; Sheppard, David; Town, Peter, "The structuring of space in family housing," *Progressive Architecture* (November, 1974), p. 106.
11. Rabeneck, Andrew; Sheppard, David; and Town, Peter, "Housing flexibility/adaptability?", *Architectural Design* (February, 1974), vol. XLIX.
12. Federal Housing Administration, *Minimum Property Standards for Multi-Family Housing.* Washington, D.C.: U.S. Government Printing Office, 1963, p. 62.
13. Conway, Donald (Ed.), *Social Science and Design: A Process Model for Architect and Social Science Collaboration.* Washington, D.C.: American Institute of Architects, 1973.
14. Beck, Robert, "User generated research information requirements for roles engaged in the design, management, building, protection, teaching, informing and use of the environment," *Man-Environment Systems* (April, 1976), p. 1.
15. Deasy, C. M., *Design for Human Affairs.* Cambridge, Mass.: Schenkman Publishing Co., 1972, p. 40.
16. Letter from Becker, Franklin, August, 1976.
17. Fitch, James Marston, "Architectural criticism: Trapped in its own metophysics," *Architectural Educ.* (April, 1976), vol. XXIX, no. 4, p. 3.

Bibliography and References

Books

Alexander, Christopher; Ishikawa Sara; Silverstein, Murray; Angel, Shlomo; King, Ingrid; Jacobson, Max, *Pattern Language.* New York: Oxford University Press, 1976.

Back, Kurt W., *Slums, Projects, and People.* Durham, N.C.: Duke University Press, 1962.

Cooper, Clare C., *Easter Hill Village: Some Social Implications of Design.* New York: The Free Press, 1975.

Deasy, C. M., *Design for Human Affairs.* New York: John Wiley & Sons, 1974.

Festinger, L.; Schachter, S.; and Back, K., *Social Pressures in Informal Groups.* New York: Harper and Brothers, 1950.

Gans, Herbert J., *The Urban Villagers.* Glencoe: The Free Press, 1962.

Goodman, Robert, *After the Planners.* New York: Simon & Schuster, 1971.

Hall, E. T., *The Hidden Dimension.* New York: Doubleday, 1966.

Jacobs, Jane, *The Death and Life of Great American Cities.* New York: Random House, 1961.

Jephcott, Pearl, *Family Life in High Flats.* Edinburgh: Oliver & Boyd, 1971.

Kuper, Leo, "Blueprint for living together," in *Living in Towns.* London: The Cresset Press, 1953.

Lang, Jon et al. (Eds.), *Designing for Human Behavior.* Stroudsberg, Pa.: Dowden, Hutchinson, and Ross, 1974.

Lawton, M. Powell, *Planning and Managing Housing for the Elderly.* New York: John Wiley & Sons, 1975.

Michaelson, William, *Man and His Urban Environment: A Sociological Perspective.* Reading, Mass.: Addison-Wesley Publishing Co., 1970.

Newman, Oscar, *Defensible Space.* New York: Macmillan, 1972.

Sommer, Robert, *Personal Space: The Behavioral Basis of Design.* Englewood Cliffs, N.J.: Prentice-Hall, 1969.

Stevenson, A., Martin, E. and O'Neill, J., *High Living: A Study of Family Life in Flats.* Melbourne, Australia: University Press, 1967.

Whyte, William F., Jr., *The Organization Man.* New York: Simon & Schuster, 1966.

Periodicals and Reports

Alexander, Christopher, *Houses Generated by Patterns.* Berkeley: Center for Environmental Structure, 1969.

Appleyard, Donald, *Environmental Planning and Social Science: Strategies for Environmental Decision Making.* Working Paper No. 217. Berkeley: Institute for Urban and Regional Development, 1973.

American Society of Landscape Architects' Foundation, *Barrier Free Site Design*, Washington, D.C.: U.S. Department of Housing and Urban Development and U.S. Government Printing Office, 1975.

Architecture Research Unit, *Courtyard Houses, Inchview, Prestonpans.* Edinburgh: Department of Architecture, University of Edinburgh, 1966.

Bauer, Catherine, "Social questions in housing and community planning," *J. Social Issues,* vol. VII, nos. 1 and 2, 1951, pp. 1–34.

Beck, Robert, "User generated research information requirements for roles engaged in the design, management, building, protection, teaching, informing and use of the environment," *Man-Environment Syst.,* vol. 6, no. 3, May 1976, pp. 151–162.

Becker, Franklin and Friedburg, Lawrence, *Design for Living: The Resident's View of Multi-Family Housing.* Ithaca, New York: Cornell University, 1974.

Brill, William and Associates, *Controlling Access in High-Rise Building: Approaches and Guidelines* (Draft Rep.). Washington, D.C.: U.S. Department of Housing and Urban Development, 1976.

Chicago Housing Authority, *The Livability of Low-Rent Public Housing.* Chicago, Ill.: Chicago Housing Authority, 1950.

Conway, Donald (Ed.), *Social Science and Design: A Process Model for Architect and Social Science Collaboration.* Washington, D.C.: American Institute of Architects, 1973.

Cooper, Clare and Hackett, Phyllis, *Analysis of the Design Process at Two Moderate-Density Housing Developments.* Berkeley: Center for Planning and Development Research, University of California, June 1968.

Cooper, Clare and Marcus, Stephen, *Observations at Three San Francisco Redevelopment Agency Housing Developments.* (Mimeographed.) San Francisco: San Francisco Redevelopment Agency, June 1971.

Cooper, Clare, "St. Francis Square: Attitudes of its residents," *Amer. Inst. Architects J.* (December, 1971), pp. 22–25.

Cooper, Clare, "Resident dissatisfaction in multi-family housing," in *Behavior, Design and Policy Aspects of Human Habitats,* Smith, William M., Ed. Green Bay, Wisc.: University of Wisconsin, 1972.

Cooper-Marcus, Clare, "Children's play behavior in a low-rise inner-city housing development," in *Proc. 5th Annu. Conf. Enviironmental Design Res. Assoc.* Stroudsberg, Pa.: Dowden, Hutchinson, and Ross, 1974.

Cooper-Marcus, Clare, *People Places.* Berkeley: Dept. Landscape Architecture, September, 1976.

Department of the Environment, *New Housing in a Cleared Area: A Study of St. Mary's Oldham.* London: Her Majesty's Stationery Office, Design Bulletin 22, 1971.

Department of the Environment, *Children at Play.* London: Her Majesty's Stationery Office, 1973.

Federal Public Housing Authority, *Public Housing Design: A Review of Experience in Low-Rent Housing.* Washington, D.C.: U.S. Government Printing Office, 1946.

Fitch, James Marston, "Architectural criticism: Trapped in its own metaphysics," *J. Architectural Educ.* (April, 1976), vol. XXIX, no. 4, pp. 2–3.

Fried, Marc, "Grieving for a lost home," in *The Urban Condition,* Duhl, L. J., Ed. New York: Basic Books, 1969.

Fried, Marc and Gleicher, P., "Some sources of residential satisfaction in an urban slum," *J. Amer. Inst. of Planners 27* (November, 1961), pp. 305–315.

Griffin, Mary E., *Mount Hope Courts: A Socio-physical Evaluation.* (Mimeo.) American Civilization Senior Honors Thesis, Brown University, May 1973.

Hartman, Chester, *Family Turnover in Public Housing.* San Juan, Puerto Rico: Urban Renewal and Housing Administration, Office of Research, 1960.

Department of the Environment, *The Estate Outside the Dwelling: Reactions of Residents to Aspects of Housing Layout.* London: Her Majesty's Stationery Office, Design Bulletin 25, 1972.

Hollingshead, A. B. and Rogler, L. H., "Attitudes towards slums and public housing in Puerto Rico," in *The Urban Condition,* Duhl, L. H., Ed. New York: Basic Books, 1963.

Housing Research and Development Program, *Play Areas for Low Income Housing.* Urbana-Champaign, Ill.: Housing Research and Development Program, Univ. of Illinois, and State of Illinois, Department of Local Government Affairs, and Office of Housing and Buildings (revised edition), 1974.

Housing Research and Development Program, *Families in Public Housing: An evaluation of three residential environments in Rockford, Illinois.* Urbana-Champaign: University of Illinois Housing Research and Development Program, 1972.

Howell, Sandra, "Needed: Performance specifications for using behavior science," *Industrialization Forum,* vol. 5, no. 5, 1974.

Leibman, Theodore and Melting, Alan, "Learning from experience: The evolution of housing criteria," *Progressive Architecture* (November, 1974), pp. 70–77.

Maizel, J., *Two to Five in High Flats.* London: The Housing Center, 1961.

Ministry of Housing and Local Government, *Homes for Today and Tomorrow* (Parker Morris Report). London: Her Majesty's Stationery Office, 1961.

Ministry of Housing and Local Government, *Families Living at High Density.* London: Her Majesty's Stationery Office, 1970.

Ministry of Housing and Local Government, "Housing at Coventry: A user reaction study," *Official Architecture and Planning* (December, 1967), pp. 1–20.

Ministry of Housing and Local Government, *The Family at Home: A Study of Households in Sheffield.* London: Her Majesty's Stationery Office, 1969.

Ministry of Housing and Local Government, *Family Houses at West Ham: An Account of the Project and an Appraisal.* London: Her Majesty's Stationery Office, 1969.

Montgomery, Roger, "Pattern language," *Architectural Forum* (January, 1970), pp. 52–59.

Newman, Oscar, *Design Guidelines for Creating Defensible Space* (National Institute of Law Enforcement and Criminal Justice and U.S. Department of Housing and Urban Development). Washington, D.C.: U.S. Government Printing Office, 1976.

Rabeneck, Andrew; Sheppard, David; and Town, Peter, "Housing Flexibility?", *Architectural Design,* vol. XLIII, (November,1973), pp. 198–227.

Rabeneck, Andrew; Sheppard, David; and Town, Peter, "Housing flexibility/adaptability?," *Architectural Design,* vol. XLIX (February, 1974), pp. 76–91.

Rabeneck, Andrew; Sheppard, David; and Town, Peter, "The structuring of space in family housing: An alternative to present design practice," *Progressive Architecture* (November, 1974), pp. 100–107.

San Francisco Planning and Housing Association, *San Francisco Public Housing: A Citizen's Survey.* San Francisco: 1946.

Shankland, Cox and Associates, *Social Survey, Childwall Valley Estate, Liverpool.* London and Liverpool: 1967.

"Social Policy and Social Research in Housing," *J. Social Issues,* vol. VII, nos. 1 and 2, 1951.

Van der Ryn, Sim and Silverstein, Murray, *Dorms at Berkeley: An Environmental Analysis,* Center for Development Research. Berkeley: University of California, 1967.

Wallace, Anthony C. F., *Housing and Social Structure.* Philadelphia: Philadelphia Housing Authority, 1952.

Zeisel, John and Griffin, Mary, *Feedback Charlesview: A Diagnostic Evaluation of Charlesview Housing, Allston, Massachusetts.* (Mimeo.) Cambridge, Mass.

Section Three
Choice and Change

7
A Framework for Industrialization

Richard Bender and John Parman

"This is the last word in condominiums—each owner hires his own architect."

MISSING THE POINT

Mystery writers often use the tactic of providing a clue that seems to point in one direction while really pointing in another. Only when we reach the end of the story and the facts start to fall in place, do we understand our confusion and see that we have missed the point.

In this chapter we are going to consider housing industrialization as if it were one of these ambiguous clues. We have reached the end of "The Mystery of Housing—Volume One," and realized that we have been deceived—or have deceived ourselves. By misusing the clue of housing industrialization, we have built a generation of unsatisfactory housing.

Our view of housing industrialization may never have been appropriate to the real situation. We have achieved a manufacturing process that is productive, but it leaves us with a narrow range of products—prisoners of the production process. And we are still stuck with the flaws of the old conceptual model—seeing housing as a product, not as a process. We have failed to understand the complexity of housing or develop technologies to support it. "Industrialized" has come to mean factory mass pro-

duced, while "housing" is synonomous with units, tracts and projects. The sense of richness and complexity that should characterize these two words is still lacking.

We find ourselves chained to an approach to production which is based on an older technology's need for standardization. We put the bulk of our efforts into organizing things for the convenience of a system which no longer serves us—one that has failed to meet our past needs adequately, and is unlikely to meet our requirements in the future.

We have at our disposal an industrial capacity so enormous that, today, its waste products are of greater concern than any problems of undercapacity. Yet, in the area of housing we continue to have production problems: we do not produce enough housing to meet the full range of our needs. We pursue our present efforts at providing housing, hoping we can somehow bring down the costs and make conventional housing more widely available. But costs have gone up and quality has gone down. Surely it is reasonable to suggest that the narrowness of our understanding of housing industrialization has been partly to blame for our problems.

Industrialized housing has been an on-again off-again "idea in good currency" over the past five decades. But it is a deceptive, ambiguous clue that, while dominating our thoughts about housing production, has been largely misconstrued. In this chapter, we would like to demonstrate this ambiguity and show that the experience of these five decades points in another direction.

LOOKING BACKWARD

Karl Popper, in talking about systems, distinguishes between "clocklike" systems—which function like clockwork, producing predictable, predetermined housing products—and "cloudlike" systems—which behave like a cloud of gnats or a school of fish, predictable in a general sense but not in terms of individual elements. We can apply this analogy to housing production.

Much effort has been spent in this century trying to industrialize housing production. These efforts have been characterized by the view of housing industrialization as a clocklike, assembly line process. Buckminster Fuller's 1927 Dymaxion I House (Fig. 7-3) is an example of such a product: mass-produced, completely

finished, and intended to be sold "fully loaded" with appliances and other mechanical amenities.

Dymaxion I was meant to be a "universal" house, produced efficiently at low cost and adaptable to any site, anywhere. It is different from much of the industrialized housing that followed (and is characteristic of Fuller) in that it casts off conventional images of housing in favor of "efficiency" in both manufacture and use.

Fuller—like many of his generation—saw industrialization as the symbol of the dynamism of society. At the time he first tried to apply the industrial methods of the aircraft and automobile industries to housing, these industries were still in adolescence—there was still a multitude of car manufacturers, and the aircraft industry was only just beginning to move into commercial aviation. Both were innovative industries with a dynamic and entrepreneurial spirit.

The Dymaxion House itself never reached production, and its impact as a housing form was negligible—its Flash Gordon style never caught on. But its impact as a scenario for a program of housing industrialization was substantial: it pictured a housing industry in which the many small builders, each operating locally and pro-

ducing relatively few houses, would be replaced by a smaller number of large firms producing hundreds or thousands of units for an aggregated, national housing market. This was the dream of housing industrialization that launched the prefabricated housing industry in the 1930s and to which people (and programs) returned in the 1940s and again in the late 1960s (each time missing the clue that industrialization might mean something other than mass production).

Ten years before Dymaxion, Corbusier introduced the Dom-ino Project (Fig. 7-4), which took a more cloudlike approach to housing industrialization. The inspiration for his approach was the typical industrial loft building of the nineteenth century, in which structure and infill could be handled separately. This allowed the industrialization of components of the structural framework, wall elements and infill, while giving users the ability to adjust these products and materials to meet their changing needs. The image of industrialization Dom-ino presents makes an important distinction between the requirements of mass production and the requirements of the user and the specific site (the general versus the particular) in which the user's requirements are met by providing incomplete housing that can be

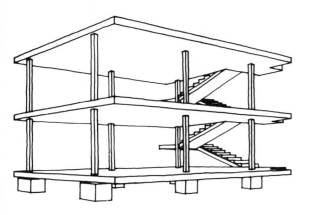

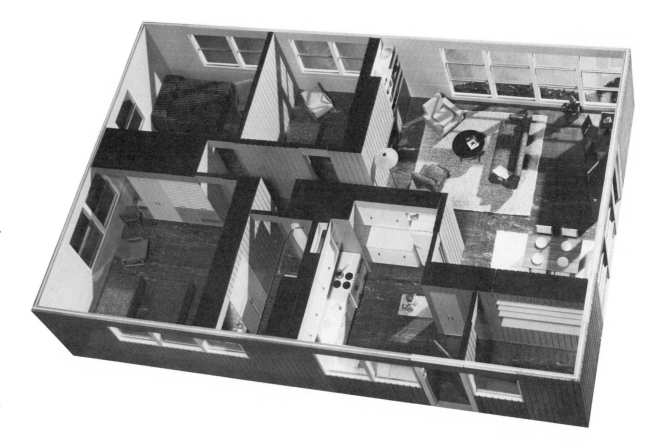

Fig. 7-4 Corbusier's Dom-ino Project took industrialization to be a cloudlike process.

Fig. 7-5 Lustron tried to implement the housing industrialization scenario first presented in Fuller's Dymaxion House.

completed using mass-produced parts. In a real sense, the structure provided is a framework for diversity. To use a familiar image, it provided a ''chassis'' and ''optional extras.''

Dom-ino was the first of a sporadic series of experiments and prototypes in Europe and the United States aimed at a cloudlike approach to housing that provides a framework but avoids anticipating the variety of forms the housing can take. Corbusier, in thinking about industrialization, caught the ambiguous clue the others had missed.

The major tendency of housing industrialization in America, however, has followed closely the scenario laid down by the Dymaxion House. The clue from abroad, that could have told us that diversity and variety in housing are also obtainable along with improved methods of production, went unrecognized. The Lustron House (Fig. 7-5), coming 20 years after Dymaxion, was a victim of this clocklike approach to housing.

Lustron was meant to be an ''ultramodern'' house, using new, highly durable materials to provide an easily maintained living environment. It arrived at the site as a factory-packed trailer of panels and parts, each part available in

Fig. 7-6 Techbuilt was a kit-of-parts house, like Lustron, but it allowed greater flexibility in accepting changes in the plan and the components at the local level.

the order of its need in the on-site assembly process. This allowed for very fast construction, while insuring the security of the components during the time between manufacture and erection.

Lustron attracted widespread interest from potential home owners. But it ran into the problem which has consistently prevented the success of factory mass production of housing in the United States: the impossibility of implementing the automobile analogy within the very different context of housing. The high cost of capitalizing a major industrial plant and setting up an adequate network of dealers was undermined by financial mechanisms which—geared to conventional housing—operated too slowly and inflexibly to accommodate mass-produced products. The mortgage system, for example, was designed for the conventional housing industry, as was the system of interim payments to builders. Builders paid for the housing components when they left the factory, but they were not paid by the house owner until the building was finished and the mortgage arranged. The result was a typical manufacturer's cash-flow problem: the faster Lustron produced houses, the faster its debts mounted. What Lustron required was prompt action on

mortgages and a single payment of interim loans, but this proved impossible. Lustron finally tried to set up an acceptance corporation like those used by the automobile industry, but it was too late.

The failure of the prefabrication firms, such as Lustron, to establish themselves as a force in the housing industry reinforced the idea among those who planned and administered housing programs that housing industrialization could not come into being until the right institutional framework could be established for it. But this conclusion missed the clue that the basic approach taken by manufacturers like Lustron—the production of a "closed" housing system whose components were all manufactured at a single, enormously expensive plant, and whose housing products were unmodifiable at the site—was basically unsuited to the realities of the housing industry. The pattern of housing demand was such that more dispersed production systems and more "open" housing—capable of modification and capable of accepting a variety of components—were inherently better able to cope with a disaggregated cyclical market.

But many people had learned from the Lustron experience. One of these was the architect

Carl Koch, who had been one of the principal designers of the Lustron House. Koch's careful studies had reduced the number of separate parts and site processes needed to build the Lustron House, while greatly improving its livability. As a result of his experience with this and other housing and component manufacturers (the Acorn House and the Conantum project, for example) and with residential design and site development, Koch emerged as a leader in the field of industrialized housing.

In the 1950s Koch launched the Techbuilt House (Fig. 7-6), a kit-of-parts house that reflected his understanding of why Lustron had failed. Koch designed Techbuilt as an "open" system that could use components that were manufactured by subcontractors or locally built versions of these components or custom-built components compatible with the system. Koch was able in this way to accommodate the need for local input and individual planning.

Techbuilt was sold through "dealerships." Local contractors worked with the owner to plan and budget the house. Techbuilt supplied a planning kit and the occasional services of an architect (the owner got two free consultations). The house was planned using Techbuilt guide-

Fig. 7-7 Conventional housing construction today makes use of a full range of industrial methods—prefabrication of components, new tools, new ways of organizing the site and construction process.

lines. Home owners had the option of staying within the system, with a clear sense of the costs involved and of the nature of the final product, or of straying outside the system to embellish the house with nonstandard plans and components. The dealers—unlike the Lustron case—were not held captive by a predetermined product, but instead took an active role in its planning and elaboration. When necessary, local techniques or materials could be substituted within the framework. The basic house "kit" was ordered by the dealer from the same parts list that the owner and his family used to plan their home—the cost of each Techbuilt part was given, and the planning process provided a way to keep a running total. Within the boundaries of the system there was confidence in cost, quality and timing; outside the boundaries of the system there was the possibility for added variety. The Techbuilt system was able to provide for the need for basic housing and the desire to extend the basic structure to meet individual requirements. Koch's genius was his understanding that this capability was a necessary prerequisite to any housing system attempting to hold its own against conventional construction in a highly localized market with built-in resistance to standard products and orthodox mass production.

Like Corbusier before him, Koch got the clue right. Although in some ways the Techbuilt House is an extension of Lustron, its spirit and its capabilities are closer to Dom-ino. Koch also got the ambiguous clue present in conventional housing construction—that it was an industrialized process far better suited to the needs of housing than the kind of industrialization proposed by the Dymaxion scenario.

THE INDUSTRIALIZATION OF CONVENTIONAL CONSTRUCTION

As Koch realized, the overall tendency in the conventional housing industry since World War II had been toward greater productivity and greater use of industrial methods—in terms of building products, new tools or new patterns of building. Today, residential construction combines prefabricated components with on-site assembly as a matter of course (Fig. 7-7). It is an industrial process that results in a custom product, and it is in many ways more sophisticated than factory mass production. The process still uses on-site labor, but many parts of the house arrive ready for installation, and by moving the production of these items to the factory, it has been possible to apply the machinery and methods of mass manufacture where they are most effective. The resulting

building products are less labor intensive and often of a higher quality than their field-produced predecessors.

Moreover, in the last decade building components have become more comprehensive—a single component can be a substantial portion of the completed housing unit. This makes for a highly simplified construction process, though one which requires special equipment. In America, mobile and modular home manufacturers follow this model most completely. Other residential construction makes use of components, but usually only those one or two men can handle—wall-frame panels, roof joists, windows and doors, and so forth.

The trend toward simplification in the construction industry has been reinforced by improvements in the fit between components. Although building products are not standardized in a strict sense, they comprise a system of basically compatible parts: walls relate to lumber and plywood dimensions; doors and windows come in certain heights and widths. It is always possible to obtain or make nonstandard parts, but these cost more. For this reason the general tendency is to use the less expensive, more widely available standard components.

Building products and tools are aimed at meeting two major objectives:

To decrease the time needed for a person to master the skills necessary to use the product or tool well. Ideally, it should be simple enough that anyone can use it after a few minutes' practice.
To increase productivity—a product or tool should accomplish more in less time, with less effort, than the product or tool it supplants. Thus, fiberglass bathtub surrounds have replaced hand tiling, and automatic nailers have replaced hammers and screwdrivers. Sometimes the development of one product has spurred the development of products that complement it—the development of the paint roller, for example, has led to improvements in latex paints.

These two objectives have made it possible for a relatively unskilled person to operate efficiently and produce at an acceptable level of quality. The products and tools meeting these objectives have also had an impact on the organization of construction. The common paint roller is an example.

Today's residential building site looks surprisingly like an assembly line, for it is laid out in a way that permits the use of large equipment for site development. In this case, the house is static; the workers move along the "line." The housing itself is assembled and completed by people whose tasks have become so standardized and specialized that they are closer to those of industrial workers than to the craftwork that once characterized housing construction.

At major building sites one can also see a variety of new devices that make multistory construction safer and easier—temporary elevators, improved scaffolding, pumping systems to deliver concrete, on-site X-ray inspection of welded joints. These devices have been coupled with new regulations—for worker safety and equal employment opportunity, for example—that have made even large construction sites much closer in their working conditions to other industries.

The pattern of industrialization quietly chosen by the housing industry has worked well—despite our failure to recognize it as such. When the President's Committee on Urban Housing (the Kaiser Committee) looked at conventional construction in 1967, it concluded that the industry was far more innovative and streamlined than many imagined and that it had, as well, developed an approach to industrialization that permitted a fair degree of housing diversity. The early years of the 1970s, when an expanded mortgage market fueled a surge in housing production, gave proof to the extent of this switch to more efficient methods.

Yet, it must be noted that the diversity in housing in terms of building form and arrangement is still much less than it could be. There is nothing inherent in the industrial methods chosen by the mainstream of the housing industry that precludes a greater amount of diversity in its products, but of course diversity has not been the industry's major goal. Its overriding concern is production and marketing, since housing development is a process born of crisis. Housing must go up fast and sell or rent quickly or the developers face penalties in interest money and taxes on empty units. Housing is therefore aimed at a finished marketable product geared to general notions of taste and living patterns, making diversity and a piecemeal approach difficult. Diversity has been handled by providing a limited number of stock plans or façade variations. The industrialization of conventional housing has permitted more diversity than is possible with factory production, but far less than would be the case if richness, individuality and diversity were also goals

STILL MISSING THE POINT

In 1967 two national advisory groups—the National Commission on Urban Problems and the President's Committee on Urban Housing—began to hold hearings to consider America's housing problem. Their final reports—the Douglas Report (after its Chairman, Senator Paul Douglas) and the Kaiser Report (after Edgar Kaiser)—pointed to a serious shortage of adequate housing, particularly for lower-income urban families. Too much housing had been allowed to deteriorate, while too little housing was being built to replace it.

The two reports are remarkable for their depth and comprehensiveness. In the programs they charted, they tried to address the full range of problems that impact on housing, the range of problems that make it one of our nation's most difficult issues. But again the clue was missed: the depth and complexity of the reports were reinterpreted simplistically (by HUD, for example) within the framework of existing subsidy programs and approaches to increased production. The reports had speculated that some 26 million housing units would be needed over a ten-year period; unfortunately, this figure was translated into the magic number of 2.6 million units per year, and the number itself began to attract much more attention than the many observations and assumptions that lay behind it.

By the late 1960s there was widespread agreement within government, industry and academia that the time had come for industrialized housing. Recent successes in space exploration had given American industry a reputation for problem solving that many felt could be applied to other national problems. Large appliance firms, aerospace firms, materials manufacturers and conglomerates suddenly began to acquire or create housing divisions, although many of these firms had little or no prior experience in housing. This was the context in which the Federal Government began to move toward larger programs in industrialized housing.

Despite the many warnings in the Kaiser Committee Report, factory-based industrialized housing grew more appealing to the Federal Government. It was seen as a way to "conquer" the housing problem. Part of its appeal lay in the nature of the Government's subsidy programs, which focused on two types of housing—low-rise and high-rise multifamily. These looked like likely candidates for industrialization. At this time, a dramatic event helped to focus interest in factory-built housing: a major hurricane destroyed much of Gulfport, Mississippi. This disaster created an immediate need for housing, which was answered by a modular housing manufacturer in upper New York State—Stirling-Homex. Stirling-Homex loaded up a trainload of modular housing units and shipped them to Gulfport, where they were quickly put to use as disaster housing. The event worked spectacularly as a public relations device, showing how quickly industrialized housing could be moved in and set up—and everyone happily swallowed the bait.

The Stirling brothers were Canadian entrepreneurs who started out in conventional housing and then moved into modulars. Their firm became one of the glamour stocks of the late 1960s, increasing in value from a fraction of a cent per share to more than 50 dollars. In 1971 the firm admitted to the SEC that it had used an accounting device—chalking up a profit for every housing unit produced, regardless of whether or not there was a firm commitment for it—that had greatly exaggerated its earnings statement. When the firm went bankrupt the next year, it was discovered that it had been producing far more housing than its real sales volume warranted. Its factory was literally surrounded by mouldering modules.

Fig. 7-8 Breakthrough housing, rooted in the Dymaxion scenario of industrialization, had less diversity in the form and the flexibility of arrangement than the tract housing it tried to replace.

Perhaps this is our best example of the ambiguous clue: how was it that Stirling-Homex had so many housing units on hand at the time of the Gulfport hurricane? If the proponents of factory production had asked this question instead of rhapsodizing over a feat of technology, we would have had an important clue to the problems that lay ahead.

The concept was not reexamined; it was pursued. In 1969 the Department of Housing and Urban Development announced a new program, Operation Breakthrough, aimed at "achieving the volume production of housing." Breakthrough was the brainchild of a new HUD Secretary, George Romney, whose view of the housing problem was conditioned by his experience as President of American Motors—a view that saw the housing problem primarily in terms of production, and saw production primarily in terms of factories and assembly lines. He felt that the methods of production of the housing industry were an anachronism, like trying to build cars in a gas station.

The program had three aims: to eliminate institutional constraints to factory production of housing; to develop new housing systems; and to create an aggregated market that could help sustain production and eventually capture

larger markets. As part of the development and initial marketing of the new systems, the program proposed to build a series of demonstration sites across the country to display prototype housing and permit some evaluation of its performance in use (Fig. 7-8).

The program brought together a managerial team drawn largely from the aerospace industry: Harold Finger, the new HUD Assistant Secretary for Research and Technology had headed NASAs facilities construction team. None of these people was very familiar with housing or with the housing industry. Although HUD indicated that Breakthrough would be a comprehensive program addressing all aspects of the housing problem, its major direction was to clear a path for factory production. Deeper probing of the housing problem was not on its agenda. And although there was a clear effort to design the program to address the right institutional issues—the problems that had made it difficult to produce housing in factories in the past—the program's insensitivity to the complexity of the housing problem was a major factor in its ultimate failure.

In simplistic terms, we can think of Breakthrough as having taken the basic Dymaxion scenario of 1927 and embellished it with the

research and development methods of the 1960s. The result, to use Marshal McLuhan's image, was like watching an expensive, high-powered and sophisticated sports car careening down a very bumpy country road, its driver focused firmly on the rear-view mirror.

Breakthrough was the wrong view of industrialization, the wrong view of housing, the wrong program altogether. It bears out Edward De Bono's observation that you cannot dig a new hole by digging the same hole deeper. Possibly, if we have really understood the clue and the story so far, Breakthrough was also the death knell of the Dymaxion scenario.

ANALOGY AND REALITY

When Alexander the Great was proposing to build a city that should redound to his credit, Deinocrates, the architect, came to him and suggested that he should build it on Mount Athos, for, besides being a strong place, it could be so fashioned as to give the city a human form, which would be . . . worthy of his greatness. And on what, Alexander asked, would the inhabitants live? Deinocrates replied that he had not thought of this.
—Niccolo Machiavelli, *The Discourses*

In the 1960s a loose confederation of Japanese architects and writers, called the Metabolists, proposed that architecture be "organic," that is, responding to human variety and changing environmental conditions. At about the same time, the Dutch architect/researcher John Habraken was beginning to write down his thoughts on housing. The Metabolists aimed for a biological analogy; Habraken wrote about "supports" and "tissue." Both began to dissect the built environment in an effort to rediscover its "life force."

Analysis is essential to understanding, but it is not always possible to recreate wholes from the parts that analysis reveals—wholes which will retain the richness of the real world. To recreate the whole we need to have images to work toward that can give life to our creations and illustrate their intricacies.

But there is one danger: Deinocrates' proposal was a city in human form, but this image in no way assured that men could live there. In the same way, the Metabolists dreamed of buildings that could grow like plants, and Habraken pictured buildings whose parts were like human viscera. These organic images have not led to buildings that have wholly succeeded in translating their organic quality. It is important

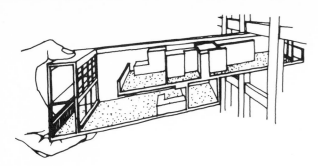

Fig. 7-9 Corbusier's Marseilles Block brought forward the idea of industrialization he presented in the Dom-ino Project.

Fig. 7-10 Corbusier thought of the Marseilles Block apartments as bottles being slid into a wine bin.

to see, however, that these images go far beyond Dymaxion's car analogy in considering the meaning of housing and what a house might be. The idea that the house could be produced like the car was the wrong idea; it concentrated on production instead of addressing housing in all its dimensions.

There are analogies and images of housing that can move beyond this narrow sense of industrialization to something richer and more varied. What such analogies try to do is to create a framework for housing that leaves the individual householder with partial or complete responsibility for the arrangement and in some cases the form of his housing. Such a framework aims at meeting the needs not only of the first users of the housing, but of each successive user who might live within the framework. This is the essence of a cloudlike system. Its aim is not to try to embody human actions and desires, but to accommodate them.

The first such analogy we might consider was posed by Le Corbusier in describing his Marseilles Block (Fig. 7-9), the enormously influential apartment building he built just after World War II. Corbusier described Marseilles as being like a wine bin, and this idea develops quite naturally from his earlier Dom-ino

Fig. 7-11 Welton Becket's Contemporary Hotel at Disney World using prefabricated steel room modules to speed completion and to build in the possibility of rapid room refurbishing in the future, applied the wine bin analogy directly.

Fig. 7-12 Kurokawa's capsule hotel extended the wine bin analogy, but its basic concept of flexibility is the same.

Fig. 7-13 The three-story volume created by the Townland System allowed low-rise housing to be fitted into a multistory framework.

Project. The housing block consists of a framework—the wine bin that holds an infill of housing—the wine bottles (Fig. 7-10). Corbusier saw the infill as something of fixed arrangement, but conceptually it could be varied a great deal. The clue lies in the image of the wine bottle: it connotes something of fixed shape and size, but containing wine of every variety.

Welton-Becket's Contemporary Hotel at Disney World (Fig. 7-11) is a direct application of the wine bin analogy: its ziggurat framework holds prefabricated steel hotel room modules which make it possible to replace or refurbish whole rooms without disrupting the operation of the rest of the hotel. They also allowed the hotel to be finished rapidly, while minimizing the number of workers who had to be brought to and maintained at the site. But, like the Marseilles block, each of the modules is basically the same as the next.

Other groups are working in this way. The London-based Archigram group's Plug-In City Project and Kurokawa's Capsule Hotel in Tokyo's Ginza District (Fig. 7-12) are both variations on the wine bin theme, except that these modules attach to the main structure, rather than fitting within it.

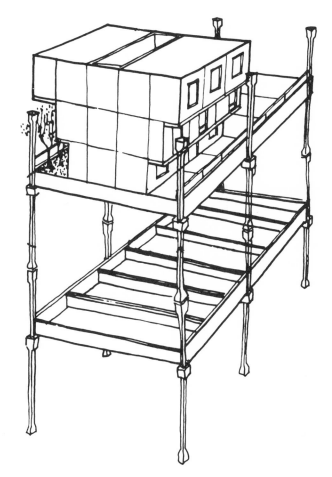

The problem with the wine bin analogy and its variations is that they depend on some outside force to remove and replace the housing modules, and they picture the modules themselves as things of fixed dimension and arrangement. Although flexibility is provided, it is limited, provided to the framework and not to the housing.

An analogy which tries to redress this problem, is one that compares the housing structure with a bookcase. This analogy was proposed by Townland, one of the competitors in the Breakthrough Program. The Townland System (Fig. 7-13) is based on the same separation of structure and infill that characterizes the wine bin analogy and its examples, but it goes a step beyond in providing the kind of ambiguous space that we associate with a bookshelf— a space that can hold not only books, but lamps, aquariums, bric-a-brac and a host of other things.

As it was first presented, Townland indeed looked very much like a bookcase (Fig. 7-14). It was pictured filled with a variety of housing types-multifamily, multistory and detached single family housing, each somewhat different from the next. At the same time, a variety of other functions could be inserted in the

Fig. 7-15 The urban homesteading movement got the clue that tenements, even ones that had been burnt out and abandoned, could serve as the shells for new housing.

framework—playgrounds, schools, stores, offices and community facilities However, as the system evolved in the Breakthrough Program, this variety was lost—Townland devised its own infill, which was a variation on the conventional multifamily housing theme, and HUD reduced the scope of the Project (in the end, the infill took over. The single Townland project finally built in Seattle reduced the "bookshelf" to a single bay) (Fig. 1-45). Few of those involved in the Breakthrough Program understood that the framework, as conceived, not only permitted variety, but made it possible to alter this variety over time to suit the needs of the community served.

Both the wine bin and the bookcase ideas are evolutions of the nineteenth century industrial loft. We can think of loft buildings as an example of the separation of framework and infill, but we can also think of them as separating the building envelope and interior space. What they provide is a sheltered interior space that can be adapted to housing and other uses. This is a case where we missed the clue: until artists and craftsmen began to create the present rich mixture of loft housing, using a wide variety of tools, products and materials to do so, we thought of lofts—and the districts where we found them—as the province of industry.

Fig. 7-16 Fuller's dome over Manhattan can be thought of as an umbrella that would begin to affect the form of the housing within it.

Today, people pay premiums to get lofts for residential use, and whole industrial areas are being converted to housing.

A similar process has marked the "urban home-steading" movement in cities like New York that have a great deal of deteriorated or abandoned brick tenement housing. By seeing that these buildings remained structurally sound, providing a sheltered space within which rebuilding could occur, tenant cooperatives have taken steps to bring their housing back to life (Fig. 7-15). They have been greatly aided in this process by organizations like the Urban Homesteading Assistance Board (U-HAB), which have provided legal, financial and tech-nical assistance to self-helpers.

We can point to several other examples of buildings that provide only a sheltered area for their owners or tenants: large shopping malls typically provide only raw space and utility hookups, placing the burden of development on the individual tenant, who is free to plan the space within a clearly stated set of rules. The same is true for some condominiums (in high-rise buildings in particular).

Our final analogy in these terms comes from the ever-fertile mind of Buckminster Fuller.

Fig. 7-17 The basic "seed" of Stephensen's summer house can serve individuals, young families and families whose children have grown.

Fig. 7-18 The "seed" can be added to in order to meet the needs of the expanding family.

Fig. 7-19 Galgebakken's garden courts function simply as ambiguous spaces that can be used in a variety of ways to suit the residents living around them.

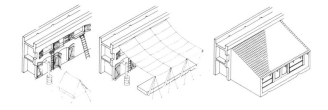

Fuller is responsible for pushing the separation of envelope and space enclosed to its logical conclusion, proposing that an immense dome be built over part of Manhattan (Fig. 7-16), thus creating an umbrella between New York and the environment. (As he pictured it, Fuller made no distinction between the housing inside the dome and the housing outside, but surely there would be some differences. We can imagine that the regulated internal climate of the dome could result in a more tropical architecture, one less dependent on bulk and mechanical equipment than its outside counterpart.)

The wine bin, the bookcase, the umbrella—each of these analogies has thought about a containing structure and the parts or spaces it contains. Is there another way of thinking about housing? The Danish architect Peter Stephensen has suggested the analogy of the seed. He had noticed that when people build second homes, they often start off with something very small—just big enough for themselves and a guest or a young child; as they get older and their children increase in size and number, they start adding on to the house; later, when the children are grown up, they may even begin to dismantle the house to whittle it down to a more manageable size. When, in 1974, the

Danish Brick Manufacturers Association sponsored a Summer House Competition, Stephensen was able to apply his seed analogy.

His entry provided a basic two-story structure as the "seed"—a building just large enough to provide the needed living and sleeping spaces for a young family (Fig. 7-17). This seed can grow with both temporary and permanent additions (Fig. 7-18). The resulting housing can take on many forms and meet the requirements of many different living patterns. It can also be pruned back if necessary, after the children have gone.

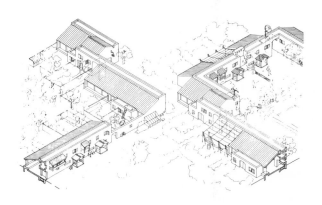

Another Danish project—Galgebakken, by Øruno, Øruno, Marcussen and Storgaard—makes a variation on this same theme by creating garden courts, shared and bounded by four houses. The courts can be used as a single large community space, or broken up to form private gardens or additions to the dwellings or some combination of these options (Fig. 7-19). The seed analogy begins to get away from the limitations inherent in the completed building at the beginning of the process. An idea about housing (and building) that goes further in this direction is the thought that the housing process is like a game, chess, for example. The

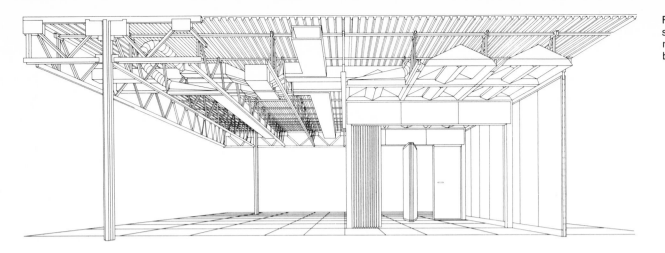

Fig. 7-20   SCSD was the first of a series of building systems that moved away from specific hardware to a more general consideration of components and building types.

different parts of the house are the board and pieces. As in chess, their ability to interact with other parts is determined by rules for their use. What results from such a game depends very much on the players; the game is played out rather than predetermined.

The Techbuilt House is an example of this type of approach. So is the SCSD (School Construction System Development) project developed by Ezra Ehrenkrantz in the 1960s (Fig. 7-20). Both involve a kit-of-parts and rules for its use. Building Systems Development, Ehrenkrantz's firm, has carried the game analogy forward by concentrating on rules rather than on the creation of custom components or completed buildings.

The direction of these analogies is away from the literalness of Deinocrates—the inhuman city in human form. But translating even the chess game analogy to built form has been problematic. It has often resulted in structures that provide flexibility and diversity, but within a framework that—crammed with redundant structure and utilities—seems ungainly and visually heavy. The artistry that accompanies a reconsideration of housing and housing production must also be brought into play in developing and applying these analogies.

We cannot simply apply analogies blindly, or think them up in isolation. Each has to grow out of a consideration of the community—its technology, its resources, its desires. A building which provides more flexibility than anyone wants, or needs, at a higher cost than anyone can afford, in a form that nobody likes, is not likely to find favor with its neighbors, regardless of the merits of the analogy that led to it. Analogies themselves are ambiguous clues— we have to try to understand them in light of the whole story.

LOOKING FORWARD

The desire to embellish the utilitarian—to go further with a technology than was originally intended—has always stretched the imagination and ingenuity of the mechanic. The same is true in building construction: churches, stadiums, greenhouses and Crystal Palaces— not the need for shelter—have led us to new tools and methods. It is our aesthetic curiosity rather than basic necessity that generates innovation and invention. Technology is closer to art than to science—it is an art that enriches our daily lives.

We had come to believe that housing is an end in itself—something monstrous that comes to life full grown and dies unchanged. Resigned to this belief, we shuffled from one house to another. But now we are beginning to understand that housing is a process—that a house is something that is born, matures, prospers, sickens, decays and dies, as a result of its own makeup and our treatment of it.

The construction of a house is the beginning of a process that can last hundreds of years. We know from the evidence of our existing housing stock that much housing is older than the oldest among us, yet still capable of meeting new living patterns and demands. We know from the urban homesteading experience that some buildings can support change. We know from the experience of industrial loft conversion that some buildings can change uses completely. When these buildings were first built, someone was able to see beyond the crush of the tenement or the noise of machinery to another era and another set of people altogether. The result was buildings that can support another's dreams.

Industrialization can be a means to our own self expression, a way for us to have an impact on housing and bring it into correspondence with our expectations. Industrialization can also be the means to such housing—a framework for a technology that allows us to magnify our self-expression, giving form to our changing image of what our house should be. This can be the goal of housing industrialization and housing technology: to be housed as we like, when we like.

Our image of industrialization has been stuck in the rut of the linear assembly line—an industrial method conceived at a time when inadequate equipment and methods forced the tradeoff between production and diversity. As long as we continue to think of industrialization in this linear way, we will keep missing the point that technology has changed, that we need not think in terms of products that are standard and repetitive, or remain chained to an industrial process that gives us only numerical satisfaction.

Housing lies at the frontier between the individual and society. The person and the community each have a role in determining the form of housing, and their interaction should have the quality of a conversation, each party hearing the other. The individual householder today is playing Charley McCarthy to an institutional Edgar Bergen. Developers, contractors, banks, building and planning departments and other organizations and agencies dominate the conversation, and have too much say in the determination of housing patterns and arrangements.

Housing technology can be "friendly," inviting us to use it, eager to help us in every way. The tools, products and equipment that go into the house are already "friendly" to the contractor and the construction worker. Building materials are already "friendly" to the home owner. But this friendliness has been limited to initial construction or to maintenance, and the emphasis has been on how quickly a person can do a job, rather than on how creatively he or she can use the technology available to alter the living environment or embellish it. A technology that is "friendly" to the user and an industrial process that provides productivity, variety, and diversity can do much to reestablish an equality of interaction between *all* those involved in the housing process. We do not really need a technical revolution. We need a switch in the way we think about housing and housing production.

If we can picture forms of housing—and housing processes—that are capable of meeting unpredictable and varied needs, and if we can imagine the kinds of resources whose richness corresponds to the fertility of the human imagination, then we can allow our housing and all the things that go into it to flow in the direction of our thoughts. We can begin with what we have now: as we discover what it is we need—and as we embellish what we have—the rest will fall into place.

Bibliography

Books

Bender, Richard, *A Crack in the Rear-View Mirror: A View of Industrialized Building.* New York: Van Nostrand Reinhold, 1973.

Bruce, Alfred and Sandbank, Harold, *A History of Prefabrication.* New York, Arno Press, 1972.

Cutler, Laurence S. and Cutler, Sherrie Stephens, *Handbook of Housing Systems for Designers and Developers.* New York: Van Nostrand Reinhold, 1974.

Habraken, N. J., *Supports.* New York: Praeger, 1972.

Kelly, Burnham, *The Prefabrication of Houses.* New York: Technology Press and John Wiley, 1951.

Le Corbusier, *The Marseilles Block.* London: Harvill Press, 1953.

Periodicals and Reports

Anon, "Operation breakthrough," *Architectural Record* (April, 1970).

Benet, James et al., *SCSD: The Project and the Schools,* Educational Facilities Laboratories, New York, 1967.

Boice, John, *A History and Evaluation of SCSD,* Building Systems Information Clearinghouse, Menlo Park, Calif.—n.d.

Building the American City: Report of the National Commission on Urban Problems ("The Douglas Commission"). Washington, D.C.: U.S. Government Printing Office, 1968.

A Decent Home: Report of the President's Committee on Urban Problems ("The Kaiser Committee"). Washington, D.C.: U.S. Government Printing Office, 1968.

189

8
Interiors—Accommodating Diversity

Sam Davis and Cathy Simon

"Dinner will be slightly delayed—jammed partition."

Sociologists generalize about the characteristics and needs of certain categories of users; market research analysts assess the goals and aspirations of various consumer groups. Their statements generate programs which (ultimately) determine the forms of available housing from which most users must choose their dwellings. Custom designed houses are generally financially out of reach.

The marvelous diversity of possible human activity is excluded from consideration for most new multifamily housing. Group characteristics take no account, for example, of whether a person might want to build furniture, or have a home office, or bathe communally, or weave tapestries, or play chamber music, or paint, or restore automobiles, or raise exotic birds or have a garden. Most available multifamily housing types cannot accommodate one of these variations from the "norm," let alone three or four.

The framework approach discussed in the previous chapter recognizes these restrictions in housing and overcomes the problem by allowing variation within each household. This approach not withstanding, building for large aggregates of people usually results in a restricted container, limited to housing certain

essential human activities—cooking and eating, bathing, relaxing, sleeping, securing goods. If such housing includes transitional *exterior* spaces (front yard, front porch, vestibule, front door which permit the occupant to impose his own symbolic imagery upon the anonymous dwelling) general acceptability may be obtained. Yet, even in the most responsive mass housing built thus far, the *interior* divisions severely limit diversity and choice.

The sizes, numbers, and often the configuration of interior spaces are regulated by code or prescribed by government agencies in subsidized housing, and by financial institutions in commercial markets. These criteria indicate how much space is necessary for each typical function and for appropriate (often minimal) equipment and furnishings. It is not uncommon, for example, for an elderly person to be unable to fit old (fashioned) furniture into a modern housing unit. Although intended for public protection, these standards have a severe negative side effect. They restrict possible configurations within the unit, legislate minima as the norm, and perpetuate the use of single-function furniture. Available choices are limited to style, materials, and color of artifacts and do not include the use of space, or adding to or substantially altering activities within the

dwelling. Though undeniably convenient to many, the proliferation of rigidly subdivided containers is frustrating and constraining to others. Change in domestic environments can currently be achieved only by moving; real variety and adaptability are available only to those who can afford to design and build their own house.

Historical Aspects of the House

One reason for most Americans' tenacious preference for the single family house is its place in our history and in the Anglo-Saxon world: a house is an enclave of security. A house was historically a statement about property, wealth and social status, and remains so today. Ignoring changing twentieth century lifestyles, the rural or semirural house was an excellent example of adaptability, of resolution of changing needs over a family's life. On a large plot of land, insulated by open space, a house could expand and contract as necessary. A room or wing would be added in a rambling sort of way, and could more easily be closed up when not in use (Fig. 8-3). The luxury of abundant space was common, and special ceremonial spaces could be accommodated. It was not unusual for a large country house to contain an elegant ballroom, used only once or twice a year.

Fig. 8-3 Rambling country house. Spaces could be added at will and closed off if unused.

Fig. 8-4 Galerie des Glaces at Versailles. Each room houses objects suggesting appropriate behavior.

In both their conception and their organization, houses today reflect these rural and semirural models, rather than their equally historical urban counterparts. In his article, "Transformations of the Interior," Kenneth Frampton describes how current feelings for housing reflect associations and experiences of the past. Frampton points out the complex development sequence of the domestic (or residential) interior from medieval times to the futuristic projections of Italian designers of the 1970s. Citing Versailles, he outlines an ancestor of modern housing (Fig. 8-4):

> Behind the crystalline illusion of the hall of mirrors, however, there lay the unhygienic labyrinth of the palace itself. Versailles effectively transformed the traditional all-purpose plan of the Renaissance palace into a complex spatial etiquette; the articulation of a pleasure dome into a caravansary of the State. From now on the *enfilade* begins to comprise a sequence of rooms each housing objects which denote specific sets of behavior; the library, the picture gallery, the gaming room, the billiard room, the orangery, the conservatory, etc.[1]

This prerevolutionary "spatial etiquette" led directly to the Victorian interior (Fig. 8-5):

> . . . codification in stone of the myth of Victorian chivalry and the construction of class structure. The meticulous designation of domestic space to specific social ends reaches its limit in this development with its elaborate differentiation of the interior into entrance hall, drawing room, morning room, gun room, billiard room, smoking room, library, gallery, bedroom, dressing room, ballroom, schoolroom, chapel and so on.[2]

In southern, middle Atlantic and northeastern America, these considerations were included, often on a reduced scale, in large houses characterized by the casual quality of American life, a love of the picturesque, and a freer definition of function. Yet there were parlors from which children were forbidden, music rooms, great halls, inglenooks and so on.

Combined with responses to modern lifestyles, materials, and costs, much of today's housing derives from these earlier house types. A typical dwelling unit with its prescribed spatial divisions is a condensation of the historical single family house pattern in which the number of specific rooms—and functions—represents the affluence of the owner. Typically, there is a game room for recreation, a breakfast room

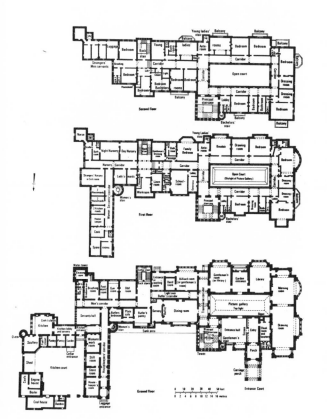

for morning meals, a dining room for formal eating, a parlor, a solarium, and so forth. Each room designates a certain behavior, and when a new activity is desired, the participants simply change settings. The range of choice and possible events in such an environment expands as one's affluence increases. In the everyman version of this stately situation each function is still desired, yet the number of spatial alternatives has been reduced. Furthermore, different family members wishing to engage in separate activities must do so within the same space. This housing form no longer resolves but creates conflicts.

Today's House: Conflict and Change

William Michelson describes a dwelling as an "opportunity structure," meaning that "the arrangement of physical space, while not determining behavior, provides more or less opportunity for behavior to occur."[3] While available space does not necessarily determine which activities will occur, the lack of it can preclude them. The reduction of the dwelling into a few very specific spaces has radically reduced the diversity of human activity the dwelling can support.

In her book, *With Man in Mind*, Constance Perin similarly discusses the space within the building as having "adaptive costs." When rooms are rigidly defined, the building has a high adaptive cost:

Contemporary alienation from and frustration with the physical environment stem, in these terms, from authoritarian environments imposed on human purposes that really require a diversity of places and spaces in order to be carried out without unwarranted adaptive cost. Overly articulated environments, at the other extreme, fail to accommodate the full range of purposes.[4]

Aside from a desired change in locale or place of employment, four types of interrelated change are most likely to require a move if the dwelling is incapable of *long-term* or life cycle flexibility.

The first major change is household size. Marriages occur, one or more children arrive, goods are acquired, children become independent and need their "own space," aging parents need accommodation, children leave home, grandchildren visit for the summer, and so on. This simplified scenario is but one of many possible life patterns. Each step has monumental spatial implications for the dwelling. For example, as children grow up, gaining independence and freedom of movement, their spatial needs increase dramatically. Problems arise when sharing a room and a younger sibling suddenly becomes intolerable, when children want a place to entertain their friends, when activities of parents and children conflict. If children go away to school or college, they leave their space ambiguously available. When they leave home more or less permanently, their space may become vestigial. In a typical cycle and typical habitation, several moves may be necessary to avoid major conflicts. Because the dwelling cannot adapt to change, the people must, often with severe consequences.

The second common type of change is an alteration in lifestyle. As people grow older, socioeconomic status, aspirations, values and self-definition change. Symbols of self which may have been appropriate at 25 become less so at 50. The dwelling must continue to fulfill these psychological needs which vary tremendously. People need to imprint their houses with their own self-image. Although the need to assert one's affluence and social position is often met by the location of the house, its character, condition and uniqueness also play an important role. For example numerous San Franciscans have distinctively painted their builder Victorian row houses to stand out from the others. By selective treatment of detail and surfaces, identical houses can be differentiated (Fig. 8-6). The profound need for a "personal statement" may be seen where people have applied symbols (moldings, railings, half-timbering, colonial pediments, false fireplaces, eclectic furniture) to otherwise anonymous structures.

This psychological need to present an image to the world is summarized in Venturi and Rauch's recent Bicentennial exhibition, "Signs of Life: Symbols in the American City," in Washington, D.C., which contains a section called "Home," devoted to the dwelling. It shows typical exteriors of a "Colonial," a suburban tract house, a working class row house, and their corresponding interiors. The three examples are lush with eclectic details and evocative ornament (Fig. 8-7). Of these Denise Scott Brown has said:

We hope people will recognize the rich heritage of themes that repeat themselves in all three rooms. They all come out of the same eighteenth- and nineteenth-century sources . . . Symbolic times, rural life, patriotic themes and estates of the rich. What it communicates is largely about social status, social aspirations, personal identity and nostalgia for rural life . . .[5]

Changing equipment is a third consideration affecting residential interiors. In this country's world of marketing and appliances, fashions for the home and its furnishings change daily. Whereas kitchens used to be composed of free-standing elements—stove, sink, refrigerator, counter—now they most frequently include such "essential" items as built-in cooktop and wall oven, dishwasher, disposal and trash compactor. Sound equipment and television sets, washer–dryers, wet bars and Jacuzzis, vacuum systems, heating systems, and fire and intrusion alarms—all these are now commonly incorporated into the building shell and are relatively difficult to add later. Changes in equipment which involve alterations to services—electrical, plumbing, gas—are expensive and complicated.

Finally, over time a dweller's desired activities may diverge from the sociologists' "norm." A person may acquire many interests having important spatial implications. Music—listening and recreational playing— may become a passion for someone. Several times a week a person may play piano informally with friends.

194

Fig. 8-6 Victorian houses in San Francisco. Differentiation of similar façades to make a personal statement.

Fig. 8-7 Urban row house interior giving symbolic messages.

A piano consumes substantial space as do four chamber musicians with seats, music stands and instruments.

Activities develop and are continually redefined. Upon leaving home for the first time, a person may know nothing about cooking. Soon food preparation becomes an immensely relaxing and satisfying activity. Cooking and eating dinner becomes a valued time when the events of the day can be rethought and discussed, when assembling a meal is a shared experience, when the family spends time together. How can this occur if the "kitchen" was designed for efficiency, for one person alone making a minimum number of steps, for some market researcher's sterile notions of a food preparation center?

In addition to *long-term flexibility*, the need for alteration of the dwelling occurs in other time frames. Although not necessitating a major move, lack of potential for change can still cause conflicts and dissatisfaction with the living environment. *Short-term* flexibility allows the dwelling to change for various ceremonial and social events, such as an elegant dinner party or holiday celebration or wedding. *Medium-term* flexibility is necessary for temporary changes in life patterns such as the need

195

to accommodate overnight or weekend visitors, or an ill or handicapped person. The potential for the house to accept changes over various time spans (long, medium, or short) is particularly critical and difficult when the activity is either social, needs specialized equipment, or has specific space requirements.

Cooking–dining is a complex human activity often involving social ceremony as well as specific equipment. Its nature, scope and spatial demands vary tremendously from the microwave oven and frozen dinner eaten informally in front of the television, to elaborately conceived and prepared dinners for parties, to group cooking projects and leisurely family meals with one or two guests. Parents may want to eat with the children or not, children with friends, and so on. People may desire informal meals most of the time, but on occasion may also want to entertain.

Bathrooms generally conform to the most rigid notions of hygiene and waste elimination. Because of typically restricted space, it is difficult if not impossible for family members to use a bathroom simultaneously. Any possible alternative bathing styles, such as Japanese baths, hot tubs, steam baths, even separate showers

are precluded in most common housing forms. Like cooking, variety and flexibility in bathing modes are made difficult by the nature of the equipment and need for connections to outside services.

The house as a workshop is another problem area. While many activities, such as stamp collecting, drawing, or reading require little room or equipment, many others demand space and special lighting or devices. Carpentry, dance, automobile repair, sewing, painting, sculpture, weaving, pottery, photography, indoor gardening, restoring furniture and on and on—consume space. Without it they must either be abandoned, be removed from the home, or conflict with the activities of others causing internal problems or a reordering of family priorities. In the worst situations, they cannot happen; in marginal cases adaptive costs are high; in the best circumstances, activities are accommodated and lives enriched.

RESOLUTIONS WITHIN THE ENCLOSURE

The dwelling must continue to fulfill certain basic needs, some of which are culturally defined. It must give shelter from the elements as well as a sense of security and protection.

It must provide for various activities such as bathing, sleeping, eating, child nurturing and lovemaking. It is a setting for an entire range of simple, repetitive domestic functions and as such, a spatial framework for people's everyday lives.

Beyond this the house must positively support and promote change rather than force users to restrict or abandon desired activities. In order to reduce the conflicts which arise from both minimal and highly defined spaces, a number of resolutions are possible which permit change and diversity. These resolutions include perceptual methods for creating privacy, actually increasing or reallocating existing space, reconceptualizing household equipment and reorganizing volume. In addition there are planning strategies which have less to do with the specific physical aspects of the dwelling than with a planning process which involves the user in decisions about the dwelling's configuration and ambience. These resolutions are often interrelated. In reallocating space within a given volume, for example, it may be necessary to rethink the nature of the appliances within that space as well. Although these ideas will be treated in separate sections, they should not be seen as mutually exclusive.

Fig. 8-8 Office landscape. Minimum spatial definition and the illusion of more personal space.

Fig. 8-9 The Japanese house. Light weight walls and floor mats determine spatial boundaries of activities.

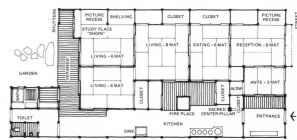

Perceptual Resolution: Privacy

In Western society, the concept of privacy implies actual separation. Visual and aural barriers are valued as a means to isolate activities. Yet another great virtue of older single family houses, with their range of separate but similar family living rooms, is the real physical privacy they provide for potentially conflicting simultaneous activities. Robert Sommer in his book, *Personal Space,* investigated the ability of humans to construct mental definitions of space and territory within which they feel secure and comfortable. The extent of these mental spatial constructs is culturally determined and may vary depending on the occasion.

Similar to "personal space," privacy may be redefined in a less simplistic and less literally physical manner. "Psychological privacy" implies the "use of social conventions and mental barriers to negate the sensory inputs the mind is receiving."[6] With reduced space in the home and an increasing need for simultaneous activities within the same space, the ability of people to develop a concept of psychological privacy becomes extremely important. Informal open plan living in which living room, dining room, and kitchen are a continuous space

would be utterly unsatisfactory if it were not for our ability to filter out certain "sensory inputs." Increasingly, psychological privacy has been reinforced by the minimal definition of boundaries through lighting, arrangement of furniture or changes of materials. In both offices and schools, this technique permits more efficient utilization of space, greater flexibility, heightened communication when desired, and gives the illusion of greater available area (Fig. 8-8).

In certain respects, open planning is analogous to the definition of separation in Japan. In the traditional Japanese house, for example, movable lightweight walls and simple floor mats are used to define and enclose various activities (Fig. 8-9). They can be rearranged quickly and simply to allow for new activities. Privacy derives more from conventional, symbolic aspects of separation than from the physical barrier in itself.

Although this perceptual resolution of the problems of choice and flexibility is simple and efficient in material expenditure, its use depends on the nature of the potentially conflicting activities. While appropriate in spaces where cooking, watching television and reading are

simultaneous activities, as activities become louder, involve more people or create increased odors, the limits of this technique are reached. At that point, high "adaptive costs" are incurred, conflicts arise, and activities must again be separated by actual physical barriers.

Extended Space Resolution

The typical and atypical dwellers in multifamily housing face static housing configurations. The freedom inherent in the traditional single family house, to extend the dwelling by adding space, is not available. Yet, there have been attempts, mostly in Europe, to implement long-term dwelling size changes. In high density, high-rise buildings there has been limited experimentation with overbuilding the structural framework to allow for expansion (Fig. 8-10). In row houses, the walls between units may simply be extended to a fixed point of ultimate growth, and extra space be left as private outdoor yard until such time as it is enclosed (Fig. 8-11). In this country, in existing low-rise, high density housing such as St. Francis Square in San Francisco, interior space has been added to the unit by enclosing the large outdoor terrace–balcony provided by the architects (Fig. 1-34). The problem with the latter two methods

Fig. 8-10 Overbuilding the structural frame for future expansion and change.

Fig. 8-11 Extended space in row houses serves as private outdoor space until enclosed.

Fig. 8-12 The greenhouse section. A simple and commercially available method of adding space.

is that as the family grows and its need for interior space increases, so does its need for the private outdoor space consumed by the interior expansion.

Within limits, small spaces may be added to existing houses or apartments: prefabricated lean-to greenhouses, bay windows, entry vestibules—all are commercially available (Fig. 8-12). Although their contribution to the dwelling's actual size is minimal, these add-ons do extend the space of the dwelling visually and psychologically. The greenhouse enclosure may be a play space during inclement weather, a place for interior gardening or simply an extended living space with a different light quality.

Resolution: Space Reallocation

Although not yet common in this country, experiments with choice and change in high density housing have been carried out in Europe. Most include user participation in decision making and apply the technology of movable walls. These are positioned at the user's request before occupying the dwelling.

In a thorough study of European flexibility experiments, architects Rabeneck, Sheppard and Town discovered that the user's realization

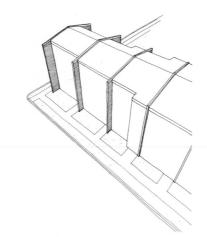

that real choices existed led to a high degree of satisfaction, even when the potential for variety was not fully exploited. In many apartments within the same structure, plans were quite similar, reflecting the homogeneous nature of the residents and the commonality of their lifestyles. These plans could have been developed by an architect and social scientist team. In a significant number of cases, however, the residents developed plans unlike anything an architect would have devised for the same space. Often a dwelling was designed around specific furniture while in other cases the dwelling was zoned into two living spaces that allowed for simultaneous activities and a high degree of privacy.

In planning flexible multifamily housing, special care must be taken that the user's arrangements correspond to fire exits, window openings and various mechanical systems. In certain experiments, the first users were given limited choices about the actual configuration of exterior walls and the nature of openings. In most cases air-conditioning systems were located subsequent to the final dwelling layout and, therefore, restricted future change. This limitation was justified on the assumption that providing choices would enhance user satisfaction and reduce turnover.

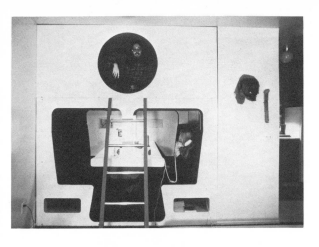

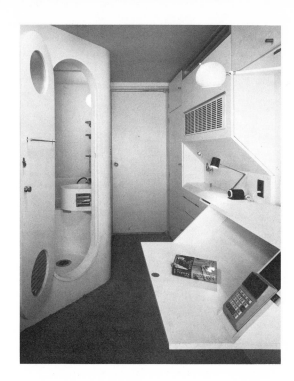

Fig. 8-13 Dining room converted to both dining and sleeping space. the design "frees" the bedroom for studio space.

Fig. 8-14 Japanese capsule dwelling. Equipment, walls, and the space within are conceptually inseparable.

Fig. 8-15 (Axonometric drawing of Fig. 8-14.)

In the future it may be possible to employ technologies currently used in other building types to provide greater housing flexibility. A raised modular "computer floor," for example, would allow electrical outlets and heating to be placed anywhere in a dwelling and changed with relative ease. Flexible plumbing could be placed beneath such a floor so that even kitchens and bathrooms could be freely located.

Space reallocation can take another form by simply rethinking the use of existing space and volume. Consider the case of a young couple in a typical two-bedroom apartment. Each is an artist and wants a separate, uncluttered "studio" space. By analyzing domestic functions and daily living patterns, they discover that sleeping and eating do not occur simultaneously as a general rule, and that sitting at a dining room table takes five feet of head room, while sleeping requires only three. They therefore convert their two "bedrooms" into individual studios, and build a sleeping loft within the dining room (Fig. 8-13). In open-plan apartment spaces, the added definition of the dining enclosure may be considered a positive feature. Although this order of invention entails a high adaptive cost, it frees the bedroom spaces for an alternative use.

Similar examples may be found, especially in high density situations where good housing is hard to find, where neighborhood is highly valued, and where moving cannot solve a housing problem. Particularly in older buildings, such as New York's brownstones or San Francisco's Victorians, space within the dwelling unit can be reallocated. Thus, a family with two children can choose to continue living in two large rooms plus kitchen by building a series of sleeping lofts. These provide privacy and free the remaining floor space for a variety of uses. The generous vertical dimensions and spacious proportions of the rooms make such resolutions possible.

Equipment Reconceptualized

The Japanese have developed a number of capsule dwellings which incorporate functional equipment into the skin of the enclosure. The equipment, enclosure, and the space within are conceived as an integrated whole. conceptually inseparable (Figs. 8-14 and 8-15). Similarly, boats and recreational vehicles optimize the use of limited space. The interior must accommodate conventional living functions, while the shell must permit mobility and encompass the devices necessary to support the activities within. Multiple use of a single space is necessary—living rooms become dining

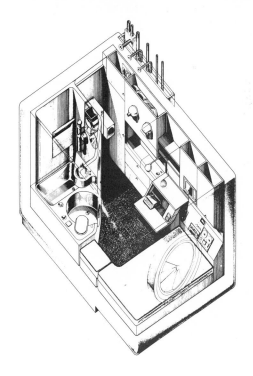

Fig. 8-16   Kit of storage components combine to make custom apartments.

Fig. 8-17   Piano bed. A multiuse object of limited usefulness.

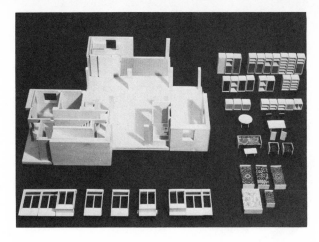

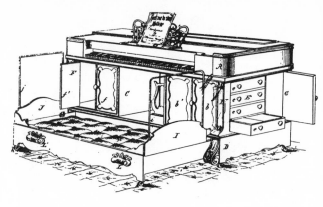

rooms and bedrooms. Every inch of the volume is explicitly organized. These environments have higher adaptive costs than conventional dwellings since there is only one setting for all activities and there must be some preparation before an activity may begin. Since these environments are recreational, however, fewer functions need be accommodated and reduced privacy is more acceptable than in the "normal" dwelling.

Because of their efficient space planning and the coordination of equipment and space, the capsule dwelling and recreational vehicle have become models for certain popularly accepted devices. With increasing frequency, modular component systems are being used both to define space and to incorporate storage and other functions. In defining space the equipment becomes a wall, as well as supplying some needed functional requirement like storage or an audiovisual center. Since it still remains "furniture" and not structure, such multiuse equipment may be moved at will allowing for flexibility. Furthermore, since the device incorporates equipment which would otherwise have to be placed within the space, the space itself is now "freed" for other uses. Portions of the restricted dwelling volume are thereby reclaimed.

Architect Jan Wampler used this technique in the renovation of an old apartment building in Boston (see p. 190 and Fig. 8-16).Each resident was given a kit of storage wall components and, with the help of the architect as an "environmental consultant," each family designed its dwelling within the confines of the existing structure. The strategy does not have to be limited to vertical surfaces. Le Corbusier used varied floor heights to conceal a roll-away bed stored under the raised floor of the adjacent apartment.

The domestic application of multiuse objects has had a long history. The advent of such devices is usually associated with the need for mobility, extremely limited space, and love of gadgetry. The lack of space in frontier and urban dwellings also elicited elaborate inventions. Their appeal is primarily their innate economy, like the common convertible bed, but historically other combinations have not been so straightforward. As Giedion points out in *Mechanization Takes Command,* the inventions have often approached the absurd. One of the most bizarre is the "piano bed," which incorporates storage, wash basin, bed, and a piano (Fig. 8-17). The trend toward convertible furnishings continued through the heyday of

American railroads, where traveler's comfort on long trips had to be accommodated. The Pullman sleeper was the direct predecessor to the pleasure craft and recreational vehicle of today.

As costs rise and square footage declines, multiuse furniture gains popularity. The familiar hide-a-bed which can change a living space into a bedroom embodies short-term flexibility with spatial implications, and new devices incorporating storage and entertainment equipment (television, stereo, recordings, bars, etc.) now occupy a prominent position in more and more dwellings. Often these objects are large and free-standing with each surface supporting an activity in adjacent areas [Figs. 8-18(a) and 8-18(b)].

Another aspect of the reconceptualization of equipment is miniaturization. Similar to multiuse furniture and seen commonly in boats and recreational vehicles, the reduction of equipment size is primarily a space-saving technique. Applied to traditional dwelling environments, this approach yields other advantages which may reduce conflicts and increase choices. A tiny kitchen can either be hidden within a wall or

Figs. 8-18 (a) and (b) Free-standing multiuse objects take up prominent positions and service the space on many sides.

Figs. 8-19 (a) and (b) Miniaturized fold-out kitchen. Many such devices may become affordable making any room a kitchen.

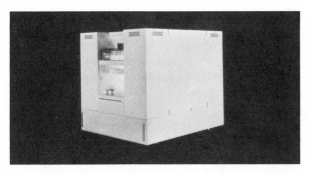

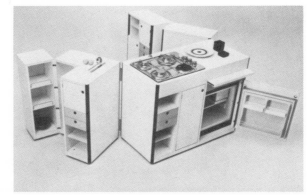

packaged as a compact, fold-up object [Figs. 8-19(a) and 8-19(b)]. Although luxury is often associated with large kitchens, miniaturized kitchens, superimposed upon flexible plumbing connections, may be moved throughout the dwelling allowing any space to become an cooking–dining area. A kitchen may even be miniaturized to the point where two kitchens become feasible, one for entertaining or for formal family meals, another for less elaborate food preparation. Children may be able to have their own kitchen if they develop an interest in cooking; a kitchen could be moved to the center of a space so that the hosts would not have to be isolated from their guests or so the guests could also participate. When the food preparation is completed the kitchen can be moved, or folded and put away. Technologies that could provide such flexibility already exist. Movable sinks with detachable supply and waste lines can plug into a floor with multiple plumbing connections in numerous subfloor locations.

Serious difficulties are encountered with the short-term flexibility designed into multiuse objects, movable walls, storage devices, miniaturized and highly mobile equipment. The nature of activities and events is understood

201

Fig. 8-20 The appropriate equipment for social occasions may become confused as short-term flexibility becomes more prominent.

through the use of mutually accepted and recognized environmental cues. These are included in building structure, in furnishings (fixed or movable) and in the relationship of these to each other and to the participants. Easily and continuously changing environments can become confusing. "As members of this culture we carry certain images as to the proprieties of the occasion and how it relates to the physical place which contains it. Is it appropriate for the dinner party to be held in the bedroom?"[7] A startling reversal of environmental expectations occurs in Luis Bunuel's film, *The Phantom of Liberty*, where behavioral conventions of dining room and toilet are exchanged (Fig. 8-20).

Space Reconceptualized

Limited spatial configurations have restricted the dwelling, not only in its ability to accommodate choice and change, but also in the manner in which space is understood and used. Although new techniques for reconceptualizing space are currently exemplified in specialized and isolated instances, their impact will influence future developments.

Partial spatial definition can add a sense of space to otherwise restricted environments, can

Fig. 8-21 The breakfast room at Lincoln's Inn Fields by Sir John Soane. Partial enclosure enough to define activity within a larger context.

Fig. 8-22 Tugendhat House dining room by Mies Van der Rohe. Minimal definition of activity area within larger space.

enhance the activities performed, and can give symbolic value and meaning to ordinary events. Sir John Soane often used partial spatial definition to emphasize the sense of enclosure of activities, with the implication of a larger space beyond, as in his Breakfast Room at Lincoln's Inn Fields. In this example, the act of eating is given an enriching shape and particularity (Fig. 8-21). By contrasting the actual space enclosure with the area beyond, the room is extended and redefined. In a similar way, Mies Van der Rohe used a curved marble wall in his Tugendhat house to define the dining space, while maintaining it as part of the larger volume of the house (Fig. 8-22). The curved plane itself becomes a wall, a screen, a beautiful object, functioning from within and without, giving a sense of scale and intimacy to the dining area. It allows the interconnected spaces of the house to flow smoothly from an open to a partially enclosed form.

The canopy bed is the paradigm for the phenomenon of implied spatial definition and symbolic value of interior space. Referentially religious (the sacred vault of heaven, the canopy of the Jewish wedding ceremony, the baldacchino), the canopy bed performs a symbolic function as well as providing shelter, warmth, security, and privacy. In effect, it becomes a

Fig. 8-23　New Canaan House by Philip Johnson. The big room with smaller volumes within.

Fig. 8-24　Interior "house" incorporates kitchen, bath, sleeping, and storage.

Fig. 8-25　Parking a fully equipped recreational vehicle *within* a large space.

Fig. 8-26　Parking a fully equipped recreational vehicle *next to* a large volume.

tiny, bed-sized room within a larger space. Its small scale heightens the sense of protection and safety it embodies, while by contast, enlarging the space that contains it.

The concept of a "big room" which contains encapsulated smaller functional volumes has had other applications. The Farnsworth house by Mies Van der Rohe and Philip Johnson's New Canaan house are simple volumes of glass and steel interrupted only by a free-standing self-contained bathroom–kitchen (Fig. 8-23). Also comparable, at least conceptually, is the interior of the Sea Ranch condominium by MLTW. The "little house" not only modulates the space and supports the adjacent activities, but also incorporates and encloses all of the dwelling equipment (bath, kitchen, storage) (Fig. 8-24). Charles Moore sees this smaller interior "house" as a place of retreat and con-trol for the user, as well as a place to contain and display the artifacts of the household.

In *The Place of Houses*, Moore categorizes domestic spaces into the "machines' domain" and "our domain," a separation similar to Louis Kahn's "served and servant spaces." This view of interior space gave rise to Moore's Sea Ranch interior. It also allows for a new vision

Fig. 8-27 A simple core includes kitchen and bathrooms
(white part) with uninterrupted volumes attached
(wood part).

Fig. 8-28

of the home similar in intent to the famous
custom houses already discussed, but achieving
aspects of choice and change in addition to
their spatial characteristics. The "machine
spaces" can either be a condensed appendage
to the house or a compact island within it,
leaving the remainder of the dwelling a
flexible activity area.

Imagine, for example, parking a well-equipped
recreational vehicle with all the necessary functional equipment within a large volume (Fig.
8-25). The space around the machine is open and
flexible and the area may be continually
altered by moving the vehicle within the space.
Another analogy is parking the vehicle next to
the large space so that the entire volume is
open and free to change (Fig. 8-26). This approach is exemplified by the mobile home designed by Davis/Glass/Shen (Figs. 9-29, 9-30,
and 9-31) and the house by Booth and Nagle
as a promotional model for a wood company
(Figs. 8-27 and 8-28). In each case, the
"machines" are incorporated into a compact
unit and the remaining free space is attached
and changeable. A proposal by Danish architect
Peter Stephenson discussed in the previous
chapter used a series of large, masonry
"cavity walls" as the basis of the house. The

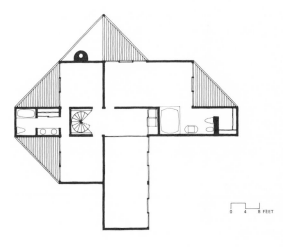

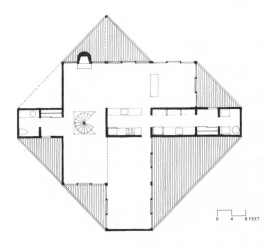

Fig. 8-29   Le Corbusier's development at Pessac. Kitchen and bathrooms are reduced to efficient "laboratories" allowing increased area for other activities.

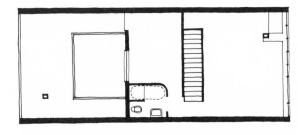

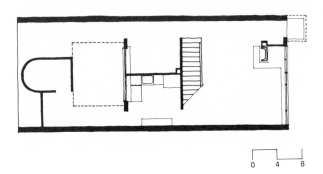

room-sized cavities contain the fixed equipment while allowing individual space interpretations to be attached at the discretion of the user (Figs. 7-17 and 7-18).

As described in Boudon's *Lived in Architecture*, Le Corbusier's development at Pessac reflects a similar approach (Fig. 8-29).

> . . . where Le Corbusier departed from normal practice was in his insistence on extremely small areas for purely functional rooms such as kitchens and bathrooms. In these rooms, which he regarded as "laboratories" and which were inspired by the galleys and bathrooms in ocean liners and Pullman cars, every object had its proper place and not a square centimetre was wasted. The space saved in this way was used to enlarge the other rooms in the house. [8]

These examples assume that the machine domains which incorporate kitchens and baths will not themselves be elements of change and flexibility, unless, of course, they are applied in a way which would allow replacement or renewal like traditional furniture. Like the framework approach, these solutions imply that certain aspects of the interior need not be alterable while other aspects must be capable

of continuous change. As the "machine spaces" become readily available consumer objects with accompanying features of obsolescence and impermanence, an interior can be developed which comprises many of the features of the custom houses of Mies, Johnson, Moore, yet differs from these in style and intent. The futuristic "superfurniture" of the recent Italian designers are "machines" which fit within a larger volume, contain the essentials of the house, and modulate the space around them; however, they are conceived as consumer objects of such neutrality that their existence is almost incidental to the activities around them (Fig. 8-30). As designer Ettore Sottsass explains it, "Let's say that the idea is to succeed in making furniture from which we feel so detached, so disinterested and so uninvolved that it is of absolutely no importance to us. That is, the form is—at least in intention—designed so that after a time it fades away and disappears." [9] Conceptually at least, the neutral and intentionally impersonal forms of the "new domestic landscape" engender a deeper relationship with the event than with the object.

In a culture where objects have always played an important role as reflections of our self-image,

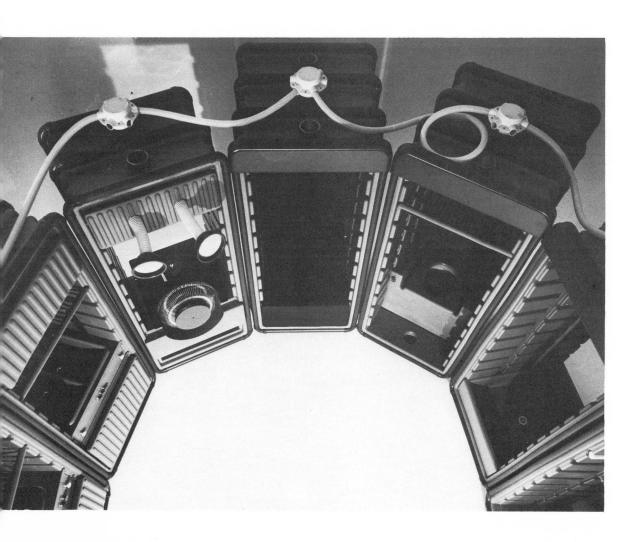

it is doubtful that impersonal objects will be acceptable until there is no longer a need for manifestation of egos through belongings. In contrast to the Italian designs, Charles Moore's "little houses" encourage and support our current need for display.

Though highly formal and specifically designed, neutral objects may be infinitely rearranged to provide for any possible configuration. As Columbo wrote:

> The space within this unit should be dynamic; that is, it should be in a continual state of transformation, so that a cubic space smaller than a conventional norm can be nevertheless exploited to the maximum, with a maximum economy in its interior arrangement. At this point, one can easily envisage the form that such a proposal should take; a series of suitably equipped furnishing units, freely placed in their allocated areas. Such furnishing units, developed to serve the various functions of the home and private life, have been differentiated so that, in turn, they may be flexible enough to be adapted to various kinds of space or to differing requirements.[10]

Fig. 8-31 "Superfurniture" accommodates varying degrees of flexibility and "function according to the various moments in which they are in use."

Fig. 8-32 A number of large-scale pieces, placed within an uninterrupted volume, creates a variety of spaces and relationships between activities.

Fig. 8-33 Kitchen pod. The entire room is movable within the interior space.

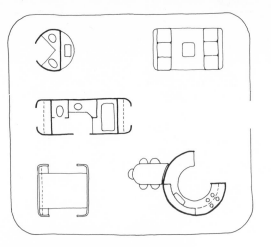

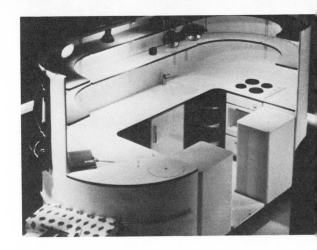

"Superfurniture" of the type suggested by the Italian designers allows for varying degrees of flexibility (Fig. 8-31). Objects may be pulled out or hidden away, depending on the desired activity: "They function according to the various moments in which they are in use."[11] Long-term flexibility is achieved by the positioning of the units within an unspecified enclosure, thereby creating free spaces between the object and the edges of the dwelling. If many superfurnitures or room pods are used, the nature of the dwelling space varies with the relative position of each device (Fig. 8-32).

There is little superfurniture on the market, even though kitchen and sleeping pods have been proposed and prototypes have appeared at exhibitions (Fig. 8-33). Only a bathroom pod is available commercially, but its location is not flexible nor does it have the potential for easy change within enclosures. Bathroom pods have been used in apartment renovation where they can be quickly added to an existing structure and connected to available city services with minimal interruption. One of the main reasons for the general lack of availability and acceptability of superfurniture is expense; more importantly, however, the restricted configurations and sizes of existing dwelling units cannot accommodate items of such scale. Unt

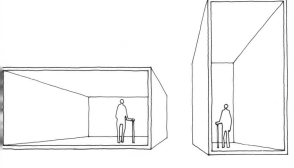

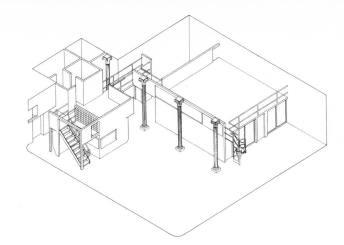

Fig. 8-34   Reorganization of the dwelling volume.
Figs. 8-35 and 8-36   Warehouse space used as dwelling.
The big room incorporates little houses within.

structures are developed with change and flexibility as a major form determinant, it will be difficult, if not impossible to reconceptualize ordinary domestic interiors.

For this reason, the building-within-a-building concept has become popular in custom-designed homes and in renovation of lofts and duplexes; the scale of these spaces can accommodate objects of large size and allow retention of a continuous spatial volume. The "small house" within the "big room" not only incorporates service spaces and privacy, but also reinforces the sense of the total volume by asking the eye to perceive an entire "building" within another. The configuration of the enclosure or the "shell" is a critical factor. Although certain types of large-scale furniture may be used with the common eight-foot ceiling height, larger devices cannot. There is little potential for real spatial variety unless the vertical dimension of the volume is 15 or 16 feet. The actual total volume need not be changed, simply the orientation of that volume (Fig. 8-34). If a typical apartment of 24 × 32 × 8 feet were changed to 24 × 16 × 16, a variety of new interiors might result without an increase of the volume.

In addition to the necessity for changing the configuration of the volume, some flexible

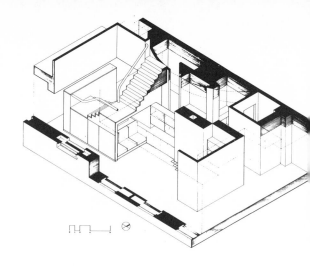

Fig. 8-37 and 8-38 Large-scale furniture becomes portions of rooms and equipment. Flexibility is reduced but space is perceived in a new way.

interpretation of building codes must also occu
In the Soho area of New York, the building
code was the major obstacle for both the habita
tion of the buildings (a change in occupancy
was needed) and for the implementation of the
more innovative environments. Codes may
govern such aspects as room sizes, configuration and the amount of exterior exposure.
Often, these buildings-within-buildings contain tiny spaces and are not on the exterior of th
dwelling and therefore have no *natural* light
and ventilation. When these devices are classified as furniture rather than rooms, code
jurisdiction is avoided (Figs. 8-35 and 8-36).
When the code must be interpreted literally,
large-scale free-standing devices usually incorporate *portions* of rooms and equipment such a
stairs, storage or seating. While the "furniture"
itself lacks many of the aspects of choice and
change which come with movability, it does
allow the space to be perceived as a continuou
volume, open to multiple domestic interpretations (Figs. 8-37 and 8-38).

In addition to the enclosure's configuration an
compliance with codes, the relationship betwee
the building enclosure and the interior device
also dictates the applicability of large-scale

Fig. 8-39 The most efficient enclosure protecting the house within. An early 1950s solution by students at MIT.

Fig. 8-40 The Carter Design Group maximum space studios in England. The horticultural greenhouse, available and simple to erect, forms a continuous volume in which to place an individualized interior.

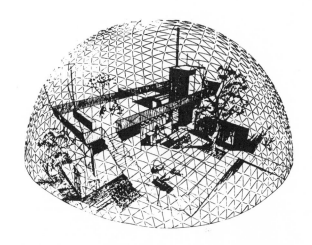

furniture. This relationship can be viewed as one of independence or one of interdependence. Because of differing life spans and flexibility requirements, the interior and exterior may be seen quite separately. The exterior relates to the scale of the site and locale while the interior is the personal environment of one family; the exterior relates contextually to other units and to a common circulation system while the interior may be unique. However, in typical dwellings, the enclosure dictates the form of the interior, separation becomes impossible, and the potential for change and variety of the interior becomes restricted.

Buckminster Fuller once commented that a house is basically a shell surrounding environmental servicing like a teepee or igloo around its fire, and his geodesic dome is one of the most efficient shells that can be placed around an activity space. The vision of this efficient enclosure around a unique interior to which it bears no physical relationship or connection was conceived by MIT students nearly 25 years ago (Fig. 8-39). They named the interior "house" encompassed by the Fuller dome a "living package." A few English architects have understood the difficulty of placing the dome

within an existing residential context and the difficulties of incorporating windows within the curvilinear skin of this enclosure. They therefore have proposed the horticultural greenhouse as a replacement for the dome (Fig. 8-40). Since the manufacture and distribution of this type of enclosure already exists, no new technologies would be required to produce it. Furthermore, the form of this structure is more congruent with normal cultural expectations of the dwelling. Like the dome, the interior can be developed independently of the structure. Also, like the dome, it can be used only in low density developments.

The "framework approach" mentioned earlier attempts to provide a building structure which allows for both high density living and individualization of the interior. In certain instances, the framework is designed in *coordination* with a flexible interior capable of change and diversity. In his book *Equipotential Space*, Renalto Severino discusses the dwelling as the combination of "frame components" and "functional objects." Although his "functional objects" or interior superfurnitures are illustrated in many configurations, their ultimate application requires a structure with higher than

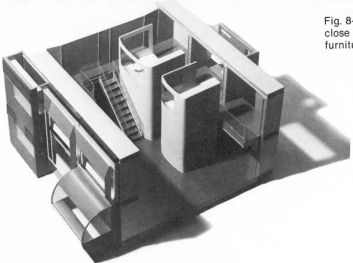

Fig. 8-41 Frame components and functional objects. A close coordination is implied between the large-scale furniture and the building enclosure.

normal ceilings (Fig. 8-41). In his early designs, the enclosure and "functional objects" were considered separately, similar to the framework approach, so that the objects could be placed anywhere within the volume. The actual interface between enclosure and furniture is minimal. The "frame components" incorporate air-conditioning, exterior exposures, and the structure of the building. The "functional objects" sit within the volume, modulate the space, and accommodate certain necessary equipment. In later developments, the frame becomes more sophisticated and the coordination of the two elements more exact. Although flexibility is still implied, the potential for an open system of interior components fitting loosely in an enclosure of varying type is diminished. As the need for technical sophistication increases, acceptance of these techniques becomes less likely. The practical appeal of the "glass house" approach is that it does not rely on new technologies or on a mechanical interdependence of the interior and enclosure.

Planning Strategies

Space is a relatively inexpensive commodity when compared to other aspects of the dwelling. Once the foundations are built, the electrical

wiring and plumbing supplied and routed, the kitchen and bath fixtures bought and hooked up, the remainder of the dwelling adds little to the cost of the house. Therefore, smaller units are often more expensive per square foot than larger dwellings since the high cost of standard equipment must be distributed over less area. Unfortunately, methods of financing housing have not followed this logic, but rather a simple cost/square foot formula. The result is that all housing space is expensive, and therefore minimal provision of space is the norm. The "life cycle" costs of the building and its suitability for many generations of diverse users are ignored.

In response to changing needs of housing users, Rabeneck, Sheppard and Town in England have developed what they call "adaptable" as opposed to "flexible" housing, to provide for ongoing change without reliance on technology or expensive hardware. Their major premise is that by alloting slightly more space than recommended by current standards and by building in as little as possible, the potential for developing different types of interiors is greatly increased. Ultimately, such space allocation is a much less expensive way of achieving a truly "resilient" and adaptable environment than

a technological approach such as the use of movable walls:

Given a 10 percent increase in space standards (about 7 percent up on cost), considerable choice is possible using only conventional gadgetry (e.g., folding doors). . . . Space in the long term, is the best buy.[12]

Room sizes, openings between rooms, and exterior openings must be carefully planned in order to make larger than usual allocations and to "avoid overt room expression" (Fig. 8-42).

Our slogan for the design of adaptable homes is "occupant choice through ambiguity." Basically, the unit is designed in such a way that there is a minimum predetermination of the patterns of use to which it will be put. Layout is designed to allow as wide a range of interpretations as possible. There is a minimum of design features that would inhibit particular choices of use. The decisions rest with the occupant.[13]

At Pessac, Le Corbusier's plans implemented some of these ideas. His villas were capable of being adapted, remodeled, reinterpreted. As Boudon states, they "facilitated and . . . even

Fig. 8-42 "Adaptable" housing purposefully creates
ambiguous areas with increases in space allocation.

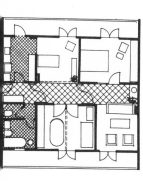

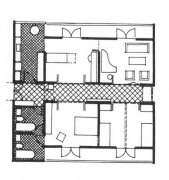

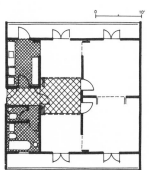

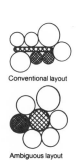

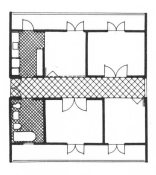

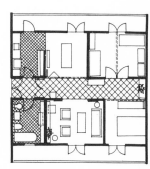

0   10'

Conventional layout

Ambiguous layout

These plans show one interpretation of
our concept of adaptability. They can
be seen as illustrative tests of one
form of generic layout. Important
features of this layout are a generous
hall space for display, shared family
storage, and service spaces large enough
to house extra domestic appliances
and/or second bathrooms. We found that
the basic choice between space and
gadgetry (i.e. movable walls) can not be
avoided. At Parker Morris space standards,
gadgetry becomes essential in order to
provide a degree of choice to occupants
At a 20 percent increase in space standards,
maximum choice can be achieved without
resorting to purpose-made components.
Space remains the best buy.

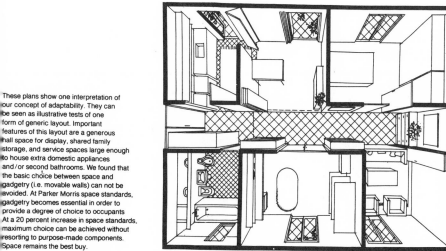

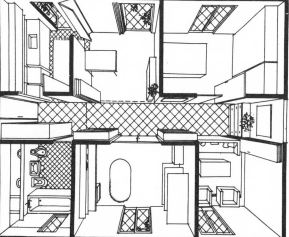

Four-room layout chosen by young family

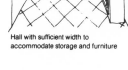

Hall with sufficient width to
accommodate storage and furniture

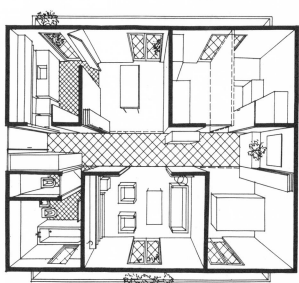

Four-room layout chosen by mature family

213

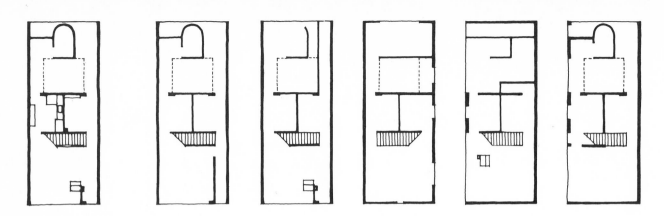

Fig. 8-43 Le Corbusier's open plan leads to user-initiated alterations.

encouraged such alterations"[14] (Fig. 8-43). In extensive interviews with the occupants, he discovered some astonishing responses:

I bought this house in five minutes flat: I didn't like the outside at all, but I saw its potential at once . . . It's the sort of house where you could introduce all manner of combinations.[15]

Converted? . . . I don't know whether it occurred to Le Corbusier twenty-five years ago, but it's quite an easy matter to convert them, in fact you can do more or less as you please . . . you can certainly arrange things to suit yourself . . . there are all sorts of possible arrangements. . . . You know, my husband has made thirty-six different designs.[16]

What I like about the house from an architectural point of view . . . from the point of view of amenities . . . is that the basic design makes it possible for the house to be *adapted* to its occupants instead of the occupants having to adapt to the house.[17]

The potential for change of Le Corbusier's dwellings at Pessac is due to the open plan, to the undefined nature of the large interior spaces (with the exception of bathrooms and kitchens, as mentioned earlier), and to the absence of built-in furniture. The dwellings provided a "basic framework within which the occupants would be able to give more or less free rein to their own ideas in both a qualitative (combinatory) and quantitative (spatial) sense."[18]

The resolutions discussed above emphasize the potential for choice, change, and individualization in the dwelling and the means by which these goals can be achieved. The main theme is to reduce conflicts which arise from static and limited housing, and to provide for increased control over the domestic environment, whether the solution lies with new technology, with revised planning strategies, or with new ways of perceiving and conceptualizing interior space.

Those approaches emphasizing technology have encountered and will continue to encounter problems of acceptability and availability. Their success will depend on economic feasibility and changes in the nature of the building process. Until then their principal value will be to provide short-term flexibility in the instances where they can be applied, such as loft buildings and renovations, and in stimulating thinking about issues of flexibility and choice.

Planning strategies which result in higher space standards—horizontally and vertically—have the greatest potential for accommodating change. These emphasize open "neutral" volumes—greenhouses, two-level maisonettes, duplexes, lofts—as the dwelling enclosure. The application of these planning concepts will be further popularized as the various methods of developing the space within (including large-scale furniture and other technologically oriented solutions) become better known and more widely available.

Footnotes for Chapter 8

1. Frampton, Kenneth, "Transformation of the interior," *Progressive Architecture* (November, 1973), p. 110.
2. Frampton, Kenneth. See footnote 1, p. 114.
3. Michelson, William, "The Case of the Equine Fountains," *Design and Environment* (Winter, 1971), p. 30.
4. Perin, Constance, *With Man in Mind.* Cambridge: MIT Press, 1970, p. 44.
5. Brown, Denise Scott is quoted. "Schlock is beautiful," *Newsweek* (March 8, 1976), p. 56.
6. Miller, Wayne, "Social occasions of the dwelling," *Housing from the Shell In*, Davis, Sam (Ed.), Berkeley, Architecture Experiment Laboratory, 1973.
7. Miller, Wayne. See footnote 6.
8. Boudon, Phillippe, *Lived-In Architecture: Le Corbusier's Pessac Revisited*, Cambridge: MIT Press, 1969, p. 121.
9. Sottsass, Ettore, *Italy: The New Domestic Landscape*, Ambasz, Emilio (Ed.). New York, Museum of Modern Art, 1972, p. 162.
10. Colombo, Joseph. See footnote 9, p. 172.
11. Colombo, Joseph. See footnote 9, p. 172.
12. Rabeneck, Andrew; Sheppard, David; and Town, Peter, "The structuring of space in family housing; an alternative to present design practice," *Progressive Architecture* (November, 1974), p. 106.
13. Rabeneck, Andrew; Sheppard, David; and Town, Peter. See footnote 12, p. 106.
14. Boudon, Phillippe. See footnote 8, p. 114.
15. Boudon, Phillippe. See footnote 8, p. 114.·
16. Boudon, Phillippe. See footnote 8, p. 115.
17. Boudon, Phillippe. See footnote 8, p. 116.
18. Boudon, Phillippe. See footnote 8, p. 120.

Bibliography

Books

Ambasz, Emilio (Ed.), *Italy: The New Domestic Landscape*. New York: Museum of Modern Art, 1972.
Boudon, Phillippe, *Lived-In Architecture: Le Corbusier's Pessac Revisited.* Cambridge: MIT Press, 1969.
Conran, Terence, *The House Book.* New York: Crown Publishers Inc., 1976.
Davis, Sam (Ed.), *Housing: From the Shell In.* Architecture Experiments Laboratory, University of California, 1973.
Eichen, Carole, *How to Decorate Model Homes and Apartments.* New York: House and Home Press, 1974.
Giedion, Sigfried, *Mechanization Takes Command.* New York: Oxford University Press, 1948.
Habraken, N. J., *Supports — An Alternative to Mass Housing.* New York: Praeger, 1972.
Moore, Charles W.; Lyndon, Donlyn; and Allen, Gerald, *The Place of Houses.* New York: Holt, Reinhart, Winston, 1974.
Perin, Constance, *With Man in Mind.* Cambridge: MIT Press, 1970.
Rapoport, Amos, *House Form and Culture.* Englewood Cliffs, N.J.: Prentice-Hall, 1969.

Severino, Renalto, *Equipotential Space.* New York: Praeger, 1970.
Sommer, Robert, *Design Awareness.* San Francisco: Reinhart Press, 1972.
Sommer, Robert, *Tight Spaces: Hard Architecture and How to Humanize It.* Englewood Cliffs, N.J.: Prentice-Hall, 1974.
Sommer, Robert, *Personal Space: The Behavioral Basis of Design.* Englewood Cliffs, N.J.: Prentice-Hall, 1969.

Periodicals and Reports

Frampton, Kenneth, "Transformation of the interior," *Progressive Architecture* (November 1973), pp. 110–115.
Rabeneck, Andrew; Sheppard, David; and Town, Peter, "Structuring space in family housing," *Progressive Architecture* (November, 1974), pp. 100–107.
Rabeneck, Andrew; Sheppard, David; and Town, Peter, "Housing flexibility," *Architectural Design* (November, 1973), pp. 698–711.
Smithsonian Institution, *Signs of Life: Symbols in the American City*, (Aperture Inc.: Washington), 1976.

Mobile Homes

am Davis

"Who's going to tell them 3750 homes have to be recalled for defects?"

would be an oversight to omit the mobile home from a book on housing in the United States. The number of mobile homes has increased so rapidly in proportion to other types of new housing that this dwelling form is now a leader in low cost and decent shelter. Although shunned and ignored for many years in the discussion of housing, by 1972 mobile homes represented nearly 20% of all new dwellings and 30% of all new single family homes, still the predominant house type desired by Americans. Of all homes under $15,000, 90% are mobile homes. The combination of a competitive market system and the established demand for low cost housing has enabled this industry to expand with natural growth, unaffected by the financial interventions of government programs.

Another reason for examining the mobile home in this study is that by isolating this industry and its products, it is possible to see how the ideas and concerns discussed in earlier chapters can influence physical form. A recurring observation of this book, particularly this section, is that housing must accommodate choice and change. Part of the success of mobile homes is their recognition of this requirement. The ability to choose from a number of models, types, sizes, and locations, thereby giving the user both variety and participation in the housing

process is a critical element of the mobile home phenomenon. The potential for moving one's entire home to another context or completely changing one's home within the same context clearly exemplifies the theme of choice and change. The technology of industrialization combined with off-site fabrication creates a consumer product, by nature responsive to market demands, and capable of long-term flexibility and change.

The growth and development of mobile home parks have not been easy. The institutional constraints of land use planning, zoning, and lending agencies have certainly affected not only form, but location. The negative image of mobile homes caused the mobile home industry to form associations similar to those for conventional home builders during the 1950s. The efforts of these associations established quality control guidelines as well as improved park layouts. Yet, the housing struggles discussed in Chapter 5 have been intense within the mobile home industry. Neighborhood groups and city governments have tried to restrict their applications. Court cases and public hearings are common and have ultimately had their own influence on design.

Although the mobile home parks are not truly

mixed-use developments (i.e., they incorporate only housing and recreation), they *are* strong enclaves of people aggregated together for security, comradery and a shared lifestyle. In an urban design context, the park must be considered a successful alternative to other forms of settlement.

The mobile home industry is a microcosm of the complex determinants and issues of housing in general. Analyzing the relationship of the mobile home form to these issues will give a better understanding of the potential of the housing industry to meet the needs and aspirations of Americans. It will also give some insight into the factors influencing the visual aspects of our environment.

A Conflict of Attitudes

The physical form of the mobile home has been greatly influenced by the conflicting nature of its two historical predecessors, the car and the house. The mobile home is a hybrid: seen from below it is a vehicle resting on wheels and axles; seen from above it is a dwelling. The very name, "mobile home," expresses an inherent conflict. Our traditional image of a home is that of a *permanent* structure forever attached to the

217

land upon which it is constructed. The earth and the home are thought of as inseparable, and it is the ownership and location of the land which contribute most to our perceived status. When land becomes valuable, so does the structure on it. Limiting the numbers of structures on a given parcel of land increases their value. The idea of our land as immovable, stable, and unchanging represents our apparent need to "put down roots."

Institutions have grown up around the housing industry which perpetuate the image of the single family house forever attached to a piece of land. The evolution of the physical form of dwellings reinforces this image. We strongly define our territory with fences. We employ substantial columns to create the sense of a structure firmly attached to the ground (Fig. 9-3). These columns and fences help to demarcate and establish the transitional spaces from the land to the inside of the house. The most apparent of the house elements, the roof, is often large and heavy looking. It usually projects beyond the walls to further connect the land visually to the house (Fig. 9-4). In this definition of house, mobility has no place.

On the other hand, although we may claim to be an agrarian society, Americans have the need

to "get up and go." Each year 20% of us move. Until very recently, the most obvious symbol of our mobility, the car, was wholeheartedly accepted by our culture. Yet we were unwilling to accept our mobility, equating rootlessness with instability, lack of commitment and even poor citizenship. Now mobility is often perceived as a manifestation of our virtuous pioneering spirit. The family with many generations living within the same household for years is dissolving into the smaller unit of the nuclear family. Our neighborhoods are in a continuous state of flux. We have less to stay put for, and are more willing to move for jobs, climate, or merely change.

One of the results of this awareness and acceptance of mobility is an increase in the status of personal belongings and artifacts, and a decreased dependency on the house for identification. In terms of social status, we tend to rely less on where we live and more on what we do and what we have. If we consider our home to be mobile, then we can move the symbols of our position in society with us. The ability to transfer our immediate personal environment and the familiar objects within it as an undisturbed entity alleviates some of the disorienting aspects of moving. A degree of stability is

achieved while maintaining the potential for mobility.

The original mobile homes, "trailer houses," were concerned less with being dwellings and more with mobility. The objects themselves exemplified movement in their form. The configuration often emphasized the wheels, with designers reducing the surfaces to alleviate friction with the wind. The development of this form was not unlike that which shaped the car pulling it. Its ultimate refinement, the Airstream Trailer, is still popular as a recreational vehicle (Fig. 9-5). As both the need for housing and the desire for a high degree of mobility increased, the conflict of mobility versus stability became stronger. The industry split into a housing and a recreational vehicle industry. The mobile home evolved into more of a dwelling and became too large to be towed by a car. By the early 1960s, some mobile homes were 10 feet wide and 50 to 60 feet long. Although technically not permanently attached to the land, the mobile home now makes only one major move from factory to site.

The House as Product

Once the dwelling is conceptually separated from the land, and mobility accepted as a positive

Fig. 9-5 The Airstream. The industry split into a home building industry and a recreation vehicle industry. Recreational vehicle emphasizes aspects of mobility rather than images of house.

circumstance, the house can be viewed as a consumer product in much the same way that we regard the objects within it. If our middle class desire to "keep up with the Joneses" persists, we can simply acquire a better dwelling, without abandoning our neighborhood and friends. The notion of a changeable dwelling or a disposable house with built-in obsolescence has been put forth by the many futurists groups and is exemplified in various analogies, like wine racks or bookshelves. Although the "plug-in" concept, where individual dwellings are applied to a permanent holding framework, is usually illustrated in a three-dimensional configuration, the mobile home is a single-level realization of the theory. The mobile home park, constructed by a developer and including service hookups, roads and community facilities, is independent of the individualized dwelling. One of the major advantages of the "plug-in" or framework is that it allows the dwelling manufacturer to continuously supply houses, independent of locational constraints. His product can fit into any framework. This is a major difference between conventional housing, which is attached to land, and mobile homes or "plug-in" housing. Conventional housing is not flexible to market demands in all locations. Once it is in place, it can affect the market only in that locality, and thus has no effect on in-

creased demand in another place. The result is housing monopoly. Conventional housing is also inflexible to changing demands within one locality. With mobile homes, if demographics change in a particular area, the appropriate dwellings may be supplied to replace the existing stock. Conventional housing must be extensively altered to accommodate such change.

Conceptualization of the house as a consumer product has other consequences on supply and demand which result in more and increasingly better houses. In order to insure future sales, manufacturers must continually increase the market. This can be done either by making better and more innovative houses so that owners will "trade up" to a new home, or by meeting more of the market through varied products. Although neither of these possibilities has been fully realized, their existence has been cause for the continued success of the mobile home industry.

The mobile home is the first generally available dwelling that is responsive in its form to individual user input. Architect designed homes allow for enormous user input, but the resulting costs are out of range of most people. Apart-

ments and speculative homes can make only tentative generalizations about the individual wishes of the user. In any consumer product, a feedback system making known the wishes of the buyer is imperative for maintenance of sales. Since most mobile homes are produced on order (like custom features on a car), the consumer has a direct influence on the ultimate form of his house. In the past, unfortunately, the dealer acted as the conduit for consumer demands to the manufacturer. New form possibilities have been limited by the images in the existing sales brochures, and by the ability of the dealer to suggest and interpret consumer desires.

The house as a product can no longer be differentiated from the other products within it. When a person buys a mobile home, all appliances—furniture, curtains, lighting—may be supplied as a part of the package. The idea of completeness is encouraged by advertisers, who sell an entire lifestyle, not just a dwelling. Those insecure about their ability to tastefully equip and design the interior of the home can overcome their fears by simply choosing a coordinated product, ranging from "Mediterranean" to "Early American." These choices are ones which reflect some positive self-image or some traditional value in society. They represent marketing

219

strategies which have had a very powerful influence on the present aesthetics and form of the mobile home.

The focus of these approaches are the two major mobile home markets—the young married and the elderly retired. Typical buyers are young couples under 35 with one child, a blue collar job and income around $7500.[1] They constitute 40% of those living in mobile homes. The "package" approach allows them to acquire their own home, its contents and image with one loan, and at the same time build some equity. Another 30% of the mobile home owners, on the other hand, are over 55 and retired. In California this figure is as high as 60%. Although not as interested in the package aspect of the product, they are more apt to respond to conventional images of luxury and status in which to live out their retirement.

These packaging techniques are valuable not only from the convenience point of view (the objects are acquired and moved simultaneously with the container from the factory), but also from the financial standpoint (the entire finished product is financed as one item). The loan techniques are similar to those for automobiles, with higher rates and much shorter periods than traditional home mortgages. They are relatively easy to obtain. As a result, the "entry" cost of owning a mobile home is substantially less than that of a conventional house. However, the monthly cost of owning a mobile home, when all aspects are considered, is usually not much less than for conventional homes of similar size. There are no personal income tax advantages for mobile homes as there are with real property and one must still pay loan and lot rental fees. As lenders realize that mobile homes are not often moved, that the mobile home is becoming a close approximation of a conventional house both in size and aesthetics, and that the owners are fiscally responsible, they are more willing to allow longer term financing and thereby lower monthly costs. Currently some loans of 15 years and longer are being made on mobile homes.

Changing values and attitudes on mobility, coupled with an inherent interest in technological approaches, have allowed mobile homes to become an acceptable form of housing for many Americans. The factory-produced house, substantially less expensive to buy than conventional houses, has brought this form of home ownership within the reach of those formerly excluded, enabling them to have a say in the design of their homes. This would not have been possible under normal home-building techniques and institutions.

Mobile Homes as "Odd Man Out"

The conventional home-building industry and its support institutions are generally conservative. Margaret Drury's major thesis in *Mobile Homes: An Unrecognized Revolution in American Housing*, is that:

> Conservatism in housing is most apparent in design, but it also permeates other segments of the housing market. It can be seen in financing, labor regulations, zoning, building codes, legislations, taxation and legal regulations concerning housing. This combination of conservative forces . . . has operated to reject the industrialized home, whether conventional or mobile.[2]

The conservatism of unions has been one deterrent to innovation in both technology and the uses of materials. Many of these innovations are meant to cut high labor costs and most labor costs are attributable to site work, which totally eliminated in the production of a factory-built home. Union resistance is therefore understandable.

...he constraints most severely affecting the form ...the conventional house are building codes. ...hey tend to be conservative in that they ...gulate the use of materials based on known ...haracteristics and performance. New materials ...d techniques are slow to be accepted ...nce they do not have an *in situ* performance ...cord. Operating outside the code restrictions, ...obile home suppliers, particularly the plastics ...dustry, have incorporated new materials ...d techniques which substantially lower the ...al cost of the house. These less expensive ...aterials, generally made to simulate natural ...aterials, are a major reason for the stereotyped ...age the industry has for making an inferior ...d shoddy product. The aspects of durability ...d fire retardation are the focus of numerous ...mplaints, many of which are outlined in a ...cent book by the Center for Auto Safety. Yet, ...en the critics of the industry recognize that the ...obile home is a decent house which might ...t be affordable if these materials were not ...nployed. A balance between quality and cost ...ust be attained in order to continue to supply ...uses which will last at a "moderate cost." ...any manufacturers of mobile homes are incor- ...orating traditional materials, particularly ...psum board. This reduces the fire danger and ...akes sturdier walls with less sound trans- ...ission. With these materials the product can

qualify as a conventional dwelling when placed on a permanent foundation.

Precisely because they were spurned by the conventional housing community and classified and registered as vehicles, mobile homes were free to develop new markets, techniques and institutions. In Drury's words: "The mobile home is virtually immune to the same financial, zoning, code, taxation and labor restrictions which apply to conventional housing. This immunity is the factor that has contributed most to the growth of the mobile home industry in the housing market."[3] This is also one of the main factors which distinguishes the success of mobile homes compared to other industrialized housing efforts.

Exclusion of mobile homes by the housing industry has been a mixed blessing. Although it allowed for changes in the nature of the product, thus placing it within the financial grasp of more people, mobile homes were not allowed in locations usually reserved for houses. Zoning ordinances have placed mobile home parks (where 60% of the mobile homes are located) into industrial areas and other less desirable city fringe locations. Local ordinances often exclude the individual mobile home from residential neighborhoods. The negative, vagabond

image of the mobile home dweller, and the visual blight of early trailer courts have perpetuated these exclusionary tactics. The fact that mobile homes were considered as vehicles—and thus the owners paid no property tax—caused further resentment. Those resisting mobile homes use the argument that mobile homes are cheap and therefore are inhabited by transients; mobile home owners pay no property tax and thus do not share the burden of city services.

Attempts to overcome both this inaccurate image and the regressive legislation that accompanies it have been less than successful. They have, however, generated three valuable side effects.

First, the mobile home industry formed organizations that paralleled the evolution and efforts of the Home Builders Associations. The Mobile Home Manufacturers, the Trailer Coach, and the Southeastern Manufactured Housing Associations are now combined into a single national group—The Manufactured Housing Association. The initial activities of these associations were basically public relations, and the collecting of data and statistics for the industry. Later, they began to offer design consultant services to developers in order to promote better park

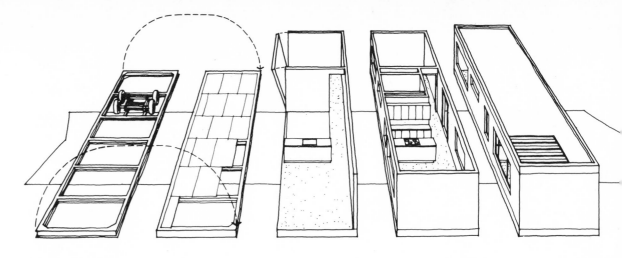

Fig. 9-6 Production of the mobile home as it moves down assembly line. Conventional-type construction takes place simultaneously rather than sequentially.

environments. This was not the first recognition of the need for better design. Many of the manufacturers had formed an independent corporation for the same purpose which dissolved in 1961. It was clear that the only way to increase the market for mobile homes was to create decent places to put them. The associations also established an industrywide standard for mobile home construction which was the first self-imposed national standard for housing of any type. These standards have had an erratic history, plagued by noncompliance, the logistics of inspection, and the lack of sanctions. Nevertheless, feeling the need to overcome the negative stereotypes, the associations continued the effort. Following the example of California, the first state to enact manufacturing standards for mobile homes, the industry groups sponsored new standards developed by the American National Standards Institute (ANSI) and the National Fire Protection Association (NFPA). These standards were based on the performance of various aspects of the dwelling, allowing the manufacturer flexibility in materials and techniques employed for meeting criteria. Conventional building codes are more limiting, often specifying materials and the manner of construction. The ANSI standards were accepted by most of the industry and the states. In 1976, the United States Congress permitted the

Department of Housing and Urban Development to adapt construction standards which would be mandatory for any mobile home manufactured throughout the country. These latest standards became law in June of 1976 and are again based on performance criteria. HUD is allowing each of the states to take responsibility for administering the law, but will also appoint their own enforcement agencies if the states request it. The long struggle over standards has now guaranteed uniformity throughout the country and has generally resulted in enhanced quality.

The second valuable consequence of attempts to improve the image of mobile homes is the consumer-oriented publications. The manufacturers' associations have developed their own publications, but Woodall's *Mobile Home and Park Directory* included the most complete and updated information on various aspects of interest to buyers and owners. Editions of this manual, published annually, included feature articles on mobile home living, advice on how to shop for mobile homes, information on moving them, repairing them, and recognizing their construction quality. Woodall's book was of great value when real mobility of mobile homes was still possible and while new parks in developing areas were rapidly being created. Since the

parks are now relatively stable, the homes too large to easily move, and the residents less transient than other segments of the population Woodall's directory has outlived its usefulness for those looking for places to put their home In mid 1976 it ceased publication after having served a valuable role in educating mobile home owners and prospective buyers.

The third effect is new legislation concerning site inspection of mobile homes. A number of safeguards causing increased cost have developed in order to insure that mobile homes, on at the site, would be free of gas leaks and improper water or sewer connections. The laws governing utility connections resulted in increased standardization of the mobile home the early 1960s which in turn limited site placement. In the future, variations in siting become more prevalent. On-site inspection is now required and this law will help overcome reluctance of developers, manufacturers, and owners to try various terrains and orientation The standards governing utility connections m be relaxed since a correct and safe "setup" will now be assured.

Pressure from within the industry and a more informed buying public have improved the nature of the product and the quality of the en

222

Fig. 9-7 Costs per square foot for mobile and conventional homes.

Fig. 9-8 Making the container look more substantial.

Costs Per Square Foot for Mobile and Conventional Homes

Source: Mobile Home Manufacturers Association;
Department of Commerce, Bureau of the Census,
Construction Reports, C25-71-B, C25-73-3.

ronment. This has stimulated more sales. As the homes and environments get better, people are more willing to invest in the product and the old stereotypes disappear.

The mobile home industry, however, wants the best of both worlds. They would like to be fully accepted as part of the conventional housing industry. This would allow the factory-built house to be placed on any site. Yet to do so would involve basic changes in the product which might offset its success as a low cost house. The paradox is further reinforced by the conflict between mass production and an individualized product, and extends to the formal design resolution of the dwelling.

Production and Design

Mobile homes are not inherently different in construction from other housing. Yet the fact that they are assembled in a factory to be shipped completed on the road originally yielded an ungainly house in which the space was allocated inefficiently. The road restriction is usually a maximum of 12 to 14 feet wide and 60 to 70 feet long. The most efficient mass-produced volume, using planar materials like plywood, is a rectangle. This provides the maximum

interior space contained within these dimensions—a long, narrow box.

The boxes are made of conventional stud walls and ceilings. The walls are produced on large tables and lifted into position as the floor framing is completed (Fig. 9-6). Two major aspects of the production of a mobile home in the factory differentiate it from the construction of a conventional house at the site: subassembly and simultaneous activities. In the factory, the walls, cabinets, ceiling trusses, can be produced separately and assembled on the production line like an automobile. While these subassemblies are connected, the various crafts can work concurrently. Electrical wiring, plumbing, and carpentry need not wait until another facet of construction is complete. Factory production allows for reduced costs through bulk buying of materials and components. Labor costs are cut by limiting the variety of tasks and the necessity for chronological coordination. Further, working within a factory allows for year-round production and for the stockpiling of materials to avoid delivery and availability delays.

The central idea behind factory mass production is standardization. However, the more standardized and efficient the production system be-

comes, the more difficult it is to appeal to individual needs and desires within the market. In the case of the mobile home, all the accoutrements of conventional single family houses—porches, picture windows, bay windows, and variety in configuration—increase the cost of the product. The line must be drawn at a point where the addition of amenities to attract more buyers begins to price the product out of the market. As conventional houses increase in cost, the ability to add features to mobile homes and still be within financial range of buyers increases. Partly because of the advantages of factory production, mobile home costs do not rise as rapidly as those of conventional houses (Fig. 9-7).

Unfortunately, the demand for mobile homes in their present form has been enough so that the need to add significant variation to the product has not arisen. The "features" that have been added are for the most part merely appliqué symbolism. These devices are an attempt to make the container seem more substantial, for instance, fake brick arches or inset windows with columns in front to give the wall the appearance of thickness (Fig. 9-8). A study done in the Department of Architecture at the University of Arkansas sums up the problem:

223

The mobile home is a package in the sense that crackers come in a package, because people buy the mobile home to get rights to use of its interior. It is a package also in that the exterior can be designed as a package—as the box which contains the crackers. Heretofore the industry has not exploited the possibilities of this, apparently because it has been mesmerized by the image of the conventional house and has tried to "house-up" the mobile home with fake siding, shutters, et al.[4]

This reluctance to allow the product to assume an aesthetic value in keeping with its use and the requirements of its production is partly a result of default on the part of designers. The designers of mobile homes have contented themselves with making refinements on the original travel trailer with the interjection of conventional home imagery. The result, when coupled with the production and shipping limitations, is an unresolved form. When compared to the automobile industry, which faced similar formal problems in its infancy, the mobile home is aesthetically backward. Automobiles were first modeled after the horseless carriage with such detailing as external lighting, but soon developed their own integrated formal vocabulary. Indeed, the portion of the trailer industry which emerged as

recreational vehicles has been more successful than the mobile home in achieving an early degree of aesthetic integrity.

Architects are usually not involved in the design of mobile homes. When they have been, they too have failed to resolve the formal conflict, choosing to adopt an existing style. The most ironic of these cases is that of the Frank Lloyd Wright Foundation design commissioned by National Mobile Homes (Figs. 9-9 and 9-10). Wright, who has contributed most to the development of a residential style in this country, saw style as an element of craft. "Style is important. A style is not," he said, and was repulsed by the proliferation of suburban speculative homes which were "stupid makeshifts, putting on some style or other, really having no integrity." Yet the Wright Foundation mobile home is simply that, a mobile home in the style of Frank Lloyd Wright.

The elements typical of the Wright houses—free-floating space linking activity areas, roof extensions which visually claim more of the site and extend interior spaces outward, and the central hearth as the focus of activity—are all nonexistent in the Wright Foundation design. The only features which remain are stylistic

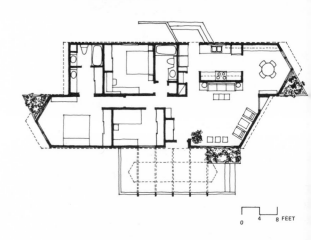

Figs. 9-11 and 9-12 Wrightian design with most of the features of the Prairie Houses.

Fig. 9-13 Reasons for stacking: higher density, new internal dimensions, more open land, privacy from overlooks.

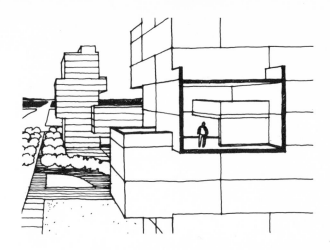

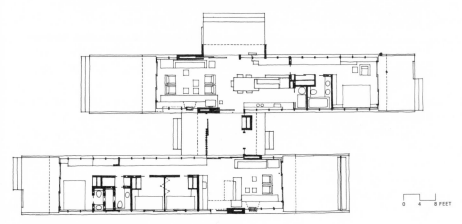

0 4 8 FEET

appliqué in the form of detailing and angles at the end of the plan. A better application of the Wrightian house features has been suggested in a mobile home designed by John Raup (Figs. 9-11 and 9-12). This solution, with its sweeping cantilivering decks and long horizontal lines not only succeeds in claiming the site but also breaks the image of the container, a feat which even the angled ends of the Wright Foundation design failed to accomplish. The comparison cannot be extended too far, however, since the Raup design is larger and was not restrained by the manufacturer's production requirements as was the Wright Foundation design.

Another architect and devoted formalist, Paul Rudolph, was intrigued by the potential of the factory-produced house, calling it the "20th century brick." His images are of modules, stacked into many faceted forms. There are four reasons for such an approach: to achieve a higher density than is possible by placing units on the ground; to produce privacy from over-looks; to allow a new internal dimension to the dwelling by opening up the volume where the units cross; to reserve more land for other purposes (Fig. 9-13). Yet in his only built at-tempt to use this newfound formal device, Oriental Masonic Gardens in New Haven

Fig. 9-14   Oriental gardens in New Haven by Rudolph. The box configuration is emphasized without many of the advantages of stacking.

Fig. 9-15   Size implications: potential for courts, decks and various window exposures.

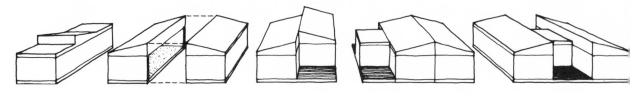

(Fig. 9-14), Rudolph made little of these potential advantages. His dwellings look even more elongated and boxy than the standard mobile home resting on the ground. The "free space," formed by the projections of the units as they stack, could have been an excellent and inexpensively gained area, but they are dark and oppressive.

Joseph Koncelik states:

> The mobile home exists as a product without aesthetic integrity. Most mobile homes are a hodge-podge of stylistic clichés and attempts to dazzle the buyer's eye with pseudo-impressions of luxury. In a sense, the mobile home lacks an image. It has yet to develop—if it ever will—a stylistic resolution faithful to its formal conception.[5]

What development there has been is in size, yet even in this there is unrealized potential. The long, slender box was clearly inappropriate for a house. It did not look like a house nor was its space efficiently allocated. Attempts were made to solve this problem by varying the roof. These were less than successful. The insufficient and ill-proportioned space was rectified, not with changes in the core structure, but simply with appended separate structures.

The major breakthrough was the double-wide which took two identical units and placed them together longitudinally. This arrangement not only added the needed space within and allowed for more efficient plans, but also accommodated better proportioned rooms. The double wide also moved the mobile home closer to the image and configuration of the conventional house by adding a roof sloped to a ridge (Fig. 9-15).

For the most part, the double-wide units are of an equal length. Outdoor entries or courts which could be provided by decreasing the length of one of the units are an uncommon form. The newer triple-wide uses a third mobile unit. This is smaller and placed midway on the side of the double-wide house, making a front and back court. Although the placement of the smaller unit between the two larger sections making an H-shaped dwelling with private courts has been suggested, it has not been marketed as yet. Once one accepts the need for a two or three unit mobile home, many configurations are possible which will yield the advantages of defined outdoor space and of multiple exposures and orientations for the rooms. Many of these configurations were experimented with in prototype models designed by Robert Lee and David Klages. They were manufactured by Golden West

Fig. 9-16 Mobile homes by Lee and Klages. Variation in configuration using multiple units.
Fig. 9-17 Lee and Klages unit plans.

obile Homes, and placed on a remote second ome development in Southern California. ome of these units used double-wides slipped ongitudinally, making courts or decks at the nds. Others used units arranged perpendicular o each other, forming an L-shaped house hich wrapped around a deck (Figs. 9-16 and 17). The location of the site and the lack of local aterials and labor precluded conventional onstruction. Yet in professional circles and in e media, the designs received enormous atten- on beyond their limited application on the te. The models have, nevertheless, not been ut into regular production.

he lack of acceptance of these and other inno- ations in the form of the mobile home can be tributed to the desire of most developers to mit land in the park. It is also a function of e growing retirement market's reluctance to ndertake responsibilities of yard work and aintenance. User demand for private outdoor ace is not strong, but the demand for in- reased amounts of enclosed space is. As a sult, the norm in mobile housing is the largest ouse on the smallest lot. The embellishment f a small amount of land in front of the unit lows for minimum recreational gardening and adequate to display the identity of the ousehold (Fig. 9-18).

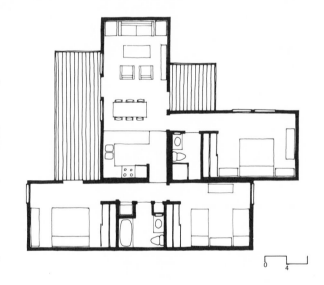

The desire for increasing amounts of *enclosed* space was first evident when the lean-to awnings covering the entry were enclosed by dwellers with canvas and screens. Many of these make- shift enclosing techniques were structurally unsound and represented fire hazards. The in- dustry responded with a permanent third element making up the triple-wide. Manufacturers claim that a courtyard or H-shaped house would induce a similar problem as owners would soon find makeshift methods of enclosing the resulting space. The desire for more enclosed space on a small lot has not led to stacked units, however, because stairs are not favored by the older retirement market. Furthermore, most developers will not allow stacked units on the smaller lots since their presence darkens what little space is allocated between dwellings.

Landing the Mobile Home

Since the mobile home is constructed away from the site, there is a problem in making it look like it "belongs" on the piece of land where it is placed. If the circumstance of mobility is ac- ceptable, then the notion that the unit be attached to the land seems incongruous. Philo- sophical movements in architecture beginning with Constructivism suggest that elements with

227

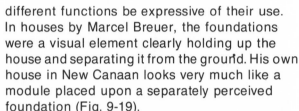

Fig. 9-18   Small yards and large houses. Embellishment without overburdening responsibility.

Fig. 9-19   Breuer House 1947. Foundations visually separate from enclosure.

Fig. 9-20   Grounding technique of berming up to the uni It is also possible to set the home into the land. Both approaches provide level entries.

different functions be expressive of their use. In houses by Marcel Breuer, the foundations were a visual element clearly holding up the house and separating it from the ground. His own house in New Canaan looks very much like a module placed upon a separately perceived foundation (Fig. 9-19).

The transportation problem is another direct conflict with "grounding" the unit since the wheels and axles take up about two feet between the ground and the floor of the dwelling. In modular homes, the unit is often shipped on a flat truck and then lifted onto a foundation. The potential for movement must remain if the mobile home continues to be considered a vehicle. Transition of indoor to outdoor space is impossible and the exposed underside of the unit is an unpleasant sight.

The need for a two-foot transition in height, plus the desire for immediately available outdoor space has led to the use of raised platforms, adjacent to the unit, covered with an awning. In most new parks, these two devices are required in order to provide a visual consistency and thus their use is perpetuated. Often the wheels are removed from the unit (the axles remain) in order to reduce its height from the ground.

Some space is still necessary for drainage and f mechanical devices usually accommodated in the walls, basements or crawl spaces of conve tional houses. This required void is a more accessible service area for plumbing connections and air ducts than is found in convention dwellings. The space has also been used to accommodate a dropped floor in the unit, pro viding a spatial amenity to the interior. Other methods to camouflage this idiosyncratic space have been successful, but of course more costly. Two solutions consist of changin the ground plane by berming up to the unit o by depressing the pad on which the unit sits (Fig. 9-20). In either case, the pad must be pre pared in a method similar to a conventional retaining wall and allowance made for ground drainage. For this reason, these solutions occ mostly in desert regions where the ground is sandy and naturally drained.

The obvious answer is also the most prevalent simply covering up the void and put stairs leading into the house. Devices which cover t underside of the house (skirting) vary in elaborateness. Some designs emphasize intended permanence of the house by constructi a brick wall, while the simplest and most prevalent skirting is an extension of the siding

Fig. 9-21 Brick skirting. Covering up the underside and adding permanence to the mobile home.

Fig. 9-22 Planters as skirting. Emphasizes permanence and connection to ground.

Fig. 9-23 Mobile home as suburban house. Few clues as to its mobile origin.

the unit (Fig. 9-21). One of the more interesting skirting designs suggested by Uri Hung in his scheme for the Reynolds Mobile Home Competition involved sloping planter/storage containers (Fig. 9-22).

The Mobile Home as Suburban House

If the overriding design concern in the mobile home industry is to produce a factory-built house which is indistinguishable from the conventional dwelling, then the most advanced product thus far is that introduced by Levitt. Using wood materials on the exterior, shake shingles, large windows, and various forms of appendages and unit sizes, the dwelling takes on the appearance of a suburban tract house without leaving a clue to its mobile origin (Fig. 9-23). Wood trim around windows is also used to cover the seam necessary between the units, so there is a consistency and sophistication of detailing. The variation in unit sizes allows for private patio space, especially when the unit is sited with one of the earth-moving techniques. The smaller units are often placed midlength on the larger units, which requires some site work to complete and match the shingling. These units are expensive and are usually never moved. This is, in theory, a modular house, capable

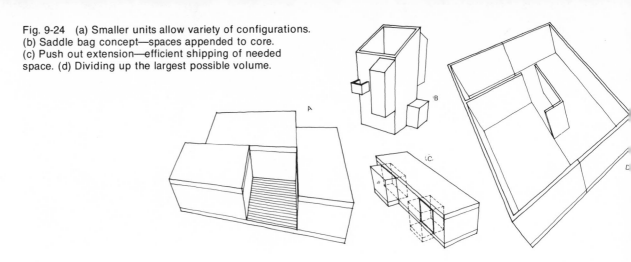

Fig. 9-24 (a) Smaller units allow variety of configurations. (b) Saddle bag concept—spaces appended to core. (c) Push out extension—efficient shipping of needed space. (d) Dividing up the largest possible volume.

of being connected to a permanent foundation. The growing trend is for the manufacturer of mobile units to switch to producing modular homes on the same assembly line. The factory costs have already been outlaid and an established marketing and distribution system exists. If a manufacturer can vary the product within these constraints and produce both modular and mobile homes, he should be able to immensely increase his market, constrained only by the necessity to stay within the economic 500 mile shipping range.

Innovative Approaches

The house seen as a consumer product must have the capability for variation by the development of new models or ideas in order to sustain or increase its market. One hopes attempts to maintain the market will lead to innovation, and ultimately to a better living environment. This potential has yet to be fully realized in the mobile home industry, although the present "top-of-the-line" mobile homes are a significant improvement in the early 9-wides or trailers.

It must be remembered that innovation and variation in product is in conflict with production requirements. A balance must be maintained between this production conservatism and the

ability to sell and supply. Thus far mobile home innovations have been in adding space and in upgrading the quality and variety of images and style packages.

The size of the unit can be approached in two ways. First, the modules can attain a maximum size, allowing for variation within the enclosure. Second, the modules can vary in size, not only allowing for variation in interior orientation and definition but also for variation and definition of exterior space (Fig. 9-24). If many smaller mobile units are used together, almost any configuration can be attained. However, the resultant setup costs for the site and the cost of increased perimeter and shipping requirements often offset the advantages. Minor variation in size (particularly length) has begun to be introduced by the industry and seems to indicate that factory production need not be limited to boxlike containers.

An early technological approach by the industry to increase unit size was the "push-out" extension (Fig. 9-24). Once the mobile home arrives at the site, this extension is pulled like a drawer from the unit. Usually this is a breakfast room addition to the kitchen space. Conceptually, this notion of extending the basic dwelling unit is similar to Charles Moore's "saddlebag"

house. Moore "starts with a simple room, empty and waiting for human action, with specific provisions—kitchen, bath, storage, and the like—appended in little sheds hung, like saddlebags, onto the central space."[6] The difference in the mobile home is that the equipment is within the central space, and special activity areas are appended. The advantage to this, beyond the additional interior space and potential for defining exterior spaces, is that the container now shipped to the site nearly empty could hold other items. This would offset the shipping cost for this additional space. The expense of shipping air has always been a matter of controversy in the mobile home industry.

One of the early luxury mobile home developments in this country, Blue Skies in Palm Springs, California, signaled an interesting and innovative compromise between the mass-produced unit and individualization. At the time of its construction, the eight-foot wide mobile home was prevalent. It was clearly insufficient in style and size for a luxury second home community. Consequently, the owners at Blue Skies, encouraged by the developer Rex Thompson, constructed their own attachments on and around the original unit. In this way, the factory produced unit supplied the core of the dwelling—including the appliance or "machine domain"

Figs. 9-25 and 9-26 Mobile home serves as basic unit. Individual features added by owner.

Fig. 9-27 Permanent structures serve as foundations.

elements—and additional living spaces were grouped around it. The structures which enshroud the mobile homes, called "Ramadas," are extremely elaborate and individualized elements (Figs. 9-25 and 9-26). This approach was presented in earlier chapters as the "seed" analogy, a means to accommodate choice and long-term change.

In a similar manner the owners of mobile homes in the Montevalle subdivision, near Santa Cruz, California, have coordinated permanent structures with their mobile homes. These elements are not only used to increase the amount of space and individualize the home, but are also used to alter a hilly site into flat areas on which to place the mobile homes. Furthermore, since residents own their lots in this development, these structures serve as a permanent foundation (Fig. 9-27).

Other attempts at variation in the mobile home are concerned with expanding the limited spatial aspects of the containers. This goal is most easily accomplished by changes in window sizes, a production step well within the constraints of the assembly line limits. Another method is to vary the ceiling plane. Since units are rarely stacked or placed next to high structures which would limit light and privacy, the use of clere-

Fig. 9-28   A standard frame with attachable components.

story skylights and "pop tops" is possible. The proliferation of roof shapes in the Reynolds Aluminum competition submissions is a function not only of the desire for light, but of the importance of the roof form in the overall aesthetics of the structure.

From the point of view of the consumer, the ultimate factory-produced house would be a set of elements, flexible enough to be assembled or reassembled in a variety of ways. This would result in an individualized house, perfectly fitted to the needs of the user and capable of change as the user's lifestyle and needs changed.

The problem with this approach is that as the components get smaller (and choice greater) we are back to the custom house. This type of factory-produced house may be the evolution of housing technology where conventional dwellings become more industrialized and mobile homes are less like containers, each accommodating interchangeable house parts. One design suggestion by Duane Kell and Craig Rafferty, cited in the second Reynolds Aluminum Mobile Home competition, approached the problem of production, choice, and environment in exactly this way. A set of components, mostly room size, was designed to fit within a

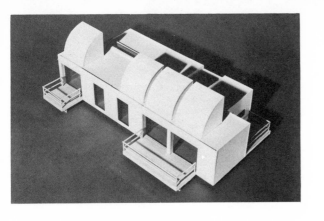

standard frame. These elements attach to the frame in a manner similar to the drawer-type extension but are less restricted in size and location (Fig. 9-28).

Combining Some Approaches

The house is relatively nontechnical when compared, for example, to a car. It consists of a few technical and equipment areas (baths, kitchens, heating, etc.), but the remainder of the dwelling is undifferentiated space. This space becomes useful when certain types of equipment are placed within it (couches, beds, chairs, etc.). An attempt to recognize these different aspects of the dwelling and to incorporate other innovative approaches to mobile homes is made in a design by Davis/Glass/Shen (Figs. 9-29, 9-30, and 9-31). In this mobile home, the service spaces are zoned into a single module. Thus, most of the equipment (water supply, drains, venting) is accommodated in one smaller 12-foot wide unit. This unit also contains all the circulation space for the house, including a recessed entry. It constitutes an efficient "machine" portion of the dwelling that could be used in conjunction with a mobile or a conventionally produced house. The larger, "living" unit consists of flexible spaces of maximum

width (14 feet allowed on the road) and is uninterrupted by circulation or by the requirements of specialized equipment. The two units are placed together in such a way that the service functions are directly across from the activity spaces they serve.

The Davis/Glass/Shen model uses clerestories to give the activity areas in the larger living unit a feeling of spaciousness and light by increasing the ceiling height. Clerestories are hinged and placed in the unit until it arrives at the site. This is possible because there is no fixed equipment in this portion of the home; it has been concentrated in the service unit.

The design allows for houses of various sizes. The service unit always remains the same, for it contains the elements essential even for houses of increased size. The "living" unit can be extended in increments, to allow for additional space according to the home buyers' needs. Since the two units are of different lengths, there are voids and changes in the perimeter which can accommodate decks, or various orientations and exposures for the rooms.

This design accepts the production restriction of the long rectangular form, and suggests that

233

it can be efficient and satisfactory spatially when used with another unit. In order to make the unit less containerized, and to allow for more connection with the exterior, voids are cut *into* the container rather extending elements *from* it. The need for increased space is handled within the existing technology by increasing the length of one of the units. The length is not concealed, however. The circulation space is linear and reinforced by skylighting to make a well-lighted, pleasant space. It should be noted that the planning concepts—particularly the core unit and living unit distinction—still permit stylization in any manner acceptable in the marketplace. There was no attempt made to "land" the home. Rather the desire was to make evident the distinction between the structure and the earth.

Although this scheme does not represent a radical departure from the current technology, it is doubtful that some of the features and the overall imagery will be acceptable in the market for some time. The living unit is relatively inexpensive, yet the use of skylights (in any form including the scoop) would be considered a risk by manufacturers. Furthermore, the acceptance of the box and the divergence from the traditional image of "house" might also be considered a negative marketing feature. The

industry has no incentive to attempt such changes even if they might yield a better living environment. Innovation and change occur in moderate doses, and usually concern choice of materials or additional household appliances. Even though its history and technology may have stimulated other forms, the conservative nature of the mobile home industry and the desire to make a product like conventional homes are the strongest forces in effect at present. The manufacturers wait for the "other guy" to experiment. They are quick to follow if he is successful, and quicker to recoil to the known quantity when he fails.

THE MOBILE HOME IN A CONTEXT

The sociology of the park and the preferences of the users are closely tied to the physical form of both the dwelling and the park planning itself. This tendency is particularly true in the adult mobile home parks of California and the retirement areas of the South. Although these park communities are not typical of the nation, they represent a growing market for mobile homes. In his sociological study of southern California parks, James Gillies called these adult communities "service oriented parks." They cater mostly to retired adults who choose the park less for economic reasons than for the

type of community and lifestyle it offers. Gillies categorizes the other major park trend as "housing oriented" developments. These are made up of young couples, many without children, who want an economical place to live near their work. They do not intend to stay in the park indefinitely and for them mobility and informality are more important than the social amenities.

The service-oriented park resident chooses that environment for reasons other than mobility and economics. Although they generally refer to the lifestyle and sense of community as their justification, there are physical aspects of the environment which support this lifestyle. These create a sense of community which may be lacking in other forms of housing.

The most complete sociological mobile home study, and one which concentrates on a "service-oriented" park, is *Idle Haven* by Sheila Johnson. Written in 1969, this extensive examination of a Northern California adult community analyzes the reasons middle aged and elderly adults (majority aged 50 to 70 years) chose the park environment. Many residents valued the park's being a recognizable neighborhood, even to the six-foot high fence around it. The fence, required by law, is a throwback to the days

when the parks were unsightly and were enclosed to protect others from visual blight. Now, however, the fence symbolizes the fortresslike nature of the park, it keeps undesirables out. This inside–outside dichotomy extends to all aspects of park life and physical form. The closeness of the units encourages casual social contact and informal surveillance. In nearly all studies of parks, the aspect of security was seen as a foremost justification of choosing park life. People feel comfortable leaving their homes for extended periods of time, knowing that their neighbors will watch out for their property. Within the walls people feel relaxed walking to the social events of the park at night.

The value of the notion of keeping "undesirables" out of the community is further reflected in the residents' tolerance of extremely severe rules and regulations. These regard not only how the units are maintained, but also the types of units and individuals allowed in the park. Antiurban sentiment and suspicion of racial minorities within the parks have long been an anathema to social planners and civil rights advocates. Nevertheless, the exclusive rules are almost unanimously supported by residents interviewed in studies. They are a major justification for renting rather than owning one's space. Residents feel that with individual ownership would

come a lack of control over the park environment. They look to the management to supply this control. Furthermore, the fact that they are not committed to the land makes it easier for residents to move their homes if they do not like their neighbors. The system is so endemic to park psychology that people comply with rules governing such minutiae as types of planting, length of grass (when allowed at all), and acceptable products which may be attached to the house. The physical characteristics resulting from these rules were outlined in Woodall's *Mobile Home and Park Directory*, a book which evaluated parks on the basis of visual consistency and excellence of landscaping.

Park residents continue to favor a single family detached house, not only because of the degree of privacy it offers over apartments, but also because it offers an opportunity to establish identity through individual landscaping. Here, however, a conflict arises. People in mobile homes choose them because of ease of maintenance. Although they like yards and gardening, the process of maintaining them is considered a burden. One response has been to eliminate the yard completely or leave its upkeep to strict governance by park rules. Thus, one person's status and environment cannot be depreciated by another's slovenliness.

The focal symbol of the community is the recreation building. It not only houses the extensive program of activities, but in many respects replaces the need for the status of an elaborate individual unit. Usually provided with great expanses of lawn, always having a pool and other luxuries, these structures stand like the castle of the kingdom. They are a substitute mansion, often designed to evoke images of aristocracy (Fig. 9-32). Brandburg, Statler, and Moore, large developers of mobile home parks in Northern California, have one development which includes a community building in the style of an Old English manor house and another with a hacienda. Within these structures are meeting rooms, game rooms, a kitchen, and often a library with a massive fireplace. In one sense they have replaced the town hall, the mansion, and the country inn as multipurpose symbols of community life, order, and decision making.

The image of a controlled, walled fortress with the castle within, self-contained, and somewhat self-governed, has led Sheila Johnson to suggest that mobile parks represent an ultimate urban solution. "Problems of local government, social control, community structure would be brought very close to the individual in the form of small, self-government enclaves, on the one hand, and there would be integration at the

235

metropolitan area level on the other hand."[7] Such a form, as she points out, is similar to the Chinese *pao-chia* system. The city of Hemet, California, with a population of approximately 12,000 has over 40 parks with a total of 7000 spaces. Hemet could be an example of the new American settlement.

The development of mobile home communities is certainly not a phenomenon limited to California, but there are unique features which are nurturing their proliferation in the state. These in turn have specific effects on physical form.

As has been said earlier, restrictive zoning has had much to do with placing mobile home parks away from important supporting city facilities and in areas often inappropriate for housing. These areas are frequently zoned commercial, and more often industrial. In California, however, rapid expansion and the accompanying freeways and suburban sprawl has left large amounts of flat land near transportation links. Although these areas are not near city centers, the migration of light industry, corporate offices and regional shopping centers outside the city has meant that mobile home parks can still be near thriving areas. Although the park sites are often zoned commercial or industrial as elsewhere, the image of industry is no longer one of

236

pollution-producing factories. Instead, there now exist industrial parks, created for light manufacturing and the "clean" industries of electronics and aerospace. These are not unpleasant neighbors for residential communities since they often are associated with large amounts of open green space.

The growth patterns and the generally positive environmental qualities of the typical California city combined with a moderate climate attract a retired population. As this land gets more expensive and the quality of the park environment improves, people may be more willing to invest in the mobile home community. Better and more expensive dwellings result, and there is a further upgrading of the quality of the environment. This, in turn, increases the market by attracting people with more to spend. Indeed, there is now a danger of pricing the product out of the range of those population groups that originally chose the parks.

Another problem, also related to land value and the development process, is that of larger parks. Whereas a large park in the mid 1970s was 300 to 400 dwellings, it is becoming 700 or 800. The community aspects of the park and the degree of security and identity will decrease as size increases. The form of the park as a viable

small community may be lost to a new form, the mini-city with its own commercial facilities.

Park Design

Originally, the trailer court was an unpleasant parking lot for units crowded as close together as possible (Fig. 9-33). This has now evolved most commonly into rows of double- or triple-wide mobile homes placed perpendicular to a street. The distance between units and the widths of streets are now outlined in industry standards and by government regulation of those parks which have approved housing. The industry's internal pressure for improved park layout and design suggestions has been effective, but generally developers still want to provide the smallest acceptable spacing possible.

Another variation catering to the same type adult community market employs some of the more traditional subdivision planning concepts, namely the green belt. These parks attempt a closer approximation of the suburban form. Units are on cul-de-sacs, and back up to a community green belt running through the park and including the community building. The use of cul-de-sacs makes for more variation in lot size and unit orientation. In addition, these parks often incorporate a natural feature or a man-

Fig. 9-33 1930s trailer park.

made lake or a golf course. The street layout is less rigid, as it winds around the open space making more corner lots than standard designs and thus allowing more units to have a "front" side or approach (Figs. 9-34 and 9-35). The major grounding technique in these parks is that of berming the earth to a level access, thus decreasing the apparent height and the boxlike form of the mobile home. The added amenities of such a plan are attractive; however, the developers point to the added expense of the green-belt planning and the question of intended use and maintenance of these common areas. More mundane parks simply avoid the issues of who owns and cares for green space by not including it.

In most parks there are no sidewalks and cars are placed next to the unit (on the right) in tandem with the entrance on the opposite side. The lots are generally 3000 square feet, the homes range from 1500 to 2000 square feet. The yards between the units and the street are 9 to 15 feet deep. Rents vary according to location within the development, with corner lots being the most expensive because of better views and light. These lots also allow the "front door" of the unit to face the side of access, or the street, as is the case in conventional housing (Fig. 9-36). This avoids the ambiguities on most lots about

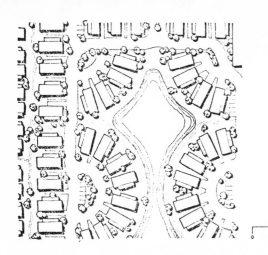

Fig. 9-34   Lake Park. Special features and more siting variety.

Fig. 9-35   Green-Belt planning. A closer approximation of suburban living.

what is "front" and "back." Other lots that are considered prime (and thus rent for more) are those that border on the community building. Again, these have more light and view and are closer to the park activities. Variations on form occur when the user group changes. For example, a park which allows children may have larger facilities. These parks are frowned upon by the more successful developers. They cost more to develop, but do not yield higher rents and management complexities are increased by the problems associated with the presence of children.

The Suburban Form

Some of the more progressive new park designs are developed in concert with the mobile home manufacturer. These are often called "closed parks" and their intention is to be as much like the modern day subdivision as possible. This type of park appeals to different buyers: those who previously owned homes, those who want to pay cash for a new home in a secure community, and those who want both a degree of privacy and a detached house. (Condominiums, the major competitor of the closed park, do not offer all of these features and are more costly.) The term "closed park" means that only

Fig. 9-36   Corner lots in mobile home parks.

certain units are allowed in the development. This rule is not only to control aesthetic integrity, but also to make the development process more lucrative. In the typical manufacture-to-park development process, profits must be shared between the manufacturer, the dealer and the developer. Many feel there is not enough profit in the industry to be divided three ways. In the closed park the developer/owner is also the dealer and thus profits must only be shared by two parties.

The best example of this type of park is Brookview in Concord, California. The park is a green-belt-type plan, relatively small (80 units) and family run by owners who held the property for many years before its development. It avoids many of the possible objections to a closed park. For example, residents are usually reluctant to bypass the developer/dealer and to go directly to the manufacturer for correcting defects in the home. They fear retaliation and possible eviction from their park. In the case of Brookview, however, the dealers take a personal interest in the quality of the product and visit the manufacturer themselves before any home is shipped to the site. Their rationale is that since the home is likely to stay in the park, problems with the product could hurt future park sales and the development in general.

In the case of Brookview, the close relationship of the developer/owner to the manufacturer has been instrumental in overcoming local objections to locating a mobile home park in a conventional suburban neighborhood. The local community was against a "tin city" mobile home park, but came to support the project when the developers took community leaders and councilmen to a Southern California exhibit of the Levitt mobile home product. This, as was mentioned previously, is wood-sided with a shingled roof making the unit indistinguishable from a subdivision site-built house (Fig. 9-37).

In addition to requiring either the Levitt or Viking shingled wood-sided units, the owners do extensive site development for each house and sell the package to the home owner at cost. Their justification is that they are thus assured of a professional installation in keeping with development plans. Since they make a profit on rent and sales, they need not do so on the site preparation (which includes a recessed pad and retaining wall with a drainage system around the unit). There is level access, a shingled carport and storage space, and an independent covered walkway. The carport and storage space belong to the residents and can be dismantled and moved with the unit if desired. Mobility of these mobile houses is illusionary, however, since the units fit snugly into the site and are, in a sense, custom designed for a particular resident and location. The homes are, nevertheless, registered as vehicles. Owners thus pay taxes only on the initial sale and through the rental of their lot. The site plan for the development is also similar to subdivisions, although at Brookview the units are closer together and the lots smaller. The lots may be legally subdivided, however, in the event that the property is converted to a condominium. Site development includes services or utilities which are operated by a local company and individual meters which run to the street from each unit.

The external pressures upon the industry by the public through both valid objections and misconceptions of mobile home communities, and the market demands for conventional houses at lower costs have determined the form of mobile homes at Brookview. The home is factory built, but not recognizable as such. It assumes an aestheticism acceptable to the immediate community and the housing industry as a whole. What should be noted is that there is no difference between this mobile home and a modular house. Indeed, the company that produces these units can make the adaptation of the product to conventional techniques and foundations. There are no significant physical differences between a residential environment such as Brookview and a conventional suburb. Although Brookview now stands as proof that factory housing can replicate existing modes of housing, its creation was not an easy process. Had the developers not previously owned the land, their uphill struggle for legal acceptance would probably have been abandoned. Still, the existence of Brookview demonstrates that the objections toward the mobile home can be overcome without sacrificing the original appeal of the product. The physical form of the dwelling and environs has been determined by the conservative forces both in and out of the industry. However, the process by which the dwelling is conceived, marketed, distributed, and potentially changed is an evolutionary departure from traditional housing.

A Vanishing Distinction

There is nothing inherent in their production, site needs, and shipping requirements which would preclude the use of mobile homes in many forms, including garden apartments and town houses. Their use to date, however, has been almost exclusively as a lower cost version of the single family detached house. This applies both to the form of the unit and the form of the park. The single family detached house continues to be the American ideal. The application of a lower cost technology has prolonged its existence when it might have otherwise been reduced to more economical forms. Though they have held the advantages of factory production and price, the mobile home industry cannot be blamed for failing to pioneer new housing forms. The mobile home business works on the free market principles of supply and demand, and the predominant demand continues to be for the single family house. Thus, it is easy to understand why the most advanced mobile home designs and park environments are indistinguishable from the forms of the suburb. In fact, any existing lines of distinction are becoming increasingly vague. The conventional home-building industry is becoming more standardized and componentized in an effort to remain competitive and the mobile home industry is becoming more flexible in an effort to increase its market. The success of the mobile home industry in terms of providing significant numbers of decent, if uninspired dwellings, may eventually be great enough to offset the desire to maintain the status quo in the conventional home-building industry. This may result in further adaptation of mobile techniques of factory production, and marketing more like that for consumer products. This, in turn, may allow increasing involvement of individuals in the formation of their dwellings and enhanced potential for choice and change.

Footnotes for Chapter 9

1. Center for Auto Safety, *Mobile Homes, Low Cost Housing Hoax.* New York: Viking Press, 1975, p. 15.
2. Drury, Margaret, *Mobile Homes, An Unrecognized Revolution in American Housing.* Ithaca: Cornell University Department of Housing and Design, 1967, p. 110.
3. Drury, Margaret, See footnote 2, p. 112.
4. University of Arkansas Department of Architecture, *The Immobile Home Syndrome,* Fayetteville, 1973, p. 33.
5. Koncelik, Joseph, "Mobile homes construction and the systems building concept," *Housing Crisis and Response,* edited by Earl W. Morris and Margaret E. Woods, Ithaca, Cornell University Department of Economics and Public Policy, 1971, p. 48.
6. Moore, Charles; Lyndon, Donlyn; and Allen, Gerald, *The Place of Houses.* New York: Holt, Reinhart, Winston, 1975, p. 51.
7. Johnson, Sheila, *Idle Haven.* Berkeley: University of California Press, 1971, p. 69.

Bibliography

Books

Center for Auto Safety, *Mobile Homes, Low Cost Housing Hoax.* New York: Viking Press, 1975.

Drury, Margaret J., *Mobile Homes: The Unrecognized Revolution in American Housing.* New York: Praeger, 1972.

Johnson, Sheila K., *Idle Haven.* Berkeley: University of California Press, 1971.

University of Arkansas Department of Architecture, *The Immobile Home Syndrome,* Fayetteville, 1973.

Waby, Marian, *Montevalle, The Story of a Dream Come True.* Felton, Calif.: Big Tree Press, 1975.

Woodall, *Mobile Home and Park Directory*, Highland Park, Ill., 1975.

Periodicals and Reports

American Institute of Architects Journal, "Mobile home, the third alternative," (December, 1971), pp. 42–45.

Cohen, Stuart, "Trailing Frank Lloyd Wright," *Architectural Design* (November, 1972), pp. 663–664.

Architectural Record, "Mobile home is the 20th century brick," (April, 1968), pp. 137–146.

Changing Times, "What living in a mobile home is like," (October, 1969), pp. 7–11.

Camarow, Avery, "The surprising new look of mobile homes," *Money Magazine* (October, 1975), pp. 92–106.

Fish, Richard, "Mobile home that doesn't look like it," *Los Angeles Times Home Magazine* (March 1, 1970), pp. 17–20.

Kendall, Elaine, "The invisible suburbs," *Horizon* (Winter, 1971), pp. 105–111.

Kneeland, Douglas, "From tin can on wheels to mobile homes," *New York Times Magazine* (May 9, 1971).

Morris, Earl W. and Woods, Margaret E. (Eds.), *Housing Crisis and Response,* Department of Consumer Economics and Public Policy, Cornell University, 1971.

Swabac, V. D., "Mobile home industry viewed by an architect," *American Institute of Architects Journal* (November, 1972), pp. 35–37.

Swaback, V. D., "Production dwellings: An opportunity for excellence," *Land Economics* (November, 1971), pp. 321–338.

Section Four
The Future

10
Futures for Housing

Richard L. Meier

"It's very 'todayness' is what I like—but what about tomorrow."

Housing, like education and health services, is produced by a highly conservative set of institutions which continue to depend upon the past for their inspiration as they face the future. Therefore, the bulk of the new housing in North America over the next several decades will resemble the recent past—tract homes, condominiums, prefabs, mobile homes, cottages, and other familiar forms. Most of the stresses felt in society do not stimulate design innovation; they merely depress the rate of building. Difficult times produce apathy rather than adaptations in form.

Designers gain their living, however, from the exceptions to this generalization. They must pursue novel forms and new directions hoping to identify and mediate some long-lasting trend, such as the public policy commitment to orderliness and cleanliness in settlements. Historically this bias has been epitomized by the Greenbelt new towns, even the migrant workers' camps depicted at the end of Steinbeck's *Grapes of Wrath* launched more than 40 years ago, but more recently by slum clearance reformulated as urban development. The most pervasive policy trend followed by house designers has been the elaboration of suburban types stimulated by the provisions of federal loan guarantees. Given any other financial backing,

designers have a fair chance for obtaining commissions allowing them to work outside the accepted paradigms. Once in place, such designs may be improved upon and eventually integrated into the mainstream.

Imaginative models produced as poems for living (Soleri's *arcologies* fit into this category) or as satires (perhaps the Archigram efforts provide the best example) stay alive as public fantasies that express the times (Figs. 10-3 and 10-4). Nevertheless, exceedingly few people are likely to be found living in them for the long term.

Currently, our best renderings of utopian futures are found in journals like *The Futurist*, a periodical published on this side of the Atlantic, and *Futures*, its internationalist, cosmopolitan competitor. Roy Mason, writing in the former (1976), has compiled a series of architects' images of the future, assembled from the last two decades of publication. However, interestingness alone does not produce livability in tomorrow's world. Historian I. F. Clarke, when he appears in the second journal, pokes gentle fun at our own utopianism by pulling Victorian and Edwardian etchings from the archives illustrating their images of the period in which we are now living (Fig. 10-5).

Some designers expect to see their work lived in if they hang onto the coattails of national housing policy, since it aims at guiding the progress of dwelling construction activity. However, the policies that are acted upon are concerned with supply, not design. Great debates ask how the masses shall acquire homes of their own. Advocates of the "huddled poor" demand places to live that are modestly comfortable, serviced with utilities and schools, and convenient to their places of work. A Housing Agency alternately kicks and shoves, pets and cajoles, to induce change in a slowly evolving technology. With very rare exceptions, innovations in housing do not arise from investments in research and development for design and construction, as attempted in Operation Breakthrough, but from external forces (such as new modes of recreation, household mobility, and novel materials and compositions) that are generated outside the realm of social policy and urban planning. Faddish minor variations upon the conventional, such as split-levels, are built, and then advertised as significant innovations.

A student of the future in the service of the designer finds this situation very frustrating, because his bag of instruments—the various models of social forecasting assembled by the

Fig. 10-4 Archigram designers illustrate contemporary logic regarding *habitat* carried to its ultimate conclusions.

Fig. 10-5 Any resurrected future that had been forecast during an earlier time looks absurd to people living through the period itself. Although visualized relationships and scales have often been realized, or even exceeded, the styles impressed upon the vision enable us to date the era that imprisoned the imaginations of the forecasters.

Fig. 10-3 Idealized proposals for *habitat* are not aimed at the middle-of-the-market but at the dreams people have about what life could be like. Paolo Soleri creates images that appeal to people willing to entertain a drastic reordering of life.

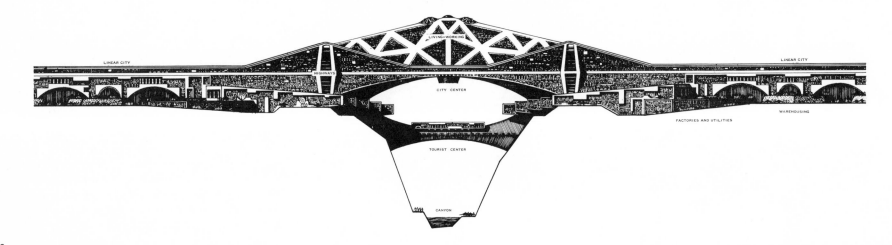

Commission on the Year 2000 and parallel groups in Europe and Japan—does not allow him to distinguish forthcoming courses of events that are noteworthy. Everyone suspects that remarkable changes in domiciles could be in the offing, but the graphic plots of growth curves and cycles, combined with statements of national intentions, do not throw light upon the kinds of transitions to be expected, nor reveal their timing.

To allow a heightened perspective, and explore a wider base of facts and trends, the futurist is forced to remove himself from regular contacts with the society. Instead of scrutinizing change as an informed observer viewing the action from the *inside*, as most planners and prognosticators prefer, he should somehow achieve an overview.

The most sweeping outlook in both space and time appears to be that offered by a *living systems* perspective. That part which encompasses organisms interacting with their environment—ecology—has become an immensely fashionable subject. The younger generation of the educated classes has become indoctrinated with its principles, and the language of the discipline is increasingly used in daily communications. Curiously, although ecological

insights have been repeatedly introduced to explain the anthropological features of housing in various societies, exercises in forecasting based upon experience with change in living systems are not found.

The appropriateness of the terms drawn from ecology now seems self-evident. Thus, at the Stockholm Conference on the Environment, it appeared perfectly logical that ecological language be drawn upon for the follow-up Conference on Human Settlements, so it was called "Habitat." Will deeper ecological analysis uncover any surprises for the experts or have any utility for the policy makers? There is no way to tell in advance other than going through the effort of fitting the phenomena of housing to the theory and the practice, hoping that not too many paradoxes and conflicts will be generated in the process. The huge stock of knowledge about living systems already accumulated should suggest new thoughts about the possible directions for housing change.

THE ECOLOGY OF HUMAN HABITAT

Living species appearing in the world before man have repeatedly interacted with their environment to produce a more congenial interface. First came tough membranes, and then

individual shells. Eventually organisms became social and collectively produced termite colonies, ant hills, wasp nests, and beehives. Birds' nests and mammalian dens followed much later. The complete habitat contained a *range*, or territory, for obtaining a livelihood by food gathering or predation, or both, and a defensible locus for bearing and nurturing the young, the *dwelling* (Fig. 10-6).

The dwelling possesses an order imposed upon a small piece of environment by an individual or a group: therefore it contains, under the more ideal circumstances, a great deal of information about life processes at a microlevel. The range, as introduced above, is more extensive; it contributes sources of livelihood (for humans this means jobs), a place for learning and play (school and avocation), materials of construction (stores and salvage centers), places to deposit waste (sewers and dumps), and a network of paths that are repeatedly retraced. In a low density society (supported by food gathering and hunting) ranges rarely overlap. If it should occur, threat of violence is likely, causing the weaker contestant to retreat. Joint uses of territory increase with rising density of settlement; they are based upon an accumulating body of accommodations and agreements by the settlers.

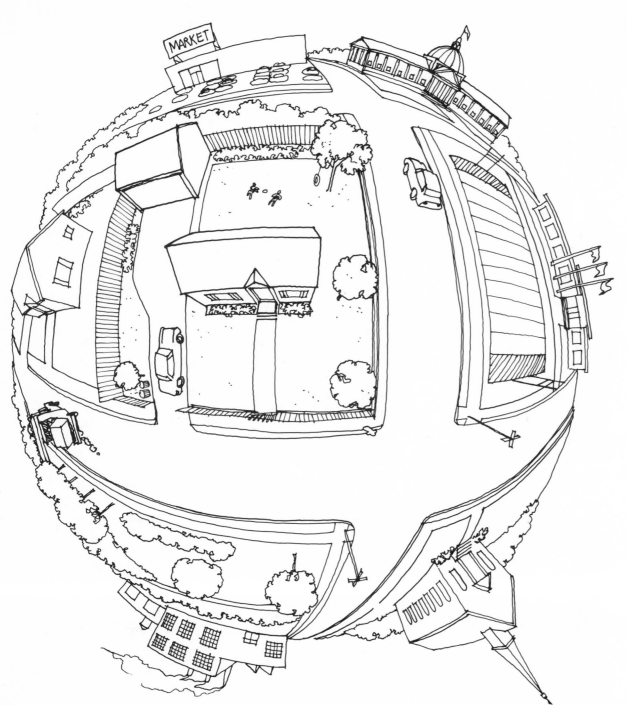

Fig. 10-6 Ecological principles can be applied to the little world of the modern household. The full extent of the regular daily movements is called *range*, home is a *dwelling* but temporary shelter may be erected at a distance next to the *source of livelihood* or sites for *play*, while somewhere in the vicinity are also found *materials and supplies*, sources of *services*, environments for *learning*, and depositories for *waste*.

Systematists among biologists can become quite ecstatic upon finding a particularly well-preserved hive or nest. Emerson, in his lectures, called such artifacts "frozen behavior." *Each species carries within itself unique instructions for making something out of its environment.* In times of prosperity the instructions are carried out quite completely, while in times of scarcity and stress there are omissions and skimping of effort. As the species evolves, the physical characteristics, the features of the design, are at least as likely to be modified as the organism itself.

Full expression of genetic instructions (and of accumulated negotiations with neighbors) is to be expected when robust members of the species experience uncommonly favorable conditions for growth and development. These instances become a statement of the *ideal form* impressed upon the environment for the full development of the community supporting such fortunate colonies of builders.

When food and materials in human society are plentiful, and the death rate due to epidemic disease is at the lowest possible level, the ideal conditions laid down above are present. Under those circumstances, meeting the requirements for subsistence takes little time or trouble, so more effort can be devoted to the preparation and management of the habitat and the rearing of the young. A curious unexpected conclusion arises from this ecological analysis of optimal conditions of life. Small groups favored with the highest potentials for welfare—superior social status, security from attack, health, fertility, nutritional surplus, and opportunities for leisure—overwhelmingly choose the same kind of environment. Despite the biases of environmentalists and other intellectuals, the evidence forces us to conclude that the contemporary suburb offers the nearest to optimal welfare conditions for Homo sapiens. *Therefore, the current classical expression for human dwellings, especially their form and organization, should be found in suburbia.* This point can be made more emphatically in the inverse: Where else could an attractive young couple of good breeding and excellent prospects, already possessing a bank account, automobiles, and pets, and planning children very soon, settle down to live? The alternatives are exceedingly scarce.

It cannot be claimed that the suburban house is genetically inscribed in the variant of humanity called *americanus*, but the characteristics of the built environment already assembled, es-

pecially the *impedimenta* accumulated to enable full participation in the society, suggest this form of home site. The plot size and floor area are determined by: 1) the need to exhibit a green circumference, 2) space to park vehicles, 3) storage of equipment (mostly sporting) suited to distant parts of the range, and 4) activity space for small children and pets. The imagery imposed upon the dwelling site is eclectic, being affected by climate, local traditions, choices of neighbors made earlier, suggestions arriving through the mass media, and a few inspirations by artists and architects.

FORECASTING HOUSING DEMAND

Ecological theory may also be used to estimate how many dwellings will be required over the next two to three decades. The field work that produces the basic information requires first taking a census of individuals to find out about age, location, parentage, functional role or social status, race, and other stigma revealing membership in a subpopulation. From such data the degree of subspeciation can be inferred, as well as some responses to abnormal density, the presence of special forms of climatic stress, the localized scarcity of resources, and the propensity to cluster in space.

The rules for the appearance of a new dwelling can be inferred from the study of human population dynamics. One unit will be built whenever:

1) a new sexual union is formed and settles upon a site;
2) a primary group (almost always including a sexual union) migrates to another site seeking more favorable circumstances;
3) much time is spent at the far end of the range (so a temporary habitation is set up); and
4) long trips are carried out under threat of inclement weather, so portable or hired shelter becomes advisable.

Once an original occupant dies or abandons a dwelling, however, that unit may be reoccupied and refurbished several times; most dwellings are expected to have a lifetime much longer than that of the founder, or any single member of the human species. Also, a dwelling unit may undergo fission in the course of changes in occupancy, being transformed into two or more adjacent units. The reverse also may be observed, particularly in prosperous periods.

It is possible to construct a *life table* for dwellings to which a cohort is added each year, and a number of "deaths" is subtracted from the population as a whole. This technique for registering census data allows us to make some forecasts of the *demand* for dwelling units when matched against a comparable table for human "home makers." The population of dwellings, like the populations of automobiles and livestock, is dependent upon the special conditions found in the human population.

The performance of the housing forecasters working within the system, adding up trends from many locales, is exceedingly poor for any time span greater than the gestation period of a house. It is useful, therefore, to expose the logic that may be employed by an outsider using the population dynamics features of *living systems* to arrive at more dependable projections. Forecasts of the number of new dwellings to appear on the scene 2 to 75 years in advance should improve significantly, because a great deal of generational information can be introduced.

New construction, the number of dwellings being created each year, should (under conditions of normal stress) be equal to the number of new human households being formed by young adults plus a number equal to the destruction

and abandonment. This number rarely coincides with the actual volume of construction because other factors are quite influential. The geographic mobility of humans always leaves a few percent of the dwellings vacant in normal times: Shifts in *mobility*, regardless of whether they can be attributed to the maturation of an earlier "baby boom," a foreign war, or better transport services, will have marked effect upon year to year forecasts. Simultaneously, the huge amount of effort expended upon the construction of modern dwellings (three to four man years per unit, and at least an equal amount invested in the range or infrastructure that supports it) tends to create lags. Thus, it is not unusual that the assemblage of new human habitat comes in spurts which result in some extra vacancies, and in lags during which independent householders may temporarily share dwellings.

This ecological perspective allows us to project the effects of a notable transition. In the past, male dominance was taken for granted, therefore households had *heads*, and the head most often sought a separate dwelling at the age of 25 to 35. He provided most of the necessary livelihood and was active over a larger range than the other members. Now there are almost

as many employed females in the younger age brackets as there are working males. Moreover, most young people resent the concept of "head" for a household. Therefore, with increasing frequency the sexual unions provide equal status to the partners, who also have roughly equal ranges. Nevertheless, it still seems likely that women will be "at home" over their lifetime more than men; so that henceforth it will be more appropriate to match adult women with the supply of dwelling units instead of "heads of households." Until now the effects of this transition were to be observed out in the range rather than in the dwelling, but soon we must expect accommodating changes in the design of the dwelling itself.

The possible forms that dwellings can take will be more influenced by *household size* than any other demographic characteristic. The most common household sizes attached to a dwelling in the next several decades seems likely to be three, one, two and four persons, in that order of frequency, although the actual occupany on a given date will be quite variable due to hospitality. The demand for units suited to single occupancy will be high for a while because for each woman reaching the age of 20 to 25 years, there will also be demand by a male of

Fig. 10-7 If we say the present "head of household" concept is obsolete, and instead equate the number of dwelling units with the number of women over 20 years of age, matching "vintage" in the stock of housing against age of women, and following up with estimates of dwelling "mortality," we arrive at an estimate of the prospective demand for housing created by women already born.

equivalent age, with their requirements merging somewhat later for the more traditional 2 to 5 person units. The average number of persons per household in America is due to fall below three, as against five to six in poor societies.

Interaction between a population of humans and a population of dwellings (Fig. 10-7) suggests that experience with the analysis of living systems may lead to other insights about what *kinds* of dwellings will be added in the future. Looking more closely at the "birth process" for dwellings, for example, it appears now that the insemination stage is the subdivision of land, since it is followed by the extension of circulation networks—streets, pipe grids, and wires. The time that the environment is "pregnant" with a dwelling is variable, a matter of several months to several years. In America the likelihood of "miscarriages" or "abortions," involving the scrapping of the structure before completion, and "infant mortality" which implies abandonment shortly after construction (as in the boom towns that become ghost towns), is now very low. These are indicators of a robust, generally healthy, well-organized society; four to five decades ago, such wastage was far more frequent.

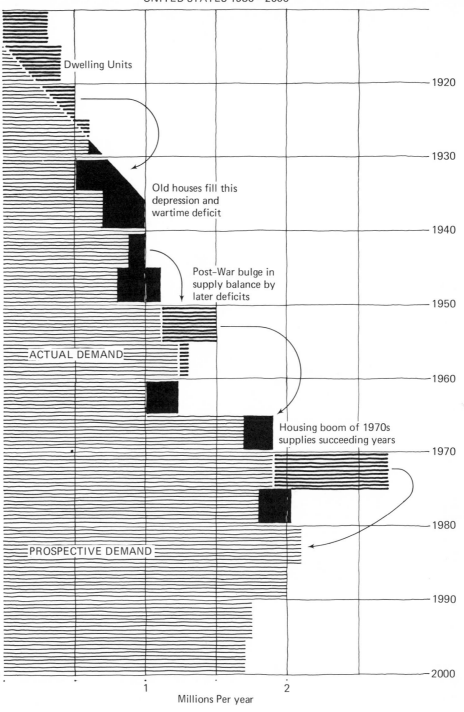

RELATIVE FUTURE DEMAND FOR HOUSING IN THE UNITED STATES 1980 – 2000

Dwelling Units

Old houses fill this depression and wartime deficit

Post-War bulge in supply balance by later deficits

ACTUAL DEMAND

Housing boom of 1970s supplies succeeding years

PROSPECTIVE DEMAND

1920
1930
1940
1950
1960
1970
1980
1990
2000

1   2

Millions Per year

Fig. 10-8 Life cycle of a dwelling: implantation, gestation, youth, maturity, senility, decease.

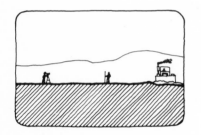
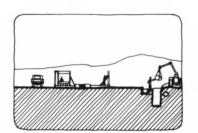

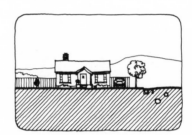
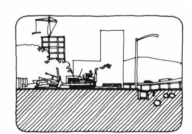

The ecological *image* of the dwelling says a great deal about its health. The "infancy" of a dwelling is healthy when associated with the planting of trees and shrubs, laying out of lawns, introduction of dogs, cats, goldfish, and other domesticates, attachment of several vehicles, powered and otherwise, all of them symbiotic with the house and its occupants. A normal mature dwelling will have outgrown shrubs, shade from full-grown trees, lines across the thinning lawn from the shortcuts taken, gaps in the hedges and fences, replacement of pets, and more elderly occupants on the average. The desires expressed at this stage for "cosmetic treatment" are understandable (Fig. 10-8).

Studying the completion of the life cycle—analysis of death, especially its causes and consequences—is absolutely essential to the outsider undertaking a forecast, but the reasons for the death of a dwelling are exceedingly difficult to classify. Fire, windstorm, flood, and earthquake are indubitable causes of mortal injury, but they seem to account for a very minor share of the deaths of dwellings.

The records of a reporting system need to be inspected before we can ascribe causes for the demise of each dwelling, such as exists on he death certificates of the human occupants. Although the records are not as comprehensively maintained as for the human occupants, it is possible from the incidental statistics and some observations to connect mortality in dwellings with some other changes in the society and the environment in recent times. In the period 1953–73, for instance, dwelling units in the path of freeway construction were demolished. Invasions by airports and harbors had similar repercussions in a number of larger settlements. These were all "violent" deaths, since the occupants were evicted, the interior was stripped of valuables, and large machines were brought in to smash the dwelling and haul away the debris. In out of the way places evidence of natural deaths can be seen; weather-beaten structures, leaning downslope or downwind, curtainless windows staring into space, surrounded by yards full of weeds, scraggly shrubs, and half-buried abandoned machines and furniture are indications of a long senile existence prior to expiration.

The issue of vulnerability to "disease" is worthy of consideration. Is there an epidemiology for the population of dwellings that operates independently of the health of their inhabitants? How do buildings become incapacitated? Specialists note that maintaining *rent controls*

seems to lead to a high (and increasing) death rate. Premature decease is attributed to neglect by proprietors and residents; not enough human effort is devoted to maintenance to keep them viable. However, we cannot be absolutely sure of the importance of this factor because quite a few other metropolises and cities must cope with significant amounts of abandonment around their cores, even though growth at the periphery is abundant and appears healthy. Is some kind of nutrient, or source of vitality, being extracted from the sites in the interior which is acquired by the habitat at the boundary? Bank offices seem to be involved; they are large and prosperous at the very center, quite rare in the core areas, and prevalent around the periphery. It readily comes to mind that they may be a nutrient conduit.

Premature death in components of a population suggests that some kind of *stress* must exist which is experienced most by the nonsurvivors. This familiar ecological principle seems to fit all the situations found in the urban cores. Observers must look for the correlates of these imputed stresses. They note that higher than usual density precedes abandonment, but that the prior emigration of jobs to districts on the periphery is at least equally significant. Stresses upon dwellings can also be observed in

the immediate locale where facilities for jobs are being installed, since the structures are either refurbished and expanded or displaced by slabs and blocks densely packed with dwellings. The pockets exhibiting ill health appear to be matters of concern, but they do not presage overall disintegration of the urban ecosystem. A few truly ancient dwellings are found wherever the stresses remained moderate.

This ecological view of human settlements encourages a holistic comprehension of the situation that is otherwise fragmented into groupings conducted by disciples serving the causes of sociology, economics, anthropology, and government. In particular, it aids our thinking about the effects of various kinds of stress upon habitat. This is important because the capacity to overcome new stresses is the basic formula for survival.

A MORE TURBULENT ENVIRONMENT

Despite sharp turnarounds in the production of dwellings, the past three decades are believed to represent a quiet period in the natural history of North American society. It seems quite likely that the physical, political, economic, social, and cultural aspects of the environment will be more variable in the future.

Fig. 10-9 Current experiments are leading the way to an even more intimate relationship between urban settlement and the production of perishable foods.

Consider first the physical shifts in the world at large. Climatologists now agree that the weather between 1940 and 1970 was extremely mild as compared to the range that the Earth has experienced over the past two millennia. While North American weather has not deviated too far from the norm since then, several very serious droughts in the wheat-growing parts of Asia have exhausted almost the whole of the American reserve stocks of food. Crop failures of equal seriousness on this continent now seem to be quite likely; the Great Plains are the most vulnerable. The world has become so closely integrated that famine anywhere will cause distress due to price rises everywhere. The expected response in North American cities would be to convert small patches of land, even rooftops, to the growing of potatoes, cabbages, beans, and similar semistaples (Fig. 10-9). The most salable new dwellings would then feature garden plots, either in allotments sited to exploit the most fertile soils or in the backyard. Growing things restricts movements of householders during the season, so their effective range would shrink. For those households without gardens the food budget would become a larger share of income; the overall income rise lags behind the price rise in the majority of the cases, so the portion of the income dedicated to mobility would be reduced. With less

mobility the area of the defensible range diminishes. Taken together, the prospective stresses, which are often at extremes in oscillations, may well produce premature failures of existing dwellings.

Climatic conditions could very easily resemble those inducing the last Ice Age. Analysis of prehistoric sediments suggests that a new Ice Age is due in our era. Such a transition might have an onset of only a few decades while triggering a 400-foot lowering of the oceans. However, the climate may also advance to a condition currently referred to as "Hot House Earth." That would set off a melting of the polar ice cap and add a few hundred feet to the sea level, thereby flooding out the world's most productive urban populations, established in estuarine and coastal settlements. Either of these extremes is certain to stimulate huge migrations, followed by the construction of habitat in new locales. However, the flows of refugees in the case of warming due to the "greenhouse effect" would be in directions opposite to those generated by an Ice Age.

A different source of stress can be identified with much greater assurance—the global production of natural gas and petroleum reaches a peak sometime during the next decade. From those top levels, supplies fall off ever more rapidly. The North American maxima were recorded in the 1970s, and the current rate of decline suggests what must be expected for the world as a whole.

Ecologically speaking, liquid and gaseous fossil fuels serve as an injection of energy that can only stimulate higher rates of material consumption, heavier investment in the physical environment, and more metabolic activity—especially mobility. These scarce mineral fuels can be replaced or substituted, but only with the aid of huge investments based upon coal and nuclear energy, later also solar energy, raising householder costs. Higher costs for energy, like those for food, cause reductions in individual ranges. General stresses reinforcing local capital shortages, such as those felt by New York, St. Louis, and Detroit tend to set off accelerated abandonment of habitat in their most threatened districts. Only predators and scavengers are expected to obtain the wherewithal to build, and most of them are inclined to build an aerie on some isolated hilltop.

ADDED SOURCES OF TURBULENCE

The present situation in the international political environment is so terrifying it paralyzes all rational considerations. Two great nations have built up, positioned, and targeted intercontinental ballistic missiles armed with multimegaton hydrogen bombs in sufficient quantity to kill each other several times over. The existing detente could be quasi-stabilized were it not for a handful of other nations racing to create their own stockpiles and the small circles of terrorists intent upon acquiring superweapons.

Even a partial exchange of blows would poison a large share of the habitat of North America. Survivors are able to flee from an irradiated sector, but dwellings cannot. Any significant use of nuclear weapons would result very quickly in a complete evacuation of larger settlements after the huge initial fatality rates were sustained. Induced leukemias and cancers would continue to cut down the survivors for decades thereafter. These refugees are forced to find niches in strange, sometimes alien, communities. They will build dwellings like those at "home," or like the archetypes in their adopted community. An understandable alternative would be slightly disguised bomb shelters to protect them to some degree from a repetition of the catastrophe.

Economic Policy

A number of archaisms cause the North American economic system to stumble from crisis to crisis, each causing a steeper and deeper cut in production. Committed to providing a job to everyone who wishes to be employed, it reports failure for 7–10% of the individuals. These promises could be met quite easily if minimum wage laws and a 40-hour week tradition did not exist. However, if either or both of these reforms were enacted, registered unemployment would disappear only to be replaced by a large number of "working poor." These poor are unable to produce or support full-fledged dwelling units from their own resources. The character of their crowded neighborhoods would run from seedy to slummy, unless subsidized by a formula for achieving equity. However, as ecologists know, wherever sustenance flows freely parasites of all kinds move in to get their share (in human settlements the parasites are unintended users, freeloaders and racketeers), so no formula for subsidy continues to be effective for housing the poor, whether employed or not.

Perusal of the study for the United States Department of Housing and Urban Development, *Housing in the Seventies* (Washington, 1974) suggests that the best hope for the poor is for further economic growth. It notes that the "trickle down" processes by which older houses of decent quality are made available to families with lower incomes is now working quite well. Nevertheless, the most probable outlook for the economy is for zigzag fluctuation in output, with surpluses of standard dwellings (as indicated by high vacancy rates) appearing on the down side of the business cycle, and localized scarcities on the up side.

Meanwhile the modern national economies of the world advance into the *post-industrial* era possessing mutual support arrangements still difficult to imagine. For example, about 80% of the active populations will no longer be engaged in the production of goods, but in providing services for each other. What are the new services to be rendered to dwellings? "Improvement of fit" and "retrofit" say the architects, who expect otherwise to be numbered among the unemployed.

Social Dislocations

The demographic milieu also inherits some major consequences from past decisions that have yet to be worked out. One of the most fasci-

nating of these has been illuminated by Peter Morrison. He notes that the tendency to migrate in America is very much a function of having moved before. Thus, whether impelled by hard times or distant opportunity, each stream of migrants creates counterstreams. Many return to the region of origin long after the original migration occurred. Once separated from their original community matrix, quite a few people move on to some beckoning potential. This fraction of the migratory population tends to move into the high amenity or high pay regions. The popular parts of North America include: 1) the Pacific coastal belt, 2) Florida, 3) the Washington metropolitan area, and 4) areas adjacent to the front range of the Rocky Mountains. People obviously prefer to recreate out-of-doors or obtain secure jobs adjacent to a clean suburbia.

To an important extent the Census interregional projections anticipated these flows, but they did not take into account the effect of loosened community links caused by the expansion in the share of the cohort obtaining higher education, which occurred particularly since Sputnik, and which still continues. Higher education is at least as alienating from the home community as the first migration, even if the student lives at home during the course of his studies.

Thus it seems quite likely that the nation has set into motion a massive matching of the educated tastes of the individual with the image presented by the environment, and the four above-mentioned regions are likely to remain the favorites. Given the competition for employment in the target areas a large share of the residents, natives and immigrants alike, are expected to work part time for pay while gradually creating with their own efforts the kind of dwelling or commune they appreciate (Fig. 10-10). Migratory pressures like these, reinforced by other sources of turbulence, could cause the populations of the favored regions to triple in the course of 30 years. Fortunately, there is more than sufficient room for all the popular kinds of human settlement, despite opinions voiced to the contrary, because per capita consumption of energy would decline somewhat, and typical ranges for humans would shrink in area. Rapidly improving telecommunications allow overlapping use of space without added congestion, since movements can be better coordinated. Finding this "good life" elsewhere means that the factory towns of the North Central region and the villages of the agricultural Midwest will be vacated and allowed to regress.

Those who arrived earliest in the favored regions will do everything in their power to keep inter-

Fig. 10-10 Emptier areas of the South and West are preferred by educated, new immigrants, many of whom work part-time while creating dwellings to fit their own tastes and life styles. A sample of the "woodbutcher's art" is presented here.

Fig. 10-11 New religions arriving from Asia are creating settlements with new and unexpected forms. This is the image toward which converts in a Tibetan Buddhist community north of San Francisco are working.

lopers away; they will invent many formulas, like the "no growth" ordinances of Petaluma (California), to restrict settlement within their borders. Nevertheless, partly in response to the "crowding" threat, the progeny of the original settlers will invent ways of occupying the empty areas of the globe, converting them to habitat for humans. The urge to pioneer—a basic trait of living populations—remains strongest in the West. More will be said about this phenomenon when those new environments are considered.

Religious Conversions

Shocks to value systems affecting the form and locus of housing seem to be arriving principally from Asia (Fig. 10-11). This shows up in part because religions from India, China, Iran, Korea, and Japan have been gaining many adherents among young people but it is probably much more attributable to a basic openness in the American urban culture which encourages the borrowing of esthetic concepts and intellectual postures. Acceptance of new symbols, images, and rituals from these other parts of the world has the effect of eliminating demand for large bulky furnishings inside the dwelling unit, allowing major pieces to be displaced by cushions, pads, trunks that serve as benches, and low tables that can be put away. The diet shifts

accordingly, either to more eating in public or to a more vegetarian cuisine that adapts to the high price of meat, thus putting fewer demands upon the kitchen.

Given this forecast of exigencies, what can be said about adjustments to be made which will provide satisfactory housing in the future? It appears that the *fitness* of a dwelling design to survive, compete, and be replicated will depend henceforth upon the following characteristics: 1) ability to function adequately with less energy, or else be oriented so as to capture its requirements directly from the sun or the wind; 2) access to land or water surface suited to intensive food production and minimal dependence upon refrigeration; 3) ability to economize upon water consumption, mainly through more intensive recycling, during periods of scarcity; 4) arrangements to share motor vehicles with others and to employ low to no-horsepower vehicles for many more purposes; 5) enhanced use of telecommunications and computing devices for immediate environmental controls and for transacting business.

These properties determine the *form* and the siting of new homes the further the society moves into the future.

Fig. 10-12   The single family ranch-style suburban house with double garage situated in a tract development is likely to retain its popularity for some years to come. Previously deprived minorities, rising to credit worthy status, strongly aspire to it. This archetype would be complete with an American made car parked in front.

With such requirements in mind it is possible to consider the expected gradual evolution of familiar types of dwellings. Present theories of evolution argue that specialized or unusual types will appear and survive when isolated sub-populations that have succeeded in meeting challenges are introduced into the mainstream again.

FROM ARCHETYPE TO "THROWBACK"

The single family ranch-style suburban house with double garage, *sfrssh-2g* (if this coding resembles that of a popular selling hybrid strain, the likeness is intended), epitome of the species proliferating in North America during the 1970s, and a symbol of modest success at the job, is ill-suited to a future with rapidly declining petroleum supplies, but it will not die easily (Fig. 10-12). Millions of school age youth of all races and ethnic groups now struggling in inner cities, industrial suburbs, and small towns will pay extra, once they acquire the credit rating. However, the subsidies that helped build them started disappearing in the 1970s, so hence-forth it will take at least a "Mercury station-wagon" level of success to acquire a new one, instead of the former "Ford sedan." How will the characteristics of this house type be affected by the stresses and opportunities that the knowable future holds, short of cataclysmic change?

Part of the answer is regionally conditioned. Prospects for new cohorts of the *sfrssh-2g* type in Middle America, from Winnipeg to Tulsa, and Pittsburgh to Omaha, are exceedingly poor. Because emigration pressure from this region is very strong, the secondhand versions will inhibit new growth. The Atlantic coast mega-lopolis, which fashions control networks for the nation and the world with top professional man-power selected for managing the new control circuits, offers the income and power to a minority to build the house of their dreams. The Virginian versions seem likely to become more numerous than the New Yorker examples. On the other hand, the renaissance of the South (from Charleston to Dallas), reinforced by the counterstream migrations desiring to demon-strate gracious, informal affluence while still strongly endowed with the Protestant Ethic, seems likely to sprout many small tracts and a few new towns, predominately "Pinto class," for a generation to come.

The West, origin of the protoimage image for the *sfrssh-2g*, is the favored region for evolving variants and crossbreeds. As suggested earlier, it is expected to absorb many more immi-grants who bring their college-fostered adapta-tions, and the terrain is so differentiated, that this region will remain the heartland of the type. The "Toyota class" will accept economical prefabs in many catalog models, but "Cadillac" households will insist upon crafted versions hidden in the hills.

Starting early in the 1980s we should expect the characteristics to be strongly modified. Berms will often be built-up window level for energy conservation and creating a more nestled look. Irrigated lawns would become more vestigial, often displaced altogether by prettified desert or Japanese rock gardens wherever water shortages pinch. Space for the second car is often taken over by a fixit shop, a summer kitchen, or a guest room; commuting and visiting are increasingly served by integrated bus lines and jitney–taxis, as a consequence of unpredictable fuel scarcities (which affect these low density settlements seriously, but do not render them unlivable). Backyards will be designed for conversion to vegetable plots, which displace the flowers during times of food shortage.

Going into the early decades of the twenty-first century the standard image of the 100-foot

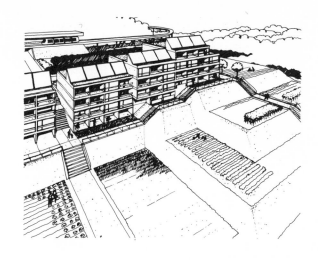

Fig. 10-13 When fossil fuels are very scarce, a generation hence, the affluent average American is expected to prefer living more compactly with immediate access to intensive gardens. The garden will require less water and the inhabitants fewer vehicles than at present. There will be more reliance on telecommunications and instrumented environmental controls.

frontage *sfrssh-2g* will have noticeably changed. Trees will be mature, high shrubs will mark many boundary lines, and their combined shade will thin out the grass. The vintage years of the 1960s and 1970s will already be growing some moss on the north side. The large quantities of speculatively held land in the south and northeast, after being long unsuccessful in establishing tracts of new housing, will have grown up into forest, thus becoming suited to the matured image.

Will nostalgic house types be taxed selectively, if they are evident drains upon natural resources? Such taxes are probably too unpopular to enact while the average voter is in his late 40s. The *sfrssh-2g* type may often be converted, however, to shelter two to four households, thus justifying a continued existence.

HIGH DENSITY CLUSTERING

Since the expansive, suburban version of the human dwelling rarely fits the resource-conserving requirements set by the future, yet the demand for units remains high for many years to come, it seems reasonable that the next building cycle will exhibit a propensity for strong clustering. This is logical, but can higher density overcome the prejudices that restrict

such construction at present? Let us look more closely at another common type in the dwelling stock, the multihousehold apartment cluster with one car families, *mhac-1cf*, and trace out its prospects.

The point has by now often been made that clustering, whether in high-rise or walkups, can compete effectively on the energy conservation front. Insulation costs per unit are low, and the radiative surface in the winter is minimal, while density is high enough to allow a grid of pipes to be laid down for a district heating system distributing steam or hot water produced with waste heat. In a continental climate, where summers can be as uncomfortable as winters, the same grid can be used for cooling. Eventual 30–50% savings in domestic energy use will need to be paid for by more complicated construction effort. A hundred square meters of floorspace (1075 square feet) may be advertised at $40–60,000 (1977 dollars). Attempts to use solar energy for the heating would push projects to the highest end of the cost range, while fitting solar equipment to the need for summer cooling as well would raise costs still higher.

To save fossil fuel expenditure on automobile transport these clusters should occupy sites

with mixed uses, such as near the center of metropolitan settlement, or at least along the inner high-volume transport corridors. That would simplify the commute to post-industrial kinds of employment, and allow a wide variety of specialized services within a small range. Long before the New Ice Age begins, energy conservation stresses bring Montreal and Twin City designs for preventing heat loss a thousand kilometers farther south.

Recycling waste water, the degree of reuse depending upon the frequency of short-run scarcity of metropolitan water supplies, is accommodated by higher density clustering of jobs, services, and dwellings. Paradoxically the highest uses for waste water and sewage are often found in intensive gardening. Therefore, once a worldwide food shortage strikes, those versions of the *mhac-1cf* which promote availability of gardens (or arrange cooperatives with access to allotments or surpluses from truck garden producers) should gain an advantage over competitors. The values and motives are so different from the present subtype known as *garden apartment*, it seems likely that a new name will be found (Fig. 10-13). When the Manila region in the Philippines was recovering from an extreme flood, followed by a severe

Fig. 10-14 Vacated spaces in the built-up areas entice the artisan and Bohemian elements who create ad hoc dwellings suited to low rents. This was a loft intended for light industries or warehousing, but both activities have largely fled the central city.

drought, and the Government sponsored gardening in all empty urban lots, city residents spoke of "green revolution" plots, relating them to the attached dwelling units.

Two major impediments to the construction of the *mhac-1cf* type dwellings are encountered by an ecologically minded futurist. One is the prevalence of predation (robbery, rape, rackets) in many of the central, high density districts. The reputation for such conditions retards investment in what would otherwise be the most suitable sites for installing carefully designed clusters. Feelings of insecurity are strongly reinforced by reports of racial prejudice, since many older neighborhoods in the core of the metropolis are now dominated by neighborhoods of blacks, Spanish-speaking peoples, and white addicts (gambling, alcohol, and harder drugs). "Red-lining" a district (i.e., excluding it from mortgage loans) is a response to risk, but it also accelerates the decay.

The second is a problem engendered by action behind the scenes, and is therefore difficult for an outsider to assess. It stems from a pyramiding of veto groups and agencies when density is high and human activities are strongly entwined. Consider, for example, the promoter who must pick up an option on land, come to agreement with an architect regarding the best image to impose upon the project, bargain out agreements with three sources of capital regarding acceptable risk and rate of return, negotiate with a contractor, press for permits from several urban agencies, and manipulate the mass media in order to merchandise the product. He must then send out at least ten thousand messages in order to find one potential occupant with the desire and the resources to make a commitment. At one moment this sequence of operations fails because of a scarcity of loan capital, at other times it is the uncertainty in the minds of many participants caused by inflation. It could also fail because of world shortages in critical supplies, or local difficulties with labor union organizations. The foreseeable future is a period in history when clear paths to the speedy provision of units with the complexity of the *mhac-1cf* type are not evident. The supply may well lag considerably behind demand.

People can create high density housing for themselves if they are permitted to do so (Fig. 10-14). In San Francisco—a unionized yet fastidious city, hardly uptight—many abandoned warehouses and empty lofts have been converted by cooperatives of artisans into complexes of small apartments, studios, and communal facilities. Until recently, equivalent attempts in New York City and elsewhere have been frustrated by authorities insisting upon the letter of the law. Breakdowns in local administration, similar to those experienced in New York's budgetary crises of 1975–76, seem likely to result in greater permissiveness, so a system of self-organized house construction, using part-time self-help, may come into vogue. Insufficient employment for architects in many locales makes it possible for most of them to become co-conspirators and promoters; their professional knowledge assures that elementary fire, structural, and other safety precautions will be observed. A significant share of these hivelike clusters are organized by recently introduced religious communities which need special spaces for their ritual and recreational activities.

Other kinds of existing structures pose similar challenges. It would not be surprising to see, quite soon, some bankrupt parking garages converted into mobile home parks, with as much time and organization dedicated to tidying up the immediate environment as is exhibited in contemporary mobile home courts. If the adaptations are successful, entrepreneurs may finally try to sell "lots" in steel and concrete space frames with plug-in utilities for the insertion of independent prefab dwellings—an idea previously interesting only for architects (Fig. 10-15). If the household retained a car, it would be parked alongside, or in the basement. This approach requires the householders to arrange for the finance of 60–80% of the cost by using their own credit resources instead of those of the builder.

Another kind of salvage operation awaits birth. Many metropolitan cores have seriously overbuilt modern office space. Is it not possible to convert less desirable office blocks into living space desired by special subgroups of urban inhabitants? When it is decided which of the downtown towers will go bankrupt, and asking prices for floor space are sufficiently deflated, it may also be possible to down-zone. Some interestingly different interiors ought to result from low cost alterations (a private suite without a private bath, but a sauna down the hall?).

A rapidly growing potential demand for centrally located dwelling space is revealed by further consideration of the population dynamics of the North American ecosystem introduced at the beginning of this futures analysis. Quite sizable cohorts are approaching the expected retirement age: they will contain an even larger proportion of females than is observed at

261

Fig. 10-15 In the recent past, mobile homes have allowed moderately high density clustering of dwelling units in the otherwise thinly settled peripheral areas of American metropolises. The cluster of mobile homes in locales with mild climates can go one step further.

present. The phenomenon seems likely to encourage the formation of cooperative groups of independent adults. Already these age classes, unsure of their ability to continue driving their own cars, tend to collect in the older, lower rent buildings on the fringes of the down town area. In two decades their number could treble, because the so-called retirement communities appear to fit the needs of a diminishing fraction.

The greatest deterrent is the common belief that central districts are dangerous at night. However, a major hope for the future can be detected in the same age distributions of urban residents. Criminal activity, it should be noted, has a strong tendency to decline after the socialization process is completed (about age 25) and also when productive roles are made available to unemployed males. Once the current sharp decline in birth rate works its way through to the age most likely to relinquish crime and violence (1985–90), not only would the supply of potential petty criminals diminish but the scarcity of people willing to take entry jobs in the labor force should also be evident. Thus, reduced numbers of youths as well as reduced unemployment, combined with a sizable expansion of the self-sufficient middle-aged population, should cause the fre-

Fig. 10-16 Year-round settlement of communities above the Arctic Circle are needed for economical extraction of energy resources, but the settlers will have been accustomed to temperate climates, so designers expect that they will need to install enclosed public gardens to enhance "livability."

quency of being a victim to be reduced by more than 50%. Moreover, the fraction that continues to live by violence and coercion has by then learned how to organize and is therefore able to prey upon the richer pickings on the periphery. This does not mean that concern regarding vulnerability to crime will disappear, because the level of concern is observed to have a low association with rates of victimage, but that other, more pressing, problems should cause attention to be diverted from fear of violence.

HARSH ENVIRONMENTS

The importance of design increases with the stressfulness or turbulence of the environment. Use of a living systems, or ecological, model of analysis assists us in understanding how a population continually tests neighboring territories in search of new habitat. A small colony is established shortly after a formula for survival has been found. Analogs throughout the animal and vegetable world suggest what should be looked for when assessing human pressures against what were once felt to be natural boundaries for habitat.

Normally parties of explorers and prospectors are sent out to look at the beckoning open space.

It is first occupied by lone males who camp and try to "live off the territory," exploiting its most valuable resources. These camp dwellers test out various proposals for permanent occupation. In earlier times these prospectors went out with mule or canoe, but nowadays they are likely to use a Landrover, or a snowmobile similarly equipped. After proving the potential of a high-grade resource, a number of light rugged carriers equipped as campers, or else pulling trailers, are dispatched to undertake preliminary development; either a road is blasted through to civilization or a port is prepared for aircraft or vessels. A permanent camp is assembled which houses men for a brief season, or increasingly now, a two-week shift followed by two weeks off. After the water supply has been secured, an appropriate technique of construction worked out, and clinics and schools have been installed, the way has been cleared for the establishment of a human community that may continue over many generations. Such a community is likely to make rather novel adjustments, especially in the manner in which they conduct their play. These adjustments are then reflected in the form of the dwellings that follow and in the organization of the community services.

Arctic areas offer the biggest prizes at the moment—petroleum, natural gas, and uranium. Equipment requirements for testing and exploiting each of these are vastly complicated, so every form of transport is brought into use. Canadians and Alaskans will be participating in the settlement of year-round communities at or above the Arctic circle within a few years (Fig. 10-16). Enterprising households will be learning how to fit into these quarters, along with indigenous Indians and Eskimos. The end product is expected to be a set of dense clusters, perhaps eventually tempered by a dome that transmits sunlight, allowing the summer to be extended by a colorful spring and fruitful autumn, but resists the transmission of the infrared portions of the spectrum, thus warming the protected precinct during the winter. However, at most only a few hundred thousand people are expected to be recruited for resource development in the North.

The antithesis, that of settling in the hot desert, seems to be far more popular. Since water is often extremely scarce, it must be strictly conserved in and around the household, and it should only be used for growing high-valued crops. When bands of desert dwellers herded animals, much of the water was needed for

Fig. 10-17 Underground houses can be energy efficient and inexpensive while the density can be quite high (say a hundred units per hectare) without casting shadows. Popular expectations about form for this genus do not yet exist, so it will pay to explore the implications of cheap tunneling techniques for dwelling design.

forage; henceforth it is expected to be utilized through hydroponics—soil-less cultivation of plants—to produce three or more crops per year from a given plot. This is a technology that is being rapidly advanced by Arab and Iranian interests after taking root in California and Arizona in the 1960s. The future oasis will be marked by a battery of plastic-sheeted hemi-cylindrical structures served by one or more block houses protecting pumps and mixing tanks.

Heavy adobe walls covered by a thick overhanging roof used to be the appropriate solution for achieving relative comfort in desert regions. It amounted to pulling up a cover of soil (both briquetted and kiln-cured) and placing it around the human habitation as insulation and protection from fearsome windstorms (Fig. 10-17). It is now evident that a more effective way to live under desert conditions is to burrow deeply into the clay or sand, disturbing as little of the surface as possible. What remains above the surface for such a house is a ventilator window, sometimes periscoped, for introducing air and light, while a framed-in-concrete hole in an adjacent mound allows descent to the living quarters, and a bit of greenery will sprout from the waste waters associated with modern living.

Fig. 10-18 The plastic arts combined with energy and space-conserving strategies suggest wraparound houses with walls and roof made of rigid polyurethane (coated or treated for fireproofing) for the do-it-yourself trade.

Fig. 10-19 American houseboats are merely aquatic mobile homes. In a suburban backwater (Alameda, California) they can be designed to project a middle class image.

Growing up in harsh environments—high altitudes, extreme heat or cold, high wind, continuous rain—produces skills and outlooks utterly different from those encountered in either rural or urban settings. In sparsely populated territory each person, male and female, becomes a jack-of-all-trades. His employment record is likely to show striking changes, such as from hard rock miner to short order cook to commercial air pilot in less than a year, with the range of avocations being still more extensive. Social status in their circles depends upon mastery of the machines that operate on the environment, and an ability to cope coolly with the emergencies that inevitably arise. Whether "wood butchers" or working in portable new materials such as polyurethane foam, they design for themselves, with helpful hints from professionals who have fled from the cities; they build when they are ready, usually with the aid of catalogs and through exchange of services. The forms are idiosyncratic, sometimes highly unusual; the details are pragmatic, often appearing ingenious (Fig. 10-18).

SEAWARD SETTLEMENT

The high seas offer the blandest, most commonplace of the harsh environments. A curious feature of the marine boundary to human settlement is the steepness of the dropoff from some of the richest and most active urban precincts to absolute emptiness. About 90% of the major cities on this continent have a watery edge, often with a few finger piers that trail out into a protected harbor. A significant amount of ship, barge, and recreational traffic is to be observed, yet the number of households to be found offshore runs from zero to a maximum of a hundred.

Western societies have always regarded the sea as a desert to be crossed with cargo, or a range for hunting fish, but otherwise fit only for camping. Ship's crews routinely leave their families behind. More recently platforms of various sizes have been installed offshore, but they are manned again as camps. By 1975 more than 10,000 men and a handful of women were at work on drilling and production platforms. Even with this number still rapidly growing, there are no new villages or towns. In contrast, the Asians have developed several traditional modes of village life for "water people" living away from land.

Problems of safety for life and property (small craft insurance rates are set about ten times the level for a house at waterside) are now coming under control. Objections that living afloat would pollute the marine environment can now be overridden in fact, if not in opinion. Structures are now known and tested for every recognized dwelling arrangement, and for some of them the solutions are more economical than for the terrestrial equivalent. They can be discussed in order, from the smallest to the most complex.

Parallel to the road-bound mobile home is the houseboat limited to protected waters (Fig. 10-19). Simplest is a cabin resting on a platform of planking supported by a few old, replaceable oil barrels. A design that is still serviceable and inexpensive would employ a special ferroconcrete hull. In estuaries rented outboard engines are attached for the purpose of changing location, analogous to the tractor-truck hired to shift a mobile home. Although factory-built houseboats can be bought, most are still self-built by owners with the assistance of marine craftsmen. The vast majority are used as second homes for a household, but a number have found their way into permanent occupation with the aid of a wink from the law. In Sausalito, California, where a whole village scale community has grown up under the protection of a rich pier owner, the Marin County law, as represented by the sheriff, has been frustrated

Fig. 10-20 Converted canal barges in Amsterdam make excellent town houses in restored "old city" precincts. Retirement of marginal waterways creates a ready supply of hulls.

through collective vigilance and active opposition when arrests were attempted. Houseboat owners are regarded as squatters, a phenomenon that cannot be tolerated in a respectable resort town.

The equivalent of the apartment building, or the rehabilitated warehouse, is a barge with several decks and suites. Although an obvious step, this approach to grouping dwelling units has so far been encouraged only in the Arab Emirates (designed and built in Singapore). Relatively uninformed landlubbers have objected, on the ground that either pollution would result or that some other as yet unknown environmental impact would be felt. The onset of comprehensive coastal planning, with its attendant delay of decisions, has not brought rationality. Amsterdam, drawing upon an estuarine tradition, does a fine job in the design of small apartments on barges moored in its canals (Fig. 10-20).

The first marine "new town" was launched from Okinawa in 1975. Designed cooperatively between Hawaii's ocean engineers and Japanese architects (Craven, Kikutake), a resort community (in Japan, a "gay district") took shape as part of an international exposition (Fig. 10-21). It is the permanent structure that remains

Fig. 10-21 Designers from two archipelagos (Japan and Hawaii) have combined to create the first modern floating community, now anchored off Okinawa.

after the fair is over. Another in the same series is proposed for a site just outside Honolulu— a new addition to the Hawaiian archipelago, but held in place fixed on stars by dynamic positioning. A stable base for a floating platform in deep water, invulnerable to storms, requires flotation tanks of a scale exceeding that of a space satellite launching station. Cost of living space in the first model is already less than the standard rent for living in Tokyo, while the cost in time and money of a regular 4–6 km ferry trip is considerably less than the normal metropolitan commute ticket.

A potentially limiting factor is the lack of job opportunities for those who hope to settle communities farther out at sea. The range is too thin to allow people to live on fishing, since the biomass per unit area is no greater than that of grassland, which historically developed nomadic tribes, not towns. The petroleum wells are controlled largely automatically once they are in place, while the metallurgy of manganese nodules brought up from the floor of the ocean may require one or two deep water installations to fill total world requirements. Proposals are being developed now for the transfer of certain land-based bulk-handling industries— superports for docking and storing cargoes from the very large ore and oil carriers, energy islands for coal-burning and nuclear power plants, airports to handle noisy jets, and a few others. Nevertheless, the number of dwelling units tied to these facilities are very few and so far quite incidental to other purposes. One interesting possibility—a technology recently actively explored—is a settlement based upon the harvesting of marine kelp where the yield can be several times greater than the best forests. If it could produce something valuable, like synthetic paper, along with by-products of protein and methane, some very interesting town sites and lifestyles could evolve.

Most coastal metropolises can now start a floating suburb that offers a contrasting image and another way of life. A romantic demand for houseboats and housebarges, supported by modern marinas, is detectable. Much of the interest arises among the present mobile home dwellers, and the bulk of the remainder from present owners of smallcraft. Once permitted by coastal planning agencies and by land-based communities (San Francisco began opening up its China Basin in 1976) without too many restrictions, it seems likely that tens of thousands of dwelling units would be built for occupation offshore, and an equal number in reservoirs and lakes. For the first decade or two rapid changes in neighborhood design must be expected, with the old-fashioned, obsolescent developments relegated to becoming havens for pensioners. Avant-garde communities would provide access to support systems for the fullest possible range of aquatic avocations, just as condominium communities in mountain resorts grew up in sites convenient to skiing, fishing, hunting, kayaking, and horseback riding.

Bits of information gleaned by a variety of investigators from the few thousands who have already found niches in marinas and fishing harbors suggest that the marine environment stimulates the synthesis of a new lifestyle. Because living space is so compact, households do not collect gear or inventory the way they do on land; such property would only break, mildew, or corrode. At sea the junk that might otherwise lay around and rust would either be collected for salvage, or sink into the muck at the bottom.

Life is lived as a round of warm human associations, permitted but not produced by the dwellings. Food from a galley, for example, is rarely served very elegantly. Residents make their living most often through expression— arts, music, journalism, broadcasting, architecture, equipment maintenance, small-scale contracting, and human services. Personal ambition is rare; ad hoc groups are easy to organize. This is a way of life that finds it easy to live with zero growth of the economy.

OUTER SPACE

In the 1960s, when the first man walked upon the moon, speculation was rife that a moon colony was imminent. However, the investment requirements were so extravagant that the zeal of even the most optimistic speculators was dampened. A great deal more wealth needed to be accumulated before this phase of science fiction would come to life. Physicist–novelist Arthur C. Clarke's idea that manufacture of solid-state components in the high vacuum of outer space might provide the essential economic base justifying such settlements did not appear productive enough.

Then quite suddenly, in Princeton University's Physics Department during the years of 1974–75, a new concept for human habitat arose out of a series of calculations. It was reinforced by the publication of Clarke's new novel *Rama II*,

Fig. 10-22 NASA scientists envisage a space colony in the twenty-first century of 10,000 persons that is constructed through the reduction of moon rocks. They may be justified economically if they build and maintain robot satellites for the collection of solar energy, converting it to microwaves and supplying land-based cities in need of electric power.

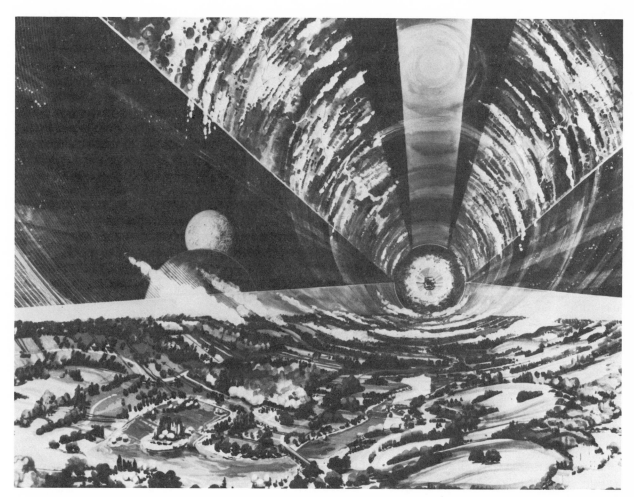

which seems to be based upon completely independent calculations for constructing a viable habitat. Human settlement now seems technically feasible some time early in the twenty-first century, and the incentive provided by Gerald K. O'Neill, originator of this novel pioneering potential, is the production of solar energy by means of reflectors and equipment for converting that radiation to microwaves beamed at an antenna field near an Earthborn metropolis which converts energy into electric power.

Consider a future world with many well-meaning people tormented by the impacts of their energy supply problems. Many of them continue to regard nuclear energy to be too dangerous; others are equally worried about the sulfuric acid adsorbed on the fly ash produced from the burning of coal. Geothermal energy, once touted as "clean," often releases hydrocyanic acid. Hydroelectric power subjects settlers downstream to risk of flood in the event of an earthquake, and indirectly causes erosion among the beaches and cliffs at the seaside. Solar energy would appear to be the permanent solution, if the storage costs were not so excessive and the technical equipment so ugly. Perhaps, say the worriers, the bulk of the North American population will be forced to move to the equatorial zone by the twenty-second century when the gas and oil are used up.

O'Neill comes to the rescue by proposing to fabricate pairs of Earth satellites out in space, mostly from soil on the moon. To operate them he needs communities in the small region (astronomers call it the L-5 Lagrangian libration point) where they are stable with respect to the Earth, its moon, and the sun. Habitat for the builder society is maintained within gigantic rotating cylinders, with people walking and working according to biorhythms they have inherited from Earth (Fig. 10-22).

Man understands himself better once he sets out to design a total environment. In order to take advantage of this "technological fix" such an environment would have to be maintained on Earth for decades, perhaps at the South Pole, or in the mid-Pacific, so that a stable ecosystem would have time to establish itself. An L-5 Society has already been formed for the colonization of outer space. Thus, there is strong incentive to occupy empty spaces on Earth as a step to outer space settlements, which in turn could solve our long-run energy supply prob-

lems. The composition of moon rocks suggests that those dwellings would have to be constructed from aluminum and glass or ceramic. The forms these buildings take will hardly be left to architects; the volunteers will almost certainly assert their freedom to create their most immediate environment.

SUMMARY

Taking the broadest possible view, employing ecological principles for systematic exploration, it appears that the quiet years are behind us. Despite strong conservative forces in the institutions responsible for the provision of housing in North America, the need to cope with global shortages, massive catastrophes, and harsh environments should stimulate diversity in form.

Continuation of low birth rates is expected to eliminate the industry of house building as it is now organized by the 1990s within most parts of the continent, leaving vestiges only in regions targeted by migrants. Most efforts will be addressed to adapting the existing stock of dwellings to changing conditions.

The necessary economies in the use of resources are best achieved through clustering of dwellings to economize on vehicular use; reoccupation of abandoned inner-city structures; integration with intensive vegetable growing; and introduction of underground construction techniques. Novel qualities will be added in coastal metropolises through the accretion of houseboats, apartment structures on barges, and even full-size communities on stable platforms on the high seas.

Increased levels of skill and sophistication in the population (and less time spent in organized work) will encourage personal design and self-help construction. The outcomes may range from wholly plastic houses to those that are hand wrought from natural materials. Condominiums, cooperatives, communes, and other associations will find ways of fitting environments to their values.

These explorations could lead the way to the total synthesis of human habitat suited to the occupation of outer space some time in the next century.

Further Reading

The futures we foresee cannot be documented in the same manner as reports on achievements and discussions of methods. Therefore, a series of suggestions for following up the ideas put forward is presented as an alternative.

The special ways of thinking within the framework of ecological principles can be extracted first from any of the recent textbooks. That reading can be followed with selections from general sources containing overviews, such as Ecological Monographs or Annual Reviews of Ecology and Systematics, along with occasional presentations in *Science*, which contained, for example, R. L. Meier, "A stable urban ecosystem, vol. 192, (4 June 1976), pp. 962–978.

For a still more comprehensive outlook see J. G. Miller, "The nature of living systems," *Behavioral Science 16*, pp. 277–301, 1971, then following up references cited there. Thereafter, one can browse in the yearbooks and journals of the Society for General Systems Research for examples of argument by homology rather than analogy.

Ready approaches to the literature on futurism and ecology are provided in the introduction to this chapter, but see also Michael Marien, *Societal Directions and Alternatives*, Information for Policy Design, LaFayette, New York 13084, 1976.

For assessments of recent American housing policy, see Bernard J. Frieden and Marshall Kaplan, *The Politics of Neglect*, MIT Press, Cambridge, 1975, and Arthur P. Solomon, *Housing the Urban Poor*, MIT Press, Cambridge, 1974. They offer critical appraisals of official documents and the statistics.

For implications of approaching steady state in population size, one finds a quantitative demographic analysis in Tomas Frejka, *The Future of Population Growth*, John Wiley, New York, 1973, and a qualitative evaluation of a broad range of accompanying phenomena in R. L. Meier,

Planning for an Urban World, MIT Press, Cambridge, 1974, and R. W. Burchell and David Lostoken, Eds., *Future Land Use,* Center for Urban Policy, Rutgers University, New Brunswick, N.J., 1975.

For the influence of environment, particularly the attractive forces of a mild or invigorating climate, upon migration see L. M. Svarts, "Environmental preference migration," *Geographical Review 66* (July, 1976), pp. 314–330.

The prospects for settlements in marine environments, especially the possible ways of making a living from marine resources, was recently reviewed by the Conference on Seaward Advancement of Industrial Societies and fully abstracted in the March 1975 issue of the *Marine Technology Society Journal.* The human settlements potentials offshore were considered in some detail by R. L. Meier in *Planning for an Urban World.*

A full analysis of the feasibility of dwellings underground is provided in Frank Moreland (Ed.), *Alternatives in Energy Conservation: The Use of Earth Covered Buildings,* National Science Foundation, U.S. Government Printing Office, Washington 1976.

Potentials for colonies in outer space are introduced by Gerald K. O'Neill, "Space colonies: The high frontier," *The Futurist,* vol. 10 (February, 1976), pp. 25–33.

About the Authors

Gerald Allen is an architect in New York and an Associate Editor of *Architectural Record*. He holds degrees in English and Architecture from Yale University. He is coauthor, with Charles Moore and Donlyn Lyndon, of *The Places of Houses* and, with Charles Moore, of *Dimensions: Space, shape & scale in Architecture*. His designs have appeared in major architectural magazines in the United States and abroad.

Richard Bender is Dean of the College of Environmental Design at the University of California, Berkeley. Formerly the Chairman of Berkeley's Department of Architecture, he has also taught at Harvard University, Columbia University and the Cooper Union. Bender has been a researcher, writer and consultant on many projects relating to industrialized housing and systems building. His background is in civil engineering, building construction engineering, and architecture with degrees from the City University of New York, the Massachusetts Institute of Technology, and Harvard's Graduate School of Design.

Clare Cooper Marcus is an Associate Professor in the Department of Landscape Architecture at Berkeley. She was born in England and emigrated to this country as a graduate student, receiving degrees in geography from the University of Nebraska and City Planning from the University of California, Berkeley. Her book on the design objectives and residents' responses to the environment of a public housing project in Richmond, California is called *Easter Hill Village*.

Sam Davis is an Associate Professor of Architecture at the University of California, Berkeley. A graduate of the Schools of Architecture at Berkeley and Yale, he is now a housing design consultant and his work has appeared in many journals in the United States and abroad. He was the recipient of a First Place Award in the Roosevelt Island Housing Competition sponsored by the Urban Development Corporation of New York.

Chester Hartman received his Ph.D. in City Planning from Harvard. He has been on the planning faculties at Harvard, Yale and the University of California, Berkeley and was Senior Planning Associate at the National Housing and Economic Development Law Project, University of California, Berkeley. His books include *Housing and Social Policy, Yerba Buena: Land Grab and Community Resistance in San Francisco,* and *Housing Urban America,* co-edited with Jon Pynoos and Robert Schafer.

Donn Logan is Professor of Architecture and Urban Design at the University of California, Berkeley and principal in the firm of Elbasani/Logan/Severin of New York and Berkeley. He holds degrees in Architecture from Arizona State and Harvard's Graduate School of Design. His firm is responsible for a number of nationally known projects and his building designs and articles have appeared in journals in this country and abroad. The firm has been the recipient of many design awards including six major national design competitions.

Richard L. Meier is Professor of Environmental Design at the University of California, Berkeley. Trained as a physical scientist, he went on to undertake studies of social consequences of advances in scientific thought, thus joining the ranks of the planners and futurists. Much of his recent work on the design of resource conserving urbanism is set forth in his book, *Planning for an Urban World*.

Roger Montgomery is a Professor of Urban Design in the Departments of Architecture and City and Regional Planning at the University of California, Berkeley. He attended Harvard's Graduate School of Design, practiced architecture and planning, and taught previously at Washington University in St. Louis. He has contributed to many books and journals and is co-editor with Daniel R. Mandelker of *Housing in America*.

John Parman is in the Ph.D. Program of the Department of Architecture at Berkeley in Building Technology and is also associated with the Energy Conservation Assessment Program at Lawrence Berkeley Laboratory. He was trained in architecture at Berkeley and at Washington University.

Cathy Simon is an Associate in the architectural firm of Marquis and Associates in San Francisco and a lecturer in the Department of Architecture at the University of California, Berkeley. She holds a degree in Art History from Wellesley and a Master in Architecture from Harvard's Graduate School of Design. Her work and articles have appeared in journals in this country and abroad.

Photo and Illustration Credits

Fig. 0-1, p. xiii. Photo credit: Sam Davis. Fig. 0-2, p. xiv. William and Carol Glass. Fig. 1-1, p. xx. Thomas Airviews. Fig. 1-2, p. 1. Alan Dunn and Architectural Record Books. From *Architecture Observed.* Fig. 1-3, p. 2. The Institute of Architecture and Urban Studies. Fig. 1-4, p. 3. William and Carol Glass. Fig. 1-5, p. 5. Photo credit: David Hirsch. Architects: Prentice/Chan Ohlhausen. Fig. 1-6, p. 5. Photo credit: Josh Freiwald. Architect: Ratcliff, Slama, Cadwalader. Chart: Herbert McLaughlin and *Architectural Record.* Fig. 1-7, p. 6. Photo credit: Sam Davis. Fig. 1-8, p. 7. Photo credit: Foundation Le Corbusier. Figs. 1-9, 1-10, and 1-11, p. 9. Gerald McCue and Bobbie Sue Hood. Fig. 1-12, p. 10. A. J. Diamond and Associates. Fig. 1-13, p. 11. William and Carol Glass from a drawing by Roger Sherwood. Figs. 1-14 and 1-15, p. 13. Photo credit: Sam Davis. Architects: MacKinley, Winnacher, McNeal. Figs. 1-18 and 1-19, p. 15. Photo credit: Backen, Arrigoni & Ross, Architects. Figs. 1-22 and 1-23, p. 17. Photo credit: Donn Logan. Architect: Jorn Utzon. Fig. 1-24, p. 17. Fig. 1-25, p. 18. William and Carol Glass. Fig. 1-26, p. 18. Photo credit: David Hirsch. Architect: Louis Sauer Associates. Fig. 1-27, p. 18. Photo credit: Norman McGrath. Architect: Louis Sauer Associates. Fig. 1-30, p. 19. Photo credit: David Hirsch. Architect: Louis Sauer Associates. Fig. 1-31, p. 20. Photo credit: Vernon DeMars, Architect. Fig. 1-33, p. 21. Photo credit: Karl H. Riek. Architects: Marquis and Stoller. Fig. 1-34, p. 21. Photo credit: Sam Davis. Fig. 1-36, p. 23. Photo credit: Norman McGrath. Architect: Charles Moore. Fig. 1-37, p. 23. William and Carol Glass. Fig. 1-38, p. 24. Photo credit: Institute for Architecture and Urban Studies, Architects. Fig. 1-40, p. 25. Photo credit: L. Bezzola. Architect: Atelier 5. Figs. 1-41 and 1-42, p. 26. Photo credit: Barry Evans. Architects: DeMars and Reay. Fig. 1-43, p. 26. Photo credit: Moshe Safdie, Architect. Fig. 1-44, p. 27. William and Carol Glass from a drawing in *Ordinariness and Light,* MIT, 1970. Fig. 1-45, p. 27. Photo credit: Townland Marketing and Development Corporation, New York. Fig. 1-46, p. 28. Photo credit: Norman McGrath. Architects: Davis-Brody and Associates. Fig. 1-47, p. 29. William and Carol Glass. Fig. 1-49, p. 30. William and Carol Glass. Fig. 1-50, p. 31. Photo credit: William and Carol Glass. Architects: Sert-Jackson Associates. Fig. 1-51, p. 31. Photo credit: Steve Rosenthal. Architects: Sert-Jackson Associates. Fig. 1-52, p. 32. Photo credit: Inger Abrahamsen. Architects: Hoberman and Wasserman. Fig. 1-55, p. 33. Photo credit: Norman McGrath. Architects: Hodne and Stageberg. Fig. 1-56, p. 34. Photo credit: Hodne and Stageberg, Architects. Fig. 1-57, p. 35. Photo credit: C. Hadley Smith. Architects: Koetter and Wells. Fig. 1-59, p. 35. Photo credit: George Pohl. Architects: Venturi and Rauch. Fig. 1-60, p. 36. Photo credit: Kyu Sung Woo, Architect. Fig. 1-61, p. 36. Photo credit: Ed Stoecklein. Architects: Stern and Hagmann. Fig. 1-62, p. 37. Photo credit: Michael Severin. Architects: Sam Davis and ELS Design Group.

Fig. 2-1, p. 40. Photo credit: Byron. Permission of the Byron Collection of the Museum of the City of New York. Fig. 2-2, p. 41. Alan Dunn by permission of Architectural Record Books. From *Architecture Observed.* Fig. 2-3, p. 42. Litchfield Historical Society. Fig. 2-4, p. 42. William and Carol Glass. Fig. 2-5, p. 42. Photo credit: Wendy Tsuji. Fig. 2-6, p. 42. William and Carol Glass. Fig. 2-7, p. 43. Photo credit: Wendy Tsuji. Fig. 2-8, p. 43. Courtesy New York Historical Society, New York City. Fig. 2-9, p. 43. Photo credit: Wendy Tsuji. Fig. 2-10, p. 44. William and Carol Glass. Fig. 2-11, p. 45. William and Carol Glass. Fig. 2-12, p. 46. Permission of the Foundation Le Corbusier. Fig. 2-13, p. 46. Permission of the Museum of the City of New York. Fig. 2-14, p. 47. Photo credit: Wendy Tsuji. Fig. 2-15, p. 47. William and Carol Glass from a drawing in *Architectural Forum,* Jan.-Feb. 1967. Fig. 2-16, p. 49. Courtesy O. M. Ungers, Architect. Fig. 2-17, p. 49. Courtesy Lawrence Halprin Associates. Fig. 2-18, p. 50. Photo credit: Aero photographers. Fig. 2-19, p. 51. Photo credit: Vernon DeMars, Architect. Fig. 2-20, p. 51. Photo credit: Steve Rosenthal. Fig. 2-21, p. 52. William and Carol Glass. Fig. 2-22, p. 53. ELS Design Group, Architects. Fig. 2-23, p. 54. Photo credit: Donn Logan. Fig. 2-24, p. 55. Photo credit: Donn Logan. Fig. 2-25, p. 55. Photo credit: Booth and Nagle, Architects. Fig. 2-26, p. 55. Permission of the Museum of the City of New York. Figs. 2-27 and 2-28, p. 56. Photo credit: Joshua Freiwald. Architects: Fisher/Friedman. Fig. 2-29, p. 57. Photo credit: Backen, Arrigoni & Ross, Architects. Fig. 2-30, p. 58. Courtesy Gruen Associates. Fig. 2-31, p. 58. Courtesy Harvard Graduate School of Design. Fig. 2-32, p. 59. Photo credit: William and Carol Glass. Fig. 2-33, p. 59. Photo credit: Paul Rudolph, Architect. Fig. 2-34, p. 60. William Turnbull, Architect. Fig. 2-35, p. 60. Photo credit: Rob Super. Fig. 2-36, p. 60. Photo credit: Cervin Robinson. Architect: Don Lyndon. Fig. 2-37, p. 60. Photo credit: Jonathan Green. Architect: Don Lyndon. Fig. 2-38, p. 61. Photo credit: Norman McGrath. Architects: Davis/Brody & Associates. Fig. 2-39, p. 61. Davis/Brody & Associates, Architects. Fig. 2-40, p. 62. Photo credit: John Fulker. Architect: Diamond and Myers.

Fig. 3-2, p. 65. Alan Dunn by permission of Architectural Record Books. From *Architecture Observed.* Fig. 3-3, p. 69. Photo credit: Hedrich-Blessing. Fig. 3-10, p. 73. Photo credit: Randolph Langenbach. Fig. 3-11, p. 73. Photo credit: Jan Corash. Fig. 3-12, p. 73. Photo credit: Jan Corash. Fig. 3-14, p. 74. Photo credit: Steve Rosenthal. Fig. 3-18, p. 75. Photo credit: Phokion Karas. Fig. 3-21, p. 76. Photo credit: Phokion Karas. Fig. 3-22, p. 76. Photo credit: Phokion Karas. Fig. 3-23, p. 76. Photo credit: Rolin R. LaFrance. Fig. 3-25, p. 77. Photo credit: Ron Gordon. Fig. 3-26, p. 77. Courtesy Harry Weese & Associates. Fig. 3-28, p. 78. Photo credit: Gerald Allen. Fig. 3-29, p. 79. Photo credit: Morley Baer. Figs. 3-30, 3-31, and 3-32, p. 79. Photo credit: Thomas Brown.

Fig. 4-1, p. 82. Photo credit: Sam Davis. Fig. 4-2, p. 83. Alan Dunn by permission Architectural Record Books. From *Architecture Observed.* Fig. 4-4, p. 86. United States President's Committee on Urban Housing, *A Decent Home* 1968. Fig. 4-5(a), p. 88. Photo credit: Roger Montgomery. Fig. 4-5(b), p. 88. Photo credit: Ray Belknap and the SWA Group. Fig. 4-6, p. 90. Photo credit: *NAHB Journal of Homebuilding.* Fig. 4-7, p. 91. Photo credit: Roger Montgomery. Figs. 4-9(a) and (b), p. 94. Kevin Lynch. From *Site Planning,* MIT Press. Fig. 4-10, p. 97. Photo credit: Thomas Airviews. Fig. 4-11, p. 97. Photo credit: Wayne Thom. Fig. 4-12, p. 98. Photo credit: Morley Baer. Fig. 4-13, p. 98. Photo credit: Thomas A. Abels. Architects: Sandy and Babcock. Fig. 4-14, p. 99. Photo credit: Roger Montgomery. Fig. 4-15(a), p. 100. Photo credit: Roger Montgomery. Fig. 4-15(b), p. 100. Photo credit: Ernest Braun. Architects: Anshen and Allen. Fig. 4-16(a), p. 102. Photo credit: Roger Montgomery. Fig. 4-16(b), p. 102. Photo credit: Joshua Freiwald. Architects: Fisher/Friedman. Fig. 4-17, p. 106. Photo credit: Mac Mizuki. Fig. 4-18, p. 107. Photo credit: Roger Montgomery. Fig. 4-19, p. 109. Photo credit: Moore/Grover/Harper, Architects.

Fig. 5-1, p. 112. Photo credit: Ted Milikin. Fig. 5-2, p. 113. Alan Dunn by permission of Architectural Books. From *Architecture Observed.* Fig. 5-3, p. 114. McCue/Boone/Tomsick, Architects. Fig. 5-4, p. 115. Photo credit: Aero Photographers. Fig. 5-5, p. 115. Photo credit: Aero Photographers. Fig. 5-6, p. 117, Robert Herman, Architect. Figs. 5-7(a), (b), (c), and (d), p. 118. Photo credit: Ira Nowinski. Figs. 5-8(a), (b), (c), and (d), p. 119. Photo credit: Ira Nowinski. Fig. 5-9, p. 122. Photo credit: Ted Milikin. Fig. 5-10, p. 123. Photo credit: Ted Milikin. Fig. 5-11, p. 123. Photo credit: Ted Milikin. Fig. 5-12, p. 124. Photo credit: Ted Milikin. Figs. 5-13 and 5-14, p. 127. Photo credit: Ken Sower. Fig. 5-15, p. 127. Ralph Rapson, Architect. Fig. 5-16, p. 128. Photo credit: Ken Sower. Fig. 5-17, p. 129. Ralph Rapson, Architect. Fig. 5-18, p. 130. Ralph Rapson, Architect. Fig. 5-19, p. 133. Photo credit: Ann Waterhouse.

Fig. 6-2, p. 139. Alan Dunn by permission of Architectural Record Books. From *Architecture Observed.* Fig. 6-3, p. 140. William and Carol Glass from a drawing by Clare Cooper Marcus. Fig. 6-4, p. 141. Copyright 1956 by William Whyte Jr. Permission of Simon and Schuster. From *Organization Man.* Fig. 6-5, p. 142. Copyright 1975 Russell Sage Foundation. From *Sociology and Architectural Design* by John Zeisel. Figs. 6-6(a) and (b), p. 143. Architecture Research Unit, Edinburgh. From *Low Rise High Density Housing Study,* 1970. Fig. 6-7, p. 144. Permission of the Controller of Her Britannic Majesty's Stationery Office. Fig. 6-8, p. 144. Permission of *Official Architect and Planning* (now *Built Environment*). From "Housing at Coventry—A User Reaction Study." Figs. 6-9 and 6-10, p. 144. Permission of the Controller of Her Britannic Majesty's Stationery Office. From *Family Houses at West Ham: An Account of the Project with an Appraisal.* Fig. 6-11, p. 145. Alan Dunn by permission of Architectural Record Books. From *Archi-*

tecture Observed. Figs. 6-12(a) and (b), p. 146. Center for Environmental Structure. Figs. 6-13 and 6-14, p. 147. Center for Urban Development Research. Cornell University. From *Design for Living: The Resident's View of Multi-Family Housing*. Photo credit: Lawrence P. Friedberg. Fig. 6-15, p. 149. Housing Research and Development Program, University of Illinois at Urbana-Champaign. Fig. 6-16, p. 150. Permission of Macmillan Publishing Company. From *Defensible Space*, copyright 1972 by Oscar Newman. Fig. 6-17, p. 151. Photo credit: Clare Cooper-Marcus. Fig. 6-18, p. 152. Clare Cooper-Marcus. Institute of Urban & Regional Development, University of California at Berkeley. Fig. 6-19, p. 153. Permission of the Controller of Her Britannic Majesty's Stationery Office. From *Space in the Home*, Design Bulletin No. 6. Fig. 6-20, p. 154. Center for Urban Development Research, Cornell University. From *Design for Living: The Resident's View of Multi-Family Housing*. Fig. 6-21, p. 155. Permission of the Controller of Her Britannic Majesty's Stationery Office. From *Choosing Your House*. Fig. 6-22, p. 156. Permission of the Controller of Her Britannic Majesty's Stationery Office. Fig. 6-23, p. 156. Macmillan Publishing Co. From *Defensible Space*, copyright 1972 by Oscar Newman. Fig. 6-24, p. 157. Institute for Architecture and Urban Studies. Fig. 6-25, p. 158. Center for Urban Development Research, Cornell University. From *Design for Living: The Resident's View of Multi-Family Housing*. Fig. 6-26(a), (b), and (c), p. 158. Center for Urban Development Research, Cornell University. From *Design for Living: The Resident's View of Multi-Family Housing*. Photo credit: Lawrence P. Friedberg. Fig. 6-27, p. 159. Andrew Rabeneck. Fig. 6-28, p. 160. Housing Research and Development Program, University of Illinois at Urbana-Champaign. Fig. 6-29, p. 162. Permission of the Controller of Her Britannic Majesty's Stationery Office. From *Children at Play*. Fig. 6-30, p. 162. Center for Urban Development Research, Cornell University. From *Design for Living: The Resident's View of Multi-Family Housing*. Photo credit: Franklin Becker. Fig. 6-31, p. 163. Alan Dunn by permission of Architectural Record Books. From *Architecture Observed*.

Fig. 7-1, p. 172. Warner/Burns/Toans/Lunde. Fig. 7-2, p. 173. Alan Dunn by permission of Architectural Record Books. From *Architecture Observed*. Fig. 7-3, p. 174. Office of R. B. Fuller. Fig. 7-4, p. 175. William and Carol Glass from a drawing by Le Corbusier. Fig. 7-5, p. 175. Photo credit: Robert D. Harvey. Fig. 7-6, p. 176. Photo credit: Alderman Studios. Fig. 7-7, p. 177. Photo credit: Richard Bender. Fig. 7-8, p. 180. Photo credit: Richard Bender. Fig. 7-9, p. 182. William and Carol Glass. Fig. 7-10, p. 182. William and Carol Glass from a drawing by Le Corbusier. Fig. 7-11, p. 183. Photo credit: Welton Becket, Architects. Fig. 7-12, p. 183. Photo credit: Tomio Ohashi. Architect: Kisho Kurokawa. Fig. 7-13, p. 183. Warner/Burns/Toan/Lunde. Fig. 7-14, p. 184. Warner/Burns/Toan/Lunde. Fig. 7-15, p. 185. Photo credit: Don Terner. Fig. 7-16, p. 186. Office of R. B. Fuller. Fig. 7-17, p. 187.

Peter Stephensen, Architect. Fig. 7-18, p. 187. Peter Stephensen, Architect. Fig. 7-19, p. 187. Photo credit: Peter Stephensen. Fig. 7-20, p. 188. Building Systems Development, Inc.

Fig. 8-1, p. 190. Jan Wampler, Architect. Fig. 8-2, p. 191. Alan Dunn by permission of Architectural Record Books. From *Architectural Cookbook*. Fig. 8-3, p. 192. William and Carol Glass. Fig. 8-4, p. 192. From *The Sun King*, Harper and Row: New York, 1966. Fig. 8-5, p. 193. From *The Victorian Country House*, by Mark Girouard, Clarendon Press: Oxford, 1971. Fig. 8-6, p. 195. Photo credit: Sam Davis. Fig. 8-7, p. 195. From Signs of Life: Symbols in the American City, by Venturi and Rauch. Renwick Gallery of the National Collection of Fine Arts, Washington, 1976. Photo credit: Stephen Shore. Fig. 8-8, p. 197. Photo credit: Ezra Stoller. Architects: Skidmore, Owings and Merrill. Fig. 8-9, p. 197. William and Carol Glass from a drawing in *Japanese Architecture* by Heinrich Engel. Fig. 8-10, p. 198. Photo credit: Hans Kundig, Architect. Fig. 8-11, p. 198. William and Carol Glass. Fig. 8-12, p. 198. Photo credit: Marvin Buchannon. Architect: Peter Behn. Fig. 8-13, p. 199. Photo credit: Sam Davis. Designer: Joe Cucchiara. Figs. 8-14 and 8-15, p. 199. Photo credit: Tomio Ohashi. Architect: Kisho Kurokawa. Fig. 8-16, p. 200. Photo credit: Jan Wampler, Architect. Fig. 8-17, p. 200. United States Patent No. 56,413, 17 July 1866. Figs. 8-18(a) and (b), p. 201. Alberto Seassaro, Designer. Figs. 8-19(a) and (b), p. 201. Tecnico Snaidero, Designer. Fig. 8-20, p. 202. From "Le Fantome de la Liberte," a film by Luis Bunel. Courtesy Greenwich Film Production, Paris. Fig. 8-21, p. 203. Photo credit: Sidney Newbery. Sir John Soane's Museum, London. Fig. 8-22, p. 203. Photo credit: Mies Van der Rohe Archive, The Museum of Modern Art, New York. Fig. 8-23, p. 204. Photo credit: Alexandre Georges. Architect: Philip Johnson. Fig. 8-24, p. 204. Photo credit: Morley Baer. Fig. 8-25, p. 204. William and Carol Glass. Fig. 8-26, p. 204. William and Carol Glass. Figs. 8-27 and 8-28, p. 205. Booth and Nagel, Architects. Fig. 8-29, p. 206. William and Carol Glass from a drawing in Phillippe Boudon's *Lived in Architecture*, MIT, 1969. Fig. 8-30, p. 207. Photo credit: Centro Kappa. Designer: Ettore Sottsass. Fig. 8-31, p. 208. Joseph Colombo, Designer. Fig. 8-32, p. 208. William and Carol Glass. Fig. 8-33, p. 208. Photo credit: Joseph Cucchiara. Fig. 8-34, p. 209. William and Carol Glass. Figs. 8-35 and 8-36, p. 209. Photo credit: Ed Stoecklein. Architect: Jon Michael Schwarting. Figs. 8-37 and 8-38, p. 210. Photo credit: Ed Stoecklein. Architects: Stern and Hagmann. Fig. 8-39, p. 211. *Architecture Association Quarterly*, Summer 1972. Fig. 8-40, p. 211. Photo credit: Carter Design Group, Architects. Fig. 8-41, p. 212. Photo credit: Renalto Severino, Architect. Fig. 8-42, p. 213, Andrew Rapeneck, Architect. Fig. 8-43, p. 214. William and Carol Glass from a drawing in *The Place of Houses*, by Charles Moore, Gerald Allen, and Donlyn Lyndon.

Fig. 9-1, p. 216. Photo credit: Julius Shulman. Architects: Lee and Klages. Fig. 9-2, p. 217. Alan Dunn by permission of Architectural Record Books. From *Architecture Observed*. Fig. 9-3, p. 218. William and Carol Glass. Fig. 9-4, p. 218. William and Carol Glass. Fig. 9-5, p. 219. Photo credit: Sam Davis. Fig. 9-6, p. 222. William and Carol Glass. Fig. 9-7, p. 223. From *Housing in the Seventies*. HUD, p. 224. Fig. 9-8, p. 223. Photo credit: Sam Davis. Fig. 9-9, p. 224. Photo credit: F. L. Wright Foundation, Architects. Figs. 9-11 and 9-12, p. 225. John Raup and Reynolds Aluminum. Fig. 9-13, p. 225. William and Carol Glass. Fig. 9-14, p. 226. Photo credit: Donald Luckenbill. Architect: Paul Rudolph. Fig. 9-15, p. 226. William and Carol Glass. Fig. 9-16, p. 227. Photo credit: Julius Shulman. Architects: Lee and Klages. Fig. 9-18, p. 228. Photo credit: Sam Davis. Fig. 9-19, p. 228. Photo credit: Marcel Breuer, Architect. Fig. 9-20, p. 228. Photo credit: Sam Davis. Fig. 9-21, p. 229. Photo credit: Sam Davis. Fig. 9-22, p. 229. Uri Hung and Reynolds Aluminum. Fig. 9-23, p. 229. Photo credit: Sam Davis. Fig. 9-24, p. 230. William and Carol Glass. Figs. 9-25 and 9-26, p. 231. Photo credit: Sam Davis. Figs. 9-27, p. 231. Photo credit: Dan Gregory. Fig. 9-28, p. 232. Duane Kell and Craig Rafferty and Reynolds Aluminum. Figs. 9-29 and 9-30, p. 233. Sam Davis/William Glass/Carol Shen. Fig. 9-32, p. 235. Photo credit: Sam Davis. Fig. 9-33, p. 237. Photo credit: *The New York Times*. Fig. 9-35, p. 238. Photo credit: Sam Davis. Fig. 9-36, p. 239. Photo credit: Sam Davis. Fig. 9-37, p. 240. Photo credit: Sam Davis.

Fig. 10-1, p. 244. National Aeronautics and Space Administration, Ames Research Center. Fig. 10-2, p. 245. Alan Dunn by permission of Architectural Record Books. From *Architecture Observed*. Fig. 10-3, p. 246. Cosanti Foundation and MIT Press. Fig. 10-4, p. 246. Peter Cook. Fig. 10-5, p. 246. *FUTURES*. Fig. 10-6, p. 248. William and Carol Glass. Fig. 10-8, p. 252. William and Carol Glass. Fig. 10-9, p. 254. Minimum Cost Housing Group, School of Architecture, McGill University. Fig. 10-10, p. 257. Photo credit: Sam Davis. Fig. 10-11, p. 257. Odiyan: Center of Nyingma Culture. Fig. 10-12, p. 258. Photo credit: Sam Davis. Fig. 10-13, p. 259. William and Carol Glass. Fig. 10-14, p. 260. Photo credit: Potters Williams, Architect. Fig. 10-15, p. 262. Photo credit: Elmer W. J. Frey. "SkyeRise Terrace" by the Frey Building Company. Fig. 10-16, p. 263. Photo credit: Bill Gonsales, Architect: Wallace, Floyd, Ellenzweig, Moore. Fig. 10-17, p. 264. Photo credit: Norman McGrath. Architect: Malcolm Wells. Fig. 10-18, p. 265. Photo credit: Sam Davis. Fig. 10-19, p. 265. Photo credit: Sam Davis. Fig. 10-20, p. 266. Photo credit: William and Carol Glass. Fig. 10-21, p. 267. Photo credit: Mitsubishi Heavy Industries. "Aquapolis" Architect: Kiyonori Kitautake. Fig. 10-22, p. 269. National Aeronautics and Space Administration, Ames Research Center.

Index

Index